CW01551699

Contemporary Research in Accounting and Finance

Abdelghani Echchabi · Rihab Grassa ·
Welcome Sibanda
Editors

Contemporary
Research
in Accounting
and Finance

Case Studies from the MENA Region

Editors
Abdelghani Echchabi 🆔
Higher Colleges of Technology
Dubai, United Arab Emirates

Rihab Grassa 🆔
Higher Colleges of Technology
Dubai, United Arab Emirates

Welcome Sibanda 🆔
Higher Colleges of Technology
Dubai, United Arab Emirates

ISBN 978-981-16-8266-7   ISBN 978-981-16-8267-4 (eBook)
https://doi.org/10.1007/978-981-16-8267-4

Cover illustration: © Alex Linch shutterstock.com

This Palgrave Macmillan imprint is published by the registered company Springer Nature
Singapore Pte Ltd.
The registered company address is: 152 Beach Road, #21-01/04 Gateway East, Singapore
189721, Singapore

PREFACE

In spite of its socioeconomic importance to the growth and development of the global economy and its unremittingly increasing role in transforming current and future social and economic trends, the Middle East and North Africa (MENA) region is consistently ignored when researching and discussing business-focused social sciences. While academic research on economics, business management, accounting and finance systems from a developed markets standpoint is indisputably abundant, research focusing on the MENA framework is still in embryonic stages. Consequently, a closer investigation of these topical business management issues within the MENA context while merited is long overdue since the region is on the cusp of an unprecedented socioeconomic transformation that warrants some research traction. Research in the region will help shed valuable insights on the existing regional state of an economically developing bloc, help unlock socioeconomic opportunities, broaden academic research in business, economics, finance and accounting systems, policy makers craft policy as well as inform wider readership.

The book is as timely as it is essential in plugging the knowledge gap from a MENA region perspective and is set to assist readers in focusing on the most successful accounting and finance practices. The volume presents a set of fourteen previously unpublished meticulously chapter articles peer-reviewed by internationally acclaimed academics in monograph form straddling the entire range of a consolidated blend of empirical research, conceptual models, theoretical aspects, and applied case scenarios. The chapters are presented such that each is independent, with articles focusing on interconnected themes of practice of accounting and financial systems, with the main emphasis on generating output that highlights modern research developments from a MENA regional context.

The book explores the importance of these themes and advances their theories, and in the process, enunciates an opinion in accounting and finance from the regional perspective. This profoundly influences the understanding of contemporary research challenges from a different viewpoint. The book lays the ground by briefly explaining each article, how and why each chapter article transforms the way we think about accounting and finance, providing clear insights as to the fundamentals of how to successfully exploit such systems and processes. The book will become a valuable reference resource for academics, practitioners, policy makers, and students interested in and fascinated by the interdisciplinary areas of accounting and finance.

Society critically depends on high-quality accounting and financial models for decision-making for a large part of their business procedures and processes. Therefore, policy makers, students, practitioners, and researchers alike must adeptly reach robustly informed decisions in this fast-paced global economy of digital technologies. This comes on the heels of the fact that for a diversity of reasons, systematic applied research exploiting robust samples and methods, and generating robust results are scarcely obtainable for the MENA region. Thus, there is an unquestionable need for employing large robust samples on strong empirical methods, for their generation, dissemination, and application of more meaningful results. This book presents a diversity of data sampling, theory-based empirical, and applied studies and methodologies.

Each chapter article models theoretically and empirically informed experimentation that places research results output in an unrelenting interchange with theoretical concepts. Reflections subsequent to each chapter narrate the research's trajectories of diverse business finance ecosystems and their influence in research. Eventually, this fertile nexus of ideas enlightens business finance scholars on how to appropriately employ analytical business finance systems research theory to produce results that are concurrently hypothetically inspired, methodically engaged, and empirically evocative. This is an excellent approach since most empirical research skirts the exploitation of theory, generates and provides analytical results, with negligible or no business finance rationalization. Conversely, theoreticians infrequently investigate their ideas with empirical projects. As this inventive manuscript clearly indicates, neither empiricism, data nor theory is independently sufficient to the task of business finance explanation.

Instead in a fluid and globalized economy, they rather condition and apprise each other as the investigative process unfolds, bridging the outdated theory-research-application conundrum by expounding how research can and does exploit vital business finance theory to decide applicable empirical research strategies, and broaden the investigative and occasionally applied prowess of sampling, testing, and interpretation. While emphasis is on applied methodology, due consideration is given to econometric analysis for an audience with an advanced appreciation for statistics.

Dubai, United Arab Emirates

Abdelghani Echchabi
Rihab Grassa
Welcome Sibanda

CONTENTS

Editors and Contributors

About the Editors

Abdelghani Echchabi is an Assistant Professor of Finance at the Higher Colleges of Technology, United Arab Emirates. Earlier, he served in similar positions in South Korea, Oman, and Saudi Arabia. His areas of research and teaching interest cover a wide range of finance and Islamic finance topics, as well as entrepreneurship and social entrepreneurship. He participated in several international conferences in finance and Islamic finance, and has published significant research papers in internationally recognized journals.

Rihab Grassa is an Assistant Professor of Accounting at the Higher Colleges of Technology in Dubai, as well as external associate researcher for the Laboratoire Interdisciplinaire de Gestion, in the High Institute of Accounting and Business Administration, University of Manouba, Tunisia. She worked as a Researcher in KPMG Global Islamic Finance in Dubai and as a manager for Islamic finance services in KPMG Tunisia.

Welcome Sibanda is an Assistant Professor of Finance at the Higher Colleges of Technology in Dubai. Prior to joining HCT, Welcome was an Assistant Professor of Finance at Heriot-Watt University's Dubai Campus. He has served as an Associate Editor of the *International Journal of Research in Banking and Finance* and Portfolio Manager at Barclays

Wealth, Barclays Bank, London. He has also been a Visiting Lecturer at the Geneva Business School, London School of Economics' UAE Affiliate College, and the University of Bolton. His research interests span bank performance, asset allocation and portfolio dynamics, FinTech models, and SME Business Dynamics.

List of Contributors

Abdolkarim Abootaleb Abbasi is a finance student at the Higher Colleges of Technology in United Arab Emirates. His areas of interest include Islamic financial management, Islamic insurance (Takaful), and Islamic capital markets.

Sonia Abdennadher is an Associate Professor of finance at the Higher Colleges of Technology in the United Arab Emirates. She holds a Ph.D. from University Paris Sud 11. She has about 15 years of teaching experience. She taught finance and accounting courses for undergraduate, postgraduate, and continuing education levels in universities and in business schools. She published several research papers in PRJ and co-authored a Springer publisher book. She published in peer-reviewed international journals including a recent article in Financial Times top 40. Her research interests are in FinTech, corporate governance, CSR practices, and managers' adoption decisions.

Hareb Abdulla is an accounting student at the Higher Colleges of Technology in the United Arab Emirates. His area of interest is Blockchain technology, audit, accounting, and assurance services.

Mohammed Ali Akour is an Associate Professor with more than 20 years of international academic and industrial experience in USA, Jordan, and Oman. He is specialized in instructional psychology and technology, technology management, innovation, and application of information and communication technologies in business and education settings. He is a member of executive, steering, and editorial board committees in a number of international conferences and journals.

Omar Abdulaziz Alabdulla is an accounting student at the Higher Colleges of Technology in the United Arab Emirates. His area of interest is credit control, audit, and credit management.

Abdulla Alfalasi is an accounting student at the Higher Colleges of Technology in the United Arab Emirates. His area of interest is Blockchain technology, audit, accounting, and assurance services.

Salim Al-Hajri is an Assistant Professor of Management Information Systems (MIS) at A'Sharqiyah University in Oman. He obtained his Ph.D. in MIS from Victoria University, Melbourne, Australia. He has published a book, edited several book chapters, and published many papers in distinguished international journals in the MIS area. He is a reviewer for several esteemed international scientific journals and an academic promotion reviewer in several academic institutions. Furthermore, he is a presenter of many papers in many International conferences. Formerly, he also worked as an MIS department director and chaired many committees.

Ahmad Al-Hiyari is an Assistant Professor of Accounting at Liwa College of Technology since 2019. He holds a Ph.D. in Accounting from University Utara Malaysia. His research interests focus on financial accounting and corporate governance with a specific interest in auditing, financial reporting, and the role of accounting information in capital markets. His teaching interest includes financial accounting, managerial accounting, auditing, and financial management. He published in a number of reputable international journals such as *Journal of African Business, Social Responsibility Journal*, and *Journal of General Management*.

Saeed Ahmed Saeed Alkaabi has recently graduated from the Higher Colleges of Technology in the United Arab Emirates (UAE) and obtained his bachelor's degree in Finance with a concentration in investments. He is currently working for Al Ain Municipality in the UAE.

Abdulla Abdulmajid Alkhaja is an accounting student at the Higher Colleges of Technology in the United Arab Emirates. His area of interest is credit control, audit, and credit management.

Obaid Meshal Almansoori is an accounting student at the Higher Colleges of Technology in the United Arab Emirates. His area of interest is credit control, audit, and credit management.

Saeed Ali Almarri is an accounting student at the Higher Colleges of Technology in the United Arab Emirates. His area of interest is credit control, audit, and credit management.

Ahmad Obaid Almheiri is an accounting student at the Higher Colleges of Technology in the United Arab Emirates. His area of interest is credit control, audit, and credit management

Mohammad Bader Almheiri is a finance student at the Higher Colleges of Technology in the United Arab Emirates. His areas of interest include investment and portfolio management, Islamic financial management, and Islamic insurance (Takaful).

Ali Salem Alshebli has recently graduated from the Higher Colleges of Technology in the United Arab Emirates. He obtained his bachelor's degree in Finance with a concentration in investments. He is currently working at Yahsat Company in the UAE.

Abderazak Bakhouche is an Assistant Professor of Economics and Finance at the Higher Colleges of Technology, United Arab Emirates. He holds a Ph.D. degree in Banking and Finance. Abderazak has taught several modules in Economics, Banking, and Finance at both undergraduate and graduate levels. His primary area of research interest covers issues related to banking systems such as structure, competition, and efficiency.

Sarra Baroudi is an Assistant Professor of Accountancy at Heriot-Watt University in Edinburgh. She is the Global Course Leader for Undergraduate and postgraduate courses, and her teaching has a strong focus on relating academic concepts and theories to what happens in the real world. Sarra worked previously as an Assistant Professor at Woosong University in South Korea. Prior to joining academia, she worked as an Auditor at KPMG.

Sonia Benghida is a faculty in the Sociology Department at McGill University. She holds a doctorate in Glottopolitics and Education from Rouen University, France, as well as a doctorate degree in Policy Planning from Cardiff University, UK. She formerly worked as an Assistant Professor of Sociology and Cultural Studies at Woosong University, South Korea. She has published in the fields of language planning and education, government policies, management structures, and economy, as well as a variety of sociological topics. She has regularly served on peer review committees for internationally renowned journals and publishers.

Anca Bocanet is currently an Assistant Professor and Program Team Leader at the Higher Colleges of Technology in the United Arab Emirates. She earned her Ph.D. in Science and Technology Management from University of Naples Federico II, Italy. Her current research interests include complexity theory and systems, organizational learning, and innovation and entrepreneurship. Her latest research contributes to the debate on corporate innovation–productivity trade-off in the context of new ventures creation.

Neila Boulila Taktak is a Professor of accounting at IHEC Carthage, University of Carthage. She is the author of many scientific publications dealing with earnings management, Islamic banking and finance, and corporate governance. She is a member of the editorial board for Journal of Islamic Accounting and Business Research.

Mohamed Lotfi Boulkeroua is an Assistant Professor of Finance at the Higher Colleges of Technology in the United Arab Emirates. He holds a Ph.D. in Accounting and Finance from the University of Manchester, UK, and an M.Sc. in Investment Management from City University London, UK. He has held various positions of leadership within academia, and he has an extensive experience in designing and managing curricula in business disciplines. He also has a significant industry experience. His research interests include capital markets, corporate risk premia, corporate governance, SMEs, family business, and education.

Raida Chakroun is an Associate Professor of Accounting at the Higher Business Studies Institute at Carthage (Institut des Hautes Etudes Commerciales), Tunisia. She teaches research methodology, taxation, financial accounting, and internal audit. Her main research interests include international accounting, earnings management, voluntary disclosure, corporate social responsibility, and corporate governance. Her research papers have been published in several scholarly international journals. She served as a reviewer for many journals and supervised many research projects in accounting. She is a member at LIGUE (Manouba University, Tunisia), and she is the Vice President of Tunisian Accounting Association.

Israa Elbendary is an Assistant Lecturer at the Department of Business Administration, Faculty of Commerce, Cairo University, Egypt. She is also a Ph.D. candidate in strategic management and dynamic capabilities at Xi'an Jiaotong University, China. Her research interests focus on the areas of business, human resources management, and strategic management studies.

Randa Elchaar is a business faculty at Higher Colleges of Technology in the United Arab Emirates. She received her master's degree in Money and Banking from the American University of Beirut. Her current research interests include policy and compliance in the finance sector, and the role of Small and Medium Enterprises (SMEs) in achieving economic stability.

Sherif El-Halaby holds a Ph.D. from Plymouth University. He is an Assistant Professor at the Arab Open University in Kuwait. He has many published papers, book chapters, and books with renowned publishers. He has also presented several papers in international academic conferences. He serves as a reviewer for several international journals. His research interests focus on AAOIFI, Islamic banking and finance, corporate governance, and disclosure and earnings management.

Ali Ahmad Al Falasi is a finance student at the Higher Colleges of Technology in the United Arab Emirates. His areas of interest include investment and portfolio management, Islamic financial management, and Islamic insurance (Takaful).

Teheni El Ghak is an Assistant Professor of Economics at Higher Institute of Management, Tunisia. She started her career as a teacher since 2005 at Higher School of Economic and Commercial Sciences, University of Tunis, Tunisia. She obtained her Ph.D. in economics with distinction from the Faculty of Economics and Management of Tunis in 2011. Her main research interests are growth, productivity, financial development, and entrepreneurship. She is the author of several research studies published in refereed journals and has presented papers in various international conferences.

Syed Ghayas holds an M.Sc. in Software Engineering and an M.S. in Mobile Computing from the University of Bradford, UK. He carried out research on accessible user interfaces, user experience design, emotional design, technology-enhanced learning, technology acceptance, and user-centered design domains. His research activities merge components of Humans' behavior, Human perception, and technologies that enable better designs and learning methods. He is also interested in exploring the area of human perception, positive computing, social virtual reality, and user experience domains.

Asma Hkimi holds a Ph.D. degree in Accounting from the Institute of Advanced Business Studies (IHEC Carthage). She has a substantial academic experience in several Tunisian higher education institutions including ESSECT and ESPAF. Her areas of teaching and research interest include corporate governance, auditing, risk management, and Islamic banking and finance.

Asma Houcine is an Associate Professor of Accounting at the Faculty of Business, Emirates College of Technology (ECT), Abu Dhabi. Prior to joining ECT in 2014, she worked as an Assistant Professor at the Higher School of Economics and Business (ESSECT), University of Tunis, Tunisia. She has published numerous research papers in peer-reviewed high-ranked indexed journals. Her main research interests include financial reporting, earnings management, auditing, corporate finance, corporate governance, Islamic finance, and stock market reaction to COVID-19.

Mohamed Chakib Kolsi is an Associate Professor of Accounting at Liwa College of Technology, Abu Dhabi, United Arab Emirates and an Associate Professor of Accounting at the University of Sfax, Tunisia. He served as head of the accounting department for 10 years and internal assessor for 3 years. He has more than 18 years of teaching experience. He published many research papers in highly ranked journals and supervised numerous research projects. He also served as a reviewer for many journals. His research interests include Islamic finance, corporate governance, disclosure policy, earnings management, auditing, and corporate social responsibility.

Moez Labidi is a Professor of Economics at the Faculty of Economics and Management, University of Monastir, Tunisia, and a Research Director at DEFI (Développement Financier et Innovation). His main research interests are monetary policy, financial inclusion, macroprudential policy, and financial instability. Between 2011 and 2012 Moez Labidi was a member of the Board of Directors of the Central Bank of Tunisia. Between 2016 and February 2020 he was a Member of Stock Exchange Index Committee. Between 2016 and 2018 Moez Labidi was the Advisor to the Minister of Finance and to the President of Government in 2020.

Nadia Mansour is an Assistant Professor at the University of Sousse, Tunisia and a Visiting Researcher at the University of Salamanca, Spain. Her research centers on finance, banking, FinTech, DSGE model, and climate change. She is the chair and editor of several international conferences. She has published several papers, conference proceedings, and book chapters and served as reviewer and speaker in various conferences, and as editor in various journal editorial boards. She is a member of several international organizations and associations.

Mohamed Marie is an Assistant Lecturer at the Department of Business Administration, Faculty of Commerce, Cairo University, Egypt. He is currently a Ph.D. candidate in corporate governance and banking at Xi'an Jiaotong University, China. His research interests include corporate finance, Islamic banking, and corporate governance.

Hussien Mohsen is an Assistant Lecturer at the faculty of commerce, Helwan University, Egypt. His fields of expertise are financial reporting, board governance, earnings management, and information technology with special focus on the convergence between accounting standards and developing local standards, forward-looking disclosure, accounting estimates, and economic reality. His academic research has been published in various reputable journals.

Anissa Naouar is an Economist specialized in banking regulation, governance, and risk management. Prior to joining the MENA College of Management, she was an Assistant Professor in Economics and Finance at High Institute of Commerce in Tunisia and a faculty at Paris Sorbonne in Abu Dhabi. Previously, she worked as a Research Assistant for the Center of European Policy Studies in Brussels and as project manager for the French Prudential Supervision and Resolution Authority at the French Central Bank. Her areas of research include applied macroeconomics, macroprudential bank supervision and regulation, credit risk management, corporate governance, financial inclusion, and sustainable development.

Mohamed Adel Saleh is a finance student at the Higher Colleges of Technology in the United Arab Emirates. His areas of interest include Islamic banking and finance, real estate finance, and portfolio management.

Haykel Hadj Salem is a Research Professor in economics in different Tunisian and French universities. He is a Macroeconomist, specialized in computable general equilibrium modeling and DSGE models. He teaches macroeconomics, economic behavior, macroeconomic modeling, national accounts, international economics, sustainable development, and social and solidarity economy.

Maher Salem received his M.Sc. from Duisburg-Essen University and Ph.D. degrees from Kassel University. He is currently an Assistant Professor of cyber security and forensics and an HEA fellow. He has more than 15 years of industrial and academic experiences in Cyber and Network Security, Intrusion Detection Systems, and Security Engineering. His research interest includes Security of IT Infrastructure, Advanced Persistence Threats, Intrusion Detection, and Blockchain Technology. He is an active member in educational platforms and certified in various professional developments of online learning, hybrid learning, and blended learning methods.

Salha Ben Salem is a Ph.D. student at the Faculty of Economics and Management of Sousse, University of Sousse, Tunisia, and a researcher at the Financial Development and Innovation Research Unit (DEFI) in Tunisia. Her research interests focus on banking vulnerability, macroeconomic, DSGE models, financial stability, Big Data, business tourism, innovation, monetary policy modeling, macroprudential policy, and financial friction. She has presented various scientific papers in the indexed international and national conferences. She also has several articles and book chapters published by renowned international publishers. She has also co-edited books with internationally renowned publishers.

Eman Zabalawi is an Assistant Professor who holds a DBA in Excellence Leadership and Innovation. She also holds an M.Sc. in Excellence Management from Leicester University, UK. Her experience varies between consultancy services, entrepreneurship, and academia. Eman is currently working at Amity group as a consultant and corporate trainer in mapping corporation strategic directions, policy, and outcomes with excellence models. She is also a member of the Board of Directors of the Specialized Women, Arab League. Her primary research interests cover strategic leadership, excellence models, efficiency of performance, quality competition, standardization, improvement innovation, knowledge management, and employability.

Hajer Zarrouk is currently an Assistant Professor at Higher Colleges of Technology, UAE. She holds a Ph.D. in economics from the University of Mediterranean, France, and University of Tunis El-Manar, Tunisia. She has over 18 years of teaching experience. She has a strong interest in FinTech, Islamic finance, investment, financial development, economic performance, and entrepreneurial orientation. She is the author of several research studies published in refereed journals and has presented papers at many international conferences. She received "Emerald Literati Awards, 2018" and "The ADEC Award for Research Excellence." She is an Accredited SME Consultant (ASMEC) by AASBC.

LIST OF FIGURES

Blockchain in Dubai: Toward a Sustainable Digital Future

Feasibility and Exploratory Study of Implementing the Blockchain Technology in the UAE Financial Markets

LIST OF TABLES

Efficiency and Market Power in Tunisian Banking

*Abderazak Bakhouche, Anissa Naouar,
Mohamed Lotfi Boulkeroua, Randa Elchaar, Anca Bocanet,
and Eman Zabalawi*

1 INTRODUCTION

In banking, competition can serve as a valuable instrument in attaining an efficient allocation of funds, especially in the markets where asymmetric information and agency problems and uncertainties are widespread (Grossman & Stiglitz, 1980; Hart, 1983). Under the agency framework, managers are driven by their own utility-maximisation goals, such as effort minimisation, which contrast with the profit-maximisation goal for the owners. These managers may cause the firm to underperform

A. Bakhouche (✉) · M. L. Boulkeroua · R. Elchaar · A. Bocanet
Business Department, Higher Colleges of Technology, Dubai,
United Arab Emirates
e-mail: abakhouche@hct.ac.ae

M. L. Boulkeroua
e-mail: mboulkeroua@hct.ac.ae

R. Elchaar
e-mail: relchaar@hct.ac.ae

A. Bocanet
e-mail: abocanet@hct.ac.ae

© The Author(s), under exclusive license to Springer Nature
Singapore Pte Ltd. 2022
A. Echchabi et al. (eds.), *Contemporary Research in Accounting
and Finance*, https://doi.org/10.1007/978-981-16-8267-4_1

1

by resorting to inefficiency and slack, increasing the risk of default and bankruptcy (Hart, 1983). The diffusion of competition will incentivise management to reduce and eliminate managerial slack by operating close to their production frontier.

A strand in the industrial organisation literature examining the competition-efficiency nexus in banking emphasises the importance of competition and market power for bank performance. In particular, numerous studies support that banks in more concentrated, less competitive markets exhibit higher inefficiencies. Lower competition indicates higher market power, which measures a financial institution's ability to price output at levels above marginal cost. The finding of a negative relationship between market power and efficiency is commonly explained by the *Quiet Life Hypothesis* (QLH).

The *quiet life hypothesis* proposed by Hicks (1935) is a special case of the *market power hypothesis* (Bain, 1952) and has been intensively tested in the literature on banking. The hypothesis postulates that under less competitive conditions, banks with higher market power are less incentivised to pursue greater efficiencies (Koetter & Vins, 2008; Rhoades & Rutz, 1982). Hicks (1935) asserts that under less competitive conditions, the managers of monopolistic firms can extract rent through exercising their market power. Consequently, they are less motivated to pursue efficiency plans as they are not aligned with their utility. Hicks (1935) argues that when discipline from the product market is not sufficiently punitive, managers avoid difficult decisions and exert less effort.

There is a tendency for *a quiet life* to prosper in the banking systems where the maximisation of owners' wealth or firms' profits is not the primary goal for bank management. This view is most observed in systems where government ownership dominates. In principle, government banks have goals linked to the government's goals, which are not necessarily

A. Naouar
Economics Department, MENA College of Management, Dubai,
United Arab Emirates
e-mail: anissa.naouar@mcm.ac.ae

E. Zabalawi
Strategic Leadership, Amity Group, Dubai, UAE
e-mail: ezabalawi@amityuniversity.ae

market-driven. In the absence of an effective and efficient corporate governance and monitoring system, managers will use their "politically" influenced position to serve their own goals. These poorly monitored banks managers may pursue unfavourable and non-competitive pricing policies consistent with holding their *politically influenced* positions rather than seeking efficiency gains and maximising profit. As a result, the financial system will experience a substantial delay in attaining more deepening and efficient allocation of capital, with potential losses in social welfare (Williams, 2012).

Against this background, this study tests the relevance of the relationship between bank competition and efficiency under the aegis of the *quiet life hypothesis* in the context of Tunisian banking between 2005 and 2019.

The banking industry in Tunisia has experienced significant changes in corporate governance, manifested by the reduction in the size of government ownership accompanied by an increase of foreign ownership. Nevertheless, although privatisation has enhanced the role of non-state banks in the industry, the still significant presence of government ownership may be considered the main factor behind the banking system's recent adverse performance, among other factors.

The market power and performance conditions in banking are influenced by sector government policies. Since the late 1980s, the financial system in Tunisia has been characterised by progressively structural transformation. The effectuation of profound financial sector liberalisation reform signalled a policy shift towards the IMF-endorsed market-based management of the economy and the financial sector in particular (Jbili et al., 1997). Several direct and indirect, quantitative and qualitative financial liberalisation measures were introduced in anticipation that such measures will alleviate impediments to enacting a more efficient and competitive financial intermediation. The deregulation of interest rates, the reduction of government intervention and ownership in the banking sector, the reform of the nonperforming loans situation and the modernisation of the regulation related to capital adequacy and lending may affect banks' market structure, profitability and efficiency.

The remainder of this study is organised as follows. Section 1 provides the theoretical framework of the analysis. Section 2 reviews numerous studies on the relationship between efficiency and competition. Section 3 presents the methods used to estimate efficiency and market power, provides the specification liking market power to efficiency, and outlines the data and variables. Section 4 presents the empirical results. Section 5 summarises, recommends and concludes.

2   LITERATURE REVIEW

2.1   Bank Efficiency

In the last three decades, a sizeable body of studies has emerged estimating and analysing the factors which influence bank cost and profit efficiencies in various contexts (Berger & Humphrey, 1997). A well-developed literature has focused on developed banking systems in the context of consolidation activities and deregulation (Grabowski et al., 1994), ownership structure (Berger & Bouwman, 2013) and more recently, the effect of the 2008–2009 financial crisis (Asimakopoulos et al., 2018).

Studies using data from emerging and less developed countries have focused on the effect of the financial sector's reforms, especially the role of foreign capital (Bonin et al., 2005; Dadzie & Ferrari, 2019; Djalilov & Piesse, 2019; Williams, 2012; Yildirim & Philippatos, 2007) the difference between Islamic banks and conventional banks (Mohanty et al., 2016; Srairi, 2010) and the effect of the financial crisis (Kamarudin et al., 2016). These studies have employed different methodologies and reported significant cost and profit inefficiencies in most banking systems, and that profit inefficiencies are more widespread than cost inefficiencies, indicating a difficult environment for profit generation.

Additionally, bank efficiency analysis is extended beyond estimation to address factors and variables that affect magnitude. These factors can be divided into four sets: the set of bank-specific factors (size, capitalisation, liquidity, credit risk and market power, type ownership, business model), the set of industry-specific variables (concentration), the set of institutional variables (quality of corporate governance, political stability, quality of government) and the set of economic variables (GDP growth, inflation, and other macroeconomic indicators).

By focusing on the effect of ownership on bank performance, existing research reports inconclusive findings (Yildirim & Philippatos, 2007). Hasan and Hunter (1996), Mahajan et al. (1996) and Chang et al. (1998) find that domestically owned US banks are substantially more cost efficient than foreign-owned banks. DeYoung and Nolle (1996) conjecture that foreign banks are overwhelmed by the goal of market share expansion upon entry. To reach this goal, foreign banks will incur more costs, broaden the deposit base, set up extensive delivery channels, and accept lowering margin and possibly increase risk-taking.

By contrast, the efficiency studies in less developed banking markets generally find that private banks are more efficient than non-private banks and that foreign banks are more efficient than either state-owned banks or domestic private banks (Claessens et al., 2001; Kamarudin et al., 2016). However, there are some exceptions. Bonin et al. (2005) find that domestically owned private banks are not significantly more cost efficient than government-owned banks in Central and Eastern European countries. Yildirim and Philippatos (2007) find that in transition countries, foreign banks are more cost efficient but less profit efficient than domestically owned banks, both private and state.

Berger and Hannan (1998) summarise the reasons that may explain the influence of market structure, as a proxy for market power, on efficiency. First, in a highly concentrated market, managers may not have incentives to work as hard to keep costs under control, and therefore, they can set prices above marginal costs to obtain higher profits. Monopoly power is the main force driving managers to relax their efforts. Second, market power may allow managers to pursue objectives other than profit maximisation (such as expense preference behaviour). Third, in a non-competitive setting, managers devote resources to obtaining and maintaining market power, raising costs and reducing cost efficiency. Fourth, if banks enjoy market power, incompetent managers can survive without a wilful shirking of work efforts.

2.2   Competition-Efficiency Nexus: The Quiet Life Hypothesis

The investigation of the bank market power-efficiency relationship under the aegis of the quiet life hypothesis has engendered substantial interest within the literature on bank performance and structure. However, empirical evidence suggests unclear-cut findings, especially in emerging markets. Berger and Hannan (1998) find that banks in more concentrated markets are associated with lower cost efficiency, supporting the QLH. More recent studies re-examine the depth and cogency of the quiet life hypothesis in various contexts. Maudos and de Guevara (2007) test the quiet life hypothesis by examining the relationship between cost efficiency and the Lerner index in the EU-15 countries over 1993–2002. The results support a positive relationship between market power and cost efficiency, permitting the rejection of the quiet life hypothesis. The lower pressure from competition to increase the quality of banking services and lower monitoring and screening costs may explain the negative relationship between competition and efficiency. Results show that higher market power causes more welfare losses than inefficiency, supporting enacting economic policy measures to reduce the barriers to competition.

Similarly, Solis and Maudos (2008) estimate the social costs of market power and test the quiet life hypothesis in the Mexican banking system over the 1993–2005 period. The results reject the quiet life hypothesis in the deposits market but cannot reject it in the lending market. Banks with greater market power can offer lower quality of their services to lower operating costs and increase efficiency. Furthermore, the evidence is favourable to this hypothesis in the loans market.

Koetter and Vins (2008) tested the QLH by estimating cost and profit efficiency for all savings banks operating in Germany between 1996 and 2006, using a stochastic cost and profit panel frontier analysis, as well as the market power (Lerner index). They found a negative relationship between cost efficiency and the Lerner index, supporting the QLH and implying that more market power induces banks to incur more slack in their business's operations.

Chortareas et al. (2011) test the market power and efficiency hypotheses for several Latin American countries for the 1997–2005 period. Similarly, Williams (2012) tests the "quiet life" for a sample of 419 Latin American commercial banks between 1985 and 2010. Since the 1990s, banking in Latin America was subjected to a financial liberalisation programme, which stimulated foreign investments and active consolidation activities, and also may have caused financial crises. The wave of mergers and the increase in market concentration has questioned possible rise in banks' market power with potential effects on consumer welfare. The results of both studies reject the quiet life hypothesis, concluding that bank restructuring reforms in Latin America has promoted competition and generated efficiency gains. Instead, both studies support the efficient structure (ES) hypothesis, disregarding any collusion in the banking sectors of Latin America.

Fu and Heffernan (2009) analyse the nexus between the market power and efficiency hypotheses for a sample of Chinese banks over the period 1985–2002, a period characterised by important banking sector reforms launched in 1992. No evidence is found to support the quiet life hypothesis. Strict interest rate controls prevented state banks from earning monopoly profits. Färe et al. (2015) find that the QLH only operates for some financial institutions because depending on the level of market power and the type of bank. Almounsor and Mensi (2016) find support for the QLH in Saudi banking.

Dadzie and Ferrari (2019) reveal that ownership reforms implemented in Ghana had an overall positive impact on efficiency, primarily attributable to the relaxation of entry restrictions and foreign banks' technological superiority. The study shows that heightening competition did not contribute to efficiency gains, as the macroeconomic weaknesses did not enable smooth transmission of competition into the sector.

González et al. (2019) test the four hypotheses on the market structure, profitability and efficiency relationships using a set from the MENA region during the 2005–2012 period. Contrary to the SCP and ES hypotheses' expectations, the results show that market concentration can negatively influence efficiency. In regions like the MENA, some banks operate in risky and undeveloped environments, parallel with significant technological delay and limited competition. In this sense, the results contribute to explain an environment propitious to the QLH but where the explanation for inefficiency is not only the more relaxed position of the monopolist but also the difficult conditions to develop the activity.

Yin (2021) investigates the relationship between competition and efficiency using a dataset covering 148 countries over 1995–2015. This study finds evidence to propose that competition has delirious effects on banks' cost efficiency, in plain disagreement with the precepts of *the quiet life hypothesis*. The regulatory and institutional environment in which banks operate constitutes the catalyst factor affecting the competition-efficiency nexus. The author finds that the regulation related to activity restriction and capital requirements are more conducive to cost inefficiency, while factors related to easing information asymmetries such as effective supervisions and information sharing of credit registries bring about further more cost efficiencies. Hence, Yin (2021) proposes improving efficiency through bank supervisions and information sharing and strengthen the competition-efficiency link through effective bank regulation.

The inconclusiveness about the validity of the *quiet life* hypothesis leaves the question about the relationship between efficiency and competition open to empirical investigation. As such, the fundamental goal of this study is to test the *quiet life* hypothesis in Tunisian banking.

3   METHODOLOGY AND HYPOTHESES DEVELOPMENT

3.1   Estimation of Bank Cost Efficiency

Cost efficiency measures a banking firm's performance relative to the best-practice bank that produces the same output bundle under the same exogenous conditions. Profit efficiency measures how close a bank is to attaining the maximum possible profit as a best-practice firm on the frontier for given levels of input and output prices (quantities) and other exogenous market variables. Both estimates measure the extent to which banks achieve optimisation objectives of cost minimisation and profit maximisation.

Studies on cost and profit efficiency have used two main approaches to estimate cost and profit efficiencies: the data envelopment approach (DEA) (Chortareas et al., 2011; Diallo, 2018) and the Statistic frontier approach (SFA) (Berger & Humphrey, 1997; Dadzie & Ferrari, 2019; Yildirim & Philippatos, 2007).

The DEA approach is a non-parametric linear programming technique, which does not require the specification of a functional form from the relationship between output, input and input prices. By contrast, the SFA asserts that inefficiency is observed by estimating a function and some distributional assumptions of the error term. Most studies that employ the SFA specify a multiproduct translog functional form to estimate the cost and alternative profit. Based on Battese and Coelli (1995), Allen and Rai (1996), this study estimates cost and profit efficiency for a sample of banks from the specification of a translog function within the SFA. The definition of the input, output and input prices variables in the specification frameworks is performed using the intermediation approach (Sealey & Lindley, 1977). It assumes that banks act as financial intermediaries that purchase funds to generate earning assets.

Profit efficiency is estimated from the alternative profit specification. The alternative profit specification employs the same set of exogenous variables as the cost function in Eq. (1), with the only difference that profit replaces total cost as the dependent (Berger & Mester, 1997).

In this transformation process, banks incur costs (TC): cost of purchased funds (W1), cost of labour (W2) and cost of physical capital (W3). Following Phan et al. (2016), total costs and input prices are normalised by the input price of physical capital (W3) to impose linear homogeneity in input prices. Accordingly, bank efficiency estimated is derived from the following translog functional form:

For cost efficiency:

$$\ln\left(\frac{TC_{it}}{W_{3it}}\right) = \alpha_0 + \alpha_1 \ln Q_{1it} + \alpha_2 \ln Q_{2it} + \beta_1 \ln\left(\frac{W_{it}}{W_{3it}}\right) + \beta_2 \ln\left(\frac{W_{2it}}{W_{3it}}\right)$$

$$+ \frac{1}{2}\alpha_{11}\left(\ln Q_{1it}\right)^2 + \alpha_{22}\frac{1}{2}\left(\ln Q_{2it}\right)^2 + \frac{1}{2}\beta_{11}\left(\frac{W_{1it}}{W_{3it}}\right)^2$$

$$+ \frac{1}{2}\beta_{22}\left(\frac{W_{2it}}{W_{3it}}\right)^2 + \frac{1}{2}\beta_{12}\ln\left(\frac{W_{1it}}{W_{3it}}\right)\ln\left(\frac{W_{2it}}{W_{2it}}\right)$$

$$+ \beta_{111}\ln Q_{1it}\ln\left(\frac{W_{1it}}{W_{3it}}\right) + \beta_{112}\ln Q_{2it}\ln\left(\frac{W_{1it}}{W_{3it}}\right)$$

$$+ \beta_{122}\ln Q_{2it}\ln\left(\frac{W_{2it}}{W_{3it}}\right) + \upsilon_{it} + \mu_{it} \tag{1}$$

For profit efficiency:

$$\ln\left(\frac{\pi_{it}}{W_{3it}}\right) = \alpha_0 + \alpha_1 \ln Q_{1it} + \alpha_2 \ln Q_{2it} + \beta_1 \ln\left(\frac{W_{1it}}{W_{3it}}\right) + \beta_2 \ln\left(\frac{W_{2it}}{W_{3it}}\right)$$

$$+ \frac{1}{2}\alpha_{11}\left(\ln Q_{1it}\right)^2 + \alpha_{22}\frac{1}{2}\left(\ln Q_{2it}\right)^2$$

$$+ \frac{1}{2}\beta_{11}\left(\frac{W_{1it}}{W_{3it}}\right)^2 + \frac{1}{2}\beta_{22}\left(\frac{W_{2it}}{W_{3it}}\right)^2$$

$$+ \beta_{12}\ln\left(\frac{W_{1it}}{W_{3it}}\right)\ln\left(\frac{W_{2it}}{W_{2it}}\right) + \beta_{111}\ln Q_{1it}\ln\left(\frac{W_{1it}}{W_{3it}}\right)$$

$$+ \beta_{112}\ln Q_{2it}\ln\left(\frac{W_{1it}}{W_{3it}}\right) + \beta_{122}\ln Q_{2it}\ln\left(\frac{W_{2it}}{W_{3it}}\right)$$

$$+ \upsilon_{it} + \mu_{it} \tag{2}$$

where TC denotes total costs of bank i at time t; Q1 and Q2 denote output proxied by total loans and total earning assets, especially; W1 is the price of purchased funds proxied by the ratio of total interest income to total purchased funds; W2 is the price of labour and denoted by total labour expenses to the number of employees; W3 is the price of physical capital proxied by the ratio of depreciation to fixed assets; υ_{it} is an error term assumed to be independent of other variables; and μ_{it} is error term indicating a rise in production costs due to managerial inefficiency.

The coefficients of the function are estimated by the maximum simulated likelihood method, u_{it} has a half-normal distribution truncated at zero to signify that each bank's cost lies either on or above (on or below) the cost (profit) frontier. Deviations from the frontier are interpreted as evidence of the quality of bank management. The choice of distribution for the inefficiency term is arbitrary, and other distributions are employed elsewhere in the literature (see Greene, 2008). The standard restrictions of linear homogeneity in input prices and symmetry of the second-order parameters are applied.

3.2   *Measuring Competition: Learner Index of Market Power*

This study measures the degree of competition in Tunisian banking by estimating the Lerner index of market power. This indicator captures the competitive conditions better than structural indicators such as the concentration ratios. It has the advantage of capture market power at the bank level, across time and by considering different geographic and product markets (Capraru et al., 2020).

The Lerner index of market power is estimated as the mark-up of outputs price over marginal cost (MC). Marginal cost (MC) reflects the price of output if perfect competition prevailed. Higher (lower) values of the Lerner index indicate greater (lower) market power, therefore lower (greater) competition. Under these conditions, the bank faces lower degrees of competition and is said to operate in the market structure of monopolistic competition.

The following equation can define the conventional Lerner index:

$$\text{Lerner}_{it} = \frac{P_{it} - MC_{it}}{MC_{it}} \tag{3}$$

where i and t describe bank i and time t, P denotes output price, and MC is the marginal cost.

The price of output is proxied as the ratio of operating revenues to total assets. MC is derived from a translog cost function with a single output, which is total assets (Turk-Ariss, 2010)

$$\ln\left(\frac{TC_{it}}{W_{3it}}\right) = \alpha_0 + \alpha_1 \ln A + \beta_1 \ln\left(\frac{W_{1it}}{W_{3it}}\right) + \beta_2 \ln\left(\frac{W_{2it}}{W_{3it}}\right) + \frac{1}{2}\alpha_{11}(\ln A)^2$$
$$+ \frac{1}{2}\beta_{11}\left(\frac{W_{1it}}{W_{3it}}\right)^2 + \frac{1}{2}\beta_{22}\left(\frac{W_{2it}}{W_{3it}}\right)^2 + \beta_{12}\ln\left(\frac{W_{1it}}{W_{3it}}\right)\ln\left(\frac{W_{2it}}{W_{3it}}\right)$$
$$+ \beta_{111}\ln A \ln\left(\frac{W_{1it}}{W_{3it}}\right) + \beta_{121}\ln A \ln\left(\frac{W_{2it}}{W_{3it}}\right) + \upsilon_{it} + \mu_{it} \tag{4}$$

The estimation of the equation above requires imposing the symmetry and homogeneity of degree one in input prices. The values of marginal cost (MC) are calculated from Eq. (4) by obtaining the partial derivative of the cost function with respect to the output variable A. Therefore, MC is derived from the following Eq. (5):

$$
MC_{it} = \frac{\partial \left(TC_{it} / W_{3it} \right)}{\partial Y_{it}} = \frac{\left(TC_{it} / W_{3it} \right)}{Y_{it}}
$$
$$
\left[\alpha_1 + \alpha_{11} \ln Y + \beta_{111} \ln \left(\frac{W_{1it}}{W_{3it}} \right) + \beta_{121} \ln \left(\frac{W_{2it}}{W_{3it}} \right) \right] \tag{5}
$$

The values of the Lerner index are expected to range between zero and one. A value that is closer or even higher than one indicates full market power characterising monopolistic conditions. By contrast, a Lerner closer to zero indicates weaker market power and therefore more competitive conditions. A value within the range of these two poles suggests monopolistic competition. Lerner can carry a negative value, indicating that the firm sets prices below marginal costs. It is possible in firms that pursue goals other than profit maximisation (Huang et al., 2018), such as firms owned by the government, which tend to have a crowded set of goals.

3.3   Econometric Model

Prior studies on bank efficiency employ two primary approaches to assessing the relationship set of bank-specific and country-specific factors and efficiency: the single country setup and the cross-country. In a cross-country setup, one provides insight into the average relationship between competition and stability for the set of countries under investigation (e.g. developing countries as in Turk-Ariss (2010), developed countries as in Berger et al. (2009), the European Union as in Schaeck and Cihak (2014), while controlling for other country-specific factors such as macroeconomic conditions, regulation and supervision. However, single-country studies (such as Boyd et al., 2006; Keeley, 1990; Salas & Saurina, 2003) document a large degree of variance in the competition-stability relationship. Therefore, the following baseline setup is adopted:

Bank efficiency = f(Competition, Bank Controls, Other Controls)

More specifically, we specify four models for each cost and profit efficiencies: one without ownership dummies and one with ownership dummies and interactions terms:

$$EFF_{i,t} = \alpha + \beta_1 \, LERNER_{i,t} + \beta_2 SHARE_{i,t} + \beta_3 \, SIZE_{i,t} + \beta_4 \, CAPITAL_{i,t}$$
$$+ \, \beta_5 \, LIQUIDITY_{i,t} + \beta_6 \, LLP_{i,t} + \beta_7 \, DIV_{i,t} + \beta_8 \, GROWTH_{i,t}$$
$$+ \, \beta_9 \, CRISIS + \varepsilon_{i,t} \tag{6}$$

where the dependent variable Efficiency is the cost or profit efficiency of bank i at time t estimated from Eqs. (1) and (2); LERNER is the main independent variable and is measured by Eq. (3); SHARE is a proxy for annual bank-level assets market share; SIZE is measured by the log of total assets; CAPITAL measures capital adequacy; LIQUIDITY is measured by the ratio of total loans to total deposits; LLP is the ratio of total loan loss provisions to total loans, and is a proxy for credit risk; DIV is measured by the ratio of total non-interest income to total operating income, and is the proxy for income diversification: GROWTH is the annual growth rate in real GDP and is a measure for business cycle and economic conditions: CRISIS is used to measure the effects of the 2008–2009 global financial crisis. It takes the value of one for the year 2009 and zero otherwise and ε is a random disturbance.

In Eq. (6), the coefficients on the market structure variables, Lerner and market Share, indicate whether the *quiet life hypothesis* holds. In this sense, the *quiet life hypothesis* holds if the coefficients on Lerner and market share are negative and statistically significant. Alternatively, the *relative market power hypothesis* holds if the variable Share is statistically significant in the profit efficiency model and insignificant in the cost efficiency model.

Additionally, to assess the role ownership in the competition-efficiency relationship, other models which incorporate Ownership dummies and their interaction with each of the competition measure (LERNER) market share (SHARE) and SIZE are estimated. There four ownership dummies: STATE as a proxy for government-owned banks; FOREIGN as a dummy variable assigned to foreign-owned banks; PRIVATE as a dummy variable for domestic privately owned banks; and MIXED as a dummy variable for banks which are controlled by the Tunisian government and foreign governments. Therefore, for each type of efficiency and ownership, the following three equations are specified:

For interaction between ownership and competition:

$$\begin{aligned}
\text{EFF}_{i,t} = {} & \alpha + \beta_1 \text{ LERNER}_{i,t} + {} + \beta_2 \text{OWNERSHIP\_ DUMMY} \\
& + {} + \beta_3 \text{ LERNER}_{i,t} \times \text{ OWNERSHIP\_DUMMY} \\
& + \beta_4 \text{ SHARE}_{i,t} + \beta_5 \text{ SIZE}_{i,t} + \beta_6 \text{ CAPITAL}_{i,t} \\
& + \beta_7 \text{ LIQUIDITY}_{i,t} + \beta_8 \text{ LLP}_{i,t} + \beta_9 \text{ DIV}_{i,t} \\
& + \beta_{10} \text{ GROWTH}_{i,t} + \beta_{11} \text{ CRISIS} + \varepsilon_{i,t}
\end{aligned} \tag{7}$$

For interaction between ownership and market share:

$$\begin{aligned}
\text{EFF}_{i,t} = {} & \alpha + \beta_1 \text{ LERNER}_{i,t} + {} + \beta_2 \text{ SHARE}_{i,t} \\
& + \beta_3 \text{ OWNERSHIP\_DUMMY} + \beta_4 \text{ SHARE}_{i,t} \\
& \times \text{ ONWERSHIP\_DUMMY} + \beta_5 \text{ SIZE}_{i,t} \\
& + \beta_6 \text{ CAPITAL}_{i,t} + \beta_7 \text{ LIQUIDITY}_{i,t} + \beta_8 \text{ LLP}_{i,t} \\
& + \beta_9 \text{ DIV}_{i,t} + \beta_{10} \text{ GROWTH}_{i,t} + \beta_{11} \text{ CRISIS} + \varepsilon_{i,t}
\end{aligned} \tag{8}$$

For interaction between ownership and market share:

$$\begin{aligned}
\text{EFF}_{i,t} = {} & \alpha + \beta_1 \text{ LERNER}_{i,t} + \beta_2 \text{ SHARE}_{i,t} + \beta_3 \text{ SIZE}_{i,t} \\
& + \beta_4 \text{OWNERSHIP\_DUMMY} + \beta_5 \text{ SIZE}_{i,t} \\
& \times \text{ ONWERSHIP\_DUMMY} + {} + {} + \beta_6 \text{ CAPITAL}_{i,t} \\
& + \beta_7 \text{ LIQUIDITY}_{i,t} + \beta_8 \text{ LLP}_{i,t} + \beta_9 \text{ DIV}_{i,t} \\
& + \beta_{10} \text{ GROWTH}_{i,t} + \beta_{11} \text{ CRISIS} + \varepsilon_{i,t}
\end{aligned} \tag{9}$$

In the above equations, the statistical significance, sign and magnitude of the coefficients on interaction terms will inform on the role of ownership type on the relationship between competition and efficiency. More specially, it will inform whether the *quiet life* hypothesis holds for a specific type of ownership.

Besides, there is a strong possibility for "reverse causation" running from bank efficiency to competition in congruence with the efficient structure hypothesis. As such, the impact of market structure on cost efficiency in Tunisian banking is estimated through a panel data 2SLSIV regression model. We employ the instrumental variables method (2SLS) to address the potential bias from endogeneity problems. We retain the one-period lag of each of the competition variables as an instrumental variable for the corresponding competition LERNER variable (Koetter et al., 2012; Williams, 2012).

3.4   *Data Description*

This study investigates the efficiency-competition nexus of Tunisia's banking industry. Relevant bank-level variables are compiled from the individual balance sheet and income statements, published by the Tunisian Professional Association of Banks and Financial Institutions (APTBEF). The analysis is conducted for the 2005–2019 period, which has spawn path-changing external and internal events in the political, economic and financial spheres. All banks are involved in commercial and universal activities. The sample contains three small and recently entered Sharia-compliant banks: Baraka bank, Zitouna Bank and Al-Wifak Bank. The unbalanced dataset includes 23 banks, with a total of 321 bank year observations. All variables are ratios; therefore, there it is unnecessary to deflate the nominal values.

The definition of variables used in estimating efficiency and marginal cost (MC) follows the intermediation proposed by Sealey and Lindley (1977). This approach suggests that banks function as intermediaries transforming purchased funds into earning assets by incurring input costs. Due to the small number of banks in our sample, two output (Loans and Other Earning Assets) and three inputs are employed to calculate cost and profit efficiency, and one output (Total assets) and three inputs are used in the calculation of marginal costs.

The set of inputs consists of purchased funds (X1) retained as the sum of total deposits and borrowing; labour (X2) proxied by the number of full-time employees; and physical capital (X3) proxied by the total fixed assets. The corresponding prices of input are as follows: the price of purchased funds (W1) is proxied by the ratio of total interest expenses to total purchased funds, the price of labour (W2) is computed by the ratio of personnel expenses to the total number of full-time employees, the price of physical capital (W3) is held as the ratio of other operating expenses to total fixed assets. Total costs are retained as the sum of interest expenses, personnel expenses and other operating expenses.

Table 1 summarises the dataset used in the estimation of cost and profit efficiencies and marginal cost analysis, and presents the descriptive statistics of the control variables used in the regression.

Table 1 Total costs, total profit and output variable, and input prices variables

	Mean	Std	Kurt	Skew	Min	Max	Count
TC = Total Operating Costs	154.35	177.40	3.87	1.81	0.60	960.18	321.00
W1 = Price of purchases funds	0.03	0.02	29.92	3.34	–	0.22	321.00
W2 = Price of labour	0.02	0.02	37.11	5.79	0.01	0.13	321.00
W3 = Price of physical capital	4.33	39.97	300.88	17.10	0.11	706.82	321.00
A = Total assets	2,943.71	3,185.44	1.75	1.40	16.31	16,331.77	321.00
LOANS = Total net loans	2,095.86	2,338.19	1.41	1.36	0.11	10,676.70	321.00
Other earning assets (total other earning assets)	355	485	2	2	–	2,087	321
Π = total operating profit	62.46552336	85.70699	5.921387	2.077028	−24.166	569.063	321

Source Authors' calculation based on data collected from Tunisian Professional Association of Banks and Financial Institutions (APTBEF)

4   Empirical Results

4.1   Estimation Results for Bank Efficiency and Lerner Index of Market Power

Table 2 provides the average estimated cost efficiencies, profit efficiencies, price, marginal costs and the Lerner index of market power for the 23 banks by year and ownership type from 2005 to 2019. Table 2 shows that inefficiencies are widespread in Tunisian banking. Cost efficiency is found to be about 0.77, implying that banks in Tunisia can make cost savings of 23% had they operate on the best practice frontier. González et al. (2019) find average cost efficiency of 9.77 for the MENA region between 2005 and 2013. Otero et al. (2019) report cost efficiency of 0.82 for Tunisian banks for the period 2005–2012.

Table 2   Cost efficiency, profit efficiency and Lerner values

Year	Cost efficiency	Profit efficiency	Price	MC	Lerner index
Panel 1 = per year					
2005	0.8002	0.5682	0.0672	0.0518	0.2072
2006	0.8022	0.5904	0.0714	0.0545	0.2218
2007	0.7430	0.6020	0.0677	0.0524	0.2054
2008	0.7499	0.6497	0.0689	0.0529	0.2159
2009	0.7338	0.6967	0.0597	0.0461	0.1937
2010	0.7392	0.7142	0.0569	0.0457	0.1375
2011	0.8015	0.6120	0.0577	0.0507	0.1051
2012	0.7911	0.6084	0.0555	0.0489	0.1130
2013	0.7696	0.5871	0.0632	0.0553	0.1424
2014	0.7704	0.5746	0.0657	0.0620	0.0873
2015	0.7904	0.5241	0.0687	0.0685	0.0680
2016	0.7601	0.5124	0.0681	0.0678	0.0704
2017	0.8067	0.5484	0.0723	0.0734	0.0529
2018	0.7451	0.5105	0.0801	0.0790	0.0561
2019	0.7155	0.4982	0.0879	0.0867	0.0381
Panel 2 = per ownership type					
Foreign	0.7278	0.5803	0.0691	0.0552	0.1820
Mixed	0.8101	0.5455	0.0691	0.0542	0.2202
Private	0.7804	0.6972	0.0732	0.0511	0.2756
State	0.7971	0.5737	0.0631	0.0737	−0.0556
Period average	0.7678	0.5838	0.0674	0.0603	0.1241

Source Authors' calculation based on data collected from Tunisian Professional Association of Banks and Financial Institutions (APTBEF)

Likewise, the average profit efficiency is 0.59, implying that banks can make the current profit with 41% less operating cost had they adopt best practices. The correlation between cost efficiency and profit efficiency is found to be $-.075$ (p-value is 0.17), which implies that banks that are cost efficient are not necessarily profit efficient. Berger and Mester (1997) find a similar result for US banking, manifested by a negative correlation between cost estimates and profit estimates.

Cost efficiencies are commonly found higher than profit efficiencies in many studies (Maudos et al., 2002). For instance, Berger and Mester (1997) report values of 0.86 and 0.50 for average cost efficiency of 0.86 in US banking. Yildirim and Philippatos (2007) find an average cost of efficiency of 0.77 and average profit efficiency of 0.72 for a sample of banks from 12 East European countries.

The cost efficiencies for Tunisian banks tend to be superior and less volatile than profit efficiencies, which reflect difficult profit-related environmental conditions. Similar superiority is reported by Williams (2012) for Latin American banking.

The Lerner value for the whole period is about 0.12, indicating relative lower market power in Tunisian banking and therefore higher competition. A number of observations should be made at this level. First, cost efficiency decreased from about 0.80 in 2005–2006 to about 0.74 in 2007–2010, possibly relating to the negative effect of the 2008–2009 financial crisis. Between 2011 and 2017, cost efficiency fluctuated between 0.76 and 0.80 then declined from about 0.81 in 2017 to 0.72 in 2019. This decline may be due to the increase in the cost of compliance with the new regulation of 2016. Foreign banks are the least efficient with 0.73, whereas other types of banks have a relatively equal level of about 0.80.

Second, profit efficiency maintained a rising trend between 2005 (0.57) and 2009–2010 (0.70). However, profit efficiency plummeted to 0.61 in 2011 and continues to decline to reach 0.50 in 2019. This decline may reflect the adverse effect of the post-2011 political change in Tunisia, which may have has reduced profit-making opportunities. Private banks are the most profit efficient with 0.70, whereas other types of ownership have values between 0.54 and 0.58.

Third, the Lerner index of market power maintained a stable level of about 0.20 from 2005 to 2009. Lerner witnessed a declining trend from 0.19 in 2010 to 0.04 in 2019, mirroring heightened competitive conditions in the banking sector. The structural transformation that occurred in the post-2010 period has yielded a new "competitive and regulatory" environment with strong implications n market power. Private banks exhibit higher Leaner values (0.28), followed by mixed banks (0.22) and foreign banks (0.18). State banks have negative values for Lerner (−0.06), reflecting an absence of market power for this category of banks and that they may be still operating away from the principles of wealth and profit maximisation. Conventional banks (0.09) have more market power than Islamic banks (0.06).

4.2   *The Estimation Results for the Market Power-Efficiency Nexus*

The estimation strategy is to run the 2SLSIV model to control for simultaneous and endogenous relationship between bank efficiency and indicators of market power: Lerner, market share and size.

Table 3 displays the 2SLSIV estimates from the regressions where cost and profit efficiencies are the dependent variables. In both specifications, the coefficients on the two market structure proxies of Lerner and market share carry the *plus* sign, suggesting a positive relationship between market power and efficiency. While the relationship is statistically significant for Lerner in both profit and cost efficiency specifications, for Market share, it is significant only for the profit efficiency model.

The results show that the Lerner index of market power and market share as a measure of relative market power positively affect efficiency. The higher the market power, the higher efficiency, which implies that lower competition fosters efficiency in Tunisian banking. Hence, a finding consisting of a positive and significant coefficient for the variable Lerner as a measure of competition refutes the validity of the *quiet life* hypothesis in the context of Tunisian banking.

Alternately, there is an indication that the relative market power hypothesis (RMP) holds in Tunisian banking. Table 3 shows that the variable proxying market share is statistically insignificant in the cost efficiency model, whereas it is positive and statistically significant in the profit efficiency model. A similar finding applies to the variable proxying size. The results show that market share positively affects (profit) efficiency, suggesting banks with higher market share tend to be more (profit) efficient.

These results may indicate that Tunisian banks face different competitive conditions in the input markets and the output markets. Generally, the statistical significance of market share supports the relative market

Table 3   Relationship between market power and efficiency

	Model 1: Cost efficiency	Model 2: Profit efficiency
Constant	−0.1447 (0.9133)	−5.2759 (1.7858)***
Lerner	1.5795 (0.4195)***	1.3976 (0.8202)*
Share	0.0127 (0.0508)	0.253 (0.0993)**
Size	−0.0257 (0.0476)	−0.2255 (0.0931)**
LLP	−0.8252 (0.3866)**	−0.5084 (0.756)
Capital	−1.1231 (0.2813)***	4.2449 (0.5501)***
DIV	−0.1671 (0.0512)***	−0.1164 (0.100)*
Liquidity	0.0528 (0.0172)***	−0.1123 (0.0337)***
CRISIS	−0.1248 (0.0591)**	0.1027 (0.1156)
GDP Growth	−0.8099 (0.9111)	−1.471 (1.7814)
Number of observations	298	298
Wald chi2	58.87 (0.000)***	1893.58 (0.000)***
R-squared	0.1373	0.8637
Root MSE	0.24663	0.48224
Tests of endogeneity		
Durbin (score)	6.715 (0.009)*	4.042 (0.044)**
Wu-Hausman F-statistic	6.616 (0.011)**	3.95 (0.048)**
Estat first stage		
Minimum eigenvalue statistic	42.36 (0.000)***	42.36 (0.000)***
Tests of overidentifying restrictions		
Sargan (score) chi2	23.36 (0.003)***	14.51 (0.070)*
Basmann chi	23.81 (0.003)***	14.33 (0.074)*

Standard errors are reported between parentheses
*Statistical significance at the 10% level
**Statistical significance at the 5% level
***Statistical significance at the 1% level
Source Authors' calculation based on data collected from Tunisian Professional Association of Banks and Financial Institutions (APTBEF)

power hypothesis (RMP). Hence, the relative market power (RMP) hypothesis cannot be rejected for Tunisian banking. Banks in Tunisia may have been pursuing differentiation tactics to enhance their market power and extract profit.

An increase in competition through privatisation in favour of foreign capital (at the expense of the still large government-owned banks) and entry of new Islamic banks (as a sign for differentiation) may have posed a threat to incumbent dominant banks, which fear the loss of market share. To protect market share, they may have resort to pricing their products and services below marginal costs. To counterbalance this behaviour, foreign and private banks may have used differentiation plans to enhance performance over the already relatively troubled state banks.

Alternatively, the main finding that higher levels of competition may have detrimental effects on bank performance measured by cost and profit efficiency accords with the "banking specificities" hypothesis (Pruteanu-Podpiera et al., 2008). As state (and mixed) banks still occupy a significant portion of the banking sector, their response to competitive pressures from other private and foreign banks has affected the sector's competition-efficiency nexus. To face the trivariate threat to market share and dominance from the private and foreign banks, state banks set prices of their products and services below marginal costs.

Table 3 shows the results for the relationships between other bank-specific variables, GDP growth and Crisis and efficiency. First, both cost and profit efficiencies are found to be negatively related to bank size. While this relationship is statistically significant with a larger magnitude for profit efficiency, it is insignificant for cost efficiency. These results suggest that size is irrelevant for the cost (input market), whereas it is emphasised for the profit (output market). On average, larger banks are less efficient than smaller banks indicating diseconomies of scale. Banks in Tunisia are not operating at the right size, with strong important policy ramifications on the area related to bank assets growth through consolidation activities. These results differ from Yildirim and Philippatos (2007), who find a positive and statistically significant impact of size on cost efficiency but insignificant for profit efficiency.

Second, as expected, banks with higher credit risk proxied by the ratio of LLPs to total net loans have lower cost and profit efficiencies in line with The size of LLPs is more significant on the cost side than on the profit side, which shows than Tunisian banks incur additional costs to recover and monitor bad doubtful loans. Additionally, higher and rising LLP ratios indicate poor loan quality and regulatory requirement to enhance LLPs when they are inadequate. Improving the quality of loans may require additional operating costs relating to bad loans management, such as enhancing credit approval control, foreclosing bad loans, bad loans recovery expenses and other expenses related to loan restructuring. Poor quality of loans indicates bad management and penchant for risk-taking and unfavourable institutional and economic conditions, in line with the bad management hypothesis and bad luck hypothesis

(Berger & DeYoung, 1997; Kwan & Eisenbeis, 1997). Additionally, large volumes of doubtful loans were accumulated by state banks from lending to government-owned enterprises, *secteur publique*.

Third, the variable LIQUIDITY is found to have a significant relationship with both types of efficiency. However, while the relationship is negative for cost efficiency, it is positive for profit efficiency. In other words, banks with higher liquidity measured by the ratio of total net loans to total net deposits appear to be less cost efficient but more profit efficient.

Three explanations may justify this finding. First, the insignificance of the coefficient in the cost efficiency model may reflect that banks finance their assets with lower cost suggesting lower deposits rates in the market. Second, banks may have reduced the cost of generating loans and collecting deposits. A higher liquidity ratio indicates that increasing the loan origination functions of banks translate into higher returns (Alhassan et al., 2016). Third, the ratio of net loans to deposits can also be used to proxy for banks' funding structure and the efficiency of financial intermediation functions of banks. As such, banks might be struggling to direct deposit to profit-making with higher returns projects in very difficult economic conditions, especially in the aftermath of the 2011 structural transformation.

Fourth, regarding the variable controlling for income diversification, DIV, the associated coefficient in both cost and profit efficiency models are negative and statistically significant. This result suggests that income diversification in Tunisian banking does not aid bank cost and profit efficiency. This result conforms with the results of Berger et al. (2010) on Chinese banking that both product and geographical diversifications lead to higher costs and lower profits. It is also consistent with those, results of Abuzayed et al. (2018) on GCC banking that income or asset diversification strategies do not enhance bank stability. Thus, banks with a higher diversification ratio seem to be less efficient. This may suggest that income from non-interest activities (investments in government and non-government securities) does not measure up to the related incurred costs and does not yield sufficient profit. As this finding may imply concerns related to the business environment where banks are operating, banks may need to review the feasibility of non-intermediaries activities.

Fifth, capitalisation is found to harm cost efficiency but improves profit efficiency. In both models, the relationship is significant. Well-capitalised banks have lower cost efficiencies and higher profit efficiencies. Berger and

Mester (1997) and Yildirim and Philipatos (2007) report higher efficiency levels for better-capitalised banks.

The positive and significance of the coefficient on the CAPITAL variable suggest that higher bank capitalisation may have pursued better policies to reduce information asymmetries related to the profit-generating investment projects. However, the negative sign on capital for cost efficiency has not reduced the cost of funds to undertake intermediation. The successive rounds of recapitalisation to comply with *upgraded* capital adequacy regulations have increased costs for banks. However, other economic agents may have preferred dealing with banks with better capital ratios as a sign of sound financial health.

Finally, Table 3 shows the negative but insignificant impact of economic growth on bank efficiencies, indicating that the volatile and adverse economic conditions have affected bank performance. Further, the sign on the CRISIS dummy is negative and significant in the cost efficiency model but positive and insignificant in the profit efficiency model. These results imply that the 2008–2009 financial crisis caused banks to incur costs possibly related to NPLs.

4.3   *The Estimation Results for the Impact of Market Power, Market Share and Size for State Banks*

Table 4 shows the estimates from the profit and cost efficiencies' regressions in which the state ownership is the primary independent variable. Our focus is on the coefficients related to the ownership dummies of State, Lerner, market Share, Size and the interactions terms. Table 4 shows that the coefficients on the STATE dummy variable are positive and statistically significant in the models that accommodate interactions terms with Lerner and Size. While the coefficient is positive for the model with no interactions terms, it is only significant in the profit efficiency model. For the models where State interacts with market Share, the coefficients on the State is negative.

The quiet life hypothesis implies a negative relationship between competition and inefficiency. In more concentrated markets, bank management lacks sufficient motivations to engage in outcome-maximisation behaviour, be it profit, profit efficiency, cost efficiency or wealth, because management has attained its own utility maximisation through this situation. As a consequence, inefficient bank management

Table 4 The relationship between market power, market share and size for state banks

	No interaction		Interaction with Lerner		Interaction with share		Interaction with Size	
	Cost efficiency	profit efficiency	Cost efficiency	profit efficiency	Cost efficiency	profit efficiency	Cost efficiency	profit efficiency
Constant	−0.163 (0.9195)	−6.2273 (1.7415)***	−5.787 (1.2209)***	−14.4433 (2.3959)***	−0.4842 (0.9332)	−7.891 (1.7037)***	−0.9232 (0.9627)	−9.2027 (1.7695)***
Lerner	1.5968 (0.4347)***	2.3473 (0.8233)***	3.6768 (0.5866)***	5.3467 (1.1512)***	2.0095 (0.5052)***	4.6524 (0.9222)***	2.044 (0.4982)***	4.3169 (0.9157)***
State	0.0081 (0.0428)	0.4102 (0.0811)***	4.8417 (0.7015)***	7.4847 (1.3766)***	−0.2219 (0.1018)**	−0.6911 (0.1859)***	1.287 (0.4479)***	5.2523 (0.8232)***
Lerner X State			−3.9131 (0.5637)***	−5.7281 (1.1062)***				
Share	0.0109 (0.0518)	0.1628 (0.098)*	−0.0389 (0.0498)	0.0915 (0.0977)	0.0164 (0.0516)	0.1786 (0.0942)*	−0.006 (0.0523)	0.0891 (0.0961)
Share X State					−0.0769 (0.0318)**	−0.3711 (0.0581)***		
Size	−0.0253 (0.0477)	−0.204 (0.0903)**	0.0338 (0.0456)	−0.1176 (0.0894)	−0.0194 (0.0477)	−0.1749 (0.0871)**	0.005 (0.0486)	−0.0892 (0.0893)
Size X State							−0.0857 (0.0297)***	−0.324 (0.0546)***
LLP	−0.8272 (0.3868)**	−0.5924 (0.7326)	−1.0966 (0.3614)***	−0.9954 (0.7092)	−0.8445 (0.386)***	−0.6158 (0.7048)	−0.8526 (0.3844)**	−0.6354 (0.7066)
Capital	−1.13 (0.2859)***	3.8449 (0.5415)***	0.1654 (0.2626)	5.7695 (0.5153)***	−1.2616 (0.3041)***	3.0139 (0.5552)***	−1.2821 (0.3036)***	3.096 (0.558)***

(continued)

Table 4 (continued)

	No interaction		Interaction with Lerner		Interaction with share		Interaction with Size	
	Cost efficiency	profit efficiency	Cost efficiency	profit efficiency	Cost efficiency	profit efficiency	Cost efficiency	profit efficiency
DIV	-0.1636	0.0571	-0.0533	0.2201	-0.1557	0.0843	-0.1592	0.0642
	(0.054)***	(0.1023)	(0.0514)	(0.1009)**	(0.0539)***	(0.0983)	(0.0537)***	(0.0987)
LIQ UIDITY	0.0518	-0.1662	0.0221	-0.2094	0.0254	-0.2948	0.021	-0.284
	(0.0181)***	(0.0343)***	(0.0177)	(0.0348)***	(0.0214)	(0.039)***	(0.0212)	(0.039)***
CRISIS	-0.1245	0.1159	-0.1007	0.1508	-0.1215	0.1297	-0.1212	0.128
	(0.0592)**	(0.1121)	(0.0556)*	(0.1091)	(0.0591)**	(0.1079)	(0.0589)**	(0.1082)
GDP	-0.8099	-1.4864	-0.2075	-0.5957	-0.797	-1.4859	-0.7876	-1.4567
GROWTH	(0.9114)	(1.7261)	(0.8558)	(1.6794)	(0.91)	(1.6612)	(0.9062)	(1.6656)
Number of observations	298	298	298	298	298	298	298	298
Wald chi2 (8)	58.80	2041.91	101.70	2182.36	61.37	2339.90	63.36	2222.43
	(0.000)***	(0.000)***	(0.000)***	(0.000)***		(0.000)***	(0.000)***	(0.000)***
R-squared	0.1367	0.872	0.241	0.879	0.1393	0.8814	0.1464	0.8808
Root MSE	0.2467	0.46726	0.23134	0.454	0.24634	0.44972	0.24532	0.45093
Tests of endogeneity								
Durbin (score) chi2	6.621	7.103	7.30	7.05	6.76	12.65	6.45	10.60
	(0.010)**	(0.008)***	(0.007)***	(0.008)***	(0.009)***	(0.000)***	(0.011)**	(0.001)***
Wu-Hausman	6.499	6.984	7.16	6.91	6.61	12.63	6.31	10.51
F-statistic	(0.011)**	(0.009)***	(0.008)***	(0.009)***	(0.011)**	(0.000)***	(0.013)**	(0.001)***
Estat first stage								

	No interaction		Interaction with Lerner		Interaction with share		Interaction with Size	
	Cost efficiency	profit efficiency	Cost efficiency	profit efficiency	Cost efficiency	profit efficiency	Cost efficiency	profit efficiency
Minimum eigenvalue statistic	39.41 (0.000)***	39.41 (0.000)***	23.03 (0.000)***	23.03 (0.000)***	27.51 (0.000)***	27.51 (0.000)***	28.20 (0.000)***	28.20 (0.000)***
Tests of overidentifying restrictions:								
Sargan (score) chi2	23.39 (0.003)***	15.06 (0.058)*	23.98 (0.004)***	14.25 (0.114)	27.27 (0.001)***	13.88 (0.127)	28.31 (0.000)***	13.30 (0.149)
Basmann chi2	23.76 (0.003)***	14.85 (0.062)*	24.24 (0.004)***	13.91 (0.126)	27.90 (0.001)***	13.53 (0.140)	29.08 (0.000)***	12.95 (0.165)

Standard errors are reported between parentheses
*Statistical significance at the 10% level
**Statistical significance at the 5% level
***Statistical significance at the 1% level
Source Authors' calculation based on data collected from Tunisian Professional Association of Banks and Financial Institutions (APTBEF)

maximises its own utility by gaining market power through wasteful expenditure.

These results offer several inferences about state ownership. First, in both cost and profit efficiency models, there is a negative and significant relationship between the interaction term of LERNER and STATE and efficiency. The market power of state banks may be responsible for their inefficiencies. Managers of state banks could have fewer incentives or pressure from internal and external factors to be more efficient because they may think they have met certain efficiency threshold or achieved other goals. However, for state banks to protect *monopolistic privileges* and maintain *market power*, they may accept lower efficiency levels by purchasing expensive input and setting products at lower prices. This result is consistent with the *quiet life hypothesis*.

Second, there is a negative and significant relationship between the interaction term of market SHARE and STATE dummy in both cost and profit efficiency models, suggesting a negative market share-efficiency link for state ownership. This result implies that state banks with higher market share tend to be associated with lower cost and profit efficiencies. For state banks to protect their market share, they incur higher costs and accept forgoing profit manifested by lower (and negative) profit margins. This further supports the relevance of the *quiet life hypothesis* for state banks. To compare, Garza-Garcia (2012) find that state-owned banks' performance in Mexico is driven by market share.

Third, there is a negative and significant relationship between the interaction terms of Size and State in both cost and profit efficiency specifications. Larger state banks tend to have less cost and profit efficiencies, implying widespread diseconomies of scale.

To sum up, State banks with higher market power, market share and size tend to be the least cost and profit efficient. Hence, the quiet life hypothesis for State banks cannot be rejected.

4.4 The Estimation Results for the Impact of Market Power, Market Share and Size for Foreign Banks

Table 5 shows results from the 2SLSIV estimation for foreign banks where the main independent variable is the dummy variable controlling for foreign-owned and controlled banks, FOREIGN and its interaction terms with LERNER, market SHARE are and SIZE.

Table 5 Relationship between market power, market share and size for foreign banks

	Cost efficiency	profit efficiency	Cost efficiency	profit efficiency	Cost efficiency	profit efficiency	Cost efficiency	profit efficiency
Constant	−0.2762 (0.9046)	−5.4621 (1.7782)***	−0.1244 (0.8583)	−5.2985 (1.7568)***	−0.7496 (0.8935)	−5.5905 (1.7968)***	0.1982 (0.879)	−5.3616 (1.7877)***
Lerner	1.5762 (0.4148)***	1.393 (0.8155)*	0.6993 (0.4879)	0.5176 (0.9986)	1.6795 (0.4076)***	1.3959 (0.8196)*	1.546 (0.4003)***	1.3988 (0.814)*
Foreign	−0.0809 (0.0313)**	−0.1144 (0.0615)*	−2.9486 (0.6889)***	−2.7173 (1.4101)*	0.2873 (0.0986)***	−0.0077 (0.1984)	−1.7014 (0.3579)***	−0.4712 (0.7279)
Lerner X Foreign			2.3371 (0.5609)***	2.1212 (1.1481)*				
Share	−0.0002 (0.0505)	0.2347 (0.0992)**	0.0083 (0.0479)	0.2449 (0.0981)**	−0.0477 (0.051)	0.2218 (0.1026)**	0.0045 (0.0488)	0.2354 (0.0992)**
Share X Foreign					0.1036 (0.0264)***	0.03 (0.0531)		
Size	−0.0168 (0.0472)	−0.2129 (0.0928)**	−0.0178 (0.0447)	−0.2139 (0.0915)**	−0.0057 (0.0462)	−0.2097 (0.093)**	−0.0554 (0.0464)	−0.2214 (0.0944)**
Size X Foreign							0.1125 (0.0248)***	0.0248 (0.0503)
LLP	−0.9022 (0.3835)**	−0.6173 (0.7539)	−1.0468 (0.3665)***	−0.7651 (0.7502)	−0.9758 (0.3748)***	−0.6442 (0.7536)	−0.9969 (0.3708)***	−0.6355 (0.754)
Capital	−1.101 (0.2783)***	4.2761 (0.5472)***	−0.4908 (0.3294)	4.8806 (0.6742)***	−1.091 (0.2712)***	4.2962 (0.5454)***	−1.0139 (0.2681)***	4.2874 (0.5452)***
DIV	−0.1457 (0.0513)***	−0.0862 (0.1008)	−0.1072 (0.0502)**	−0.0474 (0.1028)	−0.165 (0.0505)***	−0.0904 (0.1015)	−0.1562 (0.0497)***	−0.0891 (0.101)

(continued)

Table 5 (continued)

	Cost efficiency	profit efficiency	Cost efficiency	profit efficiency	Cost efficiency	profit efficiency	Cost efficiency	profit efficiency
LIQUIDITY	0.0435 (0.0174)**	-0.1256 (0.0342)***	0.0285 (0.0168)*	-0.139 (0.0345)***	0.0236 (0.0178)	-0.1313 (0.0357)***	0.0216 (0.0175)	-0.1304 (0.0356)***
CRISIS	-0.1243 (0.0585)**	0.1034 (0.115)	-0.1155 (0.0554)**	0.1115 (0.1134)	-0.1278 (0.0572)**	0.1024 (0.1149)	-0.1267 (0.0565)**	0.1028 (0.1149)
GDP Growth	-0.8091 (0.9009)	-1.4699 (1.7711)	-0.4825 (0.8583)	-1.1569 (1.7569)	-0.8733 (0.8806)	-1.4828 (1.7707)	-0.88 (0.8708)	-1.4881 (1.771)
Number of observations	298	298	298	298	298	298	298	298
Wald chi2 (8)	66.88 (0.000)***	1919.19 (0.000)***	104.31 (0.000)***	1980.72 (0.000)***	83.07 (0.000)***	1921.27 (0.000)***	89.60 (0.000)***	1920.72 (0.000)***
R-squared	0.1564	0.8653	0.244	0.8691	0.1946	0.8654	0.2123	0.8654
Root MSE	0.2439	0.47945	0.231	0.47257	0.23831	0.4792	0.23566	0.47928
Tests of endogeneity								
Durbin (score) chi2(1)	6.843 (0.009)***	4.08 (0.044)**	6.56 (0.010)**	3.26 (0.071)*	6.53 (0.011)**	3.86 (0.049)**	5.48 (0.019)**	4.07 (0.044)**
Wu-Hausman F(1,288)	6.721 (0.010)**	3.97 (0.047)**	6.41 (0.012)**	3.15 (0.77)*	6.38 (0.012)**	3.74 (0.054)*	5.33 (0.022)**	3.94 (0.048)**
Estat first stage Minimum eigenvalue statistic (F(7,283))	42.21 (0.000)***	42.21 (0.000)***	28.13 (0.000)***	28.13 (0.000)***	37.91 (0.000)***	37.91 (0.000)***	38.188 (0.000)***	38.19 (0.000)***

	Cost efficiency	profit efficiency	Cost efficiency	profit efficiency	Cost efficiency	profit efficiency	Cost efficiency	profit efficiency
Tests of overidentifying restrictions:								
Sargan (score) chi2(6)	22.62 (0.004)***	14.27 (0.075)*	21.72 (0.009)***	14.24 (0.114)	25.66 (0.002)***	15.24 (0.084)*	26.32 (0.002)***	14.49 (0.106)
Basmann chi2(6)	22.92 (0.004)***	14.04 (0.081)*	21.77 (0.009)***	14.90 (0.126)	26.09 (0.002)***	14.93 (0.093)*	26.84 (0.002)***	14.152 (0.117)

Standard errors are reported between parentheses
*Statistical significance at the 10% level
**Statistical significance at the 5% level
***Statistical significance at the 1% level
Source Authors' calculation based on data collected from Tunisian Professional Association of Banks and Financial Institutions (APTBEF)

In all specifications reported in Table 5, the coefficients on the dummy variable FOREIGN are adequately significant in the cost efficiency models but slightly significant or insignificant in profit efficiency models. Further, while the sign on FOREIGN is negative in all models, it turns into positive in the model that accommodates the interaction of SHARE and FOREIGN. These results may suggest that: (i) foreign banks may enjoy similar profit effeminacy levels as other types of banks, (ii) foreign banks are associated with lower cost efficiencies and (iii) foreign banks may extend their market share through the realisation of cost savings. Overall, these conflicting results may signal that these banks may have improved efficiencies, especially since many of them were controlled by the government.

Thus, for foreign banks, the interaction terms suggest positive relationships between market power, market share and size with efficiencies in the cost efficiency models. By contrast, for profit efficiency models, the relationship with profit efficiency is weakly significant when interaction with Lerner and insignificant for interaction with market share and size.

These results imply that foreign-owned banks rely on efficiencies to foster their market power and extend their market share. These results refute the quiet life hypothesis suggesting that foreign banks do not resort to collusion to heighten performance. A significant positive relationship between the estimated efficiency and market share (and Lerner and market share) indicator supports the Efficient Structure Hypothesis (ESH), which is not the main concern f this study.

Finally, results suggest that larger foreign banks realise higher cost efficiencies, suggesting considerable economies of scale.

4.5   The Estimation Results for the Impact of Market Power, Market Share and Size for Mixed Banks

Table 6 presents the results of the 2SLSIV estimation for mixed banks. The main independent variables are the dummy variable controlling for the mixed ownership, *Mixed*, and the interaction terms of *Mixed* with *Lerner*, market *Share* and *Size*. The ownership of these banks is equally shared between the Tunisian government and governments from the GCC and Libya. In 2005, the charter of these banks was transformed from development financial institutions to universal banks subject to similar banking regulation as other banks.

Table 6 The relationship between market power, market share and size for mixed banks

	Cost efficiency	Profit efficiency	Cost efficiency	Profit efficiency	Cost efficiency	Profit efficiency	Cost efficiency	Profit efficiency
Constant	−0.0475 (0.8955)	−5.5209 (1.7612)***	−0.2352 (0.9105)	−5.5296 (1.7936)***	−0.0646 (0.8892)	−5.5093 (1.7528)***	−0.2431 (0.9053)	−5.7975 (1.7811)***
Lerner	1.2355 (0.4339)***	2.270 (0.8534)***	1.1528 (0.4674)**	2.1314 (0.9207)**	1.1629 (0.4352)***	2.0681 (0.8578)**	1.1169 (0.4564)**	2.0125 (0.8979)**
Mixed	0.1299 (0.0462)***	−0.3428 (0.0908)***	−0.8618 (1.1435)	−0.5846 (2.2525)	−0.6815 (0.4528)	−1.4056 (0.8926)	1.0818 (0.8524)	1.1236 (1.677)
Lerner X Mixed			0.8098 (0.9361)	0.2008 (1.8439)				
Share	0.0355 (0.0505)	0.1939 (0.0993)*	0.0263 (0.0507)	0.1956 (0.0999)*	0.0382 (0.0502)*	0.2012 (0.099)**	0.0275 (0.0505)	0.1843 (0.0994)*
Share X Mixed					−0.1725 (0.096)*	−0.2268 (0.1893)		
Size	−0.0201 (0.0467)	−0.2404 (0.0918)***	−0.0079 (0.0487)	−0.2372 (0.0959)**	−0.0163 (0.0464)	−0.2352 (0.0915)**	−0.006 (0.0482)	−0.2186 (0.0948)**
Size X Mixed							−0.072 (0.0642)	−0.1107 (0.1264)
LLP	−0.9138 (0.3803)**	−0.2821 (0.748)	−0.9133 (0.3792)**	−0.3071 (0.747)	−0.9304 (0.378)	−0.3267 (0.745)	−0.9278 (0.3792)**	−0.3197 (0.746)
Capital	−0.9542 (0.2845)***	3.822 (0.5595)***	−0.901 (0.3052)***	3.9089 (0.6011)***	−0.9178 (0.2843)	3.9364 (0.5605)***	−0.8831 (0.2969)***	3.9783 (0.5842)***
DIV	−0.1797 (0.0502)***	−0.0814 (0.0988)	−0.1722 (0.0516)***	−0.0748 (0.1016)	−0.1795 (0.0499)**	−0.0767 (0.0983)	−0.1715 (0.0508)***	−0.0658 (0.1)

(continued)

Table 6 (continued)

	Cost efficiency	Profit efficiency	Cost efficiency	Profit efficiency	Cost efficiency	Profit efficiency	Cost efficiency	Profit efficiency
LIQUIDITY	0.0572 (0.0169)***	−0.1236 (0.0333)***	0.0577 (0.0169)***	−0.1232 (0.0333)**	0.0593 (0.0169)**	−0.1206 (0.0333)***	0.0589 (0.0169)***	−0.1208 (0.0333)***
CRISIS	−0.1276 (0.0579)**	0.1103 (0.114)	−0.126 (0.0578)**	0.1109 (0.1138)	−0.1334 (0.0576)*	0.1028 (0.1136)	−0.1293 (0.0577)**	0.1079 (0.1135)
GDP GROWTH	−0.801 (0.8924)	−1.4872 (1.7552)	−0.7928 (0.8899)	−1.4626 (1.753)	−0.9196 (0.8883)	−1.6228 (1.751)	−0.8533 (0.8891)	−1.5533 (1.7492)
Number of observations	298	298	298	298	298	298	298	298
Wald chi2	70.33 (0.000)***	1964.15 (0.000)***	73.35 (0.000)***	1970.23 (0.000)***	75.30 (0.000)***	1983.94 (0.000)***	73.10 (0.000)***	1981.82 (0.000)***
R-squared	0.1723	0.8677	0.1774	0.8681	0.1837	0.8689	0.1798	0.8688
Root MSE	0.24158	0.47514	0.2408	0.47438	0.23991	0.47291	0.24098	0.47313
Tests of endogeneity								
Durbin (score) chi2	4.692 (0.030)**	6.276 (0.012)**	5.23 (0.022)**	5.52 (0.019)**	4.71 (0.030)**	5.38 (0.020)**	4.30 (0.038)**	5.25 (0.022)**
Wu-Hausman F-statistic	4.575 (0.033)**	6.153 (0.014)**	5.09 (0.025)**	5.38 (0.021)**	4.58 (0.033)**	5.24 (0.023)**	4.17 (0.042)**	5.11 (0.025)**
Estat first stage Minimum eigenvalue statistic	38.02 (0.000)***	38.02 (0.000)***	31.31 (0.000)***	31.31 (0.000)***	33.55 (0.000)***	33.55 (0.000)***	30.91 (0.000)***	30.91 (0.000)***

	Cost efficiency	Profit efficiency	Cost efficiency	Profit efficiency	Cost efficiency	Profit efficiency	Cost efficiency	Profit efficiency
Tests of overidentifying restrictions:								
Sargan (score) chi2	21.68 (0.005)***	15.55 (0.049)**	22.34 (0.008)***	17.45 (0.042)**	22.43 (0.008)***	17.15 (0.046)**	22.04 (0.009)***	17.10 (0.047)**
Basmann chi2	21.89 (0.005)***	15.36 (0.053)*	22.45 (0.008)***	17.23 (0.045)**	22.55 (0.007)***	16.91 (0.050)***	22.12 (0.008)***	16.86 (0.051)*

Standard errors are reported between parentheses

*Statistical significance at the 10% level

**Statistical significance at the 5% level

***Statistical significance at the 1% level

Source Authors' calculation based on data collected from Tunisian Professional Association of Banks and Financial Institutions (APTBEF)

The results in Table 6 indicate the following. First, in the model without interaction terms, the coefficient on the dummy variable, *Mixed*, is positive and significant for cost efficiency but negative and significant for profit efficiency. This finding suggests that mixed banks have been more effective in controlling and lowering their cost than maximising profit efficiencies. Second, in the models where interactions terms are present, the coefficients on *Mixed* and the interactions terms are statistically insignificant. This finding implies that mixed banks are still under transition period and they are somehow still shielded away from the impact of market disciplines, which may tend to regulate behaviour and performance. These insignificant impact of market conditions on efficiency for mixed banks may provide additional support for the *quiet Life* hypothesis and urges government intervention.

4.6   *The Estimation Results for the Impact of Market Power, Market Share and Size for Private Banks*

Table 7 shows the 2SLSIV estimation results for private banks where domestic private capital holds control and the majority of ownership. Table 7 shows that the coefficients on the *PRIVATE* dummy variable and the interaction terms of *PRIVATE* with *LERNER*, market *SHARE* and *SIZE*, are statistically insignificant. These findings suggest that private banks in Tunisia may be pursuing more objectives than standard outcome-maximisation, such as cost efficiency and profit efficiency. Further, private banks may be responding to competition from foreign banks by other factors which are not captured by our specifications.

It is worth noting that the banks controlled by domestic private capital in Tunisia are part of holding company structures. Isik and Hassan (2002) and Berger and Bouwman (2013) find that a bank owned by holding companies tends to be more efficient and has less capital. However, Athanasoglou et al. (2008) find no significant relationship between performance and ownership structure. The findings further support the exploration of the role of private banks in the market structure-performance nexus.

5   DISCUSSIONS AND CONCLUSION

Over the last three decades, the banking system in Tunisia has experienced structural configuration driven by the fundamental shifts in public policy towards market-based principles with implications for market concentration and performance.

Table 7 The relationship between market power, market share and size for private banks

	Cost efficiency	Profit efficiency	Cost efficiency	Profit efficiency	Cost efficiency	Profit efficiency	Cost efficiency	Profit efficiency
Constant	−0.1939 (0.914)	−5.4101 (1.785)***	−0.1708 (0.9133)	−5.3386 (1.7802)***	−0.1788 (0.9114)	−5.4056 (1.7845)***	−0.1009 (0.9322)	−5.0588 (1.8187)***
Lerner	1.5891 (0.4194)***	1.4255 (0.819)*	1.5846 (0.4167)***	1.4163 (0.8122)*	1.6387 (0.4164)***	1.5009 (0.8154)*	1.6008 (0.4165)***	1.4767 (0.8126)*
Private	0.048 (0.0533)	0.1302 (0.104)	−5.2048 (6.213)	−16.3386 (1.7802)	0.7927 (0.4882)	0.8265 (0.9559)	−0.7937 (1.6449)	−3.0695 (3.2091)
Lerner X Private			4.1643 (4.9252)	13.208 (9.5998)				
Share	0.0073 (0.0511)	0.2383 (0.0998)**	0.0088 (0.0511)	0.2429 (0.0996)**	0.0072 (0.051)	0.2373 (0.0998)**	0.0122 (0.052)	0.2568 (0.1015)**
Share X Private					0.3408 (0.2221)	0.3186 (0.4349)		
Size	−0.025 (0.0476)	−0.2237 (0.0929)**	−0.0264 (0.0475)	−0.228 (0.0927)**	−0.0275 (0.0475)	−0.226 (0.093)**	−0.0305 (0.0488)	−0.2446 (0.0951)**
Size X private							0.0535 (0.1045)	0.2033 (0.2038)
LLP	−0.8293 (0.3862)**	−0.519 (0.7542)	−0.8291 (0.3856)**	−0.5173 (0.7515)	−0.8268 (0.385)**	−0.5106 (0.7538)	−0.8311 (0.386)**	−0.5245 (0.7531)
Capital	−1.1227 (0.281)***	4.2447 (0.5488)***	−1.1192 (0.2794)***	4.2526 (0.5446)***	−1.1518 (0.2791)***	4.199 (0.5464)***	−1.1307 (0.2793)***	4.2098 (0.5449)***
DIV	−0.1698 (0.0512)**	−0.1239 (0.1)	−0.1713 (0.0511)***	−0.1288 (0.0996)	−0.1772 (0.0512)***	−0.1322 (0.1003)	−0.1724 (0.0513)***	−0.1338 (0.1002)

(continued)

Table 7 (continued)

	Cost efficiency	Profit efficiency	Cost efficiency	Profit efficiency	Cost efficiency	Profit efficiency	Cost efficiency	Profit efficiency
LIQUIDITY	0.052 (0.0172)***	−0.1146 (0.0336)***	0.0516 (0.0172)***	−0.1157 (0.0335)***	0.0508 (0.0172)***	−0.1158 (0.0337)***	0.0514 (0.0173)***	−0.117 (0.0337)***
CRISIS	−0.125 (0.0591)**	0.1022 (0.1154)	−0.1244 (0.059)**	0.104 (0.115)	−0.1255 (0.0589)**	0.1016 (0.1154)	−0.1251 (0.0591)**	0.1017 (0.1152)
GDP Growth	−0.81 (0.91)	−1.4717 (1.7772)	−0.8099 (0.9088)	−1.4722 (1.7713)	−0.7993 (0.9075)	−1.4677 (1.7768)	−0.8066 (0.9099)	−1.46 (1.7751)
Number of observations	298	298	298	298	298	298	298	298
Wald chi2 (8)	59.69 (0.00)***	1904.05 (0.000)***	61.11 (0.000)***	1918.74 (0.000)***	62.60 (0.000)***	1905.44 (0.000)***	60.26 (0.000)***	1909.70 (0.000)***
R-squared	0.1393	0.8643	0.1415	0.8652	0.144	0.8644	0.1396	0.8646
Root MSE	0.24635	0.4811	0.24603	0.47953	0.24567	0.48102	0.24631	0.48053
Tests of endogeneity								
Durbin (score) chi2	6.727 (0.009)***	4.07 (0.044)**	7.15 (0.007)***	4.51 (0.034)**	7.42 (0.006)***	4.60 (0.032)**	7.11 (0.008)***	4.51 (0.034)**
Wu-Hausman F-statistic	6.606 (0.011)**	3.96 (0.048)**	7.01 (0.009)***	4.38 (0.037)**	7.28 (0.007)***	4.47 (0.035)**	6.97 (0.009)***	4.38 (0.037)**
Estat first stage Minimum eigenvalue statistic	42.16 (0.000)***	42.16 (0.000)***	38.82 (0.000)***	38.82 (0.000)***	38.74 (0.000)***	38.74 (0.000)***	38.94 (0.000)***	38.94 (0.000)***

	Cost efficiency	Profit efficiency	Cost efficiency	Profit efficiency	Cost efficiency	Profit efficiency	Cost efficiency	Profit efficiency
Tests of overidentifying restrictions:								
Sargan (score) chi2	23.47 (0.003)***	14.39 (0.072)*	23.63 (0.005)***	14.25 (0.114)	24.23 (0.004)***	14.42 (0.108)	23.46 (0.005)***	14.36 (0.110)
Basmann chi2	23.85 (0.002)***	14.16 (0.078)*	23.86 (0.005)***	13.91 (0.126)	24.52 (0.004)***	14.09 (0.119)	23.67 (0.005)***	14.02 (0.122)

Standard errors are reported between parentheses

*Statistical significance at the 10% level

**Statistical significance at the 5% level

***Statistical significance at the 1% level

Source Authors' calculation based on data collected from Tunisian Professional Association of Banks and Financial Institutions (APTBEF)

The financial sector has been subjected to a comprehensive programme of price and nonprice liberalisation reforms. This consisted of implementing deregulation of interest rates, consolidation among a few ex-specialised public banks in the late 1990s, the transfer of ownership of a few distressed banks to healthier foreign-owned entities, and liberation of the balance sheets of distressed state institutions off nonperforming loans by use of public funds and successive rounds of use recapitalisation.

However, despite the remarkable progress made as evidenced by the declining concentration ratio (CR3), the Tunisian banking sector still shows numerous vulnerabilities, resulting from the significant government ownership in the industry. This study examines the banking sector's cost and profit efficiency in Tunisia, which is still transitioning to a more market-based system. The *quiet life hypothesis* represents the primary theoretical framework of the empirical analysis. An unbalanced panel of 23 banks is studied over the period 2005–2019. A two-stage approach is followed to arrive at the results. In the first stage, the cost efficiency, profit efficiency and marginal costs used to estimate the Lerner index of market power are derived from the stochastic frontier approach. In the second stage, a 2SLSIV regression is specified to measure the relationship of market power, market share, size, ownership and other bank and non-banks specific variables with cost and profit efficiency.

The results vary. First, the average bank in Tunisia deviates substantially and significantly from the best-practice frontier. The average cost efficiency level is 0.77, and the average profit efficiency is about 0.59. These estimates suggest that an average bank would have realised savings of 23% less actual costs and 41% more actual profit had it matched its performance with the best-practice bank. While foreign banks are the least cost efficient, private banks are the most profit efficient.

Second, the Lerner index of market power suggests low and declining market power for the average bank in Tunisia. Average Lerner values fell from 0.21 in 2005 to 0.04 in 2019, with an average of 0.12 over the period 2005–2019, in a clear indicator to improved competition conditions. This trend indicates that measures consisting of reducing government ownership, entry of foreign capital, and de novo Islamic banks, in addition to other liberalisation measures, may have heightened competition in the banking industry. The dichotomy of Lerner values per type of ownership shows that private banks (0.28) than mixed banks (0.22) or foreign banks (0.18). State banks have negative values of Lerner (−0.06), reflecting multi-faceted difficulties.

Third, the results of the 2SLSIV estimation report a positive and significant relationship between a bank's cost and profit efficiencies and the Lerner index of market power. Banks with higher market power are more cost and profit efficient. Banks tend to increase their efficiencies in an environment characterised by less competitive pressure. Hence, the *quiet life hypothesis* is rejected, favouring the *relative market power hypothesis*. Generally, our results are similar to González et al. (2019).

However, the breakdown of the analysis per type of ownership yields different standpoints by the *quiet life* hypothesis. The results provide evidence for the validity of the *quiet life* hypothesis for State banks (and to some extent private and mixed banks) but reject *it* for foreign banks.

Such conflicting results findings are not novel in the literature. For instance, Koetter et al. (2012) reject the quiet life hypothesis for cost efficiency but not for profit efficiency for in US banking. Färe et al., (2015) find that the quiet life to be valid only for some financial institutions in Spain (Khan et al., 2017) find evidence for both the efficient structure hypothesis and the *quiet life* hypothesis in ASEAN banking industry.

Based on the above, the following can be advanced:

> First, the widespread cost and profit inefficiencies in Tunisian banking suggest significant wastage significant social loss with implications on consumer welfare. This finding should motivate banks' management to propose cost saving plans to reduce inefficiencies by embarking on intensive investment in technology, productivity and FinTechs.
>
> Second, the results also indicate to the presence of diseconomies of scale in Tunisian banking. On average, banks are not operating at the optimal size. The policy shall implement consolidation activities, primarily through the acquisition of least efficient banks by most efficient banks.
>
> Third, non-intermediation activities tend to hurt banks' performance, reflecting difficult economic conditions, underdeveloped financial markets and the absence of alternative investments where banks extract solid non-interest revenue. The government should continue developing stable social, political and financial institutions and regulatory infrastructure and tackling non-bank sources of instability, particularly information asymmetries and macroeconomic conditions.

Fourth, the most important implication of this study can be derived from the *quiet life hypothesis* stand. The government shall review how banking is practised by state banks, mixed banks and private banks and propose plans to deal with the prevailing inertia by domestically owned banks. In particular, evidence suggests that bank state-to-foreign ownership transfer and entry of new banks has been able to reduce concentration, heighten competition and improve efficiencies over the years. However, further measures are still needed to eradicate the *quiet life* phenomenon, which tends to be more associated with state banks. Privatisation of the remaining State banks, preferably to foreign capital, may constitute one solution since foreign banks rely on improving performance to compete.

To bring robustness to our findings, we suggest that studies on Tunisia shall consider that the country is still in Transition, and therefore, studies shall consider the impact of ownership in analysis. Future research shall capitalise on the finding of these study. We recommend furthering the analysis of the market power-efficiency nexus through estimation of the social cost of the *quiet life* of state banks. The exploration of the role of ownership in nexuses such as the diversification-efficiency nexus, and efficiency-stability, and the competition-stability nexus shall also attract attention.

References

Abuzayed, B., Al-Fayoumi, N., & Molyneux, P. (2018). Diversification and bank stability in the GCC. *Journal of International Financial Markets, Institutions and Money, 57*(November), 17–43.

Alhassan, A. L., Tetteh, M. L., & Brobbey, F. O. (2016). Market power, efficiency and bank profitability: Evidence from Ghana. *Economic Change Reconstruction, 49*(1), 71–93.

Allen, L., & Rai, A. (1996). Operational efficiency in banking: An international comparison. *Journal of Banking and Finance, 20*(4), 655–672.

Almounsor, A., & Mensi, S. (2016). The implications of market structure and bank efficiency on social welfare: The case of the Saudi Arabian banking system. *Middle East Development Journal, 8*(2), 329–357. https://doi.org/10.1080/17938120.2016.1226467

Asimakopoulos, G., Chortareas, G., & Xanthopoulos, M. (2018). The Eurozone financial crisis and bank efficiency asymmetries: Peripheral versus core economies. *The Journal of Economic Asymmetries, 2018*(November), e00099.

Athanasoglou, P. P., Brissimis, S. N., & Delis, M. D. (2008). Bank-specific, industry-specific and macroeconomic determinants of bank profitability. *Journal of International Financial Markets, Institutions and Money, 18*(2), 121–136.

Bain, J. S. (1952). Relation of profit-rate to industry concentration: American manufacturing, 1936–1940. *Quarterly Journal of Economics, 65*, 293–324.

Battese, G. E., & Coelli, T. (1995). A model for technical inefficiency effects in a stochastic frontier production function for panel data. *Empirical Economics, 20*, 325–332. https://doi.org/10.1007/BF0120544

Berger, A. N., & Bouwman, C. (2013). How does capital affect bank performance during financial crises? *Journal of Financial Economics, 109*(1), 146–176. https://doi.org/10.1016/j.jfineco.2013.02.008

Berger, A. N., & DeYoung, R. (1997). Problem loans and cost efficiency in commercial banks. *Journal of Banking & Finance, 21*(6), 849–870.

Berger, A. N., & Hannan, T. H. (1998). The efficiency cost of market power in the banking industry: A test of the "Quiet Life" and related hypotheses. *The Review of Economics and Statistics, 80*(3), 454–465.

Berger, A. N., & Humphrey, D. B. (1997). Efficiency of financial institutions: International survey and directions for future research. *European Journal of Operational Research, 98*(2), 175–212.

Berger, A. N., Klapper, L. F., & Turk-Ariss, R. (2009). Bank competition and financial stability. *Journal of Financial Servies Research, 5*(2), 99–118. https://doi.org/10.1007/s10693-008-0050-7

Berger, A. N., & Mester, L. J. (1997). Inside the black box: What explains differences in the efficiencies of financial. *Journal of Banking and Finance, 21*, 895–947.

Berger, A. N., Hasan, I., & Zhou, M. (2010). The effects of focus versus diversification on bank performance: Evidence from Chinese banks. *Journal of Banking & Finance, 34*(2), 1417–1435.

Bonin, J. P., Hasan, I., & Wachtel, P. (2005). Bank performance, efficiency and ownership in transition countries. *Journal of Banking & Finance, 29*(1), 31–53.

Boyd, J. H., De Nicolò, G., & Jalam, A. M. (2006). *Bank risk-taking and competition revisited: New theory and new evidence.* IMF working paper. Retrieved from https://www.imf.org/external/pubs/ft/wp/2006/wp06297.pdf

Capraru, B., ihnatov, I., & Pintilie, N.-L. (2020). Competition and diversification in the European Banking Sector. *Research in International Business and Finance, 51*, 100963.

Chang, C. E., Hasan, I., & Hunter, W. C. (1998). Efficiency of multinational banks: An empirical investigation. *Applied Financial Economics, 8*(6), 1–8.

Chortareas, G. E., Garza-Garcia, J. G., & Girardone, C. (2011). Banking sector performance in Latin America: Market power versus efficiency. *Review of Development Economics, 15*(2), 307–325.

Claessens, S., Demirguc-Kunt, A., & Huizinga, H. (2001). How does foreign entry affect domestic banking markets? *Journal of Banking & Finance, 25*, 891–911. https://doi.org/10.1016/S0378-4266(00)00102-3

Dadzie, J. K., & Ferrari, A. (2019). Deregulation, efficiency and competition in developing banking markets: Do reforms really work? A case study for Ghana. *Journal of Banking Regulation, 20*(March), 328–340.

Diallo, B. (2018). Bank efficiency and industry growth during financial crises. *Economic Modelling, 68*(1), 11–22.

Djalilov, K., & Piesse, J. (2019). Bank regulation and efficiency: Evidence from transition countries. *International Review of Economics & Finance, 64*(November), 308–322.

Färe, R., Grosskopf, S., Maudos, J., & Tortosa-Ausina, E. (2015). Revisiting the quiet life hypothesis in banking using nonparametric techniques. *Journal of Business Economics, 16*(1), 159–187.

Fu, X., & Heffernan, S. (2009). The effects of reform on China's bank structure and performance. *Journal of Banking and Finance, 33*(1), 39–52.

Garza-Garcia, J. G. (2012). Does market power influence bank profits in Mexico? A study on market power. *Applied Financial Economics, 22*(1), 21–32.

González, L. O., Búa, M., Vivel, S., & Lado, R. (2019). Market structure, performance, and efficiency: Evidence from the MENA banking sector. *International Review of Economics & Finance, 64*(C), 84–101.

Grabowski, R., Rangan, N., & Rezvanian, R. (1994). The effect of deregulation on the efficiency of U.S. banking firms. *Journal of Economics and Business, 46*(1), 39–54.

Greene, W. H. (2008). *Econometric analysis* (6 ed.). Pearson Prentice Hall.

Grossman, S. J., & Stiglitz, J. E. (1980). On the impossibility of informationally efficient markets. *The American Economic Review, 70*(3), 393–408.

Hart, O. D. (1983). The market mechanism as an incentive scheme. *The Bell Journal of Economics, 4*(2), 366–382.

Hasan, I., & Hunter, C. H. (1996). Efficiency of Japanese multinational banks in the United States. *Research in Finance, 14*, 157–173.

Hasan, I., & Marton, K. (2003). Development and efficiency of the banking sector in a transitional economy: Hungarian experience. *Journal of Banking & Finance, 27*(12), 2249–2271. https://doi.org/10.1016/S0378-4266(02)00328-X

Hicks, J. R. (1935). Annual survey of economic theory: The theory of monopoly. *Econometrica, 3*(1), 1–20.

Huang, T.-H., Hu, C.-N., & Chang, B.-G. (2018). Competition, efficiency, and innovation in Taiwan's banking industry—an application of copula methods. *The Quarterly Review of Economics and Finance, 67*, 362–375.

Isik, I., & Hassan, K. (2002). Technical, scale and allocative efficiencies of Turkish banking industry. *Journal of Banking & Finance, 26*(4), 719–766.

Jbili, A., Enders, K., & Treichel, V. (1997). *Financial sector reforms in Algeria, Morocco, and Tunisia a preliminary assessment* (IMF Working Papers). https://doi.org/10.5089/9781451955170.001

Kamarudin, F., Sufian, F., & Nassir, A. M. (2016). Global financial crisis, ownership and bank profit efficiency in the Bangladesh's state owned and private commercial banks. *Contaduría y Administración, 61*(4), 705–745.

Keeley, M. C. (1990). Deposit insurance, risk, and market power in banking. *The American Economic Review, 80*(5), 1183–1200. https://www.jstor.org/stable/2006769

Khan, H. H., Kutan, A. M., Naz, I., & Qureshi, F. (2017). Efficiency, growth and market power in the banking industry: New approach to efficient structure hypothesis. *The North American Journal of Economics and Finance, 42*(C), 531–545.

Koetter, M., & Vins, O. (2008). *The quiet life hypothesis in banking—Evidence from German savings banks (Finance and Accounting Working Paper Series 190).*

Koetter, M., Kolari, J. W., & Spierdijk, L. (2012). Enjoying the quiet life under deregulation? Evidence from adjusted Lerner indices for US Banks. *The Review of Economics and Statistics, 94*(2), 462–480.

Kwan, S., & Eisenbeis, R. A. (1997). Bank risk, capitalization, and operating efficiency. *Journal of Financial Services Research, 12*(2), 117–131.

Mahajan, A., Rangan, N., & Zardkoohi, A. (1996). Cost structures in multinational and domestic banking. *Journal of Banking & Finance, 20*(2), 283–306.

Maudos, J., & de Guevara, J. F. (2007). The cost of market power in banking: Social welfare loss vs, cost inefficiency. *Journal of Banking & Finance, 31*(7), 2103–2125.

Maudos, J., Pastor, J. M., Perez, F., & Quesada, J. (2002). Cost and profit efficiency in European banks. *Journal of International Financial Markets. Institutions and Money, 12*(1), 33–58.

Mohanty, S. K., Lin, H.-J., Aljuhani, E. A., & Bardesi, H. J. (2016). Banking efficiency in Gulf Cooperation Council (GCC) countries: A comparative study. *Review of Financial Economics, 31*, 99–107.

Otero, L., Razia, A., Cunill, O. M., & Mulet-Forteza, C. (2019). What determines efficiency in MENA banks? *Journal of Business Research, 112*(May), 331–341.

Phan, H. T., Daly, K., & Akhter, S. (2016). Bank efficiency in emerging Asian countries. *Research in International Business and Finance, 38*, 517–530.

Pruteanu-Podpiera, A., Weill, L., & Schobert, F. (2008). Banking competition and efficiency: A micro-data Analysis on the Czech banking industry. *Comparative Economic Studies, 50*(2), 253–273.

Rhoades, S. A., & Rutz, R. D. (1982). Market power and firm size. *Journal of Monetary Economics, 9*(1), 73–85.

Salas, V., & Saurina, J. (2003). Deregulation, market power and risk behaviour in Spanish banks. *European Economic Review, 47*(6), 1061–1075. https://doi.org/10.1016/S0014-2921(02)00230-1

Schaeck, K., & Cihák, M. (2014). Competition, efficiency, and stability in banking. *Financial Management, 43*(1), 215–241.

Sealey, C. W., & Lindley, J. T. (1977). Inputs, outputs, and a theory of production and cost at depository financial institutions. *Journal of Finance, 32*(4), 1251–1266. https://doi.org/10.1111/j.1540-6261.1977.tb03324.x

Solís, L., & Maudos, J. (2008). The social costs of bank market power: Evidence from Mexico. *Journal of Comparative Economics, 36*(3), 467–488.

Sraïri, S. A. (2010). Cost and profit efficiency of conventional and Islamic banks in GCC countries. *Journal of Productivity Analysis, 34*(1), 45–62.

Turk-Ariss, R. (2010). Competitive conditions in Islamic and conventional banking: A global perspective. *Review of Financial Economics, 19*(3), 101–108.

Williams, J. (2012). Efficiency and market power in Latin American banking. *Journal of Financial Stability, 8*, 263–276. https://doi.org/10.1016/j.jfs.2012.05.001

Yildirim, H. S., & Philippatos, G. C. (2007). Efficiency of banks: Recent evidence from the transition economies of Europe, 1993–2000. *The European Journal of Finance, 13*(2), 123–143. https://doi.org/10.1080/13518470600763687

Yin, H. (2021). The impact of competition and bank market regulation on banks' cost efficiency. *Journal of Multinational Financial Management, 61*, 100677.

Board Gender Diversity and CSR Disclosure: The Case of Tunisian Listed Banks

Raida Chakroun

1 INTRODUCTION

Companies disclose information on social and environmental responsibility for several reasons, such as meeting stakeholders' information needs and improving the corporate image. However, a good level of corporate social responsibility (CSR) disclosure is not always synonymous with respect for the environment and society. Indeed, some managers may adjust the company's reporting to improve its quality and meet stakeholders' requirements (Gray et al., 2001).

The reports published by companies are controlled by their governance structures and especially by their board of directors. Indeed, this board, being the most effective control mechanism (Charreaux, 2000), plays a central role in the implementation of the company's strategies, including the CSR reporting strategy.

R. Chakroun (✉)
Accounting Department, IHEC, University of Carthage, Carthage, Tunisia
e-mail: raida.chakroun@ihec.u-carthage.tn

LIGUE LR99ES24-ISCAE, University of Manouba, La Manouba, Tunisia

© The Author(s), under exclusive license to Springer Nature Singapore Pte Ltd. 2022
A. Echchabi et al. (eds.), *Contemporary Research in Accounting and Finance*, https://doi.org/10.1007/978-981-16-8267-4_2

Moreover, as diversity on the board of directors is seen as a source of enrichment of the directors' profiles, it improves control and decision-making (Cox, 1993). Kang et al. (2017) define diversity on the board as "variety in the composition of the BOD." This diversity includes, but is not limited to, nationality, age, gender, racial or ethnic origin, work experience, and training.

Gender diversity on the board of directors is a topic that has gained momentum in the field of governance (Manita et al., 2018). Numerous studies have analyzed the effect of women on the board of directors on firm value, performance, earnings management, board effectiveness, and disclosure.

Carter et al. (2003) assert the existence of a positive relationship between the proportion of women directors and firm value. They also show that the proportion of women directors increases with firm size and board size but decreases as the number of insiders increases.

Many studies have focused on the impact of board gender diversity on firm performance (Ali et al., 2020; Campbell & Mínguez-Vera, 2004; Erhardt et al., 2003; Saleh et al., 2020). Based on a sample of Jordanian banks between 2009 and 2016, Mohammad et al. (2018) find a non-significant relationship between the percentages of women directors and their appointment as senior managers, on the one hand, and the financial performance of these banks on the other.

Lenard et al. (2017) prove that the presence of women leaders (on the board or in management) decreases the likelihood of fraud-based litigation in financial reporting. Zalataa et al. (2018) show that the female representation on the audit committee reduces earnings management. Specifically, the results show that the proportion of women finance experts on the audit committee is significantly related to a low level of earnings management, whereas the proportion of male finance experts on the audit committee does not affect earnings management significantly. Arun et al. (2015) also find that the presence of women on boards in the UK is associated with a low level of earnings management. However, Arioglu (2020) shows based on a sample of Turkish firms that the presence of women directors does not affect earnings management.

Using the theoretical framework of the standards market, Srinidhi et al. (2020) explain that women directors are efficacious even without being a majority on the board. They empirically show that independent female directors are more effective than their male counterparts in changing board norms (board process) and improving governance (board outcomes). Likewise, Terjesen et al. (2016) conducted an international study of 3876 companies in 47 countries and proved that women directors improve board effectiveness.

The present work is part of the research axis that deals with the consequences of board gender diversity on CSR disclosure in the annual reports of Tunisian banks listed on the *Bourse des Valeurs Mobilières de Tunis* (BVMT) between 2012 and 2017. Most of the studies interested on this issue have been conducted in developed markets. Indeed, although the banking sector influences other sectors of activity, most of the previous studies excluded it from their samples as it is characterized by specific regulations. Therefore, our study contributes to the previous literature on CSR disclosure and board gender diversity in financial institutions in emerging countries. To the best of our knowledge, this is the first study that examines the relationship between board gender diversity and the level of CSR disclosure in Tunisia.

This paper represents an extension of the work of Chakroun et al. (2017) and aims to examine other determinants of CSR disclosure by listed Tunisian banks. Here, we adopted the content analysis method according to the grid of Branco and Rodrigues (2006, 2008) to quantify CSR disclosure. To measure the presence of women on the board of directors, we used the proportion of the female representation in the board.

The low presence of women in top management can be explained by the "glass ceiling" metaphor. This concept appeared in the 1980s in the USA and explained the inequality of opportunities between men and women. This inequality is explained by the obstacles faced by women in their work that prevent them from advancing in the corporate hierarchy. Moreover, there are no gender balance strategies or policies in Tunisia. The code of commercial companies in Tunisia does not require a female representation on the boards. However, several countries oblige companies by laws to include women on the board. For example, Norway, Spain, and France have mandated 40% female representation on boards. Other European countries also have imposed a gender quota, including Italy (33.3%) and the Netherlands (30%). Nevertheless, Tunisia is a country that belongs to the Middle East and North Africa (MENA) region and is renowned for the numerous regulations in favor of women's rights, such as the Personal Status Code (PSC) promulgated in 1956. Moreover, according to the latest report on gender equality prepared by the World

Economic Forum: "Tunisia is the leading Arab country and second in the MENA region."

Our results reveal that board gender diversity affects the level of CSR disclosure positively; thus, reinforcing the initiatives undertaken around the world to promote board gender diversity. Legislators are recommended to consider our findings in making recommendations for gender equality on boards of directors.

The remainder of the paper is organized as follows: The conceptual and theoretical frameworks of the study are presented in Sect. 2. In Sect. 3, we outline the literature review and the research hypothesis. The methodology is described in Sect. 4. Section 5 presents and discusses the results.

2   Conceptual and Theoretical Frameworks

2.1   Conceptual Framework

Disclosure is an external control mechanism that protects investors and makes the capital market more efficient (Marston & Shrives, 1991). According to Golob and Bartlett (2007), CSR disclosure is defined as: «*A key tool for communicating with stakeholders regarding a company's social responsibility activities*». CSR disclosures contain information about a company's activities, aspirations, and public image with respect to the environment, community, employees, and consumers (Gray et al., 2001).

The company that discloses CSR information enjoys numerous advantages, namely the legitimization of its activities, the improvement of its image and position on the market, the development of its relationship with the stakeholders, the enhancement of decision-making, and the improvement of financial returns.

CSR practices in the banking sector differ from other sectors due to the specific regulations that characterize it. Indeed, CSR is a principal concern for banks because they can grant credits to polluting companies that manufacture dangerous products or violate human rights.

In another vein, several previous works compared female and male leadership styles. Women have different leadership styles compared to men (Bear et al., 2010) and are more likely to support socially responsible projects (Hillman et al., 2002). They are more caring, sensitive, and sympathetic; thus, more proactive in cooperation, whereas male leaders are more autocratic, dominant, confident, and therefore more competitive

(Pucheta-Martínez et al., 2018). Along these lines, Evans et al. (2019) confirmed that women are more emotionally intelligent because they can control their emotions and work in complex scenarios. Thus, they have skills, such as active listening, communication, empathy, and multitasking (Evans et al., 2019). However, Wajcman and Martin (2002) argue that leadership styles tend to be similar with some largely context-dependent differences. Rose (2007) states that female managers are relatively aware of female stereotypes and tend to adapt their behavior, hence a convergent pattern of management behavior regardless of gender.

Board gender diversity could be a source of richness in the exchanges and discussed ideas (Shehata, 2013) and could enrich perspectives and experiences; thus, leading to improved oversight and decision-making (Cox, 1993). According to Bear et al. (2010), a high female representation on the board raises the awareness of its members to adopt socially responsible recommendations.

Women are known to be more ethical and risk-averse than men; therefore, the appointment of women directors to boards can help improve the decision-making process in companies, as they are more responsible, more civilized, and stricter than their male counterparts (Bear et al., 2010). Nielsen and Huse (2010) draw on theories of gender differences and group efficacy to examine women's contributions to boards. Their findings suggest that women directors tend to empathize with others, support them, and contribute solving relational and interpersonal problems. As a result, they conclude that women may be particularly sensitive and make decisions about certain organizational practices, such as CSR. Moreover, women directors are more likely to be responsive to the expectations of stakeholders other than shareholders.

To have social legitimacy, boards need to represent the population they serve and be more diverse and inclusive. Dewally et al. (2017) find that women are appointed when the board size is large. They also provide evidence that women's board participation is lower in areas of high religiosity, measured by church affiliation and attendance. They also provide evidence that an educated and qualified female population leads to higher female participation on the board. However, women would have to work harder and demonstrate superior skills to be nominated for higher positions, and therefore women with higher positions in the hierarchy are likely to be highly competent and diligent. Moreover, women may face additional barriers to accessing leadership positions due to social exclusion or discrimination (Mateos De Cabo et al., 2011).

2.2   Theoretical Framework

Similar to studies that examined the impact of board gender diversity on the level of CSR disclosure, our theoretical underpinnings are based on four theories: the agency theory, the resource dependence theory, the stakeholder theory, and the legitimacy theory.

The agency theory was founded by Jensen and Meckling (1976). It essentially deals with the mechanisms implemented to deal with the agency relationship and resolve conflicts of interest. The agency relationship is defined as «*a contract by which one or more persons (the principal(s)) engage another person (the agent) to perform some service on their behalf which involves delegating some decision-making authority to the agent*» (Jensen & Meckling, 1976, p. 308).

Like all other governance mechanisms, the board of directors aims to solve agency problems. Indeed, a gender-diverse board devotes more effort to oversight, thereby strengthening governance practices and reducing agency costs (Adams & Ferreira, 2009). The agency theory explains the relationship between agency problems and corporate disclosure, as it is considered one of the principal monitoring tools. Therefore, firms disclose CSR information to reduce agency costs, reduce information asymmetry, and protect their images (Htay et al., 2012; Lim et al., 2007).

Consistent with the agency theory, to develop adequate oversight functions, board members must have the capacity and experience to influence CSR reporting (Hillman & Dalziel, 2003). In the same vein, Alonso-Almeida et al. (2017) show that women's leadership style encourages CSR practices. Indeed, women directors may be more responsive to CSR activities than men (Bear et al., 2010; Harrigan, 1981; Kesner, 1988).

Several previous studies that have addressed board-related topics have used the resource dependence theory. This theory, which was developed by Pfeffer and Salancik (1978), views the firm as an open system that depends on the external environment. It also states that the primary mission of the board of directors is to provide the firm with the necessary resources. This mission refers to the board's ability to provide these resources by linking the firm to its external environment (Hillman & Dalziel, 2003). A diverse board in terms of age, gender, and nationality increases the resources brought by board members and improves the organization's access to external resources. This diversification could help managers improve their disclosure policy (Ayuso & Argandona, 2009).

According to Ibrahim and Hanefah (2016), the resource dependence theory is the theory that best explains the impact of gender diversity on the board of directors on the CSR disclosure level.

This study also relied on the stakeholder theory, which is based on the principle that the company is not only responsible to its shareholders but also has obligations to all the actors with whom it may have a relationship. Freeman (1984, p. 46) defined the concept of "stakeholders" as «*any group or individual who can affect or is affected by the achievement of the organization's objectives*».

CSR disclosure helps improve the company's image and its relationship with stakeholders (Khan, 2010). Manita et al. (2018) relied on the underlying assumption of the stakeholder theory that corporate disclosure is used to provide information to the different stakeholders, such as employees, investors, public authorities, NGOs, etc.

The inclusion of women directors on boards can be seen as an orientation signal to stakeholders as female directors have the potential to influence CSR reporting (Fernandez-Feijoo et al., 2014; Rao & Tilt, 2016). In the same vein, Hillman et al. (2002) showed that a high proportion of female directors on boards guarantees respect for stakeholders' interests. Furthermore, Larrieta-Rubín de Celis et al. (2014) found that women directors act in a socially responsible manner in favor of stakeholders and encourage companies to disclose CSR information.

Our study is also based on the legitimacy theory developed by Hogner (1982). Suchman (1995, p. 574) defined legitimacy as: "*a generalized perception or assumption that the actions of an entity are desirable, proper or appropriate within some socially constructed system of norms, values, beliefs and definitions.*" Companies tend to improve their legitimacy through the disclosure of information on their social and environmental performance (Brammer & Pavelin, 2006; Cho & Patten, 2007; Deegan, 2002).

Indeed, according to this theory, CSR disclosure is a corporate practice that is expected by society. In this sense, Muttakin et al. (2018) explained that CSR disclosure is seen as a legitimization strategy whereby the political connection could allow companies to avoid stakeholder pressure associated with potential legitimacy threats from poor CSR performance.

3   LITERATURE REVIEW AND RESEARCH HYPOTHESIS

Velte (2017) shows that the results of previous studies on the impact of board gender diversity on the quantity of CSR reporting (number of CSR-related words or phrases) are mixed, i.e., positive, negative, or insignificant. He also finds that the results of studies that use CSR disclosure indices are mixed as well. To conclude, this author asserts that half of the analyzed studies found a positive relationship between CSR disclosure and the proportion of women directors.

Majeed et al. (2015) examined the relationship between governance characteristics and CSR disclosure in Pakistan. They found that gender diversity affects CSR disclosure negatively. In the same vein, Powell and Ansic (1997) argue that women are more risk-averse and more cautious than men. The association between women directors and CSR reports may be negative, which may be due to their lack of expertise.

Manita et al. (2018) examined the relationship between board gender diversity and environmental, social, and governance (ESG) disclosure on a sample of 379 large US companies and found a non-significant relationship between the two. Using a sample of companies listed on the Helsinki stock exchange during 2008, Nalikah (2009) found that the proportion of women directors does not have a significant effect on voluntary disclosure in annual reports.

Ibrahim and Hanefah (2016) investigated the impact of the diversity of board members' characteristics, namely independence, gender, age, and nationality, on the level of CSR disclosure on a sample of 117 companies listed on the Amman Stock Exchange belonging to the financial, services, and industrial sectors between 2007 and 2011. Their results indicate that the level of disclosure increases steadily over time and that there is a positive and significant relationship between the level of CSR disclosure and the variables of board members' characteristics diversity. Al Fadli et al. (2019) show in a study conducted in the Jordanian context that the presence of women on the board has a positive and significant effect on CSR reporting. They explain their result by the fact that women play an important role in complying with good governance practices and argue that this finding motivates companies to consider gender balance on boards of directors. In the same vein, based on a sample of companies listed on the Ghana Stock Exchange, Agymang et al. (2017) find that the presence of women on the board affects the level of CSR disclosure positively. This association is stronger when a woman is the chair of the board. These authors also find that board size and board members' independence play a crucial role in determining the level of CSR disclosure. Likewise, Barako and Brown (2008) show that a high level of women directors is associated with high level of voluntary social disclosure.

Nekhili et al. (2017) conducted a study on a sample of 91 French companies over 11 years. They found that the level of CSR disclosure is higher when women are present on the board of directors. Liao et al. (2015) indicated that the higher the percentage of women directors, the higher the level of voluntary greenhouse gas disclosure is in the UK. Furthermore, Rao and Tilt (2016) provide evidence that gender-diverse boards are positively associated with social reporting practices in the Austrian context. Ben Amar et al. (2015) used a sample of publicly traded Canadian companies for the period spanning 2008–2014. They found that the likelihood of voluntary climate change disclosure increases with the percentage of women on boards.

Board members influence decisions that relate to corporate governance in general and CSR disclosure in particular. In general, women are more conservative, more risk-averse, more honest, stricter in oversight, and have a clearer overview (Vähämaa, 2017) that can influence the company's reporting. With minimal risk-taking and better ethical behavior, it is expected that women directors can affect the quality of CSR reporting positively. Based on the above developments, our hypothesis is formulated as follows:

Hypothesis: There is a positive relationship between gender diversity on the board and the level of CSR disclosure.

4   RESEARCH METHODOLOGY

4.1   Presentation of the Sample and Data Sources

The initial sample was composed of 11 Tunisian banks listed on the BVMT. Following the study of Hili and Affes (2014), we excluded the bank governed by a supervisory board (AMEN BANK) because we are interested in the board of directors. Thus, our final sample consisted of 10 Tunisian banks listed on the BVMT observed between 2012 and 2017, i.e., a total number of observations of 60. Data for our study were collected from the annual reports of the banks in our sample.

The choice of a sample composed of banks is justified mainly by two reasons. First, banks play a vital role in the Tunisian economy and widely cover the financing needs of firms and households. Second, most studies addressing the relationship between governance and CSR disclosure have been conducted on non-financial sector firms and have excluded banks and financial institutions.

4.2   Definitions and Measurement of Variables

The dependent variable of this study was the level of CSR disclosure measured by the content analysis method of annual reports. Indeed, this method for measuring CSR disclosure consists of classifying the disclosed CSR information into different categories. The content analysis method is the most used by previous studies to measure CSR disclosure in annual reports. It consists of calculating the number of words, sentences, or pages related to CSR (Agymang et al., 2017; Driss & Jarboui, 2015; Gana & Dakhlaoui, 2011; Hasseldine et al., 2005; Ibrahim & Hanefah, 2016; Nekhili et al., 2017).

To measure the level of CSR disclosure, previous studies used two approaches: The first consists of using a CSR disclosure index constructed by other researchers (Chakroun et al., 2017; Driss & Jarboui, 2015; Haniffa & Cooke, 2005; Unerman, 2000) and the second consists of constructing a CSR disclosure index by the researcher (Agymang et al., 2017; Ibrahim & Hanefah, 2016; Nekhili et al., 2017).

Here, we opted for the first approach and used the CSR disclosure analysis grid adopted by Branco and Rodrigues (2006, 2008). This grid adapted to banks has been used by many previous studies (Driss & Jarboui, 2015; Haniffa & Cooke, 2005) and has already been used in the Tunisian context by Chakroun et al. (2017).

The grid consists of 22 items divided into four categories: environmental disclosure, human resources disclosure, consumers and products disclosure, and community involvement disclosure. The "Environment" category includes disclosure of corporate environmental concerns, environmental management, lending and investment policies, natural resource conservation and recycling, and energy conservation. The "Human Resources" category covers issues of employee health and safety, employment of minorities and women, employee training, employee assistance and benefits, employee remuneration, human resources profiles, employee share ownership schemes, employee morale, and industrial relations. The category "Products and consumers" consists of three items, product quality, consumer complaints or satisfaction, and provisions for disabled,

Table 1 Summary table of variables

Codes	Variables	Measures
CSRD	CSR disclosure score	Number of items disclosed by the bank divided by 22
PWB	Proportion of women on the board	Number of women on the board divided by the total number of directors
BIND	Board independence	Number of independent directors divided by the total number of directors
WCB	Woman chair of the board	"1" if the chair of the board is a woman; "0" otherwise
AUDIT	Auditor quality	"1" if the bank is audited by a BIG 4 firm: "0" otherwise
SIZE	Bank size	Number of branches of the bank
ROE	Return on equity	Net income divided by total equity
AGE	Bank age	Number of years from the year of the creation of the bank to the year of the achievement of the study

Source Developed by the author

elderly, and hard to reach customers. The "Community Involvement" category includes charitable donations and activities, education sponsorship, arts and culture sponsorship, public health sponsorship, and sports sponsorship.

In the present study, the analysis of CSR disclosure was carried out using a dichotomous procedure that detects the presence or absence of information belonging to the four categories of the grid. We assigned "one point" if the item exists in the annual report and "zero" otherwise.

$$\text{CSRD} = \frac{\text{Total disclosed items}}{\text{Total number of items (22)}}$$

The independent and the control variables are defined in Table 1.

4.3   *The Empirical Model*

To study the effect of board gender diversity on the level of CSR disclosure, we adopted the following model:

$$\text{CSRD}_{it} = \beta_0 + \beta_1\,\text{PWB}_{it} + \beta_2\,\text{BIND}_{it} + \beta_3\,\text{WCB}_{it}$$
$$+ \beta_4\,\text{AUDIT}_{it} + \beta_5\,\text{SIZE}_{it} + \beta_6\,\text{AGE}_{it} + \beta_7\,\text{ROE}_{it} + \varepsilon_{it}$$

with:

CSRD: CSR disclosure score.

PWB: Proportion of women on the board measured by the number of women on the board divided by the total number of directors.

BIND: Board independence measured by the number of independent directors divided by the total number of directors.

WCB: Woman chair of the board. This is a binary variable equal to "1" if the chair of the board is a woman and "0" otherwise.

AUDIT: Auditor quality. This is a binary variable equal to "1" if the bank is audited by a BIG 4 firm and "0" otherwise.

SIZE: Bank size measured by the number of branches of the bank.

AGE: Bank age measured by the number of years from the year of the creation of the bank to the year of the achievement of the study.

ROE: Return on equity measured by net income divided by total equity.

5   EMPIRICAL RESULTS AND DISCUSSION

5.1   *Results of the Content Analysis*

As can be seen in Table 2, the mean score of CSR disclosure increased from 38.2% in 2012 to 46.4% in 2017. Thus, the level of CSR disclosure increased over the study period. Also, the disclosure mean scores of information belonging to the categories (environment, products and consumers, community involvement) increased between 2012 and 2017, while the mean score for human resources disclosure decreased over the study period. The most disclosed information category for the years 2012, 2013, and 2017 is "products and consumers," and for the years 2014, 2015, and 2016 is "environment."

The descriptive statistics displayed in Table 3 show that the highest CSR disclosure mean score is recorded by Attijari Bank (0.54), followed by UBCI (0.53), and BNA (0.46). However, BTE has the lowest mean score (0.22).

For the environmental disclosure category, UBCI and Attijari Bank have the highest mean (0.8). ATB, BNA, BT, BTE, STB, and UIB recorded a mean score equal to 0.6. But, BH recorded the lowest mean (0.53).

The highest mean score of human resources disclosure is that of BIAT (0.33), followed by those of ATB and Attijari Bank (0.31), and UIB

Table 2 Descriptive statistics of the CSR disclosure scores and their categories by year

		CSRD	ENV DIS	HR DIS	PC DIS	IC DIS
2012	Mean	0.382	0.58	0.2325397	0.6333333	0.28
	Std. deviation	0.1176459	0.1135292	0.1848845	0.1054093	0.3011091
2013	Mean	0.3724545	0.6	0.2214286	0.6333333	0.24
	Std. deviation	0.1091196	0.0942809	0.1047866	0.1054093	0.2796824
2014	Mean	0.4041818	0.68	0.265873	0.6333333	0.22
	Std. deviation	0.1312595	0.1686548	0.1408466	0.1054093	0.3190263
2015	Mean	0.4	0.62	0.1992063	0.6	0.4
	Std. deviation	0.0904026	0.147573	0.1019429	0.1405457	0.2828427
2016	Mean	0.4681818	0.68	0.2174603	0.6666667	0.56
	Std. deviation	0.1114435	0.1398412	0.1001245	0	0.2796824
2017	Mean	0.4639091	0.64	0.2285714	0.6666667	0.56
	Std. deviation	0.0974882	0.0843274	0.1066633	0	0.2065591

CSRD: CSR disclosure score. ENV DIS: environmental disclosure. HR DIS: human resources disclosure. PC DIS: product and consumers disclosure. IC DIS: community involvement disclosure
Source Author's calculation based on data collected from banks' annual reports

(0.27). BH and BT recorded low disclosure mean scores for this category. We note that BTE recorded a mean value of 0. This means that it did not disclose any information about its human resources over the study period.

Among the ten banks in our sample, eight banks have similar product and consumer disclosure mean scores (Attijari Bank, BH, BNA, BT, BTE, STB, UBCI, and UIB). However, BIAT recorded the lowest mean of disclosure for this category.

For the community involvement disclosure category, UBCI has the highest mean (0.7), followed by Attijari Bank (0.63), BNA (0.6), and ATB (0.43). But, BTE did not disclose any information about its community involvement over the study period.

Table 3 Descriptive statistics of the CSR disclosure scores and their categories by bank

		CSRD	ENV DIS	HR DIS	PC DIS	IC DIS
(1) ATB	Mean	0.4469697	0.6	0.3148148	0.6111111	0.4333333
	Std. deviation	0.0531384	0	0.0836414	0.1360828	0.265832
(2) Attijari	Mean	0.5454545	0.8	0.3148148	0.6666667	0.6333333
	Std. deviation	0.057496	0.1264911	0.0836414	0	0.1966384
(3) BH	Mean	0.3409091	0.5333333	0.1851852	0.6666667	0.2333333
	Std. deviation	0.0850377	0.1632993	0.0907218	0	0.294392
(4) BIAT	Mean	0.4166667	0.5666667	0.3333333	0.4444444	0.4
	Std. deviation	0.088177	0.0816497	0.1721326	0.1721326	0.3098387
(5) BNA	Mean	0.4613636	0.6	0.2407407	0.6666667	0.6
	Std. deviation	0.019015	0	0.0453609	0	0
(6) BT	Mean	0.3404545	0.6	0.1481481	0.6666667	0.2333333
	Std. deviation	0.0901858	0	0.0573775	0	0.294392
(7) BTE	Mean	0.2277273	0.6	0	0.6666667	0
	Std. deviation	0.0011134	0	0	0	0
(8) STB	Mean	0.455303	0.6	0.2380952	0.6666667	0.3333333
	Std. deviation	0.0823426	0	0.0368856	0	0.273252
(9) UBCI	Mean	0.530303	0.8333333	0.2222222	0.6666667	0.7
	Std. deviation	0.0893811	0.1966384	0.0993808	0	0.1095445
(10) UIB	Mean	0.3860606	0.6	0.2777778	0.6666667	0.2
	Std. deviation	0.0746001	0	0.0608581	0	0.3098387

CSRD: CSR disclosure score. ENV DIS: environmental disclosure. HR DIS: human resources disclosure. PC DIS: product and consumers disclosure. IC DIS: community involvement disclosure

Source Author's calculation based on data collected from banks' annual reports

5.2   Results of the Descriptive Analyses

The results of the descriptive statistics illustrated in Table 4 show that the mean of the CSR disclosure is equal to 41.5% with a standard deviation (SD) equal to 0.11. This variable is then weakly dispersed.

As can be seen in the same table, the mean of the proportion of women on the board of directors is equal to 10.7%, which shows the low participation of women in the boards of directors of Tunisian listed banks. Compared to previous literature in other contexts, we note that this mean value is lower than that found by Manita et al. (2018) in the USA (15.85%) and higher than those found by Liao et al. (2015) in the UK (9.2%), and Ibrahim and Hanefah (2016) in the Jordanian context (2.8%). It is worth noting that the highest female representation on the Board of Directors is around 40%.

According to Fig. 1, for the year 2012, 20% of Tunisian listed banks have no women on the board of directors, while 40% have only a woman director and 40% have two women directors. Likewise, for the year 2017, 20% of the banks have no women on the board of directors, 40% also have only a woman director, 20% have two women directors, and 20% have three women directors. Accordingly, the female representation on the boards of directors of Tunisian listed banks has strengthened over time despite their low proportion. This can be explained by cultural factors that may, to some extent, avoid uncertainty and be intolerant to the inclusion of women in management positions. Although Tunisia has taken steps

Table 4   Descriptive statistics of continuous variables

Variables	Mean	Std. deviation	Min	Max
CSRD	0.4151212	0.1121645	0.2272727	0.6363636
PWB	0.1066843	0.0835982	0.00	0.40
BIND	0.1950387	0.0575268	0.1666667	0.4444444
SIZE	129.8333	47.63067	20	207
AGE	54	27.20855	30	133
ROE	0.1306409	0.1934833	−0.7034652	1.01432

Number of observations = 60; $n = 10$; $t = 6$
CSRD: CSR disclosure score; PWB: Number of women on the board divided by the total number of directors; BIND: Number of independent directors divided by the total number of directors; SIZE: Number of branches of the bank; AGE: Number of years from the year of the creation of the bank to the year of the achievement of the study; ROE: Net income divided by total equity
Source Author's calculation based on data collected from banks' annual reports

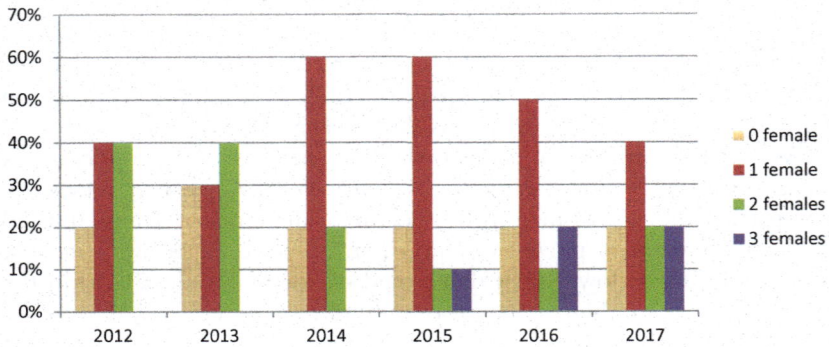

Fig. 1 Distribution of the number of women during the period 2012–2017 (*Source* Author's calculation based on data collected from banks' annual reports)

to promote the role of women in governance structures, some factors reduce their chances of accessing boards, including their perception as being inferior to men on issues, such as decision-making power, leadership ability, career aspiration, ability to manage pressure, and coping with change.

Moreover, the mean of the proportion of independent directors on the boards of listed Tunisian banks is equal to 19.50%. The minimum and maximum values are respectively 17% and 44%, with a standard deviation equal to 0.05, indicating a very low dispersion of the variable. We measured the bank size by the total number of its branches. Indeed, the minimum number of branches is 20 for BTE, and the maximum is 207 for Attijari Bank. The mean of this variable is equal to 129.83, i.e., 130 branches. The dispersion is high (SD = 47.63) because of the wide difference in the number of branches between banks. The bank age variable ranges from 30 years for (BTE) to 133 years for (BT), with an average of 54 years. The mean of the ROE variable is equal to 13%. In a previous study conducted on Tunisian listed banks during the period (2007–2012), Chakroun et al. (2017) found a value of 9.6%. We notice that the financial performance of banks has improved slightly between the two study periods.

Table 5 shows that of the 60 observations, 34 are audited by a Big 4 firm. Finally, only 20% of the board chairs of the banks in our sample

Table 5 Descriptive statistics of dummy variables

	Frequency		Percentage	
	AUDIT	WCB	AUDIT	WCB
0	26	48	43.33	80
1	34	12	56.67	20
Total	60	60	100	100

AUDIT: "1" if the bank is audited by a BIG 4 firm: "0" otherwise. WCB: "1" if the chair of the board is a woman; "0" otherwise
Source Author's calculation based on data collected from banks' annual reports

are women. This low proportion can be explained by the low female representation on the board of directors in general.

5.3 Results of the Multivariate Analyses

Table 6 shows the results of the Spearman correlation between the variables of this study. We note that no coefficient exceeds 0.7; so, we do not have a multilinearity problem. The variance inflation factor (VIF) values displayed in Table 7 vary between 1.15 and 1.28, with a mean value of 1.23. As these values are below 4, the absence of a multicollinearity problem is confirmed.

The normality condition of the dependent variable is a necessary condition for the use of the Ordinary Least Squares (OLS) regression. To verify the normality of the CSRD variable, we performed the statistical tests of kurtosis and skewness. The results depicted in Table 8 show that the distribution of the CSRD variable is normal since the values of the Skewness (0.6385) and Kurtosis (0.0883) coefficients are in the range $[-2,2]$.

We used the appropriate methodological approach to deal with panel data. Firstly, we performed the Fisher test of homogeneity (Table 9). The results show a coefficient of 3.70, significant at 1%, which confirms that the coefficients and constants are heterogeneous. Then we performed the Hausman test, whose probability is equal to 0.4222. Since this probability is greater than 5%, it allowed us to choose the random-effects model (Table 10). The R^2 of our model is equal to 61.77%, thus confirming the correct linear fit of the model.

Table 6 Spearman correlation matrix

	CSRD	PWB	BIND	WCB	AUDIT	SIZE	AGE	ROE
CSRD	1							
PWB	−0.0155	1						
BIND	−0.1770	0.0963	1					
WCB	0.1264	0.1838	−0.1915	1				
AUDIT	0.2826**	−0.0269	0.2313*	−0.0673	1			
SIZE	0.5454	−0.1296	0.1873	0.0157	0.1652	1		
AGE	0.2605**	0.4455***	0.3118**	−0.2563**	0.0350	0.0992	1	
ROE	0.3143**	0.0971	0.3359***	−0.2045	0.4447***	0.6106	0.1648	1

*, **, *** significant at the 10%, 5%, 1% level respectively

CSRD: CSR disclosure score; PWB: Number of women on the board divided by the total number of directors; BIND: Number of independent directors divided by the total number of directors; SIZE: Number of branches of the bank; AGE: Number of years from the year of the creation of the bank to the year of the achievement of the study; ROE: Net income divided by total equity; AUDIT: "1" if the bank is audited by a BIG 4 firm: "0" otherwise; WCB: "1" if chair of the board is a woman; "0" otherwise

Source Author's calculation based on data collected from banks' annual reports

Table 7   VIF test

Variables	VIF	1/VIF
SIZE	1.28	0.783333
BIND	1.27	0.786104
AGE	1.25	0.802343
PWB	1.23	0.810008
AUDIT	1.20	0.830974
ROE	1.20	0.834483
WCB	1.15	0.866271
Mean VIF	1.23	

Source Author's calculation based on data collected from banks' annual reports

Table 8   Normality test of the dependent variable

Variable	Pr(Skwness)	Pr(Kurtosis)	Prob > chi2
DRSE	0.6385	0.0883	0.1941

Source Author's calculation based on data collected from banks' annual reports

Table 9   Fisher test

F(7.43)	Prob > F
3.70	0.0032

Source Author's calculation based on data collected from banks' annual reports

Table 10   Hausman test

	Prob > khi2	Significance threshold	Selected model
Hausman test	0.4222	5%	Random effects model

Source Author's calculation based on data collected from banks' annual reports

Table 11 shows that the proportion of women on the board (PWB) variable has a positive coefficient of 0.27, significant at the 10% threshold. This result confirms that when the percentage of women directors

Table 11 Random effects model results

	Coefficients	Prob > |z|
PWB	0.2724114*	0.065
BIND	−0.4139392*	0.077
WCB	0.0412375	0.221
AUDIT	0.015055	0.703
SIZE	0.0019709***	0.001
ROE	0.0380988	0.403
AGE	0.0002121	0.852

CSRD: CSR disclosure score; PWB: Number of women on the board divided by the total number of directors; BIND: Number of independent directors divided by the total number of directors; SIZE: Number of branches of the bank; AGE: Number of years from the year of the creation of the bank to the year of the achievement of the study; ROE: Net income divided by total equity; AUDIT: "1" if the bank is audited by a BIG 4 firm; "0" otherwise; WCB: "1" if the chair of the board is a woman; "0" otherwise
***Significant at the 1% level, *Significant at the 10%
Source Author's calculation based on data collected from banks' annual reports

increases, Tunisian banks listed on the BVMT tend to disclose more information on CSR, thus confirming our hypothesis. This last finding is consistent with those of previous studies (e.g., Agymang et al., 2017; Ben Amar et al., 2015; Giannarakis, 2014; Ibrahim & Hanefah, 2016; Nekhili et al., 2017). This result also suggests that companies with gender-diverse boards can reduce agency problems, respond to stakeholder demands, and legitimize themselves by gaining the trust of a wide range of stakeholders other than the shareholders. Indeed, Women may have high levels of internalized moral identity that can translate into a focus on higher-quality corporate social responsibility (Hatch & Stephen, 2015).

Bernardi and Threadgill (2010) find that companies with a higher proportion of women directors are more socially responsible. Similarly, meta-analyses by Khlif and Achek (2017) and Guerrero-Villegas et al. (2018) confirm that female board representation promotes the levels of social and environmental disclosure. Therefore, women are more likely to report on social and environmental issues when involved in focal governance mechanisms, such as the boards of directors. Indeed, the management style of female directors is different from that of male ones (Bear et al., 2010). They may encourage ethical corporate behavior and may be more likely to support CSR disclosure than men (Hillman et al., 2002).

We found that the coefficient of the board independence (BIND) variable is negative and significant at the 10% level ($p = 0.077$). This result can be explained by the fact that a large proportion of independent directors on the boards of listed Tunisian banks tends to reduce CSR disclosure. This result is similar to those of several previous studies (e.g., Bansal et al., 2018; Eng & Mak, 2003; Haniffa & Cooke, 2005). According to Bansal et al. (2018), board independence has a negative impact on CSR disclosure because independent directors tend to avoid risky behaviors that could damage their reputation.

The coefficient of women as chair of the board (WCB) variable is positive and insignificant. This finding means that having a female board chair does not affect the level of CSR disclosure. Similarly, the coefficient of the AUDIT variable is positive and non-significant. In other words, auditor quality does not affect CSR disclosure. This result is in line with that of Doepers (2000) and Haniffa and Cooke (2005).

The coefficient of the SIZE variable is positive and significant at the 1% level. This result shows that the size of the bank positively affects the level of CSR disclosure, which can be explained by the "political visibility of the bank" factor. Indeed, the larger the bank, the more visible it is, and the more CSR information it discloses to show that it is socially responsible. This result corroborates the results found by several previous studies, such as Baccouche et al. (2010) and Chakroun et al. (2017). According to the legitimacy theory, to meet public expectations and improve their perceptions, large companies disclose more CSR information. In this sense, Cowen et al. (1987) argue that large firms are subject to public pressure.

We found a positive and insignificant coefficient for the ROE variable, proving that there is no relationship between ROE and CSR disclosure. This result confirms the results found by Eng and Mak (2003) and Boulouta (2013). The coefficient of the variable AGE is positive and insignificant; this indicates that the age of the bank does not affect the level of CSR disclosure, thus corroborating the result found by Agymang et al. (2017).

6 CONCLUSION

Several previous studies have addressed the impact of board gender diversity on CSR disclosure, but few studies have addressed this relationship in emerging countries. To fill this gap in the corporate governance literature, we studied this relationship on 10 Tunisian banks listed on the BVMT between 2012 and 2017.

To measure the level of CSR disclosure, we used the method of content analysis of annual reports. We also used the Branco and Rodrigues (2006, 2008) grid, which consists of 22 items classified into four categories: environment, human resources, producers and consumers, and community involvement.

The empirical results show that the female representation on the board of directors positively affects the level of CSR disclosure in Tunisian banks listed on the BVMT. Therefore, our hypothesis is validated. Likewise, the bank size has a positive effect on the level of CSR disclosure. However, we found that CSR disclosure is negatively affected by the proportion of independent directors on the board.

Like any research work, our study has some limitations. The main limitation is the small sample size. Besides, we will have to use other information media (such as company websites, advertisements, brochures, etc.). Another limitation is the failure to address the possible endogenous relationship between CSR disclosure and board gender diversity.

Future research can also focus on whether there is a critical proportion of female board members that can influence CSR practices.

References

Adams, R. B., & Ferreira, D. (2009). Women in the boardroom and their impact on governance and performance. *Journal of Financial Economics, 94*, 291–309.

Agymang, A., Ayamba, E., & Konadu, V. (2017). Impact of Gender Diversity on Corporate Social Responsibility Disclosure (CSRD) in Ghana. *International Journal of Economics Review & Business Research, 4*(2), 1–24.

Al Fadli, A., Sands, J., Jones, G., Beattie, C., & Pensiero, D. (2019). Board Gender Diversity and CSR reporting: Evidence from Jordan Australasian Accounting. *Business and Finance Journal, 13*(3), 29–52.

Ali, R., Sial, M. S., Brugni, T. V., Hwang, J., Khuong, N. V., & Khanh, T. T. T. (2020). Does CSR moderate the relationship between corporate governance and Chinese firm's financial performance? Evidence from the Shanghai Stock Exchange (SSE) firms. *Sustainability, 12*, 149.

Alonso-Almeida, M., Perramon, J., Bagur-Femenias, U. (2017). Leadership styles and corporate social responsibility management: Analysis from a gender perspective. *Business Ethics A European Review, 26*(2), 147–161

Arioglu, E. (2020). The affiliations and characteristics of female directors and earnings management: Evidence from Turkey. *Managerial Auditing Journal, 35*(7), 927–953.

Arun, T. G., Almahrog, Y. E., & Aribi, Z. A. (2015). Female directors and earnings management: Evidence from UK companies. *International Review of Financial Analysis, 39*, 137–146.

Ayuso, S., & Argandoña, A. (2009). *Responsible corporate governance: Towards a Stakeholder Board of Directors?* (IESE Business School Working Paper No. 701).

Baccouche, C., Errais, O., & Mzoughi, K. (2010). Les déterminants de la publication volontaire d'informations sociales: cas des entreprises tunisiennes. Working paper. *Journée «Capital immatériel: état des lieux et perspectives».* Montpellier, France.

Barako, G. D., & Brown, A. M. (2008). Corporate social reporting and board representation: Evidence from the Kenyan banking sector. *Journal of Management Governance, 12*(4), 309–324.

Bansal, S., Lopez-Perez, M. V., & Lazaro-Rodriguez, A. (2018). Board independence and corporate social responsibility disclosure: The mediating role of the presence of family ownership. *Administrative Sciences, 8*(3), 33.

Bear, S., Rahman, N., & Post, C. (2010). The impact of board diversity and gender composition on corporate social responsibility and firm reputation. *Journal of Business Ethics, 97*(2), 207–221.

Ben Amar, W., Chang, M., & McIlkenny, P. (2015). Board gender diversity and corporate response to sustainability initiatives: Evidence from the carbon disclosure project. *Journal of Business Ethics, 142*(2), 369–383.

Bernardi, R. A., & Threadgill, V. H. (2010). Women Directors and corporate social responsibility. *Electronic Journal of Business Ethics and Organizational Studies, 15*(2), 15–21.

Boulouta, I. (2013). Hidden connections: The link between board gender diversity and corporate social performance. *Journal of Business Ethics, 113*(2), 185–197.

Brammer, S. J., & Pavelin, S. (2006). Voluntary environmental disclosures by large UK companies. *Journal of Business Finance & Accounting, 33*(7–8), 1168–1188.

Branco, M. C., & Rodrigues, L. L. (2006). Communication of corporate social responsibility by Portuguese banks a legitimacy theory perspective. *Corporate Communications: an International Journal, 11*(3), 232–248.

Branco, M. C., & Rodrigues, L. L. (2008). Factors influencing social responsibility disclosure by Portuguese companies. *Journal of Business Ethics, 83*(4), 685–701.

Chakroun, R., Matoussi, H., & Mbarki, S. (2017). Determinants of CSR disclosure of Tunisian listed banks: A multi support analysis. *Social Responsibility Journal., 13*(3), 552–584.

Campbell, K., & Mínguez-Vera, A. (2004). Gender diversity in the boardroom and firm financial performance. *Journal of Business Ethics, 83*(3), 435–451.

Charreaux, G. (2000). *Le conseil d'administration dans les théories de la gouvernance* (Working paper). Université de Bourgogne.

Carter, D. A., Simkins, B. J., & Simpson, W. G. (2003). Corporate governance, Board diversity and firm value. *The Financial Review, 38*, 33–53.

Cho, C., & Patten, D. (2007). The role of environmental disclosures as tools of legitimacy: A research note. *Accounting, Organizations and Society, 32*(7–8), 639–647.

Cowen, S., Ferreri, L., & Parker, L. (1987). The impact of corporate characteristics on social responsibility disclosure: A typology and frequency-based analysis. *Accounting Organizations & Society, 12*(2), 111–122.

Cox, T. (1993). *Cultural diversity in organizations: Theory, research, and practice.* Berrett-Koehler.

Deegan, C. (2002). Introduction: The legitimizing effect of social and environmental disclosures: A theoretical foundation. *Accounting, Auditing & Accountability Journal, 15*(3), 282–311.

Dewally, M., Flaherty, S. M. V., & Tomasi, S. (2017). The impact of social norms on female corporate board membership inclusion. *Managerial Finance, 43*(10), 1093–1116.

Doepers, F. (2000). A cost-benefit study of voluntary disclosure: Some empirical evidence from French listed companies. *The European Accounting, 9*(2), 245–263.

Driss, R., & Jarboui, A. (2015). Contribution of social disclosure and organizational culture to create financial value of Tunisian companies. *Growth, Asian Online Journal Publishing Group, 2*(1), 10–19.

Eng, L. L., & Mak, Y. T. (2003). Corporate governance and voluntary disclosure. *Journal of Accounting and Public Policy, 22*(4), 325–345.

Erhardt, N. L., Werbel, J. D., & Shrader, C. B. (2003). Board director diversity and firm financial performance. *Corporate Governance, 11*(2), 102–111.

Evans, J. B., Slaughter, J. E., Ellis, A. P. J., & Rivin, J. M. (2019). Gender and the evaluation of humor at work. *Journal of Applied Psychology, 104*(8), 1077–1087.

Fernandez-Feijoo, B., Romero, S., & Ruiz-Blanco, S. (2014). Women on boards: Do they affect sustainability reporting? *Corporate Social Responsibility and Environmental Management, 21*(6), 351–364.

Freeman, R. E. (1984). *Strategic management: A stakeholder approach.* Pitman.

Gana, M., & Dakhlaoui, M. (2011). Societal information disclosure and the cost of equity: the case of Tunisian companies. *Global Journal of Management and Business Research, 11*(7), 1–8.

Giannarakis, G. (2014). Corporate governance and financial characteristic effects on the extent of corporate social responsibility disclosure. *Social Responsibility Journal, 10*(4), 569–590.

Golob, U., & Bartlett, J. L. (2007). Communicating about corporate social responsibility: A comparative study of CSR reporting in Australia and Slovenia. *Public Relations Review, 33*(1), 1–9.

Gray, R., Javad, M., Power, D. M., & Sinclair, C. D. (2001). Social and environmental disclosure and corporate characteristics: A research note and extension. *Journal of Business Finance and Accounting, 28*(3/4), 327–355.

Guerrero-Villegas, J., Pérez-Calero, L., Hurtado-González, J. M., & Giráldez-Puig, P. (2018). Board attributes and corporate social responsibility disclosure: A meta-analysis. *Sustainability MDPI Open Access Journal, 10*(12), 1–22.

Haniffa, R. M., & Cooke, T. E. (2005). The impact of culture and governance on corporate social reporting. *Journal of Accounting and Public Policy, 24*(5), 391–430.

Harrigan, K. R. (1981). Barriers to entry and competitive strategies. *Strategic Management Journal, 2*, 395–412.

Hasseldine, J., Salama, A. I., & Toms, J. S. (2005). Quantity versus quality: The impact of environmental disclosures on the reputations of UK PLCs. *British Accounting Review, 37*(2), 231–248.

Hatch, C. D., & Stephen, S. K. (2015). Gender effects on perceptions of individual and corporate social responsibility. *The Journal of Applied Business and Economics, 17*(3), 63–71.

Hili, W., & Affes, H. (2014). *Diversité en genre dans les conseils d'administration et persistance des bénéfices comptables: investigation empirique dans le contexte français* (working paper). Université de Sfax.

Hillman, A. J., & Dalziel, T. (2003). Boards of directors and firm performance: Integrating agency and resource dependence perspectives. *The Academy of Management Review, 28*(3), 383–396.

Hillman, A. J., Cannella, J., & Paetzold, A. A. (2002). The resource dependence role of corporate directors: Strategic adaptation of board composition in response to environmental change. *Journal of Management Studies, 37*(2), 235–255.

Hogner, R. H. (1982). Corporate social reporting: Eight decades of development at U.S Steel. *Research in Corporate Social Performance and Policy, 4*, 243–250.

Htay, S. S. N., Rashid, H. M., Adnan, M. K., & Meera, A. K. M. (2012). Impact of corporate governance on social and environmental information disclosure of Malaysian listed banks: Panel data analysis. *Asian Journal of Finance and Accounting, 4*(1), 1–24.

70   R. CHAKROUN

Ibrahim, A. H., & Hanefah, M. M. (2016). Board diversity and corporate social responsibility in Jordan. *Journal of Financial Reporting and Accounting, 14*(2), 279–298.

Jensen, M., & Meckling, W. (1976). Theory of the firm: Managerial behavior, agency costs and ownership structure. *Journal of Financial Economics, 3,* 305–360.

Kang, H., Cheng, M., & Gray, S. J. (2017). Corporate governance and board composition: Diversity and independence of Australian boards. *Corporate Governance: An International Review, 15*(2), 194–207.

Kesner, I. F. (1988). Directors' characteristics and committee membership: An investigation of type, occupation, tenure, and gender. *Academy of Management Journal, 31*(1), 66–84.

Khan, M. H. (2010). The effect of corporate governance elements on corporate social responsibility (CSR) reporting: Empirical evidence from private commercial banks of Bangladesh. *International Journal of Law and Management, 52*(2), 82–109.

Khlif, H., & Achek, I. (2017). Gender in accounting research: A review. *Managerial Auditing Journal, 32*(6), 627–655.

Larrieta-Rubín de Celis, I., Velasco-Balmaseda, E., Fernández de Bobadilla, S., Alonso-Almeida, M., & Intxaurburu-Clemente, G. (2014). Does having women managers lead to increased gender equality practices in corporate social responsibility? *Busines Ethics The environment & responsability, 24*(1), 91–110.

Lenard, M. J., Yu, B., York, E. A., & Wu, S. (2017). Female business leaders and the incidence of fraud litigation. *Managerial Finance, 43*(1), 59–75.

Liao, L., Luo, L., & Tang, Q. (2015). Gender diversity, board independence, environmental committee, and greenhouse gas disclosure. *British Accounting Review, 47*(4), 409–424.

Lim, S., Matolcsy, Z., & Chow, D. (2007). The association between board composition and different types of voluntary disclosure. *European Accounting Review, 16*(3), 555–583.

Majeed, S., Aziz, T., & Saleem, S. (2015). The effect of corporate governance elements on Corporate Social Responsibility (CSR) disclosure: An empirical evidence from listed companies at KSE Pakistan. *International Journal of Financial Studies, 3*(4), 530–556.

Manita, R., Bruna, M. G., Dang, R., & Houanti, L. (2018). Board gender diversity and ESG disclosure: Evidence from the USA. *Journal of Applied Accounting Research, 19*(2), 206–224.

Marston, C. L., & Shrives, P. J. (1991). The use of disclosure indices in accounting research: A review article. *British Accounting Review, 23,* 195–210.

Mateos de Cabo, R., Gimeno, R., & Escot, L. (2011). Disentangling discrimination on Spanish boards of directors. *Corporate Governance: an International Review, 19*(1), 77–95.

Mohammad, S. J., Abdullatif, M., & Zakzouk, F. (2018). The effect of gender diversity on the financial performance of Jordanian banks. *Academy of Accounting and Financial Studies Journal, 22*(2), 1–11.

Muttakin, M. B., Mihret, D. G., & Khan, A. (2018). Corporate political connection and corporate social responsibility disclosures: A neo-pluralist hypothesis and empirical evidence. *Accounting, Auditing & Accountability Journal, 31*(2), 725–744.

Nalikah, A. (2009). Impact of gender diversity on voluntary disclosure in annual reports. *Accounting & Taxation, 1*(1), 101–113.

Nekhili, M., Nagati, H., Chtioui, T., & Nekhili, A. (2017). Gender-diverse board and the relevance of voluntary CSR reporting. *International Review of Financial Analysis, 50*(2016), 81–100.

Nielsen, S., & Huse, M. (2010). The contribution of women on boards of directors: Going beyond the surface. *Corporate Governance: an International Review, 18*(2), 136–148.

Pfeffer, J., & Salancik, G. R. (1978). *The external control of organizations: A ressource-dependence perspective.* Harper & Row.

Pucheta-Martínez, M. C., Bel-Oms, I., & Olcina-Sempere, G. (2018). The association between board gender diversity and financial reporting quality, corporate performance and corporate social responsibility disclosure: A literature review. *Academia Revista Latinoamericana De Administración, 31*(1), 177–194.

Powell, M., & Ansic, D. (1997). Gender differences in risk behaviour in financial decision-making: An experimental analysis. *Journal of Economic Psychology, 18*(6), 605–628.

Rao, K., & Tilt, C. (2016). Board diversity and CSR reporting: An Australian study. *Meditari Accountancy Research, 24*(2), 182–210.

Rose, C. (2007). Does female board representation influence firm performance? The Danish Evidence. *Corporate Governance, 15*(2), 404–413.

Saleh, M. W. A., Zaid, M. A. A., Shurafa, R., Maigoshi, Z. S., Mansour, M., & Zaid, A. (2020), Does board gender enhance Palestinian firm performance? The moderating role of corporate social responsibility, *Corporate Governance, 21*, 685–701.

Shehata, N. F. (2013). How could board diversity influence corporate disclosure? *Corporate Board: Role, Duties and Composition, 9*(3), 42–49.

Srinidhi, B., Sun, Y., Zhang, H., & Chen, S. (2020). How do female directors improve board governance? A mechanism based on norm changes. *Journal of Contemporary Accounting and Economics, 16*(1), 100181.

Suchman, M. C. (1995). Managing Legitimacy: Strategic and Institutional Approaches. *Academy of Management Review, 20*(3), 571–610.

Terjesen, S., Couto, E. B., & Francisco, P. M. (2016). Does the presence of independent and female directors impact firm performance?: A multi-country study of board diversity. *Journal of Management & Governance., 20*(3), 447–483.

Unerman, J. (2000). Methodological issues—Reflections on quantification in corporate social reporting content analysis. *Accounting, Auditing & Accountability Journal, 13*(5), 667–681.

Vähämaa, E. (2017). Female executives and corporate governance. *Managerial Finance, 43*(10), 1056–1072.

Velte, P. (2017). Do women on board of directors have an impact on corporate governance quality and firm performance? A literature review. *International Journal of Sustainable Strategic Management, 5*(4), 302.

Wajcman, J., & Martin, B. (2002). Narratives of identity in modern management: The corrosion of gender difference? *Sociology, 36*(4), 985–1002.

Zalataa, A. M., Tauringanaa, V., & Tingbanic, I. (2018). Audit committee financial expertise, gender, and earnings management: Does gender of the financial expert matter? *International Review of Financial Analysis, 55*, 170–183.

Negative Earnings and the Cost of Debt: Evidence from the Emerging Tunisian Market

Asma Houcine

1 INTRODUCTION

We investigate the effect of negative earnings on the cost of debt for a sample of Tunisian firms. Since negative earnings are considered to be of lower quality than positive earnings, a shift change from positive earnings to negative earnings is considered a decrease in earnings quality, which will increase the firm's information risk. Firms with negative earnings will bear an increase in the cost of debt in the event that the increase in information risk impacts decisions of lenders.

Previous research investigating the effect of earnings quality on the cost of capital has mainly focused on developed markets, considering both the cost of equity and the cost of debt. According to Francis et al. (2004, 2005), "better earnings quality lowers the cost of capital." Earnings quality was addressed by the authors using accruals quality, accounting

---

A. Houcine (✉)
Dubai Business School, University of Dubai, Dhabi, United Arab Emirates
e-mail: asma.houcine@gmail.com

GEF2A-Lab, Higher Institute of Management of Tunis(ISGT), University of Tunis, Tunis, Tunisia

conservatism, earnings persistence, earnings predictability, value relevance, and timeliness. The findings of Zhang (2008) and Bharath et al. (2008) reveal a negative effect of earnings quality (proxied by accruals) on the cost of debt. Gray et al. (2009) and Aldmen and Duncan (2013) find that accruals quality reduces the cost of capital for Australian firms. In a cross-country study, Bhattacharya et al. (2003) examine the effect of three measures of earnings opacity (earnings aggressiveness, loss avoidance, and earnings smoothing) on firms' cost of equity for 34 countries. Their results reveal a negative association between the cost of debt and financial transparency. García-Teruel et al. (2014), find that higher accruals quality is associated with greater presence of bank debt, suggesting that higher precison of earnings favors the access of firms to bank loans. The results of Van Caneghem and Campenhout (2012) reveal that the amount and the quality of financial information are positively related to SME leverage.

As far as we know, no studies have been conducted to investigate the impact of negative earnings on the cost of debt. Companies that report negative earnings will contribute to an increase in information risk, which is expected to influence lenders' decisions by increasing the borrower's cost of debt. Indeed, more persistent earnings are more sustainable and better predictors of future cash flows, which especially important for stock valuation (Dechow et al., 2010). However, negative earnings are perceived as less persistent than positive earnings because they are seen as temporary, since shareholders have the choice to liquidate, abandon, or adapt the firm's resources to new purposes (Hayn, 1995; Berger et al., 1996). Less persistent earnings will therefore lead to an increase in the firms' cost of debt. We consider two types of companies: those that maintain at least two consecutive years of positive earnings, and those that observe a change in the sign of their earnings from positive to negative. If this change represents a decrease in earnings quality for debtors and, therefore, an increase in the information risk they face, firms observing the shift to negative earnings will bear an increase in this cost.

The results support our intuition and demonstrate that, after controlling for other determinants of the cost of debt, firms with negative earnings support an increase in that cost over the next two years.

This paper extends accounting literature by providing empirical evidence on the effect of reporting negative earnings on the cost of debt for a sample of Tunisian firms. Tunisia is a small emerging market with a legal environment structured as "code-law" in the sense described by Ball et al. (2000). Approximately 90% of companies are micro, SME sized, which means that the banking system is their primary source of funding and reporting negative earnings would increase firms' cost of debt.

The study contributes to the existing literature. First, it provides empirical evidence on the effect of reporting negative earnings on the cost of debt. Second, it adds to the scant evidence of the effect of earnings quality and information risk on the cost of debt in emerging markets. Third, the association between the quality of earnings and the cost of debt has been so far investigated for firms in "common law" countries. This paper adds to and expands the evidence of such an association in a "code-law" country. Finally, it introduces a new approach to measure earnings quality and information risk based on the change in earnings sign.

The findings of this study may be of interest to accounting literature, managers, and bankers. First, it suggests that negative earnings are of lower quality and carry more information risk than positive earnings. Second, it reinforces the idea that failing to meet certain earnings benchmarks, such as positive earnings, has negative economic consequences in capital markets, such as lower equity valuations or rating downgrades (e.g., Barth et al., 1999; Jiang, 2008; Kasznik & McNichols, 2002). Third, it provides evidence that avoiding an increase in the cost of debt may be a strong incentive for earnings management practices designed to avoid reporting losses (Degeorge et al., 1999; Bhattacharya et al., 2003).

This paper is organized as follows. Section 2 explains why negative earnings are considered of lower quality than positive earnings and develop hypotheses. The research design is discussed in Sect. 3. Section 3.2 provides the sample selection process as well as the sample characteristics. Section 1 presents the findings. The sensitivity analysis is provided in Sect. 5 and the conclusion in Sect. 6.

2   Literature Review and Hypotheses Development

Earnings are a summary measure of a company's performance that is widely used in firm valuation and contracting, such as compensation and debt contracts (Dechow et al., 1998; Lev, 1989). Dechow et al. (2010) state that higher quality earnings provide more information about the characteristics of a company's financial performance that are relevant to a specific decision made by a specific decision maker. Persistence is one of the characteristics that make earnings more relevant because more persistent and sustainable profits better predict future cash flows. Persistence is especially important for stock valuation, as more persistent earnings have a more sustainable earnings/cash flow, which translates to more inputs into stock valuation models (Dechow et al., 2010).

Negative earnings are perceived as less persistent than positive earnings because they are seen as temporary, that is, they should not last because shareholders have the option to liquidate, abandon, or adapt the firm's resources to other uses (Berger et al., 1996; Burgstahler & Dichev, 1997; Frankel & Litov, 2009). As a result, negative earnings are less accurate in forecasting a company's future performance and cash flow.

According to Francis et al. (2005), information risk is the likelihood that firm-specific information relevant to investors' pricing decisions is of poor quality. Information risk can arise from (1) information asymmetries between the firm and the investors, (2) information asymmetries between investors due to private information, and (3) and (3) imprecision (i.e., dispersion) in estimates of future cash flows based on the available information (Easley & O'Hara, 2004; Lambert et al., 2007, 2011; Leuz & Verrecchia, 2004). As a result, earnings characteristics such as persistence that improve precision in estimating a firm's future cash flows may reduce information risk and, then the risk premium required by investors and the cost of capital.

While the majority of research on persistence has focused on the utility of earnings to investors, lenders may value persistence as well because they need to forecast a firm's future cash flows to assess its default risk. Lenders will find it more difficult to assess the firm's future prospects in the presence of persistently negative earnings. As a result, the shift from positive to negative earnings reflects an increase in the information risk that lenders face.

Given that financial literature proves that information risk is a priced risk factor (Diamond & Verrecchia, 1991; Easley & O'Hara, 2004; Lambert et al., 2007, 2011), it is expected that lenders will reflect this rise in interest rates, raising them. To formalize this prediction, the following research hypothesis is formalized:

H1: The change of the sign of earnings from positive to negative leads to an increase in the cost of debt.

The bank learns about earnings when financial statements are made public, which happens around the middle of the year following the year to which earnings refer. Following this point, decisions about granting or renewing funding will reflect the information conveyed by the change in the earnings sign. As a result, the cost of debt is likely to rise in the near future. As a result, the increase in the cost of debt is likely to occur more than once after the sign change. This leads us to formulate the following hypothesis:

H2:   The change in the sign of earnings from positive to negative is delayed in relation to the moment it occurs.

3   RESEARCH DESIGN

3.1   *Model Specification*

We create two subsamples to test the effect of reporting negative earnings on the cost of debt. The first subsample consists of firms whose net income was positive in year $t - 1$ but negative in year t. The second subsample, known as the control subsample, is made up of firms whose net income was positive in year $t - 1$ and continues to be positive in year t. These two subsamples were designed so that each firm in the first subsample in year $t - 1$ matches with one firm in the second subsample of the same size, year, and industry. The firm's size was defined in terms of log total assets.

The balance sheet date of the firms examined is the year-end date, which is December 31st. Thus, lenders become aware of the firm's negative net income in year t when their financial statements are made public, which occurs in the middle of year $t + 1$. Despite the fact that a negative net income could have been predicted in year t based on accounting information provided by the firm during that year, the presentation of financial statements formalizes the existence of a negative net income.

The information conveyed by the change in the earnings sign will now be reflected in decisions related to the granting or renewal of funding. The credit conditions will be adjusted as a result of this change for at least another year, up to year $t + 2$.

Based on this scenario, the first research hypothesis is tested using a multiple linear regression model (Model 1), where the dependent variable is the variation in the cost of debt between year t and year $t + 2$, and the independent variables are: a dummy variable that indicates the change in earnings sign from positive to negative and a set of control variables to capture the effect of changes in economic and financial indicators on the cost of deb between year t and year $t + 1$. The use of two periods of variation for the dependent variable and only one period of variation for the independent variables is due to the fact that the contractual terms of a bank loan such as interest rate are determined using accounting data from the prior year. Thus, changes in the firm's economic and financial indicators between years t and $t + 1$ tend to be reflected in the cost of debt at least until $t + 2$. The model also includes, as control variables, a set of industry and year dummies that capture industry and time effects that are shared by all firms in the same industry or year.

$$\Delta \text{CostDebt}_{i,t+2} = \beta_0 + \beta_1 \text{NegEarnings}_{i,t} + \beta_2 \Delta \text{IntCov}_{i,t+1}$$
$$+ \beta_3 \Delta \text{Liq}_{i,t+1} + \beta_4 \Delta \text{Tang}_{i,t+1} + \beta_5 \Delta \text{Lev}_{i,t+1}$$
$$+ \beta_6 \Delta \text{Size}_{i,t+1} + \sum \beta_1 \text{DummyInd}$$
$$+ \sum \beta_1 \text{DummyYear} + \varepsilon_{i,t+2}$$

where:

$\Delta \text{CostDebt}_{i,t+2}$ Variation, in percentage, in the cost of debt of firm i between year t and, year $t + 2$. The cost of debt is calculated by dividing interest expense by the average interest-bearing debt.

NegEarnings$_{i,t}$ Dummy variable coded 1 if firm i has a positive net income in year $t - 1$ but a negative net income in year t, and coded 0 if firm i has a positive net income in both years $t - 1$ and t. The expected sign for this variable's coefficient is positive, indicating that firms whose earnings sign shifts from positive to negative face an increase in the cost of debt.

$\Delta \text{IntCov}_{i,t+1}$ Variation in the interest coverage ratio of firm i between year t and year $t + 1$. has implicit an increase in the firm's default risk implying and increase in the cost of debt. The interest coverage ratio is calculated by dividing earnings before interest and taxes (EBIT) by interest expense. The expected sign for this variable's coefficient is negative since a decrease in this ratio results in an increase in the firm's default risk, which implies an increase in the cost of debt.

$\Delta \text{Liq}_{i,t+1}$ Variation in the liquidity ratio of firm i between year t and year $t + 1$. The liquidity ratio is calculated by dividing current assets by current liabilities. The expected sign for this variable's coefficient is negative since a decrease in this ratio implies an increase in the firm's default risk, which implies an increase in the cost of debt.

$\Delta\text{Tang}_{i,t+1}$ Variation in the ratio of tangibility of assets of firm i between year t and year $t + 1$. The tangibility ratio is a proxy for assets that can be pledged as collateral and is calculated as property, plant, and equipment divided by total assets. The expected sign for this variable's coefficient is negative since a decrease in this ratio implies an increase in the firm's default risk, which implies an increase in the cost of debt.

$\Delta\text{Lev}_{i,t+1}$—Variation in the leverage ratio of firm i between year t and year $t + 1$. The leverage ratio is calculated as total debt divided by total assets. The expected sign for this variable's coefficient is positive since an increase in this ratio implies an increase in the firm's default risk, which implies an increase in the cost of debt.

$\Delta\text{Size}_{i,t+1}$ Variation in the size of firm i between year t and year $t + 1$. The natural logarithm of total assets is used to calculate firms' size. The expected sign for this variable's coefficient is negative since a decrease in this ratio implies an increase in the firm's default risk, which implies an increase in the cost of debt.

$\sum\beta_1$ DummyInd: a set of dummy variables coded 1 if the observation belongs to the industry and 0 otherwise. We do not make predictions about the sign of these variables.

$\sum\beta_1$ DummyYear a set of dummy variables coded 1 if the observation belongs to the year and 0 otherwise. We do not make predictions about the sign of these variables.

$\varepsilon_{i,t+2}$ the residuals.

The second research hypothesis is being tested to see if the effect of a change in the sign of earnings on the cost of debt is delayed relative to the time when the change occurs or, on the contrary, occurs closer to the time when the change occurs. This hypothesis is tested using Model 2, where the dependent variable is the variation in the cost of debt between years t and $t + 1$ (CostDebt I $t + 1$), and the independent variables are the same as in Model 1. The models will be estimated using ordinary least squares on pooled data.

$$\Delta\text{CostDebt}_{i,t+2} = \beta_0 + \beta_1\text{NegEarnings}_{i,t} + \beta_2\Delta\text{IntCov}_{i,t+1} + \beta_3\Delta\text{Liq}_{i,t+1}$$
$$+ \beta_4\Delta\text{Tang}_{i,t+1} + \beta_5\Delta\text{Lev}_{i,t+1} + \beta_6\Delta\text{Size}_{i,t+1}$$
$$+ \sum\beta_1\text{DummyInd} + \sum\beta_1\text{DummyYear} + \varepsilon_{i,t+2}$$

3.2   Sample Selection and Descriptive Statistics

All companies listed on the Tunisian Stock Exchange constitute the initial sample (TSE). However, we exclude financial institutions and insurance companies due to the unique characteristics of their asset and liability structures. Thus, our sample consists exclusively of manufacturing and services industries. We also exclude from our sample firms that do not have sufficient data for five consecutive years. These selection criteria led us to reduce the initial sample of 50 companies into a sample of 32 firms. Further, the number of the firm- year observations varies from one year to another since certain companies were not represented in the sample for each year. The study period ranges from 2008 to 2018. Accounting and financial data used in our research were hand-collected manually from the Financial Statements and "Stock Guides" provided by the Tunis Stock Exchange.

The cost of debt is calculated by using the ratio of interest expense over the average interest-bearing debt. We lag the variables in one period when calculating the average interest-bearing debt. The presence of a minimum level of interest-bearing debt is recommended in order to reduce the volatility of the estimated rates when establishing a relationship between the cost of debt and its determinants. As a result, we only consider observations with a percentage of average interest-bearing debt equal to or greater than 5% of total assets. Our measure of the cost of debt is potentially very noisy, especially where firms rollover debt throughout the year or where the level of debt changes significantly near the year-end because the average interest-bearing debt could be quite different from the interest-bearing debt that served as the basis for calculating the interest (Aldamen & Duncan, 2013). For this reason, we also eliminate observations in which interest-bearing debt during the year more than doubles or reduce by half (Minnis, 2011).

Our measure of the cost of debt is potentially very noisy, particularly when firms' renew debt throughout the year or when the level of debt changes significantly near the end of the year, since the average interest-bearing debt may differ significantly from the interest-bearing debt that served as the basis for calculating the interest rate (Aldamen & Duncan, 2013). Therefore, we exclude observations in which the interest-bearing debt more than doubled or halved during the year (Minnis, 2011).

With these observations, we calculate the remaining variables and select the firms with data for a four-year period ($t - 1$ to $t + 2$). Following that, we retain only two types of firms: (1) those that report a positive net income for at least two consecutive years ($t - 1$ and t), and (2) those that observe a change in the sign of their net income from positive to negative during this period. Following these constraints, we count 352 observations, 240 of which concern firms that report a positive net income in years $t - 1$ and t, and 112 of which concern firms that observe a change in the sign of their net income from positive to negative during this period. Table 3.1 presents the descriptive statistics for the variables of the models.

NI $t \geq 0$ and NI $t < 0$ represent, respectively, the subsample of firms that in year t report a positive net income and the subsample of firms that in year t report a negative net income. Pr > |t| is the significance of the t-test to comparing the means of the two subsamples. Pr > |Z| is the significance of the Wilcoxon test to comparing the medians of the two subsamples.

Over the years studied, the difference for firms with positive and net income is statistically different, however for total assets the difference is not statistically different between firms with negative or positive net income. Interest-bearing debt accounts for roughly half of total debt in firms with both positive and negative net income, highlighting the importance of bank credit in total debt. The average interest-bearing debt of the

Table 1 Descriptive statistics

	Mean		
	$NI_t \geq 0$ (N = 352)	$NIt < 0$ (N = 352)	Pr > |t|
NI_{It}	240	112	0.000
Total assets	17.892	17.567	0.198
Total debt	0.519	0.641	0.234
Interest-bearing debt	0.518	0.627	0.114
CostDebt	0.156	0.174	0.01r3
Tang	0.289	0.361	0.041
$IntCov_t$	0.231	0.421	0.000
Liq	0.126	0.169	0.029
$Tang_t$	0.189	0.221	0.156
Size	17.851	17.981	0.000

Source Author's calculation based on data collected from annual reports and stock exchange

two groups of firms analyzed is not statistically different. The cost of debt (CostDebt) for firms with positive net income is lower on average than for firms with negative net income. When we examine the proportion of tangible assets in total assets (Tang), we find that it is higher for firms with negative net income. This implies that these companies may benefit from lower interest rates on their loans if they provide assets as collateral.

4   EMPIRICAL RESULTS AND DISCUSSION

The estimation results for Models 1 and 2 are shown in Table 3.2. The estimation of Model 1 aims to test whether the change in the sign of earnings leads to an increase in the cost of debt. The estimation of Model 2 will examine whether that effect is delayed relative to the moment at which it occurs. The F-statistic indicates that the tests were significant, and the adjusted R^2 reveals an explanatory power of 19.21% for Model 1 and 20.89% for Model 2.

The estimation results of Model 1 show, as expected, a positive and statistically significant coefficient for the variable NegNI. This result reveals that firms that experience a change in the sign of their net income,

Table 2 The effect of negative earnings on the cost of debt

	Expected sign	ΔNI	$+\Delta NI$
Constant	+/−	0.231 (0.017)**	0.158 (0.026)**
NegNI	+	0.438** (0.031)	0.547** (0.019)
ΔIntCov	−	−0.815** (0.021)	−0.683* (−0.088)
ΔLiq	−	−0.834** (−0.043)	0.588** (0.043)
ΔTang	−	−0.126* (−0.065)	−0.331** (-0.030)
ΔLev	+	−1.124** (−0.049)	−1.291** (−0.047)
ΔSize	−	0.118** (0.013)	0.234* (0.051)
N		352	352
Adjusted R^2		19.217%	20.891%
F Statistic		3.46***	3.21***

Source Author's calculation based on data collected from annual reports and stock exchange

from positive to negative, support an increase in its cost of debt in the following two years compared to that supported by firms that maintain a positive net income. This finding supports the first research hypothesis et reveals that negative earnings are seen as less persistent and therefore of lower quality. This result means that Tunisian lenders price the information conveyed through negative earnings, which has an impact on firms' access to credit. This finding also suggests that even in an environment where lending is still based on informal and personal relationships, relationship-based lending cannot conceal the negative effect of reporting negative results. Thus, our study reinforces the view that failing to meet some earnings benchmark has unfavorable economic consequences, such as rising interest rates (Jiang, 2008).

Overall, our results corroborate previous research conducted in code-law markets (Beltrame et al., 2017; Houcine & Houcine, 2020; Reindeiro-Carmo et al., 2016; Vander Bauwhede et al., 2015 etc.) that show that better quality of earnings decreases the cost of debt.

This table presents the results of OLS estimation with pooled data, with year and industry dummies variables. ***, ** and * denotes statistical significance at 1%, 5% e 10%, respectively. t-statistic in brackets. NegNI is a dummy variable coded 1 if the observation relates to a firm that reported a positive net income in year $t - 1$ and a negative net income in year t, and coded 0 if the observation relates to a firm that reported a positive net income in both years.

For the estimation results of Model 2, the coefficient of the variable NegNI is also significantly positive and indicating that in the first year following the report of a negative net income, there is an increase in the cost of debt. This evidence suggests that the effect of a change in the sign of earnings on the cost of debt is not fully reflected during the first year following the moment when the negative income was reported, but rather is delayed relative to that moment, which supports the second research hypothesis.

In terms of control variables, the change in the interest coverage ratio (ΔIntCov) has a statistically significant negative coefficient, as expected. The coefficients for the variation in the liquidity ratio (ΔLiq) and the variation in the tangibility ratio (ΔTang) are statistically significant too. The coefficient for the variation in the leverage ratio (ΔLev) is statistically significant, but with opposite sign than expected. The coefficient of variation in the firm size (ΔSize) is significantly positive, which suggests that firms whose size increased (decreased) experienced an increase (decrease) in the cost of debt. This relationship may exist if the variation in size is a consequence of a variation in the interest-bearing debt, that is, firms that increased (decreased) their size are those that increased (decreased) their interest-bearing debt and, as a result, increased (decreased) their cost of debt.

In order to test whether the effect of the ΔSize in the ΔCostDebt is the same for firms that increased and decreased their size, Model 1 was estimated in two subsamples: one of the firms that increased their size (ΔSize > 0) and the other of firms that decreased their size (ΔSize < 0). The results of this analysis, as shown in Table 3.3, reveal that the coefficient of ΔSize is only statistically significant for firms whose size increased, suggesting that this increase could be due to the acquisition of assets using interest-bearing debt, which is the cost of debt. The coefficient of the variable NegNI is positive and statistically significant in both groups considered, indicating that changes in firm size have no effect on the relationship between negative earnings and the cost of debt. The coefficient of ΔLev is still negative as we have noted in the results of the estimation of Model 1 for the entire sample (Table 3.3). This sign may be the result of

Table 3 The effect of negative earnings on the cost of debt and changes in firm's size	*Expected sign*	Δ*Size* > 0	Δ*Size* < 0
Constant	±	0.171 (0.091)*	−0.023 (−0.063) *
NegNI	+	0,0514** (0.025)	0.044** (0.021)
ΔIntCov	−	−0.127* (−0.059)	−0.098** (−0.028)
ΔLiq	−	−0.213 (−0.115)	0.186 (0.106)
ΔTang	−	−0.104 (−0.101)	−0.113 (−0.213)
ΔLev	+	−0.755*** (−0.025)	−0.952*** (−0.043)
ΔSize	−	0.254** (0.022)	0.352 (−0.151)
N		352	3352
Adjusted R^2		19.891%	20,094%
F Statistic		2.398***	2.821***

Source Author's calculation based on data collected from annual reports and stock exchange

the proxy used for the cost of debt (Francis et al., 2005) and the relationship between total debt, interest-bearing debt, and cost of debt. As noted in the descriptive statistics, the interest-bearing debt accounts for approximately half of liabilities, thus large variations in interest-bearing debt cause large variations in the leverage ratio and the cost of debt. Thus, high positive (negative) changes in interest-bearing debt will result in high positive (negative) changes in leverage ratio, followed by high negative (positive) changes in the cost of debt.

This table presents the results of OLS estimation with pooled data, with year and industry dummies variables. ***, ** and * denotes statistical significance at 1%, 5% e 10%, respectively. t-statistic in brackets. ΔSize > 0 and ΔSize identify, respectively, those firms that have increased or decreased their size between year t and year $t + 1$. NegNI is a dummy variable coded 1 if the observation relates to a firm that reported a positive net income in year $t - 1$ and a negative net income in year t, and coded 0 if the observation relates to a firm that reported a positive net income in both years.

5   SENSITIVITY ANALYSIS

5.1   Effect of the Level of Interest Rates in year t – 1

The effect of negative earnings on the cost of debt may be conditioned by the level of interest rates prior to the report of the negative net income. In firms where these rates are already high, banks may be unable to raise them; in this case, other lending conditions, such as the requirement of collateral, may be adjusted. In order to examine whether the level of interest rates in year $t - 1$ (CostDebt $t - 1$) influences the results, we introduce the variable (CostDebt $t - 1$) into Model 1 and the interaction variable NegEarnings*CostDebt $t - 1$, yielding Model 3 below.

$$
\begin{aligned}
\Delta \text{CostDebt}_{i,t+2} = {} & \beta_0 + \beta_1 \text{CostDebt}_{i,t-1} + \beta_2 \text{NegNI}_{i,t} \\
& + \beta_3 \text{NegNIs} * \text{CostDebt}_{i,t-1} + \beta_4 \Delta \text{IntCov}_{i,t+1} \\
& + \beta_5 \Delta \text{Liq}_{i,t+1} + \beta_6 \Delta \text{Tang}_{i,t+1} + \beta_7 \Delta \text{Lev}_{i,t+1} \\
& + \beta_8 \Delta \text{Siz}_{i,t+1} + \sum \beta \text{DummyInd} \\
& + \sum \beta_1 \text{DummyYear} + \varepsilon_{i,t+2}
\end{aligned}
$$

If firms with higher interest rates in year $t-1$ support a lower variation in their cost of debt in subsequent years, the sign of the variable Cost-Debt $t - 1$ will be negative. If the level of interest rates influences the change in the cost of debt differently for firms with negative and positive net income, the variable NegNI*CostDebt $t - 1$ will be statistically significant. Results of estimation of Model 3 are presented in Table 3.4.

This table presents the results of OLS estimation with pooled data, with year and industry dummies variables. ***, ** and * denotes statistical significance at 1%, 5% e 10%, respectively. T-statistic in brackets. CostDebt is the cost of debt in year $t - 1$. NegNIis a dummy variable coded 1 if the observation relates to a firm that reported a positive net income in year $t - 1$ and a negative net income in year t, and coded 0 if the observation relates to a firm that reported a positive net income in both years.

The results in Table 3.4 show a non-statistically significant coefficient for the variable NegNI*CostDebt $t - 1$, indicating that the level of

Table 4 The effect of interest rates in year $t - 1$	Expected sign	Model 3
Constant	±	0.059 (0.061)*
CostDebt	+	−0.314** (−0.013)
NegNI	−	0.0421** (0.027)
NegNI*CostDebt	−	0.094 (0.311)
ΔIntCov	−	0.0947** (−0.026)
ΔLiq	−	0.165 (−0.123)
ΔTang	−	−0.125 (−0.173)
ΔLev	+	−1.163*** (−0.498)
ΔSize	−	0.164*** (−0.002)
N		352
Adjusted R^2		19,841%
F Statistic		3.421***

Source Author's calculation based on data collected from annual reports and stock exchange

interest rates has no effect on the cost of debt of firms that reported a negative or a positive net income. The coefficient of variable CostDebt $t - 1$ in firms with positive net income (α 1) is negative and statistically significant. The statistical significance of the coefficient of CostDebt $t - 1$ in firms with negative net income (α 1 + α 3) was assessed using the Wald test, which revealed that it is statistically significant at less than 5%. The difference in the coefficient of variable CostDebt $t - 1$ between firms with negative and positive net income was also tested using the Wald test, and it was found to be insignificant. This evidence suggests, as expected, that firms that supported a higher cost of debt in year $t - 1$ show a small change in this variable in subsequent years. This effect is the same whether the firm has a positive or negative net income. After controlling for the effect of CostDebt $t - 1$, the variable NegEarnings remains positive and statistically significant, confirming our findings.

5.2 Effect of the Change in Net Income

The approach used in this study to measure earnings quality assumes that a change in the sign of net income, from positive to negative, is the factor that determines a change in that quality and thus an increase in information risk. However, we can argue that what is being priced is the increase in the firm's default risk as a result of the earnings decline. In order to examine whether the decrease in net income affects the cost of debt, we include in Model 1 the percentage change in net income between years $t - 1$ and year t (ΔNetIncome $t+$), as well as an interactive variable between this and the variable NetNI (NegNI*ΔNetIncome t) giving rise to the Model 4 below.

$$
\begin{aligned}
\Delta\text{CostDebt}_{i,t+2} = {} & \beta_0 + \beta_1 \text{NegNI}_{i,t} + \beta_2 \Delta\text{NetIncome}_{i,t} \\
& + \beta_3 \text{NegNI} * \Delta\text{NetIncome}_{i,t} + \beta_4 \Delta\text{IntCov}_{i,t+1} \\
& + \beta_5 \Delta\text{Liq}_{i,t+1} + \beta_6 \Delta\text{Tang}_{i,t+1} + \beta_7 \Delta\text{Lev}_{i,t+1} \\
& + \beta_8 \Delta\text{Siz}_{i,t+1} + \sum \beta \text{DummyInd} + \sum \beta_1 \text{DummyYear} \\
& + \varepsilon_{i,t+2}
\end{aligned}
$$

This table presents the results of OLS estimation with pooled data, with year and industry dummies variables. ***, ** and * denotes statistical significance at 1%, 5% e 10%, respectively. t-statistic in brackets. ΔNetIncomei, t is the change, in percentage, of net income between year

$t - 1$ and year t. NegNI is a dummy variable coded 1 if the observation relates to a firm that reported a positive net income in year $t - 1$ and a negative net income in year t, and coded 0 if the observation relates to a firm that reported a positive net income in both years.

The estimation results of Model 4 shown in Table 3.5, indicate a coefficient that is not statistically significant for the variable ΔNetIncome in firms with positive net income. The statistical significance of the coefficient of the variable ΔNetIncome in firms with negative net income using the Wald test is also not statistically significant. The difference in the coefficient of ΔNetIncome between firms with positive and negative net income is not statistically significant based on the Wald test. This evidence suggests that changes in net income have no effect on the observed changes in the cost of debt. The coefficient of NegEarnings's variable has a positive and statistically significant sign, confirming the existence of the expected relationship between the cost of debt and the change from positive to negative earnings. These findings support the notion that it

Table 5 The effect of the change in net income

	Expected sign	Model 4
Constant	±	0.033
		(0.126)
CostDebt	+	0.051***
		(0.021)
NegNI	–	−0.153
		(−1.114)
NegNI*NetIncome	–	0.304
		(0.431)
ΔIntCov	–	−0.119**
		(−0.027)
ΔLiq	–	−0.128
		(−0.143)
ΔTang	–	−0.424
		(−0.316)
ΔLev	+	−1.267**
		(−0.059)
ΔSize	–	0.231**
		(0.029)
N		
Adjusted R^2		19.436%
F Statistic		3.135***

Source Author's calculation based on data collected from annual reports and stock exchange

is the change in the sign of net income, rather than the amount of the variation in net income that causes a decrease in earnings quality and an increase in information risk. This result suggests that lenders price the information conveyed through negative earnings and not the variation in earnings, since their behavior is influenced by certain thresholds and negative earnings have a psychological impact on the thresholds (Vidal, 2010).

6   CONCLUSION

In this study, we examined the effect of negative earnings on the cost of debt for a sample of Tunisian listed firms. The findings support the research hypothesis, demonstrating that firms that experience a shift from positive to negative earnings support an increase in their cost of debt following the report of a negative net income.

We conclude from the sensitivity analysis that changes in the cost of debt are conditioned by the level of the interest rates charged by banks prior to the report of negative earnings. Banks have a lower margin to increase interest rates when interest rates are already high, resulting in lower changes in the cost of debt. Additional analysis revealed that the increase in the cost of debt is determined by the change in the sign of net income, from positive to negative, rather than the amount of that change, corroborating that the report of negative earnings reflects an increase in information risk. This evidence supports the notion that negative earnings have a lower predictive value for a firm's future performance and cash flows than positive earnings (Burgstahler & Dichev, 1997; Collins et al., 1999; Hayn, 1995), posing a greater information risk to banks.

The findings of this study can be of interest to accounting literature, managers, and bankers, by providing evidence about the effects of negative earnings on the cost of debt, which may explain earnings management practices intended to avoid losses.

Our study has some limitations. One is that it is not assumed that earnings management practices to avoid losses could result in small positive earnings, so the shift from a large positive net income to a small positive net income could also represent a decrease in earnings quality and an increase in information risk.

REFERENCES

Aldamen, H., & Duncan, K. (2013). Pricing of innate and discretionary accruals in Australian debt. *Accounting and Finance, 53*, 31–53.

Ball, R., Kothari, S. P., & Robin, A. (2000). The effect of international institutional factors on properties of accounting earnings. *Journal of Accounting and Economics, 29*(1), 1–51.

Barth, M. E., Elliott, J. A., & Finn, M. W. (1999). Market rewards associated with patterns of increasing earnings. *Journal of Accounting Research, 37*(2), 387–413.

Beltrame, F., Floreani, J., & Sclip, A. (2017). Earnings quality and the cost of debt of SMEs. In G. Chesini, E. Giaretta, & A. Paltrinieri (Eds.), *Financial markets, SME financing and emerging economies* (pp. 21–39). Palgrave Macmillan Studies in Banking and Financial Institutions. Palgrave Macmillan.

Berger, P. G., Ofek, E., & Swary, I. (1996). Investor valuation of the abandonment option. *Journal of Financial Economics, 42*, 257–287.

Bharath, S. T., Sunder, J., & Sunder, S. V. (2008). Accounting quality and debt contracting. *The Accounting Review, 83*(1), 1–28.

Bhattacharya, U., Daouk, H., & Welker, M. (2003). The world price of earnings opacity. *The Accounting Review, 78*(3), 641–678.

Burgstahler, D., & Dichev, I. (1997). Earnings management to avoid earnings decreases and losses. *Journal of Accounting and Economics, 24*(1), 99–126.

Carmo, C. R., Moreira, J. A. C., & Miranda, M. C. S. (2016). Earnings quality and cost of debt: Evidence from Portuguese private companies. *Journal of Financial Reporting and Accounting, 14*(2), 178–197.

Collins, D. W., Pincus, M., & Xie, H. (1999). Equity valuation and negative earnings: The role of book value of equity. *The Accounting Review, 74*(1), 29–61.

Dechow, P., Ge, W., & Schrand, C. (2010). Understanding earnings quality: A review of the proxies, their determinants and their consequences. *Journal of Accounting and Economics, 50*, 344–401.

Dechow, P. M., Kothari, S. P., & Watts, R. L. (1998). The relation between earnings and cash flows. *Journal of Accounting and Economics, 25*(2), 133–168.

Degeorge, F., Patel, J., & Zeckhauser, R. (1999). Earnings management to exceed thresholds. *Journal of Business, 72*(1), 1–33.

Diamond, D. W., & Verrecchia, R. E. (1991). Disclosure, liquidity, and the cost of capital. *Journal of Finance, 46*(4), 1325–1359.

Easley, D., & O'Hara, M. (2004). Information and the cost of capital. *Journal of Finance, 59*(4), 1553–1583.

Francis, J., LaFond, R., Olsson, P., & Schipper, K. (2004). Costs of equity and earnings attributes. *The Accounting Review, 79*(4), 967–1010.

Francis, J., LaFond, R., Olsson, P., & Schipper, K. (2005). The market pricing of accruals quality. *Journal of Accounting and Economics, 39*(2), 295–327.

Frankel, R., & Litov, L. (2009). Earnings persistence. *Journal of Accounting and Economics, 47*, 182–190.

Jiang, J. (2008). Beating earnings benchmarks and the cost of debt. *The Accounting Review, 83*(2), 377–416.

García-Teruel, P. J., Martínez-Solano, P., & Sánchez-Ballesta, J. P. (2014). The role of accruals quality in the access to bank debt. *Journal of Banking & Finance, 38*, 186–193.

Gray, P., Koh, P. S., & Tong, Y. H. (2009). Accruals quality, information risk and cost of capital: Evidence from Australia. *Journal of Business Finance and Accounting, 36*(1/2), 51–72.

Hayn, C. (1995). The information content of losses. *Journal of Accounting and Economics, 20*, 125–153.

Houcine, A., & Houcine, W. (2020). Does earnings quality affect the cost of debt in a banking system? Evidence from French listed companies. *Journal of General Management, 45*(4), 183–191.

Kasznik, R., & McNichols, M. F. (2002). Does meeting earnings expectations matter? Evidence from analyst forecast revisions and share prices. *Journal of Accounting Research, 40*(3), 727–759.

Lambert, R., Leuz, C., & Verrecchia, R. E. (2007). Accounting information, disclosure, and the cost of capital. *Journal of Accounting Research, 45*(2), 385–420.

Lambert, R. A., Leuz, C., & Verrecchia, R. E. (2011). Information asymmetry, information precision, and the cost of capital. *Review of Finance, 16*, 1–29.

Leuz, C., & Verrecchia, R. E. (2004). *Firm's capital allocation choices, information quality and the cost of capital.* The Wharton Financial Institutions Center.

Lev, B. (1989). On the usefulness of earnings and earnings research: Lessons and directions from two decades of empirical research. *Journal of Accounting Research, 27*, 153–192.

Minnis, M. (2011). The value of financial statement verification in debt financing: evidence from private U.S. firms. *Journal of Accounting Research, 49*(2), 457–506.

Rendeiro Carmo, C., Cardoso Moreira, J. A., & Souto Miranda, M. C. (2016). Earnings quality and cost of debt: Evidence from Portuguese private companies. *Journal of Financial Reporting and Accounting, 14*(2), 178–197.

Van Caneghem, T., & Campenhout, G. (2012). Quantity and quality of information and SME financial structure. *Small Business Economics, 39*(2), 341–358.

Vander Bauwhede, H., De Meyere, M., & Van Cauwenberge, P. (2015). Financial reporting quality and the cost of debt of SMEs. *Small Business Economics, 45*, 149–164.

Vidal, O. (2010). Gestion du résultat pour éviter de publier une perte: Les montants manipulés sont-ils marginaux? *Comptabilité, Contrôle, Audit, 16*, 11–40.

Zhang, J. (2008). The contracting benefits of accounting conservatism to lenders and borrowers. *Journal of Accounting and Economics, 45*, 27–54.

Board Effectiveness, Corporate Cash Holdings, and Financial Performance Across MENA Region

Hussien Mohsen, Mohamed Marie, Sherif El-Halaby,
and Israa Elbendary

1 INTRODUCTION

Over the past two decades, companies globally have increased their cash holdings (CH) extremely. Amess et al. (2015) mentioned in their study a report by Deloitte that stated that over $2.8 trillion in cash is held by 1000 global non-financial companies. Furthermore, the CH of U.S firms

H. Mohsen
Faculty of Commerce, English section, Helwan University, Cairo, Egypt
e-mail: hussein.mohsen.saber@commerce.helwan.edu.eg

M. Marie · I. Elbendary
Faculty of Commerce, Cairo University, Giza, Egypt
e-mail: Mohamed_Marei@foc.cu.edu.eg

I. Elbendary
e-mail: Israa_Mohamed@foc.cu.edu.eg

S. El-Halaby (✉)
Faculty of Business, Arab Open University, Kuwait, Kuwait
e-mail: sismail@aou.edu.kw; shielhalaby@msa.edu.eg

A. Echchabi et al. (eds.), *Contemporary Research in Accounting and Finance*, https://doi.org/10.1007/978-981-16-8267-4_4

reached almost 13% of total assets, which is equivalent to 10% of yearly U.S Gross domestic product. During 1989–2006, Bates et al. (2009) report that CH increased by 46% annually. Juliane and Palazzo (2021) stated that, over the last 35 years, firms with large cash reserves in the stock market have intensively invested more in numbers of research and development, which support them to create a competitive advantage and sustainability to survive for the long term. The mentioned numbers reflect the importance of CH, which drives the researchers to examine in depth its antecedents and consequences on FP.

The conflict of interest between managers and shareholders inter-acts with corporate governance (CG), resulting in the agency problem. However, the weak CG may lead managers to exploit CH for personal benefits (Amman et al., 2011). One of the most important indicators for internal CG is board structure, as it has a critical role in determining the firms' policy. Masood and Attaullah (2014) concluded that to hold an optimal level of cash, firms are required to apply good CG mechanisms. In this respect, the causal relationship between CG and corporate CH is still vague in previous studies, which motivates us to explore in depth in this association.

The empirical research that measures the impact of CH and CG on the FP didn't report conclusive results, which requires more investigation. Furthermore, It is necessary to investigate the impact of CH on company outcomes (Amess et al., 2015). The prevailing literature on CH is replete with indications from the United States and developed markets with slight consideration given to the developing markets as MENA region. Plentiful influences make CH varied in developing compared with developed markets. The institutional factors could influence a business's financial practices, such as CH. This is likely to raise the level of uncertainty in transactions and inspire a range of unproductive practices as cash retention (Al-Najjar, 2013).

Our study comprises banks for countries in the MENA. This sample is valid for a variety of reasons. First, since these countries are now part of the EU's regional policy, they follow a common economic restructuring path. Though, they reflect the conflicting degree of financial reform and development. Therefore, they provide conducive environment for comparative study that connects CG and CH. Second, the MENA region, which includes Gulf Cooperation Council (GCC) countries, has unique business practices as an emerging market. GCC is an oil-rich area, the share market is comparatively immature, and an Islamic banking system is present, t and the legal origin is based on Sharia Law. Two of the utmost significant features of Islamic values relating to corporate financing are Islamic law forbidding interests and Zakat's commitment (Islamic Tax) (Al-Nodel & Hussainey, 2010). Third, many scholars have considered CG in other developing markets; CG has often been ignored in the MENA region. For instance, Dittmar et al. (2003) include just Jordan and Egypt from the MENA region in their universal sample of 45 nations, but Ramirez and Tadesse (2009) include only Egypt in their international sample and Al-Najjar and Clark (2017) include nine countries from the MENA region. Otherwise, To the authors' knowledge, there is no evidence in the banking sector about the correlation between cash holdings and CG in MENA countries. Finally, there is enough variety to allow for comparative study. In the GCC countries and Jordan, for example, CG rules include essential provisions for board composition, shareholder reporting, and other characteristics. In some countries in the region, such as Egypt, codes remain voluntary, and companies and regulations serve as the major basis for governance practices.

The originality of this paper can be presented by explaining to what extent it differs from the previous studies. For example, Guizani (2017) focuses on one country (KSA), whereas this study used data for multi regions (GCC). Most of previous studies explore CH have been conducted for the Anglo-Saxon countries such as the United States (Dittmar & Mahrt-Smith, 2007); an European framework (Ferreira & Vilela, 2004), the UK (Al-Najjar & Belghitar, 2011), in Spanish (Garcia-Teruel & Martinez-Solano, 2008), while our research focused on different context which is GCC region. Also, Al-Najjar (2013) investigates the financial determinants in some developing economies, but without including CG in his models. Whereas Al-Najjar and Clark (2017) and Conheady et al. (2015) examine the effect of internal and external CG factors on the CH actions, this study used data for financial institutions. Finally, none of the prior research—as far as we know—measure the impact of board effectiveness on both CH and FP.

Little literature has focused on examining CH in Aran or MENA region. Ben Naceuret et al. studied Companies that have been privatized in the MENA region and found that these firms increased operating performance. Chahine and Tohmé (2009) investigate CG in the Arab environment. According to Tunisian companies, El-Mehdi indicates a weak governance impact on FP. Elsayed (2007) considers the effects of CG on corporate financial performance in Egypt. As a result, we detect a strong desire to investigate the MENA region. However, the impact of CG in the Middle East and North Africa has yet to be fully investigated. This research intends to bridge that gap by employing a broad sample of financial institutions from MENA regions.

Our study provides several imperative contributions to the literature. To the best of our knowledge, no existing has been conducted on the banks across the GCC region. Thus, our paper adds to previous literatures by investigating the consequence CH decisions of banks across GCC. This study shows that board effectiveness is concerned with board independence, gender diversity, board size, and CEO duality explains a significant portion of the cross-country variations in CH. Despite the growing number of studies on CH, Only a dearth of literature has focused on the relationship between CH and FP. Thus, the current work adds to the literature by determining whether banks have a peak cash level at which their FP is empirically optimized. We also present a preliminary assessment of the factors influencing the association between FP and CH levels in order to further our understanding of CH behavior and provide evidence on how to appropriately adjust CH for listed banks based on their board effectiveness' determinants. Moreover, we focus on Islamic and conventional banks as previous research on the determinants of CH concentrated on non-financial firms and conventional banks. Given that Islamic banks are one of the world's fastest growing financial institutions, the lack of attention to them is quite unexpected. Furthermore, GCC is capturing 70% from investing in the Islamic finance industry across the globe. This study adds value for how board effectiveness can be a mediator in determining the level of CH and FP. Our paper introduces an interdisciplinary perception in empathetic corporate CH, which encompasses the literature in accounting and the theories of the multinational firm for the banking sector in a different context which is MENA.

To the best of our knowledge, this is one of the top studies in the MENA region that assesses the influence of board effectiveness in managing CH and FP for the banking sector. To conduct the analysis, we used a sample of 106 banks that combine Islamic and Conventional banks across GCC for 2010–2017. The findings reveal that CH has a negative relationship with board independence and board gender diversity. The outcome also supports for the positive association between CH and board size as well as the Chief executive officer (CEO) duality. Interestingly, our analysis finds an insignificant effect for board effectiveness on the FP. Finally, our result is not matching with the theoretical base and the previous literature that supports the impact of CH to enhance the FP. The structure of the study is as follows: Sect. 2 presents the theoretical background. Section 3 reviews the related studies on CH, board effectiveness, and FP, then formulate the hypotheses. Section 4 describes the research design. Section 5 reports the main results. Finally, Sect. 6 presents the findings, limitations, and future research directions.

2 THEORETICAL BACKGROUND

Here, we discuss theoretical background of CH, which involves four theories, these theories are pecking order theory (Myers & Majluf, 1984), free cash flow theory (Jensen, 1986), trade-off theory (Myers, 1977), and agency theory (Jensen, 1986). Because we measure association between different variables (CH, FP, and CG), we believe that adopting several theories will be applicable background to justify these multi associations. In the literature review, adopting numerous theories as a theoretical framework for corporate cash holdings is used differently (e.g., Weidemann, 2018).

2.1 Free Cash Flow Theory

It is believed that if the company has poor investment opportunities, it's preferred by entrenched managers to keep cash instead of increasing payouts to shareholders. Financing from capital markets is no longer needed if there is excess cash flow; as a result, managers won't be monitored by cash providers; however, agency problems could be severe with high levels of free cash flows (Jensen, 1986). According to Dittmar and Mahrt-Smith (2007), CH is unworthy when agency difficulties are severe. According to Opler et al. (1999), managers would maintain additional income in order to reduce their undiversified risk and fulfill personal goals.

2.2 Pecking Order Theory

CH has been widely discussed by Myers (1984); they found that CH has no optimal level. Pecking order theory analyzes the hierarchy of CH and explains how corporations prefer to fund internally, as Chen (2008) stated that the cost of internal funds is lower than external debt. As a result, corporations raise CH to fund their investments; also, firms can repay debt (Ferreira & Vilela, 2004).

2.3   Trade-Off Theory

This theory states that firms are balancing between marginal costs and benefits of keeping cash, which end up with setting an ideal level of CH (Kariuki et al., 2015). According to Myers (1977), firms can take superiority of investment opportunities; as a result, the optimal CH yields profits. Martinez-Sola et al. (2013) show that there is a robust link among FP and CH; in this respect, if cash exceeds the optimal level, FP reduces. Mainly, there are two reasons why firms keep cash on hand. First, there is the transaction cost, which means that corporations keep more cash due to the costs of external funding. Firms can avoid these costs by selling assets, issuing shares, or lowering dividend payments. Second, due to investment costs, protective incentives, i.e., investments, could be lowered (Ozkan & Ozkan, 2004).

2.4   Agency Theory

CG instruments are related to agency theory, where the owner of the firm delegates operational responsibility to the manager (Kusumaningtyas & Yendrawati, 2015). Jensen (1986) mentioned that managers aim to gain discretionary power, holding more cash. Agency theory stated that companies with a high extent of CH might face agency struggles if this cash is not invested in lucrative tasks. Chen (2008) believes in situations with high CH, directors, directors' flexible power. The high level of cash reserves makes directomakesapable for follow their individual interests.

Consequently, the board may be involved in negative NPV investments when cash is kept, negatively affecting FP. Further, firms are required to have good and effective governance mechanisms to reduce agency problem (Harford et al., 2008), as a consequence, managers who keep a high level of cash, are viewed as self-opportunistic that lead for agency clashes. Lasfer (2006) stated that CG mechanisms such as board structure could help in sinking the agency costs. Here, we examine whether decent CG practices inspire directors to spend or keep cash and to what extent cash holdings may positively affect the FP.

3 LITERATURE REVIEWS AND HYPOTHESES DEVELOPMENT

3.1 Board Effectiveness and FP

An effective board is dominant to agency theory's instruction for resolving the glitches of ownership separation. Varied outcomes were found for the association between FP and CG. Bebchuk et al. (2009) propose a positive connection between fit governed corporations and FP. Conheady et al. (2015) detect a link between board effectiveness for the company and future market performance. Moreover, Arcot and Bruno (2007) find, based on non-financial corporations in the UK, that CG is meaningfully related to FP. Ntim (2013) found a positive link between CG practices and FP across South African listed companies. However, Amanti and Venusita (2012) state that CG is negatively associated with FP. It is due to business's practice of CG is not completely applied through corporations accordance with codes of GC. Selvaggi and Upton (2008) report a robust negative correlation between FP and CG. In contrast, could not find an association between FP and board structure.

3.1.1 Board Size

Each board member has ability to develop the effectiveness of decision-making. Isshaq et al. (2009) support this debate by showing that board size positively affects FP. Orozco et al. (2018) reported similar results. On the other side and through using data from U.S corporations, Palaniappan (2017) documents a negative relationship based on Indian manufacturing industry through using Tobin's Q, ROA, and ROE. Bozec (2005) finds that board size negatively influences the sales margin based on Canadian companies. However, according to Chinese listed businesses, Shao (2019) finds no There is a link between board size and FP. Accordingly to previous mixed result, we expect a positive link between board size and FP.

H1: There is a positive association between board size and FP.

3.1.2 Board Independence

Evidence concerning board independence and FP is mixed. Jaffar and Abdul-Shukor (2016) find that structure of independent board members has showed a significant positive influence on business FP in the context of Malaysian companies. Suhadak et al. (2019) and Chung et al. (2003) sustain this positive relationship. In contrary, Afzalur (2019) find that board independence and FP do not positively influence each other. It can be claimed that the board has real independent members that can decrease board excesses and further agency costs, thus positively affecting FP.

H2: There is a positive relationship between board independence and financial performance.

3.1.3   CEO Duality

For agency theory based on Fama and Jensen (1983). The degree to which BOD members can release their fiduciary responsibilities is harmed when the CEO and chairman roles are combined. CEO duality problems for board efficiency appear as CEOs are mainly well situated to obtain superior gen around the corporation. The readiness of CEOs to ensconce themselves can guide them to capitalize on precarious information required for evaluating the quality of the board. According to Brockmann et al. (2004), cover-up information reinforces the unrestricted influence of CEO, particularly those who concurrently work as heads of BOD. Merging CEO and chairperson characters damages the management's controlling purpose (Kim et al., 2009). Shao (2019) finds CEO duality has a negative consequence on FP. The findings based on Augustine et al. (2016) are constant with arguments innovative by agency theory that CEO duality might decrease business performance by managerial entrenchment.

H3: The FP is lower for banks with CEO duality.

3.1.4   Board Gender Diversity

As individuals with a diverse gender might have inquiries that may not be derived from executives of the same gender, board diversity may enhance board decisions (Arfken et al., 2004). Additional benefits include a greater understanding of the market, increased innovation, and an increase in a company's desirability. By presenting the board with unique perspectives, raising arguments, and facilitating the interchange of ideas, diversity promotes organizational value and performance (Carter et al., 2003). Previous Literatures analyze the influence of gender diversity on FP whichever positive (e.g., Dani et al., 2019), alternatively no significant (e.g., Campbell & Minguez-Vera, 2008), or negative (e.g., Thi & Phan, 2017). Dani et al. (2019) find that, in a varied BOD related to gender, superior directors' control may happen then the performance develops. Similarly, based on the context of Vietnam, Nguyen et al. (2015) find that variety has a beneficial influence on the FP across the board. According to Daniel et al. (2015), the increasing number of female directors on boards of directors has a beneficial impact on FP in five countries.

H4: Board gender diversity has an impact on corporate FP.

3.1.5   Board Meetings

For stewardship theory, associated with CG and FP is the concentration of board activity, measured through number of board meetings. Meeting time is a significant resource to enhancing board's efficiency (Conger et al., 1998). Vafeas (1999) found that companies experience amplified board activity resulting in share price failures. Time spent by managers is too limited for expressive discussion among themselves (Jensen, 1993). Al-Daoud et al. (2016) propose a positive relationship between the frequency of board meetings and FP for businesses listed on the Amman Stock Exchange. This proposes that board members define effective matters by engaging with every other regularity meeting to improve decision-making and, therefore, FP. Abdul Gafoor et al. (2018) have found a positive link that supports this association based on commercial banks in India. For Brick and Chidambaran (2010), applying good CG practices raises the stress on companies that are imitated in board activity. In contrast, Ofoeda (2017) observed a negative association between FP and board meetings in Ghana. According to Aryani et al. (2017), the number of board meetings seems to have little effect on FP.

H5: There is no relationship between the number of board meetings and FP.

3.2   Board Effectiveness and CH

According to Akhtar et al. (2018), CG instruments and CH have received much consideration throughout the last two decades. Effective CG control mechanisms to alleviate agency problems over excess cash holdings have been an academic curiosity since Jensen's study.

Harford et al. (2008) demonstrate that there is a lack of financial reserves in week-governed enterprises because directors spend cash on capital expenses. CG develops stockholder value by applying CH function accurately (Dittmar & Mahrt-Smith, 2007). There is an agency problem with a high amount of CH; we suppose a further operative board to moderate this problem. Active board limits a self-interested director's aptitude for cutting the isolated benefit while cash is disbursed. Hence, corporations with a great amount of cash with energetic board will not worry about damaging performance as executives are powerless to follow self-interested usages of cash. For Ferreira and Vilela (2004), companies hold less cash for European Union countries with better CG. Similarly, Roy (2018), across a sample of Indian companies shown that quality of business-level CG is significant in determining level of CH. He stated that corporations with sturdier CG incline to shrink balances of cash. However, Wenchien (2018) finds that based on publicly traded U.S. corporations, businesses with respectable CG keep more money than companies with deprived CG. The negative association between CG and CH shows that businesses with severe CG are more operative across observing directors and sinking executives' propensity to capitalize on negative NPV projects (Lee & Lee, 2009). For Al-Najjar and Clark (2017), CG actions are significant in CH choices.

3.2.1   Board Size

Jensen (1993) advocates agency costs upturn with board size because big boards are less operative in monitoring and calmer for CEO to regulate. Anderson et al. (2004) document greater board is more effective monitor of financial accounting procedures. For Harford et al. (2008), companies whose investors are better represented by superior boards will let directors have more cash holdings to avoid problematic underinvestment. Randoy and Goel (2003) propose that businesses suffer from larger informational asymmetry levels and need actual controlling to alleviate agency problems, which may stem from CH. In added evidence for this perspective, Masood and Shah (2014) demonstrate that board size is inversely associated with corporate CH based on non-financial listed companies on Karachi Stock Market. Mak and Kusnadi provide comparable evidence for companies across Malaysia and Singapore. Bokpin et al. (2011) reveal a positive association between corporate liquidity holding and board size across Ghana samples. While; Al-Najjar and Clark (2017), based on MENA region, report an inverse link among both board size and CH.

H6: The levels of cash holdings increase in relation to the board size.

3.2.2 Board Independence

Independency in the board is the utmost effective monitoring specific for CH (Anderson et al., 2004). An independent board realizes better monitoring as advancing and developing his reputation as a governance professional, especially when assigned to monitor directors as of his independence. Ozkan and Ozkan (2004) find an inverse relationship between board independence and CH. With high levels of board independence acting as a controlling device on boards, management will have severe control on financial procedures and keep fewer amounts of cash. Based on (Chahine & Filatotchev, 2008), board independence improves disclosure quality and decreases information asymmetry. Based on trade-off theory, advanced info transparency creates companies more capable of raising exterior funds for investments. Therefore, corporations would not need to hold much cash. Board independence provides enhanced stockholder protection and diminishes agency costs of CH. Stockholders are keener for accepting advanced CH for companies with further independent BOD. For Wenyen et al. (2015), an independent board allows managers to keep extra CH to avoid underinvestment and control directors' money expenditure performance. While Guizani et al. (2018), According to a sampling of French firms, independence has a detrimental impact on corporate CH.

H7: The levels of CH increase with board independence.

3.2.3 CEO Duality

According to Brickley et al. (1997), the effectiveness of board monitoring can be assessed based on the board's leadership structure. CEO/chairman would apparently have unlimited power and he may stockpile excess cash holdings to serve his individual interest at expense of stockholders' interest. It is significant for board to be active, to distinct CEO and chairman positions (Jensen, 2010). The CEO/chairman may hold large cash to minimize rising capital costs from the market to evade underinvestment by bulky retentive cash. According to Drobetz et al. (2010), there is a positive relationship between corporate CH and CEO duality across Swiss non-financial companies. For Gul and Leung (2004), BOD chaired through CEO would be less active in limiting the managerial decision over business resources concerning cash usage. A probable suggestion is that merging CEO and chair roles inspire governing stock-holders to hold bulky amounts of cash funds at their disposal. While Boubaker et al. (2015) find that businesses with boards considered effective in modifying agency problems—splitting CEO and chairperson positions—accumulate a lesser amount of cash reserves than those with less active BOD.

H8: The level of CH is higher for banks where CEO is also the chair of board.

3.2.4   Board Gender Diversity

Gul et al. (2011) link females with further transparency and decrees level of information irregularity. Reducing the information asymmetry may decrease the cost of transactions for growing exterior cash; corporations don't require large amounts of cash. According to free cash flow theory, the board of directors has an incentive to keep cash because it increases the total amount of assets under their control. A growing stream of research examines how diversity in board affects FP (Merve & Cemil, 2016), corporate social responsibility (Boulouta, 2013), and CG (Kim & Starks, 2016). Furthermore, research demonstrates that females are more severe in managing roles (Adams & Ferreira, 2009) and improve BOD efficiency. Xixiong et al. (2019), based on Chinese listed companies, find that businesses with female CFOs hold significantly more cash, which favors the protective savings-based clarification. While; Alagathurai and Kumara (2017) find gender diversity has a negative impact on CH. Markku (2015) assumed businesses run through feminine directors seek to have superior balances of cash. We specified that companies hold a huge amount of cash meaningfully than firms controlled through men's board members.

H9: Board gender diversity has a negative relationship with CH.

3.2.5   BOD Meetings

For Lipton and Lorsch (1992), a superior regularity of meetings possibly will affect a greater FP since board meetings may be measured as a degree of control efficiency and must affect firm results and financial decision as degree of cash holdings. The mainstream literature shows insignificant relationship between CH and board meetings. For example, Narwal et al.

(2017) indicate that board meetings have no effect on improving the level of CH. Similarly, Alagathurai and Kumara (2017) find no indication about the influence of board meetings on CH for Sri Lanka listed companies.

H10: There is no link between the number of board meetings and the level of CH.

3.3   Cash Holdings and Financial Performance

For Myers and Majluf (1984), financial slack makes corporations less likely to give up valued investment opportunities, implying CH might increase FP. For Jensen (1986), external shareholders may want a corporation to allocate its cash as a huge amount of cash might primarily support the interests of directors and harm FP. According to pecking order theory, businesses with high profit retain higher liquidity because profitable companies accumulate cash flow generated. Therefore, the most profitable corporations would have more cash. Managing cash is a significant decision for board because it is spending for operating all activities (Megginson et al., 2014). On the other side, Asante-Daerko et al. (2018) support that CH negatively affects performance.

Similarly, Ameer (2012) shows that growth in CH has a negative consequence on the businesses' FP and this influence slows down over time. The results display that firms with extraordinary CH caused stockholders concerned that more directors have the power to spend money on schemes that harm the value of the business. Kalcheva and Lins (2007) supported our result. Furthermore, Based on U.S. businesses, Martinez-Sola et al. (2013) discover a negative relationship between CH and FP. Additionally, Azmat (2014) supports this association by arguing that an optimum cash level maximizes the FP. Our outcome is equivalent to Pinkowitz et al. (2006). One of the plausible cause for this relationship is that profitable companies are more likely to invest in optimistic projects and thus have more funds on hand. While, Isshaq et al. (2009) state that a surplus of CH has no effect FP. Hence, we suppose FP is positively associated with cash.

H11: CH has a positive influence on the FP.

Table 1   Research sample by the number of banks

Country	N. banks	Observations	%	Country	N. banks	Observations	%
Bahrain	11	88	9.3	Jordan	9	72	7.6
UAE	12	96	8.8	Yemen	1	8	2
Qatar	6	48	5.1	Syria	6	48	5.3
Egypt	22	176	18.6	Palestine	3	24	0.8
KSA	8	64	6.8	Lebanon	10	80	8.5
Kuwait	6	48	5.1	Tunisia	6	48	5.1
Oman	6	48	5.1	Total	106	849	100

Source DataStream, Bank Scope, and Zaweya database

4   SAMPLE, RESEARCH MODELS, AND VARIABLES

4.1   Sample

To measure the association between CG and CH and FP, we use diverse databases for collecting data for our samples, such as DataStream, Bank Scope, and Zaweya database. Our sample includes 106 banks (40 Islamic banks and 66 conventional banks) across 13 MENA countries for eight years between 2010 and 2017. Our paper comprises Oman, Qatar, Saudi Arabia, Bahrain, Kuwait, United Arab Emirates (UAE), Egypt, Syria, Tunisia, Lebanon, Jordan, Yemen, and Palestine. We use DataStream and bank scope for collecting financial data. Data for characteristics of BOD were manually gathered from annual reports. Table 1 presents our sample through the number of banks in each country and total observations. The maximum number of banks in Egypt with 22 banks, then UAE with 12 banks, and Bahrain with 11 banks. The less country is Yemen.

4.2   Research Models

Model 1: Board Effectiveness and FP

$$\text{Perf}_{it} = \alpha_0 + \beta_1 \text{Board Effectiveness}_{it} + \sum_{i=1}^{n} \beta_i \text{CONTROLS}_{it} + \varepsilon_{it}$$

$$\begin{aligned}
\text{FP}_{it} = \beta 0 &+ \beta 1\, \text{B.IND}_{it} + \beta 2\, \text{B.SIZE}_{it} + \beta 3\, \text{B.DUAL}_{it} + \beta 4\, \text{B.MEET}_{it} \\
&+ \beta 5\, \text{B.DIVER}_{it} + \beta 6\, \text{M.OWNER}_{it} + \beta 7\, \text{I.OWNER}_{it} + \beta 8\, \text{AC.SIZE}_{it} \\
&+ \beta 9\, \text{AC.MEET}_{it} + \beta 10\, \text{SIZE}_{it} + \beta 11\, \text{LIST}_{it} + \beta 12\, \text{GDP} \\
&+ \beta 13\, \text{INFL} + \beta 14\, \text{CORR} + \varepsilon_{it}
\end{aligned} \tag{1}$$

Model 2: Board Effectiveness and CH

$$CH_{it} = \alpha_0 + \beta_1 \text{ Board Effectiveness}_{it} + \sum_{i=1}^{n} \beta_i \text{CONTROLS}_{it} + \varepsilon_{it}$$

$$
\begin{aligned}
CH_{it} = {} & \beta_0 + \beta_1 \text{ B.IND}_{it} + \beta_2 \text{ B.SIZE}_{it} + \beta_3 \text{ B.DUAL}_{it} + \beta_4 \text{ B.MEET} \\
& + \beta_5 \text{ B.DIVER}_{it} + \beta_6 \text{ M.OWNER}_{it} + \beta_7 \text{ I.OWNER}_{it} + \beta_8 \text{ AC.SIZE}_{it} \\
& + \beta_9 \text{ AC.MEET}_{it} + \beta_{10} \text{ SIZE}_{it} + \beta_{11} \text{ LIST}_{it} + \beta_{12} \text{ GDP} \\
& + \beta_{13} \text{ INFL} + \beta_{14} \text{ CORR} + \varepsilon_{it}
\end{aligned}
\tag{2}
$$

Model 3: Cash Holdings and Financial Performance

$$
\begin{aligned}
FP_{it} = {} & \beta_0 + \beta_1 \text{ CH}_{it} + \beta_2 \text{ B.IND}_{it} + \beta_3 \text{ B.SIZE}_{it} + \beta_4 \text{ B.DUAL}_{it} \\
& + \beta_5 \text{ B.MEET}_{it} + \beta_6 \text{ B.DIVER}_{it} + \beta_7 \text{ M.OWNER}_{it} + \beta_8 \text{ I.OWNER}_{it} \\
& + \beta_9 \text{ AC.SIZE}_{it} + \beta_{10} \text{ AC.MEET}_{it} + \beta_{11} \text{ SIZE}_{it} + \beta_{12} \text{ LIST}_{it} \\
& + \beta_{13} \text{ GDP} + \beta_{14} \text{ INFL} + \beta_{15} \text{ CORR} + \varepsilon_{it}
\end{aligned}
\tag{3}
$$

4.3   Dependent Variables

This paper comprises two dependent variables, which are FP and CH. The crucial objective of FP measures is to specify whether the company can create value and reward stockholders for risk. Return of assets (ROA) is an accounting method for measuring FP and the furthermost popular measure of profitability. ROA allows investigative the influence of implementing good board efficiency practices over FP. Chang and Choi (1988) indicate that this measure is an acceptable method of real effectiveness since developing economies and capital markets are deficient. Several authors commonly adopt ROA to measure banks' financial performance, which supported our study (e.g., Al-Harbi, 2019; Bansal et al., 2018). Our second dependent variable is cash holding, calculated as cash and cash equivalent over total assets. Similar to Dittmar et al. (2003), the natural logarithm of CH is used in this study as a robustness analysis.

4.4   Model Specification and Control Variables

To test our research hypotheses and separate the influence of board effectiveness on cash holdings and FP, we control a wide variety of firm-level variables and country-specific characteristics. Companies with less managerial ownership affect the behavior of businesses, as the board has no reason to work for stockholders' benefits, resulting in a weaker CG. Furthermore, Chen (2008) indicated that higher managerial ownership decrease cash holdings in old economy corporations. The literature proposes that if managerial ownership rises, cash holdings will decline. Moreover, Masood and Attaullah (2014) illustrated that more institutional shareholdings outcomes in more CH through companies match Harford et al. (2005), who found a positive link in U.S firms. However, Zhang and Liu (2005) found a negative association between ownership structure and CH.

Several research has documented the effects of structure ownership on share price, and McConnell and Servaes (1990) have found the percentage of inside executive shareholdings have a positive connection to Tobin's Q. Additionally, Jensen (1986) claims that agency problematic of cash flows decreases with a high degree of managerial ownership. Consequently, the influence of managerial ownership on CH should be negative. Indication from British companies thus Ozkan and Ozkan (2004) backings this association. The audit committee (AC) is an essential part of the required CG system to indicate the financial reporting process. The rise in meeting regularity is claimed to provide more active control and develop FP. CG committees and regulators have addressed the requisite for operative AC. Further, Kam and Joanne (2008) found that AC improves FP. Husam et al. (2011) disclose that smaller AC with more experience is more probable to be linked positively with FP. For Hamdan et al. (2013), AC positively affects share performance across listed firms in Amman Stock Market.

Large companies have minor information asymmetries compared to small one. To secure funding in the stock and liability markets, large corporations are able to communicate the true worth of their initiatives more easily. As a result, the ratio of liquid asset holdings to bank size is negative. The business size is predicted to be in reverse linked to the amount of cash holds. Pecking order theory suggests that the corporate provides a signal of success; hence a positive relationship among corporate size and CH is predictable (Ferreira & Vilela, 2004). Smaller companies have superior chance opportunities to grow and develop (Klapper & Love, 2004). We used listed variables to measure the impact of listed status in the stock market on FP and CH. Leyuan et al. (2018) measure whether companies benefit from listing in multiple markets. The result does not find a cross-listing premium.

We used corruption as an indicator for country level, a dimension of the Worldwide Governance Indicator created by World the Bank. Huong et al. (2017) assess corruption's influence on FP based on non-financial firms across eight countries in East Asia. They find low corruption levels encourage use of derivatives and reward national corporations with higher FP. When corruption is high, companies need to pay off functionaries and want to have fluid assets obtainable. Therefore, directors will hold high levels of cash. Inflation is projected to influence corporate holdings of liquid assets negatively. For Yanchao et al. (2014), cash-holding policy is balance between the benefits and the costs. Corporations are motivated to augment their CH policies in reply to fluctuations in buying power in line with inflation. They examine this association across China's stock market and specify a negative link between CH and inflation. Gross domestic product (GDP) proxies and regulates financial development. Predictably, CH is positively associated with GDP (Ramirez & Tadesse, 2009). Table 2 provides a summary of the wholly variables whole in this paper.

5   EMPIRICAL RESULTS AND DISCUSSION

5.1   Descriptive Statistics and Correlation

Table 3 reports the descriptive statistics for all variables used in this study. According to our findings, the average CH ratio is 1.055%, with a median value of 1.108%, suggesting that CH level for banks in MENA countries is low. These results are inconsistent with those obtained by Garcia-Teruel and Martinez-Solano (2008), they found that average cash of 6.57%. For FP, the average ROA in sample firms is 1%, with standard deviation ranges from 0.0002 to 0.030. For independent variables, the mean of board size was between 9, and there was a standard deviation of 0.093. This is consistent with, indicating that banks across MENA adopt relatively small BOD members. board members hold more than eight meetings during the year. The table shows that the CEO and chair of board are the same person by 15.9%. The average of total assets is 5.482. Diversity on the board is represented in 29% of our sample. We report that independent directors are used by 61.7% of our corporations. Therefore, there is some evidence of our companies implement CG practices by incorporating independent boards. For control variables, I.OWNER is also higher in MENA banks and approximately 80% of shares are held by the institutional investors. The average of AC.SIZE has 5 members

Table 2 Research variables, definition, and sources

Variables	Abbreviations	Definitions	Source
Dependent variables			
Cash holdings: Cash holdings ratio	(CH)	Cash and short-term investments/total assets and Logarithm for Cash and short-term investments/total assets	Bank scope and annual reports
Financial Performance:	(FP-ROA)	Performance is calculated using return on assets, which is net income over total assets	Bank scope and Zaweya database
Independent variables			
Board of directors Characteristics			
Board size	(B. SIZE)	Natural logarithm of number of directors of bank *i* at time *t*	Annual report
Board independence	(B. IND)	Percentage of number of independent directors over total number of board in bank	
CEO duality	(B. DUAL)	A dichotomous variable that equals one if CEO is also the chair of the board, and 0 otherwise	
Board meetings	(B. MEET)	The number of board of directors' meetings within the year	
Board gender	(B. DIVER)	A dummy variable is equal to "1" when the board of directors has female member directors on the board, and otherwise, it is equal to "0"	
Control variables			
Ownership characteristics			

Variables	Abbreviations	Definitions	Source
Managerial ownership	(M. OWNER)	A dummy variable which takes "1" if a shareholder with five percent or more ownership stake has the representation on the board of directors or "0" otherwise	Annual report
Institutional ownership	(I. OWNER)	Total number of shares owned by institutions divided by total number of shares	
Audit committee characteristics			
Audit committee size	(AC. SIZE)	Audit committee size is calculated based on number of audit committee	Annual report
Audit committee meetings	(AC. MEET)	The number of audit committee meetings within the year	
Bank characteristics			
Bank size	(SIZE)	Natural logarithm of total assets of a bank at the end of each financial year of bank	Bank scope and Zaweya database
Listed	(LIST)	A dummy variable that equals one if bank listed on stock exchange and 0 otherwise	Central banks
Country-specific characteristics			
GDP	(GDP)	Natural logarithm of GDP	World Bank
Inflation	(INFL)	Inflation rate	
Corruption	(CORR)	Annual rate of corruption within countries	

Source Developed by the authors

Table 3 Descriptive analysis

	CH	B. Size	B.Indep	B. Meet	B. Gend	CEO. Dual	I. Owner	Manag.O
Mean	1.055	0.961	0.617	0.796	0.292	0.159	0.805	0.330
Median	1.108	0.954	0.625	0.778	0.000	0.000	0.861	0.000
Maximum	1.919	1.176	1.00	1.204	1.000	1.00	1.000	1.000
Minimum	0.199	0.698	0.083	0.477	0.000	0.000	0.306	0.000
Std. Dev	0.340	0.093	0.211	0.125	0.4551	0.366	0.1939	0.4705
Skewness	-0.305	-0.377	-0.294	0.740	0.9125	1.863	-0.784	0.722
Kurtosis	2.202	3.104	2.326	4.110	1.8326	4.470	2.446	1.5215
Jarque-Bera	35.673	20.49	28.28	121.0	165.83	566.9	97.698	150.94
Probability	0.000	0.00	0.000	0.00	0.000	0.000	0.000	0.000
Sum	895.4	815.2	523.7	675.0	248.00	135.0	682.70	280.00
Sum Sq. Dev	98.03	7.411	37.94	13.41	175.47	113.5	31.862	187.54
Observations	848	848	848	848	848	848	848	848

	AC. Size	AC. Meet	Size	ROA	GDP	Infl	List	Courr
Mean	0.541	0.660	5.482	0.014	0.034	0.036	0.641	-0.094
Median	0.477	0.602	5.472	0.014	0.030	0.038	1.000	-0.059
Maximum	0.778	1.041	6.375	0.030	0.076	0.213	1.000	1.406
Minimum	0.3010	0.341	5.000	0.002	-0.001	-0.13	0.000	-1.760
Std. Dev	0.088	0.107	0.284	0.006	0.016	0.078	0.479	0.730
Skewness	0.9825	1.304	0.144	0.357	0.505	-0.22	-0.590	0.208
Kurtosis	2.824	4.411	2.018	3.056	2.624	2.618	1.348	2.443
Jarque-Bera	137.52	310.72	36.99	18.20	41.108	12.10	145.61	17.097
Probability	0.000	0.000	0.000	0.001	0.000	0.002	0.000	0.0001
Sum	459.33	560.06	464.9	12.23	29.021	30.60	544.00	-79.750
Sum Sq. Dev	6.673	9.858	68.33	0.030	0.233	5.233	195.01	452.026
Observations	848	848	848	848	848	848	848	848

Source Authors' calculation based on data collected from DataStream, Bank Scope, and Zaweya database

and AC.MEET SIZE was six times a year. The mean of M.OWNER is 33%, indicating that MENA banks are also strongly affected by managerial ownership. The variables associated with a country's characteristics exhibit their predictable outcomes.

Table 4 presents the correlation analysis and shows that CH had a significant positive association with board size (0.247). Conversely, a negative correlation was revealed for CH with board independence and board diversity with (-0.335, -0.083) respectively, which argues that companies with more independent boards and gender diversity in board would keep less cash. While the board meetings number and CEO duality do not appear to have a significant impact on CH levels. CH is negatively correlated with Institutional-owner, corporate size, ROA, and inflation, while it is associated positively with managerial ownership, AC size, AC meetings, listing, and corruption. Given existence of robust associations between dissimilar independent variables, we calculate the variance inflation factor (VIF) marks for every independent variable. These scores signifying that our models and analysis do not reflect the multicollinearity problematic.

5.2 Regression Analysis

We used multivariate analysis to examine the impact of board Effectiveness on firm cash holdings as well as on financial performance. In Table 5, we estimate the impact of board effectiveness on CH based on cash ratio. In Table 6, we estimate the effect of board effectiveness on CH based on logarithm of CH. Table 7 conducts additional analysis by taking into consideration the impact of control variables as an example AC, ownership, firm characteristics, and country characteristics. In Table 8, we estimate the effect of board effectiveness on FP based on ROA. In Table 9, we estimate the impact of CH on FP.

In the context of control variables, Table 6 shows that board independence, board size, board gender diversity, and CEO duality all have a significant effect on CH. Table 7 confirms the result in Table 6 regarding the impact of board effectiveness on cash holding, but does not include any control variables. Table 8 does not support any contribution to board effectiveness for enhancing FP for banks. Table 9 shows an insignificant impact for CH over FP.

Table 4 Correlation analysis

	CH	B. Size	B. Indep	B. Meet	B. Gend	CEO. Dual	Block.O	Manag.O	AC. Size	AC. Meet	Size	ROA	GDP	Infl	List	Courr
Cash.H	1.000															
B. Size	0.247	1.000														
	0.000															
B. Indep	-0.335	-0.135	1.000													
	0.000	0.000														
B. Meet	0.006	0.059	0.155	1.000												
	0.854	0.085	0.000													
B. Gend	-0.083	0.300	-0.128	0.052	1.000											
	0.032	0.000	0.000	0.127												
CEO. Dual	0.015	0.069	-0.065	0.018	0.180	1.000										
	0.032	0.023	0.069	0.582	0.000											
Block.O	0.349	-0.115	0.056	-0.275	0.112	0.015	1.000									
	0.001	0.000	0.041	0.000	0.001	0.658										
Manag.O	0.241	0.248	-0.042	0.214	0.269	-0.11	-0.37	1.000								
	0.000	0.000	0.219	0.000	0.000	0.000	0.000									
AC. Size	0.245	0.261	-0.056	0.141	0.025	0.121	0.050	0.001	1.000							
	0.000	0.000	0.000	0.050	0.121	0.000	0.050	0.958								
AC. Meet	0.098	0.023	0.047	0.243	0.039	-0.16	-0.02	-0.076	0.088	1.000						
	0.004	0.496	0.164	0.000	0.246	0.000	0.470	0.025	0.009							

	CH	B. Size	B. Indep	B. Meet	B. Gend	CEO. Dual	Block.O	Manag.O	AC. Size	AC. Meet	Size	ROA	GDP	Infl	List	Courr
Size	-0.121	0.125	-0.037	0.022	0.004	0.044	-0.02	-0.072	0.174	-0.000	1.000					
	0.000	0.000	0.280	0.504	0.885	0.191	0.485	0.034	0.000	0.994						
ROA	-0.060	-0.037	0.026	0.004	0.017	0.009	0.068	-0.069	0.120	0.010	0.022	1.000				
	0.076	0.276	0.432	0.898	0.602	0.778	0.047	0.041	0.000	0.758	0.519					
GDP	-0.049	-0.123	0.126	0.040	-0.116	-0.09	0.047	-0.031	0.017	0.025	0.040	0.143	1.000			
	0.148	0.000	0.000	0.234	0.000	0.005	0.198	0.359	0.603	0.452	0.235	0.000				
Infl	-0.241	-0.028	0.044	0.011	0.028	0.080	-0.01	0.017	-0.07	-0.157	0.001	0.002	0.068	1.000		
	0.000	0.409	0.193	0.733	0.412	0.019	0.640	0.618	0.034	0.001	0.964	0.938	0.047			
List	0.383	0.336	-0.026	0.085	-0.065	-0.09	-0.22	0.273	0.271	0.168	0.058	-0.08	0.042	-0.09	1.000	
	0.000	0.000	0.441	0.013	0.057	0.007	0.000	0.000	0.000	0.000	0.088	0.015	0.218	0.003		
Courr	0.156	-0.029	0.089	-0.000	-0.126	-0.29	0.055	-0.016	0.128	0.284	0.063	0.199	0.179	-0.32	0.203	1.000
	0.000	0.396	0.009	0.995	0.000	0.000	0.105	0.622	0.000	0.000	0.066	0.000	0.000	0.000	0.000	0.000

Source Authors' calculation based on data collected from DataStream, Bank Scope, and Zaweya database

Table 5 Regression analysis for board effectiveness impact on cash holdings by cash ratio

Variable	Coefficient	Std. Error	t-statistic	Prob
Cash holdings	1.834168	0.149526	12.26656	0.0000
BOD. Size	0.187191	0.071723	2.609931	0.0092
BOD. Indep	−0.035887	0.046437	−0.772808	0.4399
BOD. Meet	−0.074694	0.061528	−1.213978	0.2251
BOD. Gender	−0.026194	0.016052	−1.631793	0.1031
CEO. Duality	0.056090	0.025140	2.231112	0.0259
Block owner	−0.085718	0.091319	−0.938665	0.3482
Manager owner	0.079922	0.058010	1.377726	0.1687
AC. Size	0.105702	0.088327	1.196710	0.2318
AC. Meet	−0.027639	0.057243	−0.482839	0.6293
Size	−0.187180	0.012592	−14.86539	0.0000
ROA	−0.068425	0.673328	−0.101622	0.9191
GDP	0.230551	0.172926	1.333230	0.1828
Inflation	−0.234635	0.040133	−5.846390	0.0000
List	0.237129	0.056342	4.208741	0.0000
Control of corruption	−0.016207	0.017863	−0.907319	0.3645
Effects specification				
			S.D	Rho
Cross-section random			0.261208	0.9238
Idiosyncratic random			0.075030	0.0762
Weighted statistics				
Adjusted R^2	0.250000	Durbin-Watson stat		1.281885
F-statistic	19.82218	Prob (F-statistic)		0.000000

Source Authors' calculation based on data collected from DataStream, Bank Scope, and Zaweya database

5.2.1   Impact of Board Size over CH and FP

Table 5 reports an analysis of board size effects over the CH. The regression demonstrates a positive correlation, indicating that H6 should be accepted. The implication is that, across our sample in the MENA region; the presence of a large BOD contributes significantly to the increase in CH levels inside the banks by offering superior monitoring that is mirrored in the bargain level of CH. The findings in Table 5 are in the line with previse studies that show a significant relationship among board effectiveness based on board size and CH. This evidence is consistent with Bokpin et al. (2011) and Al-Najjar and Clark (2017), who concluded that board size improves CH level. Greater amounts of cash are expected to be held in the hands of insiders in corporations with higher BODs as

Table 6 Regression analysis for the impact of board effectiveness on cash holdings through logarithm of cash holdings

Variable	Coefficient	Std. Error	t-statistic	Prob	Coefficient Variance	VIF
Cash holdings	1.838013	0.230408	7.977228	0.0000		
BOD. Size	0.404964	0.118417	3.419828	0.0007	0.013915	1.433415
BOD. Indep	−0.523241	0.045884	−11.40345	0.0000	0.002076	1.094785
BOD. Meet	0.025137	0.081819	0.307224	0.7588	0.006651	1.239774
BOD. Gender	−0.104138	0.022482	−4.632164	0.0000	0.000501	1.221781
CEO. Duality	0.094731	0.027575	3.435375	0.0006	0.000755	1.191770
Block owner	−0.073467	0.056340	−1.303986	0.1926	0.003154	1.396818
Manager owner	0.087315	0.022877	3.816658	0.0001	0.000520	1.355403
AC. Size	0.534879	0.117094	4.567925	0.0000	0.013592	1.260746
AC. Meet	0.115320	0.094628	1.218658	0.2233	0.008899	1.219403
Size	−0.220629	0.033611	−6.564095	0.0000	0.001120	1.063485
ROA	−2.693598	1.627484	−1.655069	0.0983	2.589997	1.103551
GDP	−0.230072	0.608087	−0.378354	0.7053	0.340448	1.102766
Inflation	−0.773797	0.159326	−4.856686	0.0000	0.015927	1.158601
List	0.156158	0.022826	6.841166	0.0000	0.000518	1.403971
Control of corruption	0.045263	0.015790	2.866532	0.0043	0.000234	1.472004
Effects specification						
Period fixed (dummy variables)					Heteroskedasticity Test: Breusch-Pagan-Godfrey	
Adjusted R^2	0.374895	J-statistic		825.000	F-statistic	6.529106
					Prob. F	0.0000

(continued)

Table 6 (continued)

Variable	Coefficient	Std. Error	t-statistic	Prob	Coefficient Variance	VIF
Durbin-Watson stat	2.291109	Prob (*J*-statistic)		0.00000	Prob. Chi-Square	0.0000
Correlated Random Effects—Hausman Test					Breusch-Godfrey Serial Correlation LM Test:	
Test cross-section random effects					F-statistic	1154.330
Test summary	Chi-Sq. Statistic	Chi-Sq. d.f		Prob	Obs*R^2	623.7515
					Prob. $F(2,830)$	0.0000
Cross-section random	44.019208	13		0.0000	Prob. Chi-Square(2)	0.0000

Source Authors' calculation based on data collected from DataStream, Bank Scope, and Zaweya database

Table 7 Regression analysis for the association between board effectiveness on cash holdings without firm and country control variables

Variable	Coefficient	Std. Error	t-statistic	Prob
Cash Holdings	0.299797	0.158079	1.896506	0.0582
BOD. Size	0.557553	0.122684	4.544612	0.0000
BOD. Indep	−0.528043	0.049191	−10.73445	0.0000
BOD. Meet	−0.018034	0.088620	−0.203497	0.8388
BOD. Gender	−0.132570	0.024092	−5.502638	0.0000
CEO. Duality	0.047714	0.028922	1.649746	0.0994
Block owner	−0.097498	0.060288	−1.617192	0.1062
Manager owner	0.127624	0.024353	5.240553	0.0000
AC. Size	0.682406	0.120940	5.642491	0.0000
AC. Meet	0.391453	0.098347	3.980322	0.0001
Effects specification				
Adjusted R^2	0.261258	J-statistic		838.0000
Durbin-Watson stat	1.272950	Prob (J-statistic)		0.000000

Source Authors' calculation based on data collected from DataStream, Bank Scope, and Zaweya database

a common channel for fortune expropriation. This implies that BOD is dynamic in the MENA area in monitoring of corporate financial processes. Conversely, Table 7 shows insignificant relationship between board size and FP, which is aligned with through Shao (2019). Hence, a number of directors do not seem to have any influence over the FP level of MENA-based banks. Our analysis leads to reject H1, which assumes the large boards failure to provide effective control over management and raise profitability level. BOD size is improbable to capture the level to which BOD are active in their management oversight. The size of the BOD is unlikely to capture the degree to which the BOD is active in their management oversight. The obvious lack of agency costs associated with board size is linked to a massive CG literature indicating that the number of BOD associates does not matter (Yermack, 1996).

5.2.2 Impact of CEO Duality over CH and FP

A positive effect of CEO duality on CH is shown in Tables 5 and 7; however, FP has no effect on CEO duality. They lead us to accept H8 while rejecting the other two hypotheses. A company with a dual CEO is believed to have a higher level of CSR than a company with two CEOs who are not related to each other. Gul and Leung (2004) and Drobetz

Table 8 Regression analysis for the impact of board effectiveness on FP

Variable	Coefficient	Std. Error	t-statistic	Prob
ROA	0.673399	0.025495	26.41266	0.0000
BOD. Size	0.001390	0.001897	0.732861	0.4639
BOD. Indep	0.000638	0.000714	0.893655	0.3718
BOD. Meet	−0.000411	0.001266	−0.324771	0.7454
BOD. Gender	1.804758	0.000348	0.051560	0.9589
CEO. Duality	0.000301	0.000430	0.700429	0.4839
Block owner	0.000159	0.000885	0.179313	0.8577
Manager owner	−0.000114	0.000357	−0.320326	0.7488
AC. Size	0.003901	0.001831	2.130637	0.0335
AC. Meet	−0.000663	0.001460	−0.453794	0.6501
Size	0.000121	0.000525	0.230380	0.8179
GDP	0.020467	0.009974	2.051896	0.0405
Inflation	0.001484	0.002030	0.730787	0.4651
List	−0.000938	0.000355	−2.644439	0.0084
Control of corruption	0.000436	0.000247	1.764056	0.0781
C	0.000842	0.003626	0.232203	0.8164
Effects specification				
			S.D	Rho
Cross-section random			0.000000	0.0000
Idiosyncratic random			0.003916	1.0000
Weighted statistics				
Adjusted R^2	0.495140	J-statistic		726.0000
Durbin-Watson stat	2.188575	Prob (J-statistic)		0.000000

Source Authors' calculation based on data collected from DataStream, Bank Scope, and Zaweya database

et al. (2010) found that boards directed by CEOs must be less restrictive in their managerial discretion over business properties, especially when it comes to the use of cash held by corporations with intense ownership. At the same time, our result contradicts Boubaker et al. (2015), who argue that companies with CEO duality have a low level of cash on hand. An absence of a split-up between the CEO's board and controlling purposes can be indicated by higher CH in businesses with dual CEOs. When working in a corporate environment, the ability to monitor stockholders must be improved in order to gain the maximum benefit from corporate resources at the expense of additional stockholders. On the other side, CEO duality does not affect FP. This insignificant association contrasts with the majority of the previse studies' findings, which show a negative

Table 9 Regression analysis for the impact of cash holdings on FP

Variable	Coefficient	Std. Error	t-statistic	Prob
ROA	0.672450	0.025537	26.33230	0.0000
Cash holdings	−0.000393	0.000546	−0.718883	0.4724
BOD. Size	0.001551	0.001911	0.811782	0.4172
BOD. Indep	0.000429	0.000771	0.555674	0.5786
BOD. Meet	−0.000406	0.001267	−0.320683	0.7485
BOD. Gender	−2.23333	0.000353	−0.063220	0.9496
CEO. Duality	0.000341	0.000434	0.787046	0.4315
Block owner	0.000134	0.000886	0.151084	0.8800
Manager owner	−7.92564	0.000360	−0.219760	0.8261
AC. Size	0.004103	0.001853	2.214347	0.0271
AC. Meet	−0.000611	0.001462	−0.418083	0.6760
Size	3.304567	0.000539	0.061268	0.9512
GDP	0.020469	0.009977	2.051483	0.0406
Inflation	0.001199	0.002069	0.579598	0.5624
List	−0.000876	0.000365	−2.401114	0.0166
Control of corruption	0.000452	0.000248	1.820029	0.0692
C	0.001565	0.003764	0.415757	0.6777
Effects specification				
			S.D	Rho
Cross-section random			0.000000	0.0000
Idiosyncratic random			0.003917	1.0000
Weighted statistics				
Adjusted R^2	0.494746	J-statistic		725.0000
Durbin-Watson stat	2.185867	Prob (J-statistic)		0.000000

Source Authors' calculation based on data collected from DataStream, Bank Scope, and Zaweya database

effect between FP and CEO duality, which is consistent with (Augustine et al., 2016; Shao, 2019). Our findings were consistent with Gill and Shah (2012), who sampled Canadian firms and discovered that CEO duality and board size positively influence corporate CH. As a result, the board of directors and the CEO are responsible for developing policies for cash management and establishing overall business strategies. As a result, board size and CEO duality have a significant effect on the business, resulting in extraordinary CH balances and a quick cash conversion cycle have been obtained.

5.2.3   *Impact of Board Independence on CH and FP*

Our analysis related to the impact of board independence on CH provides an indication of which amount of cash reduces with a percentage of independent members on BOD. This result is supported by Guizani et al. (2018), who found that board independence is negatively associated with CH. Therefore, companies seem to experience meaningfully lower CH when BOD is more independent, which supporting H7. Our findings confirmed the debating of trade-off theory about a good CG mechanism that makes corporations more proficient in using external resources for investments, allowing businesses to avoid holding large amount of cash. As a result, a more independent board of directors appears to decrease corporate resources willingly converted into secluded remunerations. This conclusion supports the idea that independent managers are less obliged to manage and more diligent in preventive controlling stockholders' independence of action and thus the expropriation risks of available cash. In general, we determine that independent boards are active with respect to the corporate CH.

In terms of influence of board independence on FP, a coefficient estimate of board independence presents an insignificant association that lead to reject H2. In other words, board independence does not play any role in enhancing firm a business value, which supports the argument of Afzalur (2019). Our result matches Bhagat and Black (2002), who found indication that board composition is not associated with corporate performance. Furthermore, Guest (2009) identifies those independent directors are not as energetic based in UK as their counterparts in United States. The insignificant impact for independent board is also supported by Ozkan (2007). This outcome specifies that independent directors are not efficiently providing enhanced controlling activities for banks in MENA countries related to FP.

5.2.4   *Impact of Board Meetings over CH and FP*

According to our findings, the number of board meetings has a significant effect on CH and FP. Our result found that significant effect on board meetings number on CH as well as on FP. This result leads to accept both H5 and H10. This result is similar to Narwal et al. (2017) and Alagathurai and Kumara (2017), they concluded that board meetings do not improve CH. Our result is a divergence from other literature that found a positive association (e.g., Abdul Gafoor et al., 2018) or negative association (e.g., Ofoeda, 2017). Moreover, Jackling and Johl (2009) found that no association between BOD meetings and corporate economic performance across Indian corporations. The insignificance results might indicate that the relationship among the meetings number and FP or CH is more complex than a simple linear relationship, or that the increase in board activities is a reaction to weak corporate FP, which in turn affects FP (Vafeas, 1999). The expected reason for this minor effect on board meetings could be explained by viewing meetings as a routine process. It is only related to the rewards system and gaining the trust of owners by exhibiting their activity by holding many of these meetings.

5.2.5   Impact of Board Gender Diversity over CH and FP

The outcome shows the extent to which board diversity has a negative effect on the CH level, whereas FP does not. This outcome supports H9 while rejecting H4. Our findings agree with Carter et al. (2010), they found that no significant relationship among board gender diversity and FP, but do not agree with other literature that finds a positive (e.g., Dani et al., 2019) or negative (e.g., Dani et al., 2019). (e.g., Thi & Phan, 2017). This result can be clarified by reducing the females on the board numbers of companies in MENA countries, which is influenced by Arab society culture, which reduces the proportion of women in top positions in corporations. Furthermore, our findings are aligned with those of, Alagathurai and Kumara (2017), who discovered that gender diversity has a negative impact on CH. According to governance literature, including females on boards is rigid in controlling objectives (Adams & Ferreira, 2009) and improves board effectiveness, limiting managerial discretion and lowering the level of CH.

5.2.6   Impact of CH on FP

Table 9 shows how levels of CH has no effect on FP. This finding contradicts H11, which hypothesized a positive relationship. This result is aligned with findings of Isshaq et al. (2009) who argue that keeping extra cash does not significantly affect FP. However, our findings contradict past research that has confirmed the association between CH and FP, whether positive or negative, such as Asante-Darko et al. (2018), Azmat (2014), Lee and Lee (2009). Pinkowitz et al. (2006) found that relative between FP and CH is much lower in markets with poor stockholder protection than in other markets like MENA markets. Our result supports the argument of Stiglitz (1974), who argue that, in the absence of market imperfections such as MENA region, firms' financial decisions as CH would not affect financial performance. Based on this finding, outside finance is always willingly obtainable and at a rational price. Holding cash would have no opportunity cost or economic hardship due to the lack of a premium for liquidity or taxes. As a result, according to Opler et al. (2001), keeping liquid cash reserves would be inappropriate, and decisions regarding liquid asset investment would have no impact on stockholders' wealth.

In terms of the control variables for the bank and country, we report based on Table 5 strong evidence that firm size, listing statutes, and inflation are significant influences that affect decisions of CH for banks across MENA region. At the same time, we find insignificant impacts for other variables. We identify a negative linkage between inflation and CH, and therefore we provide an indication for the effect of increasing inflation ratios on MENA banks, decreasing the essential to holding cash. This result is aligned with Yanchao et al. (2014). As unpredicted, we found a negative relationship among firm size and CH. This specifies that huge banks in MENA region did not req hold cash to find their investment. This outcome matches with Ozkan and Ozkan (2004) and Al-Najjar and Belghitar (2011). Lastly, our result shows an indication for a positive association between listing status and CH. Therefore, banks that are listing in the stock market will hold more cash to transmit positive signal for investors and increase their trust in the business.

6   Concluding Remarks

Most of the previse studies that measures the effect of CG on cash holdings and firm value used data mainly for developed countries, with rare studies that used data for developing countries. To fill this gap, this research measures the consequence of board effectiveness on CH and FP for a sample of 106 banks was selected from 13 MENA countries with panel data from 2010 to 2017. After controlling firm and country characteristics, the analysis shows that when the board independence and gender diversity increase, the CH decrease in banks. Whereas, when the bank is characterized by high board size and low CEO duality, CH increase. The analysis does not support the association between board effectiveness mechanisms and FP. Finally, the result displays an insignificant link between CH and FP. The result of this paper supports the role of CG toward CH while not for FP.

The paper has significant theoretical implications as well as practical implications for different interested parties. For the theoretical implication, while our result supports the positive influence for board effectiveness over the corporate financial decisions for holding cash, it underscores that board effectiveness does not affect FP in the same way. The paper's outcomes didn't provide significant support for the theories of CH, such as Pecking Order and trade-off theory. The analysis approves that the presence of CH does not maximize the FP. This result asks different theories as a basis for this association or understands the existing theories from a different perspective to consider the impact of using different contexts over the association between CH and FP. For the practical implications, our results are significant for selecting the board members by considering the characteristics of BOD to increase the corporation's CH.

Furthermore, Papaioannou et al. (1992) approve the director's desire to have a high level of CH regularly generates the clash between executives and stockholders. Consequently, the stockholder considers these results into account before hiring managers. Our result shows to what extent regulators in the MENA countries may need to consider the BOD's features when they formulate the CG structure that banks in these countries should apply. Our results should support regulators, directors, and policyholders to determine which board geographies may help to maximize stakeholders' fortune through decisions related to CH.

The results specify that BOD's size and duality have a positive influence on corporate CH. This result is significant for stockholders, who appoint BOD to monitor agents' activities, which can benefit from liquid assets. Therefore, we will rather have hold great cash, which regularly creates conflict between shareholders and managers. It is noteworthy to policymakers for developing the role of BOD in monitoring the corporation. One possible procedure is to inspire the banks and other businesses in the MENA region to hire active independent directors and consider the CEO duality problem that may offer superior control and benefit from their capabilities. It is value observing that guidelines and procedures need to identify the particular responsibilities of managers and their selection procedures. Furthermore, emerging markets such as the MENA region are needed to improve compliance with global governance principles to maximize the corporations' FP. The consequence of CG over the business policy and FP may not be the same across diverse industries and different markets or regions. This is because businesses experience diverse business chances and challenges and own different degrees of resources for managing these challenges.

When corporations face plenty of progress chances and depend on capital-intensive investments to enhance corporate value, CG safeguards stockholder shields and adequate funds for those investment chances. While businesses in the emerging economy as MENA, may be keen for more flexible CG codes to maintain independence in decision-making. This research proposes that forming real CG mechanisms may efficiently enlarge the level of flexibility for these banks to make timely corporate decisions for holding cash and then for maximizing the FP. Additionally, our study adds value to the concerned literature by filling the gap in the previous studies, focusing sensitively on the developed rather than developing countries with sporadic studies that measure this association across the MENA region.

We acknowledge some limitations of our study, which can be considered as an indicator for future research. While this study used data for financial institutions (banks), further research may consider other business categories as non-financial and SMEs. Additional potential direction for future research is to consider the impact of culture as a moderator variable between CH and board effectiveness. Furthermore, whereas this study focuses on the internal mechanism for CG. The impact of the external CG mechanisms should be investigated in future research on the CH policy. Further research may study these associations by comparing Islamic and conventional banks with considering the Islamic CG related to Sharia Supervisory Board (SSB). While we measure FP by adopting an accounting measure as ROA, further research can use the economic measure as market capitalization and Tobin's Q. Further research may extend the period until 2021 to consider the impact of COVID-19 as a mediator over this association.

Acknowledgements This study was supported and financed through the research sector, Arab Open University-Kuwait Branch under decision number 21123.

REFERENCES

Abdul Gafoor, C., Mariappan, V., & Thyagarajan, S. (2018). Board characteristics and bank performance in India. *Management Review, 30*(2), 160–167.

Adams, R., & Ferreira, D. (2009). Women in the boardroom and their impact on governance and performance. *Journal of Financial Economics, 94*(2), 291–309.

Afzalur, R. (2019). Board independence and firm performance: Evidence from Bangladesh. *Future Business Journal, 4*(1), 34–49.

Akhtar, T., Tareq, M., Sakti, M., & Khan, A. (2018). Corporate governance and cash holdings: The way forward. *Qualitative Research in Financial Markets, 10*(2), 152–170.

Alagathurai, A., & Kumara, K. (2017). Corporate governance and cash holdings: Empirical evidence from an emerging country, Sri Lanka. *International Journal of Accounting and Financial Reporting, 7*(2), 112–135.

Al-Daoud, K., Saidin, S., & Abidin, S. (2016). Board meeting and firm performance: Evidence from the Amman stock exchange. *Corporate Board: Role, Duties and Composition, 12*(2), 6–11.

Al-Harbi, A. (2019). The determinants of conventional banks profitability in developing and underdeveloped OIC countries. *Journal of Economics, Finance and Administrative Sciences, 24*(47), 4–28.

Al-Najjar, B. (2013). The financial determinants of corporate cash holdings: Evidence from some emerging markets. *International Business Review, 22*(2), 77–88.

Al-Najjar, B., & Belghitar, Y. (2011), Corporate cash holdings and dividend payments: Evidence from simultaneous analysis. *Managerial and Decision Economics, 32*(2), 231–241.

Al-Najjar, B., & Clark, E. (2017), corporate governance and cash holdings in MENA: Evidence from internal and external governance practices. *Research in International Business and Finance, 39*(3), 1–12.

Al-Nodel, A., & Hussainey, K. (2010). Corporate governance and financing decisions by Saudi companies. *Journal of Modern Accounting and Auditing, 6*(8), 1–14.

Amanti, L., & Venusita, L. (2012). Pengaruh Good Corporate Governance Terhadap Nilai Perusahaan dengan Pengungkapan Corporate Sosial Responsibility Sebagai Variabel Pemoderasi (Studi Kasus pada Perusahaan Rokok yang Terdaftar di BEI). *Jurnal Akuntansi Unesa, 1*(1), 1–21.

Ameer, R. (2012). Impact of cash holdings and ownership concentration on firm valuation empirical evidence from Australia. *Review of Accounting and Finance, 11*(4), 448–467.

Amess, K., Banerji, S., & Lampousis, A. (2015). Corporate cash holdings: Causes and consequences. *International Review of Financial Analysis, 42*(1), 421–433.

Amman, M., Oesch, D., & Schmid, M. (2011). Corporate governance and firm value: International evidence. *Journal of Empirical Finance, 18*(1), 36–55.

Anderson, R., Mansi, S., & Reeb, D. (2004). Board characteristics, accounting report integrity, and the cost of debt. *Journal of Accounting and Economics, 37*(2), 315–342.

Arcot, S., & Bruno, V. (2007). *One size does not fit all: Evidence from corporate governance.* Available on the internet at http://ssrn.com/abstract¼88794.

Arfken, D., Bellar, S., & Helms, M. (2004). The ultimate glass ceiling revisited: The presence of women on corporate boards. *Journal of Business Ethics, 50*(1), 177–186.

Aryani, Y., Doddy, S., & Rahmawati, I. (2017). *Board meeting and firm performance.* Proceedings of International Conference on Economics (pp. 438–444).

Asante-Daerko, D., Adu Bonsu, B., Famiyeh, S., Kwarteng, A., & Goke, Y. (2018). Governance structures, cash holdings and firm value on the Ghana Stock Exchange. *Corporate Governance, 18*(4), 671–685.

Augustine, D., Raghavan, J., & Ernest, M. (2016). The dynamic relationship between CEO duality and firm performance: The moderating role of board independence. *Journal of Business Research, 69*(10), 4269–4277.

Azmat, Q. (2014). Firm value and optimal cash level: Evidence from Pakistan. *International Journal of Emerging Markets, 9*(4), 488–504.

Bansal, R., Singh, A., Kumar, S., & Gupta, R. (2018). Evaluating factors of profitability for Indian banking sector: A panel regression. *Asian Journal of Accounting Research, 3*(2), 236–254.

Bates, W., Kahle, M., & Stulz, M. (2009). Why do US firms hold so much more cash than they used to? *The Journal of Finance, 64*(5), 1985–2021.

Bebchuk, L., Cohen, A., & Ferrell, A. (2009). What matters in corporate governance? *Review of Financial Studies, 22*(1), 783–827.

Bhagat, S., & Black, B. (2002). The non-correlation between board independence and long-term firm performance. *Journal of Corporation Law, 27*(2), 231–273.

Bokpin, G., Issaq, Z., & Aboagye, F. (2011). Ownership structure, corporate governance and corporate liquidity policy. *Journal of Financial Economic Policy, 3*(3), 262–279.

Boubaker, S., Imen, D., & Nguyen, D. (2015). Does the board of directors affect cash holdings? A study of French listed firms. *Journal of Management & Governance, 19*(2), 341–370.

Boulouta, I. (2013). Hidden connections: The link between board gender diversity and corporate social performance. *Journal of Business Ethics, 113*(2), 185–197.

Bozec, R. (2005). Boards of directors, market discipline and firm performance. *Journal of Business Finance & Accounting, 32*(1), 1921–1960.

Brick, I., & Chidambaran, N. (2010). Board meetings, committee structure, and firm value. *Journal of Corporate Finance, 16*(4), 533–553.

Brickley, J., Coles, L., & Jarrel, G. (1997). Corporate leadership structure: On the separation of the positions of CEO and chairman of the board. *Journal of Corporate Finance, 3*(2), 189–220.

Brockmann, E., Hoffman, J., Dawley, D., & Fornaciari, C. (2004). The impact of CEO duality and prestige on a bankrupt organization. *Journal of Management Issues, 16*(1), 178–196.

Campbell, K., & Minguez-Vera, A. (2008). Gender diversity in the boardroom and firm financial performance. *Journal of Business Ethics, 83*(3), 435–451.

Carter, D., Frank, D., Betty, S., & Gray, S. (2010). The gender and ethnic diversity of US boards and board committees and firm financial performance. *Corporate Governance: an International Review, 18*(5), 396–414.

Carter, D., Simkins, B., & Simpson, W. (2003). Corporate governance, board diversity, and firm value. *The Financial Review, 38*(2), 33–53.

Chahine, S., & Filatotchev, I. (2008). The effects of information disclosure and board independence on IPO discount. *Journal of Small Business Management, 46*(2), 219–241.

Chahine, S., & Tohmé, S. (2009). Is CEO duality always negative? An exploration of CEO duality and ownership structure in the Arab IPO context. *Corporate Governance: An International Review, 17*(2), 123–141.

Chang, J., & Choi, U. (1988). Strategy, structure and performance of Korean business groups: A transactions cost approach. *The Journal of Industrial Economics, 37*(2), 141–158.

Chen, Y. (2008). Corporate governance and cash holdings: Listed new economy versus old firms. *Corporate Governance, 16*(5), 430–442.

Chung, K., Wright, P., & Kedia, B. (2003). Corporate governance and market valuation of capital and R&D investments. *Review of Financial Economics, 12*(2), 161–172.

Conger, J., Finegold, D., & Lawler, E. (1998). Appraising boardroom performance. *Harvard Business Review, 76*(2), 136–148.

Conheady, B., McIlkenny, P., Opong, K. K., & Pignatel, I. (2015). Board effectiveness and firm performance of Canadian listed firms. *The British Accounting Review, 47*(3), 290–303.

Dani, A., Picolo, J., & Klann, R. (2019). Gender influence, social responsibility and governance in performance. *RAUSP Management Journal, 54*(2), 154–177.

Daniel, C., Helen, R., & Rosalind, H. (2015). Board gender diversity and firm performance: Empirical evidence from Hong Kong, South Korea, Malaysia and Singapore. *Pacific-Basin Finance Journal, 35*(A), 381–401.

Dittmar, A., & Mahrt-Smith, J. (2007). Corporate governance and the value of cash holdings. *Journal of Financial Economics, 83*(1), 599–634.

Dittmar, A., Mahrt-Smith, J., & Servaes, H. (2003). International corporate governance and corporate cash holdings. *Journal of Financial and Quantitative Analysis, 38*(1), 111–133.

Drobetz, W., Gruninger, M., & Hirschvogl, S. (2010). Information asymmetry and the value of cash. *Journal of Banking and Finance, 34*(2), 2168–2184.

Elsayed, K. (2007). Does CEO duality really affect corporate performance? *Corporate Governance: An International Review, 15*(6), 1203–1214.

Fama, E., & Jensen, M. (1983). Separation of ownership and control. *The Journal of Law and Economics, 26*(3), 301–325.

Ferreira, M., & Vilela, A. (2004). Why do firms hold cash? Evidence from EMU countries. *European Financial Management, 10*(1), 295–319.

Garcia-Teruel, P., & Martinez-Solano, P. (2008). On the determinants of SME cash holdings: Evidence from Spain. *Journal of Business Finance and Accounting, 35*(3), 127–149.

Gill, A., & Shah, C. (2012). Determinants of corporate cash holdings: Evidence from Canada. *International Journal of Economics and Finance, 4*(1), 70–79.

Guest, P. (2009). The impact of board size on firm performance: Evidence from the UK. *The European Journal of Finance, 15*(4), 385–404.

Guizani, A., Lakhal, F., & Lakhal, N. (2018). The cash flow sensitivity of cash in family firms: Does the board of directors matter? *Managerial Finance, 44*(11), 1364–1380.

Guizani, M. (2017). The financial determinants of corporate cash holdings in an oil rich country: Evidence from Kingdom of Saudi Arabia. *Borsa Istanbul Review, 17*(3), 133–143.

Gul, F., & Leung, S. (2004). Board leadership, outside directors' expertise and voluntary corporate disclosure. *Journal of Accounting and Public Policy, 23*, 351–379.

Gul, F., Srinidhi, B., & Ng, A. (2011). Does board gender diversity improve the informativeness of stock prices? *Journal of Accounting and Economics, 51*(3), 314–338.

Hamdan, A., Sarea, A., & Reyad, S. (2013). The impact of audit committee characteristics on the performance: Evidence from Jordan. *International Management Review, 9*(1), 32–52.

Harford, J., Mansi, S., & Maxwell, W. (2005). *Corporate governance and a firm's cash holdings* (Working Paper). University of Washington.

Harford, J., Mansi, A., & Maxwell, F. (2008). Corporate governance and firm cash holdings in the U.S. *Journal of Financial Economics, 87*, 535–555.

Huong, T., Marina, P., & Quang, N. (2017). Multinationals and the impact of corruption on financial derivatives use and firm value: Evidence from East Asia. *Journal of Multinational Financial Management, 39*(2), 39–59.

Husam, A., Duncan, K., Kelly, S., Ray, M., & Nagel, S. (2011). Audit committee characteristics and firm performance during the global financial crisis. *Accounting and Finance, 52*(4), 971–1000.

Isshaq, Z., Bokpin, G., & Onumah, J. (2009). Corporate governance, ownership structure, cash holding, and firm value on the Ghana Stock Exchange. *The Journal of Risk Finance, 10*(5), 488–499.

Jackling, B., & Johl, S. (2009). Board structure and firm performance: Evidence from India's top companies. *Corporate Governance. an International Review, 17*(4), 492–509.

Jaffar, R., & Abdul-Shukor, Z. (2016). The role of monitoring mechanisms towards company's performance. *Journal of Accounting in Emerging Economies, 6*(4), 408–428.

Jensen, M. (1986). Agency costs of free cash flow, corporate finance and takeovers. *American Economic Review, 76*(2), 323–329.

Jensen, M. (1993). The modern industrial revolution, exit, and the failure of internal control systems. *The Journal of Finance, 48*(1), 831–880.

Jensen, M. (2010). The modern industrial revolution, exit, and failure of internal control systems. *Journal of Applied Corporate Finance, 22*(3), 3–58.

Juliane, B., & Palazzo, B. (2021). Firm selection and corporate cash holdings. *Journal of Financial Economics, 139*(3), 697–718.

Kalcheva, I., & Lins, K. (2007). International evidence on cash holdings and expected managerial agency problems. *Review of Financial Studies, 20*(4), 1087–1112.

Kam, C., & Joanne, L. (2008). Audit committee and firm value: Evidence on outside top executives as expert-independent directors. *Corporate Governance: An Intentional Review.* https://doi.org/10.1111/j.1467-8683.2008.00662.x

Kariuki, S., Namusonge, G., & Orwa, G. (2015). Firm characteristics and corporate cash holdings: A managerial perspective from Kenyan private manufacturing firms. *International Journal of Advanced Research in Management and Social Sciences, 4*(1), 51–70.

Kim, D., & Starks, L. (2016). Gender diversity on corporate boards: Do women contribute unique skills? *American Economic Review, 106*(5), 267–271.

Kim, K., Al-Shammari, H., Kim, B., & Lee, S. (2009). CEO duality leadership and corporate diversification behavior. *Journal of Business Research, 62*(4), 1173–1180.

Klapper, L., & Love, I. (2004). Corporate governance, investor protection, and performance in emerging markets. *Journal of Corporate Finance, 10*(2), 703–728.

Kusumaningtyas, R., & Yendrawati, R. (2015). The effect of company diversification toward earning management moderated by managerial ownership. *Jurnal Dinamika Manajemen, 6*(2), 178–186.

Lasfer, M. (2006). The interrelationship between management ownership and board structure. *Journal of Business Finance & Accounting, 33*(7), 1006–1033.

Lee, C., & Lee, K. (2009). Cash holdings, corporate governance structure and firm valuation. *Review of Pacific Basin Financial Markets and Policies, 12*(3), 475–508.

Leyuan, Y., Janet, D., & Steve, W (2018, August), Do multiple foreign listings create value for firms? *The Quarterly Review of Economics and Finance*, 134–143.

Lipton, M., & Lorsch, J. (1992). A modest proposal improved corporate governance. *Business Lawyer, 48*(2), 59–77.

Markku, V. (2015). Do tourism firms with female CEOs hold higher levels of cash? *Finnish Journal of Tourism Research, 11*(2), 24–44.

Martinez-Sola, C., Garcia-Teruel, J., & Martinez-Solano, P. (2013), Corporate cash holding and firm value. *Applied Economics, 45*(2), 161–170.

Masood, A., & Attaullah, S. (2014). Corporate governance and cash holdings in listed non-financial firms in Pakistan. *Business Review, 9*(2), 48–73.

Masood, A., & Shah, A. (2014). Corporate governance and cash holdings in listed non-financial firms of Pakistan. *Business Review, 9*(2), 48–72.

McConnell, J., & Servaes, H. (1990). Additional evidence on equity ownership and corporate value. *Journal of Financial Economics, 27*(3), 595–613.

Megginson, L., Ullah, B., & Wei, Z. (2014). State ownership, soft-budget constraints, and cash holdings: Evidence from China's privatized firms. *Journal of Banking and Finance, 48*(1), 276–291.

Merve, K., & Cemil, K. (2016). The effect of board gender diversity on firm performance: Evidence from Turkey. *Gender in Management: an International Journal, 31*(7), 434–455.

Myers, S. (1977). Determinants of corporate borrowing. *Journal of Financial Economics, 5*(1), 147–175.

Myers, S. (1984). The capital structure puzzle. *Journal of Finance, 39*(2), 572–592.

Myers, S., & Majluf, N. (1984). Corporate financing and investment decisions when firms have information the investors do not have. *Journal of Financial Economics, 13*(2), 187–221.

Narwal, A., Karam, P., & Jindal, S. (2017). Impact of corporate governance on the cash holding of the firms: An empirical study of Indian manufacturing sector. *International Journal of Financial Management, 7*(1), 47–52.

Nguyen, T., Locke, S., & Reddy, K. (2015). Does boardroom gender diversity matter? Evidence from a transitional economy. *International Review of Economics and Finance, 37*(1), 184–202.

Ntim, C. (2013). An integrated corporate governance framework and financial performance in South African-listed corporations. *South African Journal of Economics, 81*(3), 373–392.

Ofoeda, I. (2017). Corporate governance and non-bank financial institutions profitability. *International Journal of Law and Management, 59*(6), 854–887.

Opler, T., Pinkowitz, L., Stulz, R., & Williamson, R. (1999). The determinants and implications of cash holdings. *Journal of Financial Economics, 52*, 3–46.

Opler, T., Pinkowitz, L., Stulz, R., & Williamson, R. (2001). Corporate cash holdings. *Journal of Applied Corporate Finance, 14*(3), 55–67.

Orozco, L., Vargas, J., & Galindo-Dorado, R. (2018). Trends on the relationship between board size and financial and reputational corporate performance. *European Journal of Management and Business Economics, 27*(2), 183–197.

Ozkan, N. (2007). Do corporate governance mechanisms influence CEO compensation? An empirical investigation of UK companies. *Journal of Multinational Financial Management, 17*(5), 349–364.

Ozkan, A., & Ozkan, N. (2004). Corporate cash holdings: An empirical investigation of UK companies. *Journal of Banking and Finance, 28*(3), 2013–2134.

Palaniappan, G. (2017). Determinants of corporate financial performance relating to board characteristics of corporate governance in Indian manufacturing industry. *European Journal of Management and Business Economics, 26*(1), 67–85.

Papaioannou, G., Strock, E., & Travlos, N. (1992). Ownership structure and corporate liquidity policy. *Managerial and Decision Economics, 13*(4), 315–322.

Pinkowitz, L., Stulz, R., & Williamson, R. (2006). Does the contributions of corporate cash holdings and dividends to firm value depend on governance? A cross-country analysis. *The Journal of Finance, 61*(6), 2725–2751.

Ramirez, A., & Tadesse, S. (2009). Corporate cash holdings, uncertainty avoidance, and the multinationality of firms. *International Business Review, 18*(2), 387–403.

Randoy, T., & Goel, S. (2003). Ownership structure, founder leadership, and performance in Norwegian SMEs: Implications for financing entrepreneurial opportunities. *Journal of Business Venturing, 18*(2), 619–637.

Roy, A. (2018). Corporate governance and cash holdings in Indian firms. *Contemporary Studies in Economic and Financial Analysis, 99*(2), 93–119.

Selvaggi, M., & Upton, J. (2008). *Governance and performance in corporate Britain* (Report from ABI Research and Investment Affairs Departments). Available on the ABI website at: http://www.abi.org.uk/Bookshop/defaul t.asp

Shao, L. (2019). Dynamic study of corporate governance structure and firm performance in China. *Chinese Management Studies, 13*(2), 299–317.

Stiglitz, J. (1974). On the irrelevance of corporate financial policy. *American Economic Review, 64*(3), 851–866.

Suhadak, S., Kurniaty, K., Handayani, S., & Rahayu, S. (2019). Stock return and financial performance as moderation variable in influence of good corporate governance towards corporate value. *Asian Journal of Accounting Research, 4*(1), 18–34.

Thi, V., & Phan, K. (2017). Impact of board gender diversity on firm value: International evidence. *Journal of Economics and Development, 19*(1), 65–76.

Vafeas, N. (1999). Board meeting frequency and firm performance. *Journal of Financial Economics, 53*(1), 113–142.

Weidemann, J. (2018). A state-of-the-art review of corporate cash holding research. *Journal of Business Economics, 88*(6), 765–797.

Wenchien, L. (2018). Determinants and marginal value of corporate cash holdings: Financial constraints versus corporate governance. *The International Journal of Business and Finance Research, 12*. Available at SSRN: https://ssrn.com/abstract=3131836

Wenyen, H., Huang, Y., & Lai, G. (2015). Corporate governance and cash holdings: Evidence from the U.S. property–liability insurance industry. *Journal of Risk and Insurance, 82*(3), 715–748.

Xixiong, X., Wanli, L., Yaoqin, L., & Xing, L. (2019). Female CFOs and corporate cash holdings: Precautionary motive or agency motive? *International Review of Economics & Finance, 63*(2), 434–454.

Yanchao, W., Yu, L., Chen, X., & Song, C. (2014). Inflation, operating cycle, and cash holdings. *China Journal of Accounting Research, 7*(2), 263–276.

Yermack, D. (1996). Higher market valuation of companies with a small board of directors. *Journal of Financial Economics, 40*(3), 185–211.

Zhang, R., & Liu, C. (2005). Ownership structure, shareholder protection and listed companies' cash holdings. *Finance and Trade Economics, 2*(1), 3–19.

Credit Control for Accounts Receivable Management: A Case Study of a Pharmaceutical Company

Abdulla Abdulmajid Alkhaja, Ahmad Obaid Almheiri, Obaid Meshal Almansoori, Omar Abdulaziz Alabdulla, Saeed Ali Almarri, Randa Elchaar, and Rihab Grassa

1 INTRODUCTION

The productivity and efficiency of any management are based on its capabilities and resources in handling its various operations to succeed in accomplishing its targets. Account receivables' management is a fundamental aspect in evaluating a firm's efficiency with regards to cash flow and credit turnover. Credit management functionalities are not identified as standardized principles for firms to refer and follow, rather they are an art in the fields of accounting and finance that has been developed by

A. A. Alkhaja · A. O. Almheiri · O. M. Almansoori · O. A. Alabdulla ·
S. A. Almarri · R. Elchaar · R. Grassa (✉)
College of Business, Higher Colleges of Technology, Dubai, United Arab Emirates
e-mail: rgrassa@hct.ac.ae

A. A. Alkhaja
e-mail: H00355726@hct.ac.ae

A. O. Almheiri
e-mail: H00349926@hct.ac.ae

A. Echchabi et al. (eds.), *Contemporary Research in Accounting and Finance*, https://doi.org/10.1007/978-981-16-8267-4_5

time, technology, and comprehending past mistakes. Various large institutions, individuals, and corporations, in the world of accounting have shared plenty of details, data, and figures regarding credit control and what essential core aspects are required and demanded in every receivable management. Nevertheless, the policies of a credit control management should generate terms and conditions to preserve the rights of the firm. These policies should be exercised by well-trained, experienced, and dedicated staff, a factor that establishes the essential role of credit control policies in any industry. That being said, receivables are essential for a firm's growth and working capital. It has been acknowledged in business transactions that billing in arrears is important and that it is a must in some cases. These goods and services that are pre-delivered are receivables that should be managed efficiently in order to maintain the cash flows and guarantee revenues at minimum risk. Credit control for account receivables is considered to be an essential skill of management in any organization.

Account receivables and credit control have different definitions, but one function for management when it comes to credit control of account receivables. Account receivables are the balances from credit sales of goods and services to clients. Hence, credit control management is responsible for calculating risks related to the turnover of these receivables in a specific period of time. That is implemented through the systems and methods used to indicate clients with credit billings. The main issue with loans is that risk may never be eliminated, and that credit control manages to mitigate credit risk for a certain period of time.

Technology development contributed to the efficient application of credit control management. However, the systems do not replace human judgment, or protect the reputation of the firm or the need for analyzing

O. M. Almansoori
e-mail: H00293675@hct.ac.ae

O. A. Alabdulla
e-mail: H00355218@hct.ac.ae

S. A. Almarri
e-mail: H00324406@hct.ac.ae

R. Elchaar
e-mail: relchaar@hct.ac.ae

the financial position of the debtor. For bulk services or massive loans, the creditor examines the financial position of a firm accurately and analyzes its financial capabilities before giving consent to any kind of a loan.

Credit control management has several functions when dealing with clients of credit sales. The functions include negotiating repayment plans, reviewing customers' credit ratings, responding to payment inquiries, and making sure customers pay invoices when they are due. The policies and terms are set by management in any industry to determine the customers that should be offered trade terms and can honor their credit obligations.

Pharmaceutical industries are used to massive business transactions from their medical products. The amounts are large and clients include governments, local, and international medical and research institutes that are credited with short-term and long-term payables. It can be challenging for these industries to control their receivables worldwide, so they use credit control systems that help them collect these amounts and keep track of their clients' financial position.

This study will examine the methods applied for credit control of accounts receivables for international distributors of pharmaceuticals operating from the GCC countries and sheds light on the risks their industry encounters when the receivables become uncollectible and turn into bad debts.

2   Literature Review

Accounts receivable (AR) depict the benefit earned by customers with credit sales. The credit limit typically runs from a couple of days to months or even a year in some cases. When a business offers credit to the buyer, the invoice is generated and the transfer of credit is realized. Current assets on the balance sheet are treated as loan receivables (Bennett, Coleman & Co. Ltd., 2020).

Previous studies discussed the effect of account receivable on the performance of firms. Lazaridis and Tryfonidis (2006) show that there was a strong relationship between gross operating profit and the cash conversion cycle. Their analysis indicated that there is a positive and non-significant correlation between account receivables and two profitability-based variables, the overall asset rates and the operating profit margin. Abdulrasheed et al. (2011) found that if successful inventory control is applied, small businesses could generate more profit. However, the report used Return on Invested Capital (ROCE) as a measurement of the corporations' productivity to fill this literary void. The accounts' worth, interest loss, and expected default in liabilities of accounts receivable were used to calculate the financial worth of the listed quoted manufacturing companies in Nigeria (Akinleye & Adebowale, 2019).

Credit has become the heart of business trading, and people started seeing it as the norm of trading since the twentieth century. In the past, when trading was direct and credit wasn't available, sales would be restricted, volumes would be reduced, and unit costs would be increased at least for business to business trading. Businesses restricted the granting of credit to unknown business customers, and gave credit only to customers they knew well. However, with increased competition , the need to grow and expand has encouraged businesses to grant credit to more customers rather than the trusted ones. This has increased employment and growth in businesses both domestically and globally. Sellers considered knowing the customer, judging the amount of credit and the time period to repay, as the most important aspects of credit control. Credit also created economies of scale, and the more goods were produced and sold, the lower the price (Bullivant, 2016).

A key to understanding credit control is to see it as a policy that includes business strategies directed to increase sales of goods and services. The business strategies include extending credit to potential customers, credit to customers with good credit, and limit credit to those with weak credit to ensure payment for the goods or services. The success or failure of Businesses depends on the demand for their goods or services. With higher sales more profits are generated thus leading to higher stock prices. Delaying customers' repayments makes the purchase more attractive, where customers can pay at a later time period or break in installments, and helps them justify the purchase. Businesses also benefit from charging interest on credit balances while increased sales volumes increase profits. The credit policy framework is based on certain assumptions that set the conditions for key management decisions related to the customers who are eligible for credit extension, the length of time over which the credit is extended, the discount percentage before the end of the discount period, credit standards to qualify for credit and the collection policy. Therefore, businesses should determine what kind of credit control policy they are willing and able to implement (Kenton, 2020).

The credit policy framework determines the guidelines a certain company has to comply with to extend credit or refrain from extending credit to a customer.

The three different policy types include the restrictive, a low-risk strategy classified as hard criteria for new customers, and involves strict control for extending credit. The moderate, where businesses take some calculated risk, credit is given on some middle ground and the credit limit is set in advance. The liberal, a high-risk strategy with less control on credit availability. Large businesses with higher profitability , businesses aiming to gain market share, and businesses in a monopoly situation usually go with a liberal kind of credit policy. Successful implementation of credit policy also includes customer behavior analyses, knowing the clients, and regular monitoring of their credit standing. In addition, sending bills promptly and establishing contact after an invoice is issued, to deal with any queries and to prevent late payments. Also, applying penalties, adding late payment interest and ensuring that they have been included in the terms and conditions (Trust, 2014).

Various functions of credit control management were gathered from the United States (US) over past years. Some were from academic studies, and others were from the policies adopted by massive US corporations and their subsidiaries. The 2008–2009 financial crisis revealed facts regarding the endurance of credit control managements with many debtors relying on the aid of their suppliers to maintain the flow of operations.

An accounting system requires internal control methods for accounts receivable to decrease the risk of fraud, error, and loss. The purpose of accounts receivable internal control is to make sure that sales invoices are correctly reported and customers pay quickly by adhering to the agreed terms of business. Proper instruments and clear data can help build strong internal control for accounts receivable and management. The instruments and data monitored, set the processes to order invoice creation, to maintain and to report receivable accounts, and how to handle and record invoice payments (Brown, 2019).

Well-documented methods and procedures assigning employees' area of responsibility for accounts receivable, and how the responsibilities should be handled, is major in setting strong internal control over these accounts. There are many internal control procedures for account receivables. Firstly, the receivables policy. The business should have well-documented policies and methods on accounts receivable internal controls such as credit and collection policies, to assure that all concerned departments and employees are knowledgeable and adhere to the accounts receivable process.

Secondly, is segregation of duties, also known as separation of duties where a financial process is handled by two individuals at least, to help reduce errors and combat fraud. In practice, the segregation of duties means that the employee responsible for physical assets such as cash, inventory, and supplies, is not dealing with the registration and recording of transactions related to these assets. Finally, reducing external accounts receivable risk. Internal controls for the accounts receivable management workflow are important in preventing errors that can cause damage to the financial position of a firm. For more protection, the company should properly manage commercial risks that are beyond its control, such as an interrupted cash flow due to a delay in, or non-payment of invoices.

These procedures are not exhaustive, and every business should create its own policies and processes aligning with its goals. Internal controls applied by a business can reduce the risk of fraud and human error, and can ensure that the accounting information presented is correct and complete. Consequently, the income statements, balance sheets, and cash flow statements provided by the auditing and accounting system become a reliable source of information for management to make operational decisions (Brown, 2019).

Credit management can streamline its workflows, store key information, plan or execute several day-to-day tasks of the team responsible for credit management by integrating the appropriate credit management software. The latter will enable credit department employees to focus on the tasks of high priority first.

One of the software benefits is its effectiveness in data input, processing invoices in time, and collecting money. The company's credit management's efficacy increases by automating the processes related to the control of cash flow thus making companies pay faster and on due date. Vast quantities of data can be captured and interpreted, thus allowing maximum insight into customer behavior, including extending credit and the process of collecting receivables.

The incorporation of credit management software across the firm will facilitate the exchange of information automatically and ensures that everyone has access to the latest data, thus updating and thoroughly educating the whole enterprise on the needs of each customer. Each client should be able to access and update the stored information and generate their own registered invoices. Consequently, conflicts will be minimized because the client can observe the lending process from beginning to end.

For creating a business case, time and money must be saved by reducing human resources, speeding up payment, evaluating, and maximizing the business to gain useful insight.

Organizations are always perusing to adopt secure and well-built financial policies regarding accounts receivables, and this through their credit control management to optimize on lowering their risks. These policies are of high relevance when it comes to determining the position of the organization and to what extent these policies are being applied and exercised. Extension of credit and prioritizing the number of sales without risk assessments and efficient supervision have a material potential of creating a hole in accounts receivables that can drain the life of the organization.

Inefficiency in credit control management might force an entity to create loans and drawn in debts to satisfy their payables and obligations especially with the clients' that do not honor their payment deadlines which in its turn minimizes and snares the cash flow. Hence, the company will be unable to make investments and find potential opportunities of growth (Deloitte, n.d.).

Credit control management must recruit well-trained and experienced employees to assess and calculate risks for credit limits in a proper manner, and then exercise its credit policies efficiently by tracking the payment timeline of the customers. Managements that focus on sales with strong credit control policies and systems in place, can face the risk that half the customers are late or failing to pay (TCii, 2012).

The terms and conditions included in a contract provided to customers by the management of credit control, reserve the rights of the organization in case the customers exceed the time limit of payment or on some occasions avoid paying. Among other measures, management should adopt a system that evaluates which customers, whether new or existing, are suitable for a credit sale, are capable of meeting their obligations on time, and to what extent can they can be granted credit. The latter systems will also support the organization through automated notifications and reminders sent to the customers on due dates, and will also alert the management if they are required to take action against outstanding credit balances. It has been established that over 39% of businesses in the United Kingdom spend up to four hours per week pursuing customers for payments (Hemsley, 2017). In the United Kingdom (UK), small and medium-sized enterprises (SME's) have determined that sales are a priority and an essential objective of a business, leaving the receivables to be an asset that does not generate real cash. It is also believed that many of these sectors in the UK claim that they are not getting sufficient legal support from the government, in matters of overdue, exceeding payment deadlines, while the debtors are not being legally forced to honor their payable obligations (Bullivant, 2010). The Consumer Credit Act in the UK gave privileges to Business to Business (B2B) sectors in drafting their agreements based on their terms and conditions upon negotiation, which also includes international trading in case the exporter is based in the UK. Hence, this could build a fierce challenge for a credit control management facing the laws and procedures of various countries world-wide. These matters may also include the difficulty to initiate and pursue a legal action. Not only in manufacturing and service corporations, but also bankers were led to the conclusion that numbers on a sheet are not more important than cash received on hand. The 2008 financial crisis revealed that banking corporations in the UK and United States (US) caused the bubble to burst due to lack of control and efficient management on credits. Eventually, the responsibility lays with the credit control management as the organization will depend on their judgment in approving a credit sale.

The sales administration and the credit management should cooperate and function per terms and conditions set, and both managements should comprehend their limits and responsibilities. In certain cases, the credit control management may be under pressure from the sales staff in an attempt to force a sale when a credit may not be granted approval based on policy terms and conditions. Therefore, credit control managers should not take the guilt for rejecting a customers request for billing in arrears. In addition, the strictness in applying the policies of a credit should be taken from a professional point of view by the customers since it reflects the strong impenetrable position of the organization indicating that it is holding its professional status in the market.

3   METHODOLOGY

Previous studies stressed the importance of implementing an efficient credit management system in multinational companies to reduce insolvency and liquidity risks (Dave, 2012; Shao et al., 1997).

In this paper, we use a database of pharmaceutical distributors dealing with a multinational pharmaceutical company. Our sample consists of 57 distributors operating in six regions: the GCC region, the Levant, the Sub-Saharan region, the North African countries, Central Africa, and

Turkey. The collected data covers the period from 2016 to 2020. To study the effect of credit control on the performance of accounts receivable, we use ratios assessing liquidity, leverage, efficiency , profitability , and cash flow performance. The ability of the debtors to make payments determines the performance of the control management system.

We are interested, in this paper, to analyze multinational pharmaceutical firms for mainly two reasons. First, pharma firms have complicated operations that impact their management of credit control. The industry requires sophisticated technologies, large investments, and time to develop, manufacture, and commercialize new drugs. Second, the complexity of the process and technology used, present a challenge to control the credit balances and manage cash flows. The pharmaceutical companies, therefore, tend to form strategic alliances that facilitate information sharing which help to properly control the credit management system. Strategic alliances allow for improving both companies' credit operations as well as their competitiveness in the market.

4 RESULTS

Table 1 describes the liquidity ratio for our sample for the period from 2016 to 2019. The overall liquidity ratios of the six regions indicate that the financial position of the drug distributors is good because

Table 1 Liquidity ratios per region for the period 2016–2019

Region	Year	Average of current ratio (%)	Average of quick ratio (%)
Levant average	2016–2019	1.45	0.95
Sub-Sahara Africa average	2016–2019	1.35	0.75
North Africa average	2016–2019	1.98	1.25
Middle East average	2016–2019	19.40	4.35
Central Africa average	2016–2019	1.64	0.94
Turkey average	2016–2019	2.02	1.58
Average		4.91	1.60

Source Authors own calculation based on the collected data

they have the capacity and ability to repay their debts. In terms of the current and quick ratios, the six regions have an average of 4.91 and 1.60% respectively. It indicates that the companies' financial position in the long term is solid as reflected by the long-term assets they maintain. Therefore, they are able to offset their long-term financial obligations comfortably. However, in terms of short-term liabilities, the companies' financial standing is average. The Middle East region has the highest current ratio of 19.40% and a quick ratio of 4.35%. The lowest region in terms of liquidity ratios is Sub-Saharan Africa with a current ratio of 1.35% and a quick ratio of 0.75%. It indicates that Sub-Saharan Africa subsidiaries find difficulties in fulfilling their financial liabilities.

Table 2 describes the debt ratio for the drug distributors under study. The unhealthy short-term financial capability is basically due to the lack of stringent credit controls. An examination of the average debt ratio indicates that the six regions have an average of 63%. The debt ratio is poor as it indicates that the businesses are unlikely to generate enough cash to fulfill their debt obligations. The Middle East has the lowest percentage of 50% for the average debt ratio while the Levant region has the highest at 74%. It implies that the companies in the Levant have a high risk of defaulting compared to the Middle East region.

Cash flow ratios indicate the ability of a company to pay off its current debts with cash that it generates in the same period. An examination of the average of the operating cash flow ratios for the six regions (Table 3) reveals that the companies operating in the six regions are not generating enough money to pay for their liabilities. The Middle East region is the most affected with an average of −21.14%. The regions that have posted

Table 2 Debt ratios per region for the period 2016–2019

Region	Year	Average of debt ratio (%)
Levant average	2016–2019	74
Sub-Sahara Africa average	2016–2019	73
North Africa average	2016–2019	59
Middle East average	2016–2019	50
Central Africa average	2016–2019	63
Turkey average	2016–2019	33
Average		63

Source Authors own calculation based on the collected data

Table 3 Operating cash flow per region for the period 2016–2019

Region	Year	Average of operating cash flow ratio (%)
Levant average	2016–2019	0.04
Sub-Sahara Africa average	2016–2019	0.04
North Africa average	2016–2019	−0.07
Middle East average	2016–2019	−21.14
Central Africa average	2016–2019	0.07
Turkey average	2016–2019	–
Average		−4.10

Source Authors own calculation based on the collected data

a positive figure have an average of less than one. The Gulf region has an average of 10%, Levant 0.04%, Sub-Sahara Africa 0.04%, North Africa −0.07%, and Africa an average of 0.07%. The overall average of the six regions is −4.10%. Overall, it indicates that all the subsidiaries in the six regions are unable to pay their current liabilities from the cash that they generate. The Gulf region has the highest average of cash flow of 10%. It implies that its companies are generating some cash but not enough to settle all their current liabilities. When a company has a cash flow ratio higher than one, it indicates that it has generated cash that is enough to pay its current liabilities and it remains with some (Ahmed et al., 2016). The firms are not generating enough cash to fully settle their current liabilities with most of their cash being held in account receivables.

Table 4 describes the efficiency ratio of the drug distributors under study. Efficiency ratios indicate how well a company has used its assets to generate income. The Inventory turnover ratios are used to indicate the balance between restock rates and sales. A comparison between the six regions indicates that African countries have had the highest ratio (33.51%) while their North African region counterparts have had the lowest ratio (1.67%). A good ratio that indicates a balance between restock rates and sales is between 4 and 6%. In this case, the regions that have balanced their restock rates and sales, are the GCC countries (3.84%), the Levant region (4.57%), and the Middle East region (6.31%). The Sub-Saharan Africa region and the Central African region have high account receivables ratios, where most of the goods being credit sales. The North African countries have a lower restock rate (1.67%) than is demanded by its market.

Table 4   Efficiency ratios per region for the period 2016–2019

Region	Year	Average of inventory turnover (%)	Average of DIO (%)	Average of assets turnover ratio (%)	Average of DSO (%)	Average of DPO (%)	Average of cash conversion cycle (%)
Levant average	2016–2019	4.57	125.91	5.19	143.88	166.68	103.11
Sub-Sahara Africa average	2016–2019	9.31	135.32	5.30	94.34	153.30	76.36
North Africa average	2016–2019	1.67	255.57	5.24	155.78	169.19	242.16
Middle East average	2016–2019	6.31	130.09	8.97	113.33	88.11	155.31
Central Africa average	2016–2019	33.50	140.37	9.14	92.92	186.33	46.95
Turkey average	2016–2019	4.43	83.16	25.66	123.42	97.30	109.28
Average		11.70	139.93	7.01	128.54	146.54	121.92

Source Authors own calculation based on the collected data

Internal controls are tools, rules, and procedures executed by a company to ensure the fairness of financial and accounting information, improve accountability, and prevent fraud. Besides complying with laws and regulations and deterring employees from stealing assets or committing fraud, internal controls can help increase operational efficiency by promoting the efficiency and timeliness of financial reporting.

The ratios presented in our study reflect part of the companies' company's performance through the evaluation of account receivable and cash flows management. The average of the debt ratio, calculated by dividing total liabilities by total assets, can be a sensitive ratio regarding internal control. It is a financial ratio that shows the percentage of a company's assets that are provided through debt. In particular, when companies take a loan from the bank they provide their semi-annual or quarterly, in short interim financial statements. In both cases, if the statements show that the companies have previously taken a loan, tension might arise between investors since they are not aware of the reasons behind obtaining the loan and that can make them withdraw their money from the company. Companies also fend against their competitors by keeping their statements confidential, especially their indebtedness position should be discrete since it can show their weaknesses and exposure to financial risks arising from borrowing.

5   CONCLUSION

In a world where businesses have moved from cash to credit sale of products and services, firms should be able to determine and ensure that credit facilities are extended to customers that have the capability and capacity of making repayments in future. There are various ways of enforcing credit control in businesses. In most cases, credit controllers limit the issuance of credits by calculating and managing risks. Other methods of credit control include engaging in direct sales, rationing of credit, and increasing the amount of security and collateral that is required to provide lending. In situations where individuals or businesses are defaulting on their repayments, more credit control measures are implemented to increase the returns from lending and discourage most people from seeking credit.

In this research, we tried to study the credit control and accounts receivable management in one of the international pharmaceutical companies. Our analysis provided several important recommendations to this industry.

First, pharmaceutical companies should implement stringent credit control measures that can help in improving their cash flow. The pharmaceutical companies are burdened by the huge amount of accounts receivable. The amount of cash flow from operations is not enough to fully settle their current liabilities. This implies that they have to continuously inject external capital to remain in business.

Second, they should form strategic alliances that help in sharing credit information and implementing credit control measures. Third, there are many ways to improve internal control in a company. One way is to provide adequate training for staff. Employees should be trained and authorized to execute their tasks appropriately. It is necessary to recognize that training should be considered a continuous process and staff training needs should be periodically evaluated to consider changes in business processes, technology, new laws, and regulations, etc. Another way is to perform reconciliations regularly. Reconciliations are usually an underappreciated internal control. When executed correctly and routinely, they give a powerful control to recognize and correct errors on a timely basis. Companies should reconcile all funds and accounts at least on a monthly basis and record any important changes promptly. The reconciliation should be reviewed by an individual outside of the reconciliation process and the reviewer should sign and date the reconciliation to signify that the review has been satisfactorily completed and any differences have been resolved.

Fourth, pharmaceutical companies also have to extend credit facilities to their customers in order to expand their businesses and remain competitive. Therefore, they have to implement credit control measures that help in lowering the loss that may be incurred as a result of slow and less repayments.

This paper's findings are subject, also, to a number of limitations. First, due to the lack of literature on credit control management, we had difficulties in deconstructing the conceptual framework for this study. Second, the researchers acknowledge the limitation of data. Third, the present study also limits the scope of research by focusing on the credit control management and account receivable in 6 regions. In other words, the research findings cannot be generalized in other contexts like developed countries.

Despite this paper's limitations, the authors feel that they have contributed to the literature on credit control management in the pharma industry by moving the discussion forward on this topic through field work and analysis of the empirical data. Our findings may be regarded as a pilot to serve as the basis for further research employing a larger sample and investigating other contexts.

References

Abdulrasheed, A., Khadijat, A. Y., Sulu, I., & Olanrewaju, A. A. (2011). Inventory management in small business finance: Empirical evidence from Kwara State, Nigeria. *British Journal of Economics, Finance and Management Sciences*, 2(1), 49–57

Ahmed, Z., Awan, M. Z., Safdar, M. Z., Hasnain, T., & Kamran, M. (2016). A nexus between working capital management and profitability: A case study of pharmaceutical sector in Pakistán. *International Journal of Economics and Financial Issues*, 6(3S).

Akinleye, G. T., & Adebowale, J. O. (2019). Account receivables' management and performance of manufacturing firms. *International Journal of Economics & Business*, 5(1), 18–27.

Brown, M. (2019). *Internal control procedures for accounts receivable.* Retrieved 2020, from https://www.double-entry-bookkeeping.com/accounts-receiv able/internal-control-procedures-for-accounts-receivable/#:~:text=The%20p urpose%20of%20accounts%20receivable,the%20agreed%20terms%20of%20busi ness

Bullivant, G. (Ed.). (2010). *Credit management.* Gower.

Bullivant, G. (Ed.). (2016). *Credit management.* Routledge.

Dave, A. R. (2012). Financial management as a determinant of profitability: A study of Indian pharma sector. *South Asian Journal of Management, 19*(1), 124.

Hemsley, L. (2017, December 20). *Better credit control procedures for modern businesses.* Retrieved 2020, from https://fluidly.com/blog/better-credit-con trol-procedures-for-modern-businesses/

Kenton, W. (2020, April 28). *Working capital (NWC).* Retrieved from Investo pedia, https://www.investopedia.com/terms/w/workingcapital.asp

Lazaridis, I., & Tryfonidis, D. (2006). Relationship between working capital management and profitability of listed companies in the Athens stock exchange. *Journal of Financial Management and Analysis, 19*(1), 26–35.

Pearse Trust. (2014, January 6). *Credit control policy & procedures explained.* https://www.pearse-trust.ie/blog/bid/103142/credit-control-policy-proced ures-explained#:~:text=%22Credit%20policy%22%20consists%20of%20guideli nes,business%20with%20a%20particular%20customer.&text=Businesses%20in% 20a%20monopoly%20situation,full%20advantage%20of%20their%20monopoly

Shao, L. P., Shao, A. T., & Hasan, I. (1997). International credit management policies of US subsidiaries. *Managerial Finance.*

TCii. (2012, February 21). *Setting up a good credit control system.* Retrieved 2020, from https://www.mondaq.com/uk/management/153848/setting- up-a-good-credit-control-system

The Economic Times, Bennett, Coleman & Co. Ltd. (2020). *Definition of accounts receivable.* https://economictimes.indiatimes.com/definition/acc ounts-receivable

The Financial Friction and Optimal Monetary Policy: The Role of Interest Rate

Salha Ben Salem, Haykel Hadj Salem, Nadia Mansour, and Moez Labidi

1 Introduction

The multiplication of financial crises in many emergent and advanced countries has demonstrated the cost of systemic financial volatility and credit market frictions. Frictions, in this market, have played a central role in the short-term macroeconomic variables and the long-term growth of the economy. Crises highlight that this instability can construct up during boom periods and suddenly transmits to a great and persistent recession period (bust) which emphasizes the necessity for macro-prudential policies.

The modeling of financial friction in the DSGE framework gained the importance of several policymakers and macroeconomists. Empirical analyzes in the pre-crisis period were influenced by the study of Bernanke

S. B. Salem · H. H. Salem · M. Labidi
Department of Economics, University of Monastir, Monastir, Tunisia

N. Mansour (✉)
Department of Finance, University of Sousse, Sousse, Tunisia
e-mail: mansournadia@usal.es

University of Salamanca, Salamanca, Spain

et al. (1999), Kiyotaki and Moore (1997), and Iacoviello (2005). A crucial feather of these models is that they modeled the financial frictions only on the debtors' side credit markets, and they considered a perfect banking sector.

However, the financial crisis has proven how imperfection in the banking sector can effectively have an important effect on macroeconomic and financial stability. This fact pushing the policymaker and the central bank to question the hypotheses of these models. Recently, theoretical analysis has oriented its attention to the impact of credit cycle vulnerabilities on the conduct of monetary policy, Gertler and Karadi (2011), and how the monetary authority can improve this vulnerability via its interest rate. The problem that occurs is, with financial friction, the central bank should trade-off between price stability and financial stability.

Smets (2014) emphasizes that regrouping price and financial stability under one central bank could resolve the coordination problems that may occur from their interaction. However, at the same time, it can affect the central bank's credibility insofar as the monetary policy may rest more flexible than is inevitably for price stability because to keep financial stability (Krug, 2018).

This paper deals in this context and wake-up call for the central bank to take account of the credit cycle vulnerabilities when setting the interest rate. Our methodology consists first to analyze the characterization of the Tunisian economy through the implicit volatility of the variables and their autocorrelation. Second, we study the effectiveness of standard and augmented Taylor rules in the context of the financial bubble.

The issue of this article is how does the central bank respond to financial shock that intensifies the credit cycle vulnerabilities? Note that from 2016, the central bank of Tunisia (CBT) introduced financial stability as its second objective, so can it ensure the price and the financial stability by acting only on its interest rate?

Our notable result is that there is a correspondence between the volatility of the actual and simulated variables. Also, we note that the fluctuations of the macroeconomic variables are very close to each other except for the credit level and the credit growth to GDP ratio. Then, the financial variables are more elastic than macroeconomic variables following the triggering of shocks. We conclude that when the central bank chooses to lean against the wind, it should put a real trade-off between financial stability and price stability.

This article is ordered as follows. Section 2 presents the literature review on the effect of monetary policy on financial stability in a DSGE framework. Section 3 presents the non-linear equations of the model and describes the methodology. Section 4 describes the calibration of the keys parameters in the model. Section 5 interests to study the dynamics of the Tunisian economic cycle. Section 6 compares the results under the standard Taylor rule under a monetary rule amplified by a financial indicator. The final section resumes the conclusion.

2   THE LITERATURE REVIEW

As highlighted above, the effectiveness of monetary policy given financial stability has largely been studied after the financial crisis by Blas and Malmierca (2020) and Carstens (2020). Several economists predict that the augmented Taylor rule is more adequate to combat financial risks, while others do not agree. The key variables introduced were generally, the interest rate spreads by Gilchrist and Zakrajsek (2012), Curdia and Woodford (2009), credit over GDP by Schularick and Taylor (2012), the credit growth of assets price and credit growth by Gambacorta and Signoretti (2014). All these authors support the idea of introducing the financial indicator into the central bank's reaction purpose to weaken the fluctuation of macroeconomic and financial fundamentals.

Drehmann et al. introduce several other variables and show that the credit to GDP ratio is the greatest one for forecasting crises. Likewise, Verona et al. (2017) consider several financial indicators such as, bond spread, loan spread, total credit and find that the augmented Taylor rule that introduces these indicators is better than the standard one in the financial friction time. However, these indicators were integrated into models that combine monetary policy with macro-prudential regulation.

Although, some authors aim to evaluate the adequacy of the central bank in financial stability when using only the interest rate as an instrument, i.e., independently of the macro-prudential regulations. Beau et al. introduce a credit growth indicator in the standard Taylor rule. They show that the effect of the augmented rule turns out to be destabilizing for inflation if compared to the standard one, even when financial shocks are measured.

Christiano et al. (2010) analyze the Japanese and American economies in a period of financial expansion. They show that if the central bank concentrates on inflation targeting, it will aggravate the cycle and will end up with a financial crisis. Nevertheless, if this authority applies an augmented Taylor rule, by introducing a credit growth rate, it will reduce the price fluctuation of financial assets. Badarau and Popescu confirmed this result and show that the augmented Taylor rule has a better approximation to the financial stability in the event of financial shock.

Our main contribution to the existing literature consists to analyze how the introduction of a financial variable in the Taylor rule operates in a model with the presence of both a debtor's friction and a bank credit supply channel. And, how the monetary authority could improve the response of the economy in case of a financial shock, by only using its interest rate instrument. We simulate a DSGE model of Badarau and Popescu (2014) for the Tunisian economy. The banking sector is the primary power in the financial market, accounting for 41% of total capitalization, and offering a credit of 70% of GDP. Therefore, its health state is an important barometer of the stock market investment. The Tunisian banking sector suffers, especially after the revolution of 2011, from several limitations caused mainly by the previous regime damage and by the weakness of the national economy, which helps to paralyze its ability to increase funds for productive projects. Thereby, this sector, characterized by a misallocation of resources, contributes to the weak performance of the Tunisian economy. This situation requires the intervention of the central bank to resolve these shortcomings. We consider the interest rate as the only tool available at the central bank to remedy the frictions.

3   MODEL PRESENTATION AND METHODOLOGY

The model is constructed from the model of Badarau and Popescu (2014). It includes price rigidities and credit market imperfections in the context of the financial accelerator mechanism of Bernanke et al. (1999). To match the financial framework, the model adds the banking sector and the financial market. These hypotheses make the model fit to study the firm's balance sheet channel of Bernanke et al. (1999), and the bank capital channel of Badarau and Levieuge (2011, 2013) and constructed a boom-bust process inspired by Bernanke and Gertler (1989) and Tetlow (2005).

Overall, the model studies an economy populated by seven economic agents: households, banks, government, entrepreneurs, capital producers, retailers, and the central bank.

Households economize money in the form of bank deposits, work for entrepreneurs, and consume final goods. The government has a secondary role; so that it only collects taxes from households and exploits them to use retail goods. Entrepreneurs produce homogeneous wholesale goods in a competitive market. In the production process, they exploit capital and labor supplied by households and by themselves. To finance investments, entrepreneurs use their net worth and credit offered by the bank. Banks have two sources of funding, bank capital, and deposits of households.

The capital producer differentiates his product according to the need of the entrepreneur. The government is only an actor who collects taxes from households so that they can be used in the consumption of final goods. The retailer is introduced to incite the rigidity of prices.

These companies buy the final goods (wholesale) produced by the contractors and differentiate them free of charge. The detailed goods are exchanged in a monopolistic market. Like the New Keynesian model, the household maximizes its inter-temporal utility function under budget constraints (Pirozhkova, 2017).

The entrepreneur produces the wholesale (homogeneous) products within a framework of pure and perfect competition using the labor and capital factors. The labor force is provided by the household and by the entrepreneur. According to Bernanke et al. (1999), we adopt that the net wealth of the entrepreneur is determined by his wage and accumulated profit. However, if this producer suffers from a default on a date "t," he automatically leaves the market and consumes its residual assets.

The bank plays an intermediary role between agents who need financing (the entrepreneur) and agents who have a liquidity capacity (households). Thus, this bank has two sources of financing: its fund and the deposits of these creditors. Nevertheless, if this bank goes bankrupt, it leaves the market and transforms a part of its funds to the new or existing banks.

Like the works of Bernanke et al. (1999), Carlastrom and Fuerst (1997), the model assumes that the frictions in the credit market are due mainly to problems of asymmetric information and agency costs. According to recent literature, these imperfections are analyzed in two ways. Firstly, between bank (lender) and entrepreneur (borrower). In this case, the latter supports an additional cost on the money borrowed (the firm's external finance premium). Secondly, the focus is put on the problem of asymmetric information between the bank (as a borrower) and households (the provider of funds). To avoid the "bunk run," the bank pays an additional cost; the bank's external financing premium. These two premiums have an enhancing role in some shocks. In this model, we take into account four kinds of shocks; productivity , government expenditure shocks, monetary and financial shocks. The financial shock is known as the process "boom-bust".[1]

To avoid the effect of these shocks, the central bank presents two strategies: in a first step, it considers the case where the monetary authority aims to stabilize the level of inflation and the productivity gap applying the standard Taylor rule. It analyzes the extent to which this rule is effective in reducing fluctuations in financial and macroeconomic variables. In the second step, like the model of Badarau and Popescu (2014), incorporates a financial stress indicator (the credit growth to GDP ratio) in the standard Taylor rule. We develop our analysis by comparing the variation of interest variables for the central bank under an augmented and standard Taylor rules. This comparison is made to detect the most optimal monetary policy with real and financial shocks. Also, objective, in addition to actual targeting, could affect the fundamentals of the economy. These two steps were examined using the simulation approach.[2] Then, the model is evaluated using the Bayesian estimation method on the Tunisian data including the level of GDP, inflation , nominal interest rate, the amount of the credit, and the net value of the bank[3] from the period 2000 Q1 to 2019 Q1.

3.1   Households

The representative household is infinitely-lived who determine their consumption, C_t, savings, D, and labor supply, H, so that to maximize its utility function:

$$E_t \sum_{k=0}^{\infty} \beta^k \left[\frac{\sigma_c}{\sigma_c - 1} C_{t+k}^{\frac{\sigma_c-1}{\sigma_c}} - \frac{\sigma_h}{\sigma_h + 1} H_{t+k}^{\frac{\sigma_h+1}{\sigma_h}} \right] \tag{1}$$

---

[1] Relating to a supposed cycle in which periods of prosperity and development alternate with periods of decline.

[2] This technique makes it possible to fix the values of the structural parameters from the literature of the countries. It aims at interpreting the variation of the variables concerning their steady state.

[3] In this series, the value of banking capital is considered as an indicator that measures the financial health of Tunisian banks.

where E_t is the expectation operator, β^k is the household's subjective discount rate, σ_h is the inter-temporal elasticity associated with labor supply, and σ_c is the inter-temporal elasticity of substitution associated with consumption. This household is focus to the following budgetary constraint:

$$P_t C_t + D_t + A_t \leq W_t H_t + A_{t-1} R_t^A + D_{t-1} R_t - T_t + \Delta_t \qquad (2)$$

The household receives the real wage, W_t, remunerated deposit, A_t, at a real interest rate, R_t^A, and receives the dividend from the retailer activity Δ_t. D_t is the household's savings (money acquired at t and carried into $t + 1$) remunerated at the risk-free rate, R_t. These revenues are exploited in the purchase of retailer goods C_t at an aggregate price P_t, payment taxes T_t, and invest their deposit.

3.2 Entrepreneurs

The entrepreneur's production process is determined according to Cobb–Douglas function with a constant return of scale:

$$Y_t = O_t K_t^\alpha \left[H_t^\Omega \left(H^f \right)^{1-\Omega} \right]^{1-\alpha} \qquad (3)$$

where $(1 - \Omega)$ denotes the share of profit going to the entrepreneurial work, O is an exogenous technological parameter, H^f is the work of the entrepreneur himself amounting to 1, and H_t is the work provided by the household.

O_t is the stochastic process of productivity shocks. The first-order autoregressive processes of this shock are as follow:

$$O_t = \rho_o O_{t-1} + \varepsilon_t^o \qquad \varepsilon_t^o \sim i.i.d \ N(0.1) \qquad (4)$$

The total labor supply is composited by household labor (H_t) and entrepreneurial labor H^f : $L = H_t^\Omega (H^f)^{1-\Omega}$. The work of the entrepreneur has remunerated at a rate W_t^f. Capital accumulation evolves as follows:

$$K_{t+1} = (1 - \delta)K_t + I_t \qquad (5)$$

K_{t+1} is the capital purchase by the entrepreneur at $t + 1$, δ is the depreciation rate I_t is an investment expenditure.

3.3   *Capital Producer*

It has a secondary role in the model. He purchased, I_t, units of the final goods, and transforms them into physical capital to sell to the entrepreneurs. This process requires some "internal capital-adjustment costs $\phi(.)$," which is modeled by Badararau and Levieuge (2011), as follow:

$$\phi(I_t, K_t) = \frac{\phi}{2}\left(\frac{I_t}{K_t} - \delta\right)^2 \tag{6}$$

3.4   *Banking Sector and Credit Market Equilibrium*

To invest, the firms use their net worth, N_{t+1}^f, and request credit, B_{t+1}, from the representative bank.

$$B_{t+1} = Q_t K_{t+1} - N_{t+1}^f \tag{7}$$

Likewise, to offer credit, the bank uses its net worth (accumulated capital), N_{t+1}^b, and the funds collected from households A_{t+1}.

$$A_{t+1} = B_{t+1} - N_{t+1}^b = Q_t K_{t+1} - N_{t+1}^f - N_{t+1}^b \tag{8}$$

The bank capital is derived from the accumulated profits V_t^b, and the equity transferred from the "exist banks," t^b.[4]

---

[4] The model assumes that the bank that declares failure it exits the market and transforms part of its funds, t^b to the new or existing bank on the market.

$$N_{t+1}^b = \gamma^b V_t^b + \left(1 - \gamma^b\right) t^b V_t^b = \left[\gamma^b + \left(1 - \gamma^b\right) t^b\right]$$
$$\left[R_t^k B_t - \left(R_t S_t^b\right)\left(Q_{t-1} K_t - N_t^f - N_t^b\right)\right]$$
$$= \left[\gamma^b + \left(1 - \gamma^b\right) t^b\right]\left[R_t^k B_t - \left(R_t S_t^b\right) A_t\right] \qquad (9)$$

$\left(1 - \gamma^b\right)$ is the probability of banks that exit the market.
The residual consumption of this bank is:

$$C_t^b = \left(1 - \gamma^b\right)\left(1 - t^b\right) V_t^b \qquad (10)$$

The presentation of the bank sector is finished by the variation of the entrepreneur's net worth. In the same way, the entrepreneur's net worth is determined by profits, V_t^f, and entrepreneurial wages, W_t^f, derive:

$$N_{t+1}^f = \gamma^f \left(V_t^f + W_t^f\right) = \gamma^f \left(Q_{t-1} R_t^k K_t - \left(R_t S_t^f\right)\left(Q_{t-1} K_t - N_t^f\right) + W_t^f\right)$$
$$= \gamma^f \left(Q_{t-1} R_t^k K_t - \left(R_t S_t^f\right) B_t\right) + W_t^f \qquad (11)$$

γ^f is the entrepreneur's share remaining on the market at date t. Entrepreneurs who fail in period t consume their residual equity:

$$C_t^f = \left(1 - \gamma^f\right) V_t^f \qquad (12)$$

Due to asymmetric information between borrower and lender, the distinctive shock is personal information for the entrepreneur and is not observed by the investor. Therefore, on one hand, the bank is forced to pay an audit cost to be informed, and the firms should pay an external finance premium, S_t^f. This premium is defined as the difference between the expected return on capital[5] and the risk-free rate.

$$S_t^f = \psi^f \left(\frac{Q_t K_{t+1}}{N_{t+1}^f + N_{t+1}^b}\right), \text{ with } \psi^{f'}(.) > 0$$
$$= E_t \left[\frac{R_{t+1}^k}{R_t}\right] \qquad (13)$$

---

[5] Bailliu et al. (2015) assume that, in equilibrium, the anticipated rate of capital's return, $E_t R_{t+1}^K E_t R_t^{k+1}$ is equivalent to the anticipated cost of external funds.

According to the optimal contract rule, the external finance premium (S), rises with the entrepreneur's balance sheet situation; decline of the firms' balance sheet means a tightening of the external finance premium.

Not only do the entrepreneurs have personal information about the risk and investment's return, but banks also have personal information about the risk and the return of their credit supply. The model assumes, then, the debt contracts between banks and depositors (households) occur in an asymmetric information framework. According to Badarau and Levieuge (2011), the external finance accepted by households and banks as follows:

$$S_t^b = \psi^b \left(\frac{B_{t+1}}{N_{t+1}^b} \right), \text{ with } \psi^{b'}(.) > 0$$

$$= E_t \left[\frac{R_{t+1}^b}{R_{t+1}} \right] \tag{14}$$

The Eq. (13) shows that the external finance premium depends not only on the financial situation of the firm N_{t+1}^f, but also that of the bank N_{t+1}^b. Thus, the entrepreneur undergoes a higher interest rate that covers also the banks' external financing costs: bank capital channel, a devaluation of the banks' balance sheet means a tightening of its loaning conditions to entrepreneurs. Therefore, the banking capital channel acts as a financial accelerator, Badarau, and Levieuge (2011).

3.5   Retailers

As in Calvo's (1983) hypothesis, the model supposes that only one fraction of retailers can change their selling price in the market in a period independent from the previous period. These retailers are differentiated by the distribution of the product to the economy. The optimization condition of retailers involves maximizing the current value of their future dividends subject to the level of anticipated demand for goods from households and the government. Thus, the equilibrium solution gives a Phillips curve of the neo-Keynesian type (Philipp, 2018):

$$\pi_t = \beta E_t [\pi_{t+1}] + \kappa \rho_t$$

where π is the log deviation of inflation from its steady state, k is a parameter that depends on the retailer share θ and ρ is the retailer marginal cost.

The equilibrium in the goods and services market is described as:

$$Y_t = C_t + C_t^f + C_t^b + I_t + G_t$$

where G_t it is public expenditure.

3.6   The Process of "Boom-Bust"

The proliferation of crises before 2007 and the recent financial crisis have proved that the price of assets is subject to bubbles, which harm impact on the economy. It is believed that these bubbles reflect the damaging effect of risk accumulation. The structure of the bubble introduction was modeled according to Tetlow (2005) and Bernanke and Gertler (1989). The objective, in this case, is to know how the central bank could intervene to mitigate the fluctuation of economic fundamentals. However, the mechanism presented, here, is exogenous. So, the monetary authority can affect neither the amplitude nor the duration of these bubbles. To this configuration, we interpret the central bank's reaction on all variables, but not on the boom-bust process.

The "boom-bust" process occurs whenever the market price of capital, Z varies from its fundamental value, Q. The bubble equation is:

$$\mu_t = Z_t - Q_t$$

In this model, the boom exists as a result of a positive shock that raises the market price to a level high than their fundamental value, $Z_t > Q_t$, while the bust is followed by the decrease of the market price.

The bubble persists with a probability p, increases with a rate (aR^K/p), and collapses with a probability $(1 - p)$. The bubble is summarized as follows:

$$\mu_{t+1} = \begin{cases} \frac{aR^K}{p}\mu_t & \text{if the bubble persist, } (p) \\ 0 & \text{if the bubble not persist, } (1-p) \end{cases}$$

where $p < a < 1$.

After the bubble, the economy does not recover immediately. This creates a negative shock that leads to a recession phase when $Z_t < Q_t$.

The process of this phase is determined in the ninth period, Badarau and Popescu (2014).

The bursting of the bubble assumes the dependence between the return on capital and the speculative return on assets. This relationship is explained by the following equation:

$$R_{t+1}^Z = R_{t+1}^K \left[b + (1-b)\frac{Q_t}{Z_t} \right]$$

with: $b = a(1 - \delta)$.

3.7   Central Bank

The central bank is considered the last agent in this model. It determines its nominal interest rate according to the Taylor rule. The introduction of this rule allows us to study the transmission mechanisms of monetary policy shocks. According to the following Taylor rule, the nominal interest rate is a function of the past interest rate, output gap, and inflation

$$r_t^n = \beta_0 r_{t-1}^n + (1 - \beta_0)(\beta_\pi \pi_t + \beta_y y_t)$$

With r_{t-1}^n is the deviation of the nominal interest rate delayed from its steady state, π_t it is the difference between inflation and their target level, y_t is the output. As the process of "boom-bust" is exogenous, the central bank cannot influence it. But here, we are interested to test the way that this authority could intervene to reduce the fluctuation of economic fundamentals in case of a financial bubble. This adjustment only happens by their interest rate. In this regard, as Badarau and Popescu, it is assumed that the central bank keeps its traditional objectives of stable production and inflation and adds the effect of credit growth to GDP. Therefore, the augmented Taylor rule is as follows:

$$r_t^n = \beta_0 r_{t-1}^n + (1 - \beta_0)(\beta_\pi \pi_t + \beta_y y_t + \beta_{by} by_t)$$

by_t is the log deviation of the credit growth ratio over the GDP level from its equilibrium state.

The economy is confronted by two orthogonal AR (1) stochastic shocks; Productivity, and financial shocks.

3.8   Transmission Mechanisms

To understand the events of the recent financial crisis, it is essential to study the particular channels of how financial frictions operate and affect economic activity. That is why the main idea of this subsection is about the way the presence of friction on the credit market could aggravate the initial effect of the shock and thus threaten the mechanism of transmission of monetary policy.

The external finance premium of the entrepreneur is negatively correlated with their financial situation. Thus, if this entrepreneur borrows with a high financial effect, he will face a very large premium, which influences the cost of capital and impacts, thus, its investment decision. This is consistent with the financial accelerator mechanism outlined by Bernanke et al. (1999). Moreover, this model assumes that the contractor's external financing cost depends not only on his financial situation but also on the financial health of the bank. Therefore, the investor tolerates a very high rate, which also covers the cost of financing the bank. That is why the level of banking capital represents a financial accelerator (Féve et al., 2019); the lower the level is, the more the bank bears risks and costs. Therefore, it adopts a strategy of drying up credit. This will negatively affect the overall production, Badarau and Levienge (2011) and Meh (2011).

The appearance of the premium in the net worth function of the entrepreneur and the bank shows that the credit market is imperfect. These two premiums serve as an amplifier of any shock. For example, a positive productivity shock will enhance asset prices and the demand for capital goods. This increase has a positive impact on the net wealth and thus reduces the external financing premium. This will increase the demand for credit, and consequently amplifies the initial effect of the productivity shock. Also, a positive financial shock (boom phase) will feed the price of financial assets. This has a positive influence on the company's financial situation and thus its external financing premium. Yet, the reduction in this premium will increase the demand for credit, and thus the level of long-term growth. The opposite effect occurs during the bust period.

4   Calibration

Conversely, as is classical when simulating DSGE models, some parameters or ratios are fixed before simulation, because the data does not include adequate information to estimate them. Tables 1 and 2 list the

Table 1 The calibrated parameters

Parameter	Description	Value
σ_h	The elasticity of work disutility	0.25
B	Subjective discount factor	0.985
$1 - \theta$	Part of the retailer who does not change their selling prices	0.75
A	The capital Share in the production	0.35
$(1 - \Omega)$	The Contractor's share of total labor	0.25
Ω	Share of household labor in the total labor	0.75
δ	Capital depreciation rate	0.025
χ	The price of capital elasticity with the investment cost	0.25
t^b	Bank capital share which transferred to the other banks	0.0001
$1 - \gamma_f$	Failure firm's probability	0.1
$1 - \gamma_b$	The probability of bankruptcy	0.001
N/K	The firm's equity/capital ratio	0.3
NB/B	The bank net worth/credit ratio	0.12
$\bar{\rho}$	Marginal cost	0.875

Source Authors' calculation based on data collected from Tunisian Central Bank

Table 2 Steady-State parameters

Parameter	Description	Value
$\bar{r}$	Rate of return on assets	1.01
$\bar{r}^k$	Rate of return on assets	1.06
K/Y	The capital to GDP ratio	31.31
CF/Y	Consumption expenditure of the firm/GDP	0.006
CB/Y	Consumption expenditure of the bank/GDP	0.004
I/Y	Investment to GDP ratio	0.00782
C/Y	Consumption expenditure of the household/GDP	0.622
ϵ	The coefficient of the price of capital at time t	0.989

Source Authors' calculation based on data collected from Tunisian Central Bank

calibrated parameters. These tables contain a block of parameters that is calibrated in conformity to the empirical characteristics of the Tunisian economy, while the other parameters are calculated based on the Tunisian economy data. However, if parameters cannot be available from data, such as elasticity, their value is calibrated from similar model mechanisms.

We begin by calibrating the discount rate, β, which is equal to 0.983, Jouini and Rebei (2014), which means a quarterly steady-state ex-post return of bank, $\overline{r^K}$ of 1.017.[6] The capital contribution in production (α) and the depreciation rate of capital, δ, fixed at 0.35, and 0.025 respectively. The marginal cost $\overline{p}$ is set at 0.875, estimated by Abdeli and Belhadj (2015). The share of household labor in the total labor, Ω, is set to 0.99. The share of profit accruing to the work of entrepreneurs set at 1%.[7] For the degree of price stickiness, $1 - \theta$, we set the fraction of firms that put their price relatively fixed at 0.75, which is amply classic in the DSGE literature. This signifies an average time of four quarters. The steady-state ratio of the firm's net worth to capital, N^f/K, calibrated at 0.3, Badaraux and Popescu (2014). Based on quarterly data from 2000 Q 1 to 2019 Q1, the average banks' capital to loan supply ratio, N^b/B, equal to 0.12.

We move now to elasticity. The inter-temporal elasticity of substitution, σ^c set at 0.75, Badarau and Popescu (2014). The elasticity of work disutility, σ^h, set at 0.5, which is in line with the calibration of Abdelli and Belhadj (2015). The capital price elasticity to investment, χ set at 0.25, Sangaré (2014). For the monetary policy, the degree of interest rate smoothing equal to 0.5, policy reaction to inflation and output calibrated at 1.5 and 0.54 respectively.

The weight of labor in utility, μ, is attuned to match the historical average joblessness rate of 10%. The depreciation rate of physical capital is set to 0.025, indicating that it takes 10 years to completely depreciate.

5   THE DYNAMIC RESULT
OF THE TUNISIAN ECONOMIC CYCLE

This section aims to analyze the inter-dependence between variables that measure the frictions in the credit market: the net worth of the firm and the bank, the external finance premium, investment, inflation , the output gap, the credit, and the rate of credit growth to GDP.

To present these points, the simulation and estimation approach is employed.

---

[6] In accordance to Badarau and Popescu (2014), $\overline{r^K} = 1/\beta$.

[7] As Bernanke et al. (1999), we suppose that the wage of entrepreneurial labor is equal to unity, and then its variation does not have a significant impact on the result.

5.1   Implicit Volatility and Autocorrelation

A way to measure the effectiveness of the model is to analyze its ability to embody the characteristics of the Tunisian economy. Tables 3 and 4 show the implicit volatility of the variables (standard deviation) and the autocorrelations respectively. In Table 3, we compare the volatility of output, inflation , nominal interest rate, bank net worth, credit level, and credit growth to GDP ratio, using real data and the estimated model. All the series are adjusted by the HP filter (Hedrick and Prescott).

The third and fourth columns show the volatility according to the model and the real data. It is noted that there is a correspondence between the volatility of the real and simulated variables. However, we observe that the fluctuations of the model variables are very close to each

Table 3   The implicit volatility of key variables (in percentages)

Variable	Description	Data	Model
Y_t	Output	0.901	1.06
by_t	Inflation	1.735	1.28
r_t^n	Nominal interest rate	2.106	1.80
n_t^b	The net value of the bank	6.775	5.78
bb_t	Credit supply	8.235	9.02
by_t	Credit/GDP	9.00	8.58

Source Authors' calculation based on data collected from Tunisian Central Bank

Table 4   Autocorrelations

Variable	Order 1	Order 2	Order 3	Order 4	Order 5
Output	0.6533	0.5326	0.5022	0.5164	0.5646
Investment	0.4996	0.2101	0.0266	−0.118	0.0178
Inflation	0.8764	0.7050	0.5555	0.4752	0.5073
Interest rate	0.6633	0.2775	−0.0276	−0.1935	−0.0907
Net value of the firm	0.9437	0.8669	0.8028	0.7770	0.8103
Net value of the bank	0.9664	0.9243	0.8901	0.8765	0.8952
E.F.P (firm)	0.7278	0.5011	0.3208	0.1862	0.3146
E.F.P (bank)	0.6555	0.3710	0.1465	−0.0198	0.1335
Credit supply	0.4430	0.0615	−0.2130	−0.4244	−0.2357
Credit to GDP ratio	0.4770	0.0846	−0.2098	−0.4292	−0.2425

Source Authors' calculation based on data collected from Tunisian Central Bank

other except for the credit level and the credit growth to GDP ratio. There is, therefore, coherence between the real variables while the fluctuation of the financial variables, relative to their equilibrium levels, is important. Therefore, these variables are elastic at the onset of any shock.

Table 4 demonstrates that inflation , the net worth of the entrepreneur, and the bank are very persistent with an autocorrelation coefficient over 0.8. Also, it highlights that the persistence of the external financing premium for entrepreneurs is very important as that of the banks. Thus, in the event of a shock, Tunisian firms are more threatened than banks.

5.2   Correlation Matrix

The correlation matrix, Table 4, is a symmetric table. We note that the interest rate has a strong positive correlation with the output gap and inflation, at least 77%, so the targeting of a single variable leads to the other one. Also, there is a negative correlation between the interest rate and the net worth of the bank and the company. Hence, the higher the rate of monetary policy increases, the more the financial wealth of the economic agents decreases. To replenish their wealth, these agents increase their savings to the detriment of consumers, the so-called wealth effect.[8] It is also important to note that the model succeeds to reproduce a negative correlation between the company's equity and its external financing premium. The 1% increase in net worth will lower the cost of borrowing by 80.02%. This channel is confirmed with the financial accelerator mechanism of Bernanke et al.(1999).

Similarly, the model shows that there is a strong negative correlation between the net value of the bank and its external financing premium. As a result, the lower the financial situation of the Tunisian banks, the more they paid more costs. Furthermore, Table 5 reveals that the higher the net worth of the company is, the more it has pushed to increase its investment project. This increase will reduce the share of the non-performing loan in the GDP and, thus, reduce the default payment. All things being equal, this mechanism leads to financial stabilization.

---

[8] The results are not shown in this table, but the consumption correlates negatively with the interest rate.

Table 5 The correlation matrix

	Y	I	rpm	P	N	Nb	Pfe	Pfb	Bb	bb/GDP
Output	1	–	–	–	–	–	–	–	–	–
Investment	0.7438	1	–	–	–	–	–	–	–	–
Nominal interest rate	0.7738	−0.8871	1	–	–	–	–	–	–	–
Inflation	0.4305	0.7387	0.8438	1	–	–	–	–	–	–
Firm's net worth	0.6253	0.1409	−0.3817	−0.5717	1	–	–	–	–	–
Bank net worth	0.6636	0.2437	−0.2356	−0.4258	0.9918	1	–	–	–	–
E.F.P (firms)	−0.0913	0.4799	0.8418	0.8325	−0.8000	−0.7330	1	–	–	–
E.F.P (banks)	−0.2153	0.3423	0.7700	0.8027	−0.8797	−0.8273	0.8291	1	–	–
Credit supply	0.4616	0.9077	0.4748	0.8358	−0.2864	−0.1843	0.8547	0.7046	1	–
Credit to GDP ratio	0.3616	0.8621	0.5333	0.8538	−0.3783	−0.2757	0.8258	0.7671	0.9940	1

Note E.F.P: External finance premium
Source Authors' calculation based on data collected from Tunisian Central Bank

6   Findings

We use the impulse response functions to analyze the dynamics of key variables under the standard Taylor rule with interest rate smoothing, see Fig. 1.

Figure 1 shows the repercussion of the financial shock on financial and macroeconomic variables. The financial shock was present by the boom-bust process introduced by Bernanke and Gertler (1989). The boom is reflected by the increase in asset prices, but their effect vanishes in the fourth period when the bust process occurs. Note that the horizontal axis pints the period and the vertical axis is the percentage deviation of each variable from its steady state. We exploit this shock for Tunisia in the period pre-and post the revolution.

As shown in Fig. 1, positive financial shock leads to a rise in output, an increase in inflation, and growth of credit. The intuition is as follows. The asset prices increase leads to improve the entrepreneur's net worth and thus, lowering its external finance cost. This, in turn, leads to rises in their credit possibilities and their demand investment. The bank's net

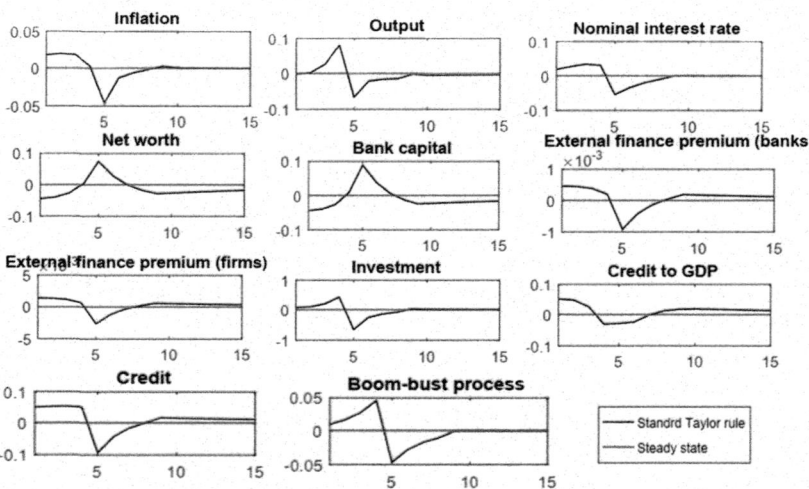

Fig. 1 Response of key variables to the boom-bust process (*Source* Authors' calculation based on data collected from Tunisian Central Bank)

worth also increases as borrowers become more solvent and thus their probability of default drops.

Inflation   also rises following the positive financial shock due to an increase in the marginal cost of the retailer, Eq. (13), and the increase of consumption. This increase pushes the central bank to increase its key interest rate.

6.1   The Dynamic of Macroeconomic and Financial Fundamentals Under the Baseline Monetary Policy

We use the impulse response functions to examine the dynamics of key variables under the standard Taylor rule with interest rate smoothing, see Fig. 1.

The figure shows the repercussion of the financial shock on financial and macroeconomic variables. The financial shock present by the boom-bust process introduced by Bernanke and Gertler (1989). The boom is reflected by the increase in asset prices, but their effect vanishes in the fourth period when the bust process occurs. Note that the horizontal axis pints the period and the vertical axis is the percentage deviation of each variable from its steady state. We exploit this shock for Tunisia in the period pre- and post the revolution.

As shown in Fig. 1, positive financial shock mains to a rise in output, an increase in inflation , and a growth of credit. The perception is as follows. The asset prices increase leads to improve the entrepreneur's net worth and thus, lowering its external finance cost. This, in turn, leads to rises in their credit possibilities and their demand investment. The bank's net worth also increases as borrowers become more solvent and thus their probability of default drops.

Inflation   also rises following the positive financial shock due to an increase in the marginal cost of the retailer, Eq. (13), and the increase of consumption. This increase pushes the central bank to increase its key interest rate.

However, once the negative shock occurs the result does not the same. The net value of the bank begins to decline slowly, which negatively influences its external finance premium and the cost of external funds of the firm. This result is confirmed with the conclusion of Dolignon et al. Badarau and Levienge (2011), in which the banking capital plays a financial accelerator role that amplifies the effect of a negative shock on real economic activity.

Concerning the credit' level, we observe that its value has increased in the first period of the bubble and remained constant throughout this phase. In the fifth phase, when the negative financial shock arises, the credit falls below its equilibrium value because it is offered at a variable interest rate (the company's risk margin will be significant following the devaluation of asset prices). Thus, even if the central bank decides to lower its interest rate, the bank cannot pass this reduction on the level of credit offered.

6.2   *Financial Shock and Augmented Taylor Rule*

We analyze the dynamics of the keys variables (GDP, inflation, credit, and credit to GDP ratio) if the central bank applied an augmented Taylor rule. Recall that the augmented Taylor rule is as follows:

$$r_t^n = \beta_0 r_{t-1}^n + (1 - \beta_0)(\beta_\pi \pi_t + \beta_y y_t + \beta_{by} by_t)$$

With by_t is the log deviation of the credit growth ratio to the GDP from its equilibrium state. β_π and β_y have the same calibration as in the standard Taylor rule.

To test the effectiveness of the augmented Taylor rule, two cases are considered: the first case where the Tunisian Central Bank does not have the objective of financial stabilization, but it monitors only the evolution of credit. According to Badarau and Popescu (2014), we consider a weak reaction of the credit growth to GDP ratio equal to 0.1, so the CBT aim only to control the evolution of credit supply. In the second case, this ratio is increased to 0.5, which implies that the CBT aims to stabilize the financial variables. The result of these two tests is shown in Fig. 2. In this figure, the black line shows the standard Taylor rule, the red line corresponds to the variation of keys variables in the context of the augmented Taylor rule. The blue line analyzes the difference of credit supply under the augmented and the standard Taylor rules.

The inclusion of a financial stress indicator in the Taylor rule means that the monetary authority has a relatively high interest rate. In the optimal case, a weak introduction of the financial stress indicator, $\beta_{by} = 0.1$, has a positive impact on the output gap and credit supply during the boom-bust process. Whereas, the reaction of inflation is volatile. Even during the first period of the booming process, it registers a low level related to the standard Taylor rule, but as the boom continues, inflation

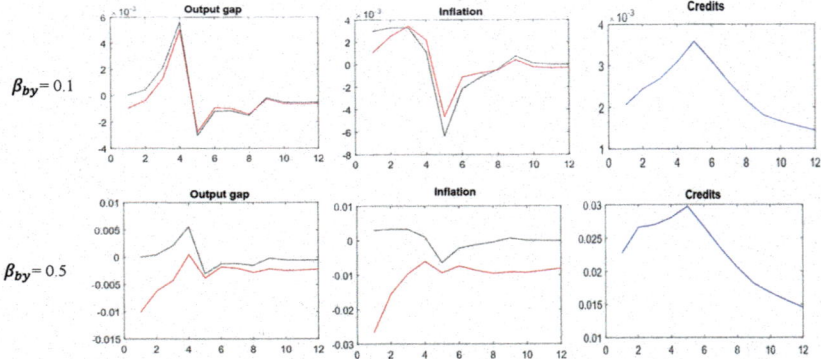

Fig. 2 The variation of the key variables under augmented and standard Taylor rules (*Source* Authors' calculation based on data collected from Tunisian Central Bank)

increase (in the third period). The bust period does not record the change in inflation , but the credit and output gap dynamics differ.

Concerning the difference of credit supply under augmented and standard Taylor rule, in the booming process the difference is positive and an upward trend (i.e., the credit provided under the augmented Taylor rule is more important than under the standard one), in the bust phase, the credit begins to fall but remain at a positive level. The shortfall in the value of the assets during the first period of the bubble increases the firm's capacity to borrow by presenting its assets' portfolio as collateral. As soon as prices drop their credit request will decrease.

Given the inflation pressure, a weak weighting of the credit growth to GDP ratio proves sufficient to control the output gap and credit dynamics but not the same for price stability. This result will be the same if the central bank decides to increase again the nominal interest rate?

Panel (b) in Fig. 2 shows that inflation remains volatile during the boom-bust process but has a very low level compared to the standard Taylor rule. However, the monetary policy tightening promotes the banking deposit and strongly penalizes the investment in equities. This pushes operators to desert the financial investment and to better position themselves in bank deposits, which causes the fall of the stock market.

On the one hand, the collapse of the stock market strengthens the under-capitalization of banks and on the other hand, it has limited the credits supply for the firms that present their assets as collateral.

7   CONCLUSION

We aim to understand how the central bank could advance the reaction of the economy in case of a financial bubble by only using its interest rate instrument. By simulating a DSGE model of Badarau and Popescu (2014), we compare the dynamics of financial and macroeconomic variables under a standard Taylor rule with those under an augmented one.

This paper highlights the amplifying consequence of the financial shock in the context of financial friction. The implicit volatility test shows that financial variables are more volatile than reals variables. Therefore, in the short term, financial variables are more affected at the beginning of any shock. This will be confirmed by the impulse response function.

We find that the booming process leads to a rise in output, an increase in inflation, and a growth of credit. However, once the negative financial shock occurs the result does not be the same. During this period financial variables, especially the credit cycle, are very volatile. Therefore, in the event of financial shock, the Standard Taylor rule finds ineffective in terms of economic stability (Xinyu et al., 2020).

The result improves if the central bank augmented the Taylor rule by a financial variable, credit growth to GDP ratio. The impulse response function demonstrates that the inclusion of a weak reaction of financial stress indicator in the Taylor rule, $\beta_{by} = 0.1$, has a positive impact on the output gap and credit supply during the boom-bust process. Whereas, the reaction of inflation remains volatile. The introduction of higher weight of credit growth to GDP ratio, equal to 0.5, in the monetary rule has sharply increased the interest rate. This monetary policy tightening reduces the inflation volatility but strongly penalizes the output and the investment on equities, which imbalance the economic stability.

We conclude that when the central bank decides to lean in contradiction of the wind, it should put a real trade-off between financial stability and price stability (Féve et al., 2019). Therefore, even the monetary authorities take charge of the macro-prudential objective in its reaction function, it should be proactive and reactive to reach a higher degree of effectiveness. The strength of policymakers resides in their flexibility to occurrence this trade-off.

REFERENCES

Abdelli, S., & Belhadj, B. (2015). The dynamic stochastic general equilibrium model for the monetary policy in Tunisia. *Global Journal of Human-Social Science Economic, 15*(1), 1–14.

Badarau, C., & Levieuge, G. (2011). Assessing the effects of financial heterogeneity in a monetary union: A DSGE approach. *Economic Modelling, 28*(6), 2451–2461.

Badarau, C., & Popescu, A. (2014). Monetary policy and credit cycles: A DSGE analysis. *Economic Modelling, 42*, 301–312.

Bernanke, B. S., & Gertler, M. (1989). Agency costs, net worth, and business fluctuations. *American Economic Review, 79*(1), 14–31.

Bernanke, B. S., Gertler, M., & Gilchrist, S. (1999). The financial accelerator in a quantitative business cycle framework. In M. Woodford & J. B. Taylor (Eds.), *Handbook of macroeconomics* (Vol. 1, pp. 1341–1393). National Bureau of Economic Research.

Blanchard, O., & Galí, J. (2007). Real Wage Rigidities and the New Keynésien Model. *Journal of Money, Credit and Banking, 39*(1), 35–65.

Blas, B., & Malmierca, M. (2020). Financial frictions and stabilization policies. *Economic Modelling, 89*(C), 166–188.

Boissay, F. (2001). *Credit rationing, output gap, and business cycles* (Working Paper BCE, n°87).

Carlstrom, C. H., & Fuerst, T. (1997). Agency costs, net worth, and business fluctuations: A computable general equilibrium analysis. *American Economic Review, 87*(5), 893–910.

Carstens, A. (2020). *Monetary policy: 10 years after the financial crisis*. Bank for International Settlements.

Christensen, I., Meh, C., & Moran, K. (2011). *Bank leverage regulation and macroeconomic dynamics* (Working Paper, Bank of Canada, n°. 11–32).

Christiano, L. J., Motto, R., & Rostagno, M. (2010). *Financial factors in economic fluctuations* (ECB Working Paper, n° 1192).

Curdia, V., & Woodford, M. (2009). *Credit frictions and optimal monetary policy* (BIS Working Papers, n° 278).

Féve, P., Moura, A., & Olivier, P. (2019). Shadow banking and financial regulation: A small-scale DSGE perspective. *Journal of Economic Dynamics and Control, 101*, 130–144.

Gambacorta, L., & Signoretti, F. R. (2014). Should monetary policy lean against the wind? *Journal of Economic Dynamic and Control, 43*, 146–174.

Gerali, A., Neri, S. S., & Signoretti, F. (2010). Credit and banking in a DSGE model of the Euro Area. *Journal of Money, Credit and Banking, 42*(1), 107–141.

Gertler, M., & Karadi, P. (2011). A model of unconventional monetary policy. *Journal of Monetary Economics, 58*(1), 17–34.

Gilchrist, S., & Zakrajsek, E. (2012). Credit spreads and business cycle fluctuations. *The American Economic Review, 102*(4), 1692–1720.

Goodfriend, M., & McCallum, T. (2007). Banking and interest rates in monetary policy analysis: A quantitative exploration. *Journal of Monetary Economics, 54*(5), 1480–1507.

Hirakata, N., Sudo, N., & Ueda, K. (2009). *Chained credit contracts and financial accelerators* (Bank of Japan Discussion Paper, n° E-30).

Iacoviello, M. (2005). House prices, borrowing constraints and monetary policy in the business cycle. *American Economic Review, 95*(3), 739–764.

Iliopulos, E., & Sopraseuth, T. (2012). *L'intermédiation financière dans l'analyse macroéconomique: le défi de la crise* (Economie et statistique, n° 451–453).

Jbeli, S. (2012). *Une analyse de l'importance des facteurs financières dans le mécanisme de transmission de la politique monétaire en économie ouverte.* Thèses de Doctorat en science économique, université de Rennes 1, 202 pp.

Jouini, N., & Rebei, N. (2014). The welfare implication of services liberalization in a developing country. *Journal of Development Economic, 106*, 1–14.

Kiyotaki, N., & Moore, J. (1997). Credit cycles. *Journal of Political Economy, 105*, 211–248.

Kolasa, M., & Rubaszek, M. (2015, December). How frequently should we re-estimate DSGE models? *International Journal of Central Banking, 11*(4), 279–305.

Krug, S. (2018). The interaction between monetary and macroprudential policy: Should central banks 'lean against the wind' to foster macro-financial stability? *Economics, 12.*

Le Moigne, C. (2013). *Les interactions entre politique macro-prudentielle et monétaire* (centre d'analyse stratégique, n°04, pp. 1–62).

Mark, M., & Sebastiaan, P. (2018). *Bank recapitalizations, credit supply, and the transmission of monetary policy* (De Nederlandsche Bank Working Paper No. 616).

Meh, C. (2011). Bilans des banques, réduction du levier financier et mécanisme de transmission. *Revue de la banque du Canada,* pp. 25–36

Meh, C., & Moran, K. (2010). The role of bank capital in the propagation of shocks. *Journal of Economic Dynamics and Control, 34*(3), 555–576.

Mishkin, F. (2011). *Monetary policy strategy: Lessons from the crisis* (NBER Working Paper, n° 16755).

Modigliani, F., & Miller, M. H. (1958). The cost of capital, corporation finance and the theory of investment. *The American Economic Review, 48*(3), 261–297.

Philipp, L. (2018). *Financial Frictions, the Phillips Curve and Monetary Policy* (Munich Personal RePEc Archive, MPRA Paper No. 89429).

Pirozhkova, E. (2017). *Financial frictions and robust monetary policy in the models of New Keynesian framework* (BCAM Working Papers 1701). Birkbeck Centre for Applied Macroeconomics.

Sangaré, I. (2014). *Chocs extérieurs et régime monétaires en Asie de sud-Est: une analyse DSGE* (Larefi Working Paper, n°02, pp. 1–55).

Schularick, M., & Taylor, A. M. (2012). Credit booms gone bust: Monetary policy, leverage cycles, and financial crises. *The American Economic Review, 102*(2), 1029–1061.

Smets, F. (2014, June). Financial stability and monetary policy: How closely interlinked? *International Journal of Central Banking, 10*(2), 263–300.

Smets, F., & Wouters, R. (2003). An estimated stochastic dynamic general equilibrium model for the Euro Area. *Journal of the European Economic Association, 1,* 1123–1175.

Tetlow, R. J. (2005). *Monetary policy, asset prices, and misspecification: The robust approach to bubbles with model uncertainty.* Bank of Canada.

Townsend, R. (1979). *Optimal contracts and competitive markets with costly state verification* (Federal Reserve Bank of Minneapolis Staff Report, n° 45).

Woodford, M. (2003). *Interest and prices.* Princeton University Press.

Xinyu, G., Xiao-Lin, L., & Zheng, L. (2020, July). The transmission of financial shocks in an estimated DGE model with housing and banking. *Economic Modelling,* 215–231.

Zhu, Q. Y. (1991). *Modèle Bayésienne à l'estimation des caractéristiques de produit finis et au contrôle de la qualité.* Thèses de Doctorat des sciences économique, l'école national des ponts et chaussées, 27 p.

Masdar Sustainable Company and the Global Reporting Initiative Standards 2016: A Case Study from the United Arab Emirates

Mohamed Chakib Kolsi and Ahmad Al-Hiyari

1 INTRODUCTION

Since many decades, the United Arab Emirates (UAE) federal authorities have adopted strategic long-term plans of sustainability, socially responsible organizations, and entities for the well-being of the community namely by the announcement of the UAE 2030 vision and the preparation for global important events (EXPO 2020, World Summit on Sustainability Abu Dhabi 2019, GITEX annual IT fair in Dubai, 2023 UN Climate Change Conference COP28 that will be held in the UAE, etc.). Such goals have been accelerated with the introduction of new emerging technologies in different fields including "paperless" administration, green

M. C. Kolsi (✉) · A. Al-Hiyari
Faculty of Business, Liwa College of Technology,
Abu Dhabi, UAE
e-mail: Mohamed.Kolsi@ect.ac.ae

A. Al-Hiyari
e-mail: ahmed.alhiyari@ect.ac.ae

M. C. Kolsi
University of Sfax, Sfax, Tunisia

economy with zero CO_2 emission target rates, artificial intelligence, and blockchain technology for financial markets' applications. The UAE is an oasis of economic and political stability allowing different business centres with numerous impressive multinational corporations to be established.

By considering the major business assistance, UAE companies are now focusing more on Corporate Social Responsibility (Hereafter, CSR) considerations and sustainability to manage the business environment. Climate changes, faster demographic growth, and natural disasters have created different problematic situations for businesses. According to Duthler and Dhanesh (2018), the practice of CSR can generate the standard pathway in dealing with the necessary market requirements while taking care of the proper financial approaches and technical prospects. For instance, charitable activities in the UAE are strongly influenced by the Islamic Shariaa (law). Managers often regard the concept of CSR to be a corporate form of Zakat, the percentage of wealth that pertains to poor people. Indeed, the federal authorities have declared CSR as a pillar of the Year of Giving, 2017. Over 400,000 companies across the country will be asked to execute mandatory CSR initiatives.[1] These CSR funds will be audited and reported to the federal authorities.

The minister of economy, *S. Al Mansouri* announced in 2017 that companies are required to register in the smart platform including areas that depend on society's expectations. This platform will also provide guides, examples, and models on how to implement CSR and share the success stories of companies. Also, companies are ranked based on the percentage of their contributions to community projects and the CSR performance index. Among the eleven initiatives of the "Year of Giving", 2017. Seven requirements are related to CSR issues including (1) Smart Platform related to CSR initiatives need in the country. (2) National CSR Index that will list companies involved in philanthropy actions. (3) CSR Passport granted to the top five performing companies, giving them priority in governmental projects. (4) Social Responsibility Label granted to companies according to their contributions to community responsible projects. (5) Companies will be evaluated upon a mandatory declaration of their CSR performance. (6) Companies with higher social responsibility contributions will be granted financial funds. Finally, (7) the full process will be assessed by a social responsibility committee.

---

[1] https://www.khaleejtimes.com/business/local/csr-to-be-compulsory-for-uae-companies.

In this regard, Masdar Company, the Abu Dhabi future energy company (Hereafter, Masdar Co.), is a leading group in renewable energy and sustainable development both in the UAE and the Middle East region. Accurate information planning related to Masdar Co. and direction also helps to specify the idea of generating proper buying decisions by gaining enough business information from the market (Gallego-Álvarez et al., 2018). The policy-making approaches within Masdar Co. become supportive where the consumers and businesspeople get strategic interests with information for long-term growth. Masdar Co.'s. commitment to follow the proper policy and fulfilment of ethical requirements assists to deal with the focused work-based integration. Moreover, focusing on both stakeholder management and following CSR business opportunities direct and manage continuous financial assistance in this prospect. The field of business ethics along with the social and environmental approaches within Masdar Co. is an important aspect to consider.

The aim of this case study is to highlight and analyze the CSR disclosure practices of Masdar Co. with regards to international standards by generating proper business integration across the globe with regards to the Global Reporting Initiative Standards (GRI, 2016).[2] Mezher et al. (2010) presented a qualitative overview based on interviews of Masdar Co. CSR practices. However, they do not measure the extent of such disclosures nor present a comparison with other companies or standards. Our study differs from Mezher et al. (2010) by the following objectives: First, we display and discuss CSR disclosure practices of Masdar Co. Second, we compare Masdar Co. CSR practices with the Global Reporting Initiative Standards GRI 2016. Finally, we propose a useful framework of best practices for companies in the UAE and abroad that adhere to CSR activities complying with international standards.

2 CORPORATE SOCIAL RESPONSIBILITY IN THE UAE: THEORETICAL BACKGROUND AND EMPIRICAL EVIDENCE

2.1 *Theoretical Background*

Corporate social responsibility is an essential concept that deals with the voluntary efforts to make the different businesses appropriate by considering key benefits to society (Al-Hiyari & Kolsi, 2021). CSR concept is

---

[2] https://www.globalreporting.org/about-gri/mission-history/.

based on many theories including: Social Contract Theory (SCT), Stakeholders' Theory (Freeman & Reed, 1983), Legitimacy Theory (Suchman, 1995), and Signalling Theory (Trueman & Titman, 1986). As suggested by Miralles-Quiros et al. (2017) argued that companies are asked to take responsibility for the impact of their activities on the environment and society and how they are managing this impact. According to The World Business Council for Sustainable Development,[3] CSR disclosure is defined as the commitment to sustainable economic development. It is achieved through continuous efforts between employees and their representatives and the public to improve the quality of life in ways that give benefit both for themselves and the business development. Definitions of CSR concept are evolving since the 1960s. Frederick (1960) defined CSR as a willingness to see that firm resources are utilized for broad social ends and not simply for the narrowly financial benefits of private persons and firms. Johnson (1971) argued that a socially responsible firm balances the interests of numerous stakeholders to encompass suppliers, dealers, employees, customers, local communities, and the nation instead of focusing on the ultimate profit maximization goal. Finally, The CSR concept will remain a primary pillar of business language that evolves with firms' strategic goals.

2.2   Empirical Evidence

Since the UAE is a leading country in the Middle East region and a Hub for various sustainable developments projects and initiatives, many empirical studies have highlighted the determinants, extent, and impact of CSR on the UAE economic tissue and capital markets using different industrial sectors (Kolsi & Attayah, 2018). For instance, Kumar and Balakrishnan (2011) used a sample of 50 organizations in the UAE to compare the existing CSR practices with the framework of the European Foundation for Quality Management (EFQM) with the best CSR practices using 5 approaches and 8 main variables. Their results show that the existing CSR fields of the UAE organizations were compared with the 5 basic approaches of the EFQM framework and validated that all those approaches had a significant impact on companies' CSR performance. Future enhancements of CSR approaches will be validated to comply with UAE 2030 strategic vision.

---

[3] http://www.wbcsd.org/.

Arshad et al. (2015) attempted first, to describe CSR disclosures of the UAE banks in response to the 2008 Global financial crisis. Second, they identified key factors determining the CSR disclosure policy of the UAE companies. Results show that both the extent and quality of CSR disclosures are enhanced after the crisis. Specifically, their findings show that bank size, board of directors' composition, and profitability level are positively associated with the CSR discloure policy of UAE banks. However, financial leverage is negatively related to CSR disclosures. Anadol et al. (2015) examined CSR awareness and related activities of UAE consumers regarding their age, gender, and location. Results show significant differences between gender in terms of complaints reporting to organizations and government and boycotting behaviour. Moreover, consumers' age significantly impacts job preferences and donation actions. Finally, consumers' opinions and behaviour in reporting products' quality vary across the seven Emirates. Nobanee and Ellili (2016) measured the extent of CSR disclosures of UAE Islamic and conventional banks. Their results show that, although the overall level of disclosures is lower for the two kinds of banks, it is more valued by conventional banks than Islamic banks. Alternatively, sustainability disclosures are positively associated with banks' financial performance.

Kolsi and Attayah (2018) highlighted three main fields of CSR disclosures: the *determinants, measure, and impact* on firm value by using a sample of sixty-one firms listed on the Abu Dhabi Stock Exchange (ADX). Their results show that firm size, leverage ratio, board size, listing history, and governmental sector, have a positive impact on CSR disclosures of ADX listed companies. However, ownership concentration, profitability ratio, and firm sector have no impact on the extent of CSR disclosures. Finally, CSR disclosures and firm value (as proxied by the market-to-book ratio) are not significantly related.

Farouk and Jabeen (2018) tested whether the ethical climate is positively associated with CSR and organizational performance for UAE public sector companies, a major component of the UAE economic tissue. By using a questionnaire addressed to public sector employees, their results show the importance of ethical climate in organizations for moral reasons and practical impact. Firms engaging in an ethical climate will benefit from positive employees' engagement and positive overall organizational performance.

In sum, most of the above studies highlighted the importance of CSR considerations for both UAE organizations and governmental authorities. Considerable efforts have been made in promoting sustainability across the country to reach international relevant standards in CSR and achieve higher levels of ESG performance resulting in the establishment of various laws, regulations, and sustainable projects. Nonetheless, additional efforts should be made by UAE companies to achieve higher levels of social and environmental performance levels.

3   RESEARCH METHODOLOGY

3.1   Company Profile

With its headquarters in Abu Dhabi, Masdar Co, or the Abu Dhabi Future Energy Company is a renewable energy company and a subsidiary of Mubadala Development Company founded in 2006. Masdar Co. is a commercially driven renewable energy company, which is a significant governmental initiative. The company tends to have a mission to invest and incubate the new strategy within the emerging industries in Abu Dhabi (Annisa, 2019). Masdar Co. is essentially involved with varied international ventures. A part of the basic business activity that is being carried out by Masdar Co. lies in the fact that the company tends to invest in and develop renewable energy technologies. In addition to this, for the sole purpose of attaining proper business growth, the company aims at developing as well as investing in high-quality sustainable and economical projects. These projects are characterized by economical clean energy projects that help in evaluating and entering bankable renewable energy opportunities and that of technologies.

As per the current business activities that are being carried out by Masdar Co, it is important to understand investments projects the company tends to carry out. The company will be launching a sustainable real estate investment trust, which would have a valuation of over 950 million AED. On the other hand, another major financial investment that is an ongoing project is that of the Masdar City project. The financial evaluation of this project accounts for over $22 billion and is a carbon–neutral, green city in the desert. Masdar City is taking care of the valuable CSR technique that helps generate future development and growth-based supportiveness to boost its brand (Anundi & Hultman, 2018). The four dimensions such as economic, legal, ethical, and philanthropic follow the CSR technique and manage coordinated relationships with society. Masdar is embracing the proper change by creating a channel with the environmental approaches where the values regarding human rights, anti-corruption, labour standards are the key principles (Masdar.ae,

2020). The global compact initiated the major change based on voluntary learning and based on the same CSR conceptualization for the UAE companies helping to build constructive development and progression (Arora & Jyoti, 2019).

The Global Reporting Initiative has proposed and managed the economic resources by directing the major idea about future development and progression based on overall requirements. The inspirational goal of Masdar Co. regarding sustainable processes by promoting the GRI standard initiative and states the significant organizational segment. Communication approaches, as well as the comparability technique, help to project and standardize the key engagement based on the quality information direction for future segments (Wójcik-Jurkiewicz & Sadowska, 2018). The stakeholders of Masdar Co. are focusing on the GRI standards and applying the best prospects that assure accountability and global comparability. Sustainability reporting related to the GRI standards initiates a reasonable and balanced work system procedure that brings a positive contribution towards the major goal. Renewable and other nonrenewable materials encompass recycled input materials by stating the proper information about natural resource management and direction.

Different UAE firms are taking help from the CSR activities and managing to generate information that focuses on supportive decision-making prospects. Continuum ranges of focused information planning and direction build supportive legal and ethical progression that builds a better work system-based perspective (Sarraj, 2018). It has been seen that corporate management assistance and coordination also follow various important resources that agree to manage constructive stakeholder strategy planning and direction.

3.2   Period Under Study and Data Collection

Data collection is a significant tool that would help in understanding the techniques required to acquire methodological perspectives. Data collection further helps in acquiring the results and findings that would help in assessing the extent to which the study gains significance. With the use of the sustainability reports that have been derived from the company website, it has managed to create a significant insight into the definite business activities and financial transactions that are being carried out by them. Hence, from this definite point of view, it can be stated that the use of proper data collection processes helps a researcher to be able to identify and assess the significant elements of research in an effective manner (Ekergil & Özgür Göde, 2017).

For the sole purpose of carrying out the research, the study was carried out using the sustainability reports of the company. It has managed to provide valuable insight into the definite ways with the help of which the company has managed to gain a significant association of the definite business activities that are being carried out by Masdar Co. Hence, based on this definite aspect, the study has been conducted with the help of sustainability reports of the years ranging between 2013 and 2019. According to the 2013 sustainability report, it has been found that Masdar Co. has managed to produce over 1,735,000 Megawatt/hour of Clean Energy. The company has further managed to advance its renewable energy and sustainable technologies, which has managed to provide them with effective business development. On the other hand, as per the 2014 sustainability report, the company has come forward to embrace the association of digital transformation that would help them to unlock substantial new economic growth. Lastly, the 2019 sustainability report of Masdar Co. has gained significant financial growth that has aided in achieving a sustainable financial market globally.

3.3   Research Methodology

Research methodology is a significant key element in the context of a research study. It helps in the proper identification of the methodological tools that are required for the conducting of research effectively. The research study is associated with the proper assessment of the definite business activities that are being carried out by Masdar Co. Hence, based on this assessment, content analysis has been selected. The aspects of content analysis are a significant research tool, which helps in the acute determination of concepts within a given qualitative data. In the context of this research, the content analysis will be carried out with the information that is derived from the sustainability reports of Masdar Co. This procedure would eventually encompass a comparative analysis of the CSR disclosures of the company each year and the extent to which Masdar Co. has managed to carry out an extensive assessment of the GRI 2016 standards effectively.

4   DISCUSSION OF THE RESULTS

4.1   *Analysis of the Universal Disclosures Standards (GRI 100) Results*

Analysis of both Table 1 and Fig. 1 shows that "management approach standards" are the most disclosed GRI 103 item across the full period rather than general and foundation approaches. This indicates that Masdar Co. leaders stressed mainly on the strategic mission and vision of the company for the long run to assure sustainability. Managing the working group-based approaches and creating regulatory assistance also requires to be stated particularly in this segment. The helpful coordination and supportive information planning-based direction related to the different policies also need to be considered and generated. Job security standards along with the information confidentiality assistance can be helpful to

Table 1   Universal disclosure standards distribution (2014–2019)

Year	GRI 101	GRI 102	GRI 103
2014	1	1	19
2015	1	2	12
2016	1	1	3
2017	0	0	7
2018	0	0	4

Source Authors' summary based on data collected from Masdar Co.

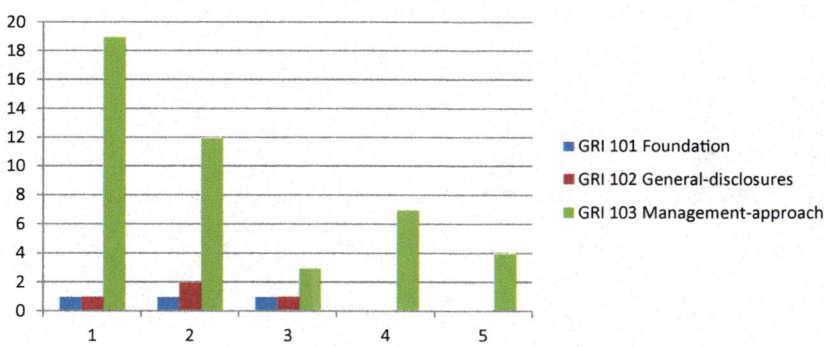

Fig. 1   Universal disclosure standards (GRI 100) for the full period (*Source* Authors' summary based on data collected from Masdar Co.)

regulate and manage the coordinated employees. The proper digital use and security standards also are not focused particularly, and it has generated different issues for the company as it cannot be able to concentrate on the development, planning, and affirmation for action implementation.

4.2   Analysis of Economic Disclosures Standards (GRI 200) Results

Both Table 2 and Fig. 2 summarize economic disclosure standards GRI 200. Both economic performance GRI 201 and market presence GRI 202 are the most disclosed items indicating the leading position of Masdar Co. both in the UAE and the region. In fact, Masdar Co. coupled with its affiliate Masdar City lead the investment efforts in sustainable projects since their creation. The specification followed that Masdar Co. has concentrated on the supply procedure by managing the focused work

Table 2   Economic disclosure standards distribution (2014–2019)

Year	GRI 201	GRI 202	GRI 203	GRI 204	GRI 205	GRI 206	GRI 207
2014	225	5	23	28	3	5	1
2015	78	8	14	14	3	7	0
2016	33	8	5	7	3	2	0
2017	16	48	7	3	0	1	4
2018	14	15	4	0	1	0	0

Source Authors' summary based on data collected from Masdar Co.

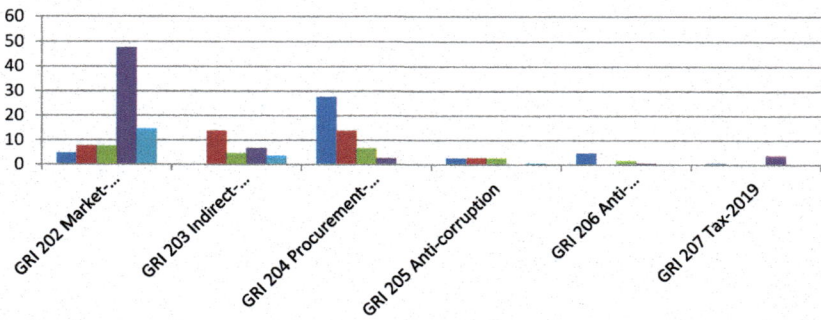

Fig. 2   Economic disclosure standards (GRI 200) (*Source* Authors' summary based on data collected from Masdar Co.)

system planning that directs a systematic understanding of the market requirements. Effective products and service coordination by generating stakeholder integration follow and correlate with the co-innovation structure and accessing better technological assistance. Global Sustainable assistance and helpful projection support the applicable meeting with the stakeholders by accessing demand-side management planning. However, the tax-related standard GRI 2019 still lacks disclosure magnitude due to the newly emerging tax regulations in the UAE and the GCC region starting 2018. Finally, both GRI 205 and GRI 206 related to anti-corruption and anti-competitive behaviour are disclosed with a minimum level due to the transparency and efficiency of Masdar Co. strategies and procedures that eliminate any unethical and anti-competitive behaviour.

4.3   Analysis of Environmental Disclosure Standards (GRI 300) Results

Both Table 3 and Fig. 3 show that Masdar Co. stressed on environmental disclosure GRI 300 more than other standards. Being one of the leading companies in the region and abroad in terms of clean energy use and sustainability, Masdar Co. has complied with a greater extent with GRI standards over the full period (2014–2019). The "GRI 302 energy" and "GRI 303 water-saving" were the most disclosed items that comply with the goal of Masdar Co., followed by environmental protection and waste management & recycling. Table 3 shows that environmental standards are the most important disclosed items through the full period.

Finally, analysis of Table 4 and Fig. 4 shows greater importance of GRI 402 Labour-management-relations, GRI 403 Occupational health and

Table 3   Environmental disclosure standards distribution (2014–2019)

Year	GRI 301	GRI 302	GRI 303	GRI 304	GRI 305	GRI 306	GRI 307	GRI 308
2014	31	245	114	12	18	80	103	32
2015	13	114	47	6	12	50	42	29
2016	9	45	19	2	2	4	10	20
2017	20	307	235	45	45	60	43	1
2018	1	92	47	25	25	24	6	0

Source Authors' summary based on data collected from Masdar Co.

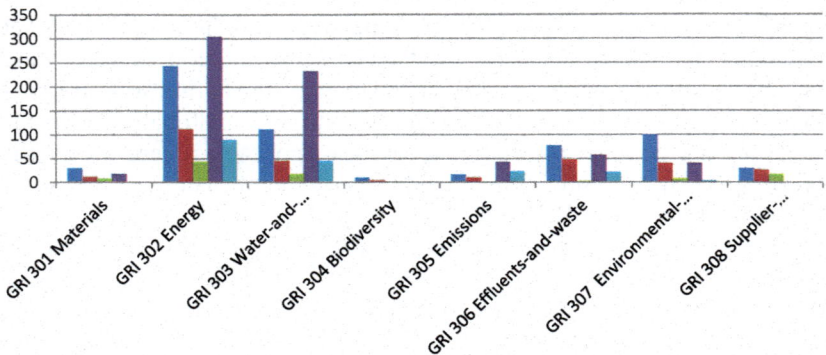

Fig. 3 Environmental disclosure standards (GRI 300) (*Source* Authors' summary based on data collected from Masdar Co.)

safety-2018, GRI 404 Training and education, and GRI 405 Diversity-and-equal-opportunity, followed by GRI 414 supplier-social-assessment, GRI 415 public policy, and GRI 416 customer-health and safety. Such standards follow the general policy of both Masdar Co. and UAE federal authorities in implementing Emiratisation strategy and providing higher-skilled employees for all companies across the UAE through continuous training and development programmes. The gender diversity in the leading positions is highly followed by Masdar Co. Finally, both worker's and customer's safety instructions are of greater interest for Masdar Co.

5   CONCLUSION

The aim of this case study is to highlight CSR disclosure practices of Masdar Co. with regards to the Global Reporting Initiative GRI 2016 standards. The success of Masdar's Co. has been attributed to the greater compliance with CSR initiatives effectively as well as through efficient managing of its business aims. Masdar Co. approaches are supportive to both customers and stakeholders. The corporate commitment has been followed through policies as well as its fulfilment in the ethical requirements for assisting the work-based integration. Masdar's Co. has used CSR opportunities in the UAE and boosted its brand by considering the valuable CSR practices to generate future growth and development. The crucial dimensions such as ethical, legal, and philanthropic are used

Table 4 Social disclosure standards distribution (2014–2019)

Year	GRI 401	GRI 402	GRI 403	GRI 404	GRI 405	GRI 406	GRI 407	GRI 408	GRI 409	GRI 410	GRI 411	GRI 412	GRI 413	GRI 414	GRI 415	GRI 416	GRI 417	GRI 418	GRI 419
2014	5	19	83	15	17	2	1	6	4	5	2	9	12	32	14	15	4	14	0
2015	5	21	5	11	10	2	1	6	4	4	1	9	6	29	5	11	3	11	0
2016	4	15	18	6	4	2	0	6	5	2	0	0	9	20	1	6	1	4	0
2017	1	14	14	22	0	2	0	0	1	1	0	1	4	1	15	4	3	4	0
2018	1	30	5	0	2	0	0	2	2	15	0	0	2	0	10	0	0	0	0

Source Authors' summary based on data collected from Masdar Co.

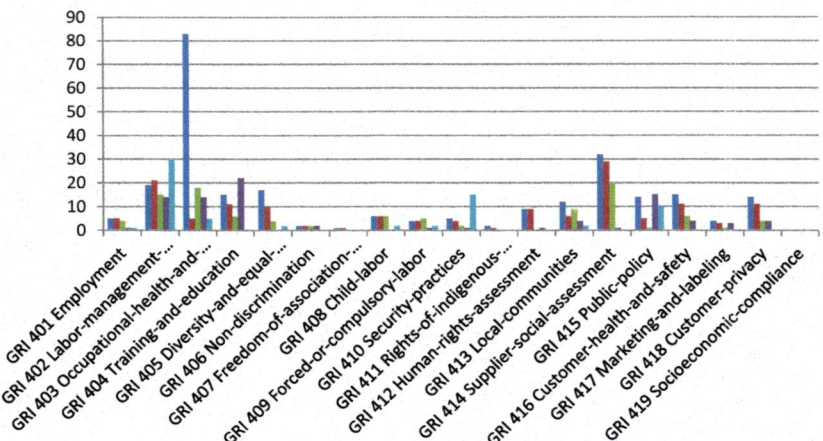

Fig. 4 Social disclosure standards (GRI 400) (*Source* Authors' summary based on data collected from Masdar Co.)

for managing as well as coordinating the effective interactions with the society. Results also show that Masdar Co. was successful to a greater extent with GRI 2016 standards compliance in general disclosures GRI 100, economic disclosures GRI 200, environmental disclosures GRI 300, and finally social disclosures GRI 400.

However, some limitations related to proper implementation of the GRI Standards as well as the sustainability assessment have not been applied properly. Moreover, we notice that CSR practices of Masdar Co. lack proper structuring as many other organizations focus on the same procedures to ensure future growth and this prospect is generating various issues. Following the ESG 2019 standards' guide issued by the Abu Dhabi Securities Exchange Market (ADX) that encompasses 31 ESG indicators, sufficient information planning and leadership engagement of Masdar Co. follow necessary attention about the senior management criteria. The performance assessment with the followed business-based reflection requires stating the talent management planning by focusing on those KPI accomplishments for Masdar Co. Generate feedback from the employees, create standard assistance, and improve employees' performance criteria deal perfectly with reward planning and career development. Setting up organizational and employee-based assistance within Masdar Co. by directing the acceptable corporate behaviour helps to initiate focused work planning and direction. Lastly, Masdar Co. is a pioneering company in the UAE and the Middle East region offering a unique sustainable experience that should inspire other entities both locally and abroad.

APPENDIX A: FULL GLOBAL REPORTING INITIATIVE STANDARDS

	Standards	Label
Universal Standards	GRI 101	Foundation
	GRI 102	General disclosures
	GRI 103	Management-approach
Economic Standards	GRI 201	Economic performance
	GRI 202	Market-presence
	GRI 203	Indirect-economic-impacts
	GRI 204	Procurement-practices
	GRI 205	Anti-corruption
	GRI 206	Anti-competitive behaviour
	GRI 207	Tax-2019
Environmental Standards	GRI 301	Materials
	GRI 302	Energy
	GRI 303	Water-and-effluents-2018
	GRI 304	Biodiversity
	GRI 305	Emissions
	GRI 306	Effluents-and-waste
	GRI 307	Environmental compliance
	GRI 308	Supplier-environmental-assessment
Social Standards	GRI 401	Employment
	GRI 402	Labour-management-relations
	GRI 403	Occupational-health-and-safety-2018
	GRI 404	Training-and-education
	GRI 405	Diversity-and-equal-opportunity
	GRI 406	Non-discrimination
	GRI 407	Freedom-of-association-and-collective-bargaining
	GRI 408	Child-labour
	GRI 409	Forced-or-compulsory-labour
	GRI 410	Security-practices
	GRI 411	Rights-of-indigenous-peoples
	GRI 412	Human-rights-assessment
	GRI 413	Local communities
	GRI 414	Supplier-social-assessment
	GRI 415	Public policy
	GRI 416	Customer-health-and-safety
	GRI 417	Marketing-and-labelling
	GRI 418	Customer-privacy
	GRI 419	Socioeconomic compliance

APPENDIX B: MASDAR COMPANY
GRI SAMPLE DISCLOSURES

GRI Standard	Label
GRI 101	Preparing a sustainability report by considering the specific standard and information from Masdar. The full balance picture of the organization by considering different impacts has been managed and initiated in this prospect to deal with the focused approaches based on relevant reference The basic process of the GRI Standards regarding sustainability reporting and manage to create better principles and related approaches GRI standards will be used in any specific claims that follow better information coordination and processes
GRI 102	GRI sustainability reporting considers the general disclosure of information by finding contextual information about the overall procedure. Masdar is the renewable energy company that incubates Abu Dhabi's energy leadership
GRI 103	Serves in Abu Dhabi and access the world by stating the holistic business model of Masdar follows research and development, managing higher education and sustainable reporting. The changing need of the market by GRI standard has been managed and coordinated
GRI 200	Economic performance assessment by considering the current approaches has been stated and projected in this segment. Over $1.7 billion in equity investments for Masdar across renewable energy projects has been seen
GRI 300	Material and topic-based GRI Standard has been initiated that indicates environmental context. The corresponding claim based on GRI integration and overall supportiveness has been focused and directed by managing the power plant of Masdar. Reporting environmental requirements and communication also concentrates on better sustainable management by dealing with a performance management context
GRI 400	Employment standards have been projected by stating the idea about current market requirements and the organization's planning. To ensure corporate governance structure, it is important to state the idea about focused work-based committees to foster proactive efforts and channels. The legal representative along with the effective procurement procedure also has been started properly. The internal audit segment as well as the anti-corruption policies for the employees within Masdar present for the work-based betterment
GRI 410	Structured security assessment by stating the idea of specific claims to manage any negative aspects
GRI 411	Rights of indigenous people 2016 concentrates on the different guidelines to manage their requirements and take better action in the future

(continued)

(continued)

GRI Standard	Label
GRI 412	Proper human rights assessment that focuses on employee management, proper agreement, and right clauses to generate and state the human rights screening

Source Authors' summary based on data collected from Masdar Co. and GRI

REFERENCES

Al-Hiyari, A., & Kolsi, M. C. (2021). How do stock market participants value ESG performance? Evidence from Middle Eastern and North African Countries. *Global Business Review*, 1–23.

Anadol, Y. G., Youssef, M. A., & Thiruvattal, E. (2015). Consumer reaction towards corporate social responsibility in United Arab Emirates. *Social Responsibility Journal, 11*(1), 19–35.

Annisa, M. (2019). Economic and Environmental Disclosures on ASRR 2018 Companies' Sustainability Report Based on GRI Standards.

Anundi, L., & Hultman, M. (2018). Följder av en standardförändring. *GRI Standard*, 56.

Arora, B., & Jyoti, D. (2019). Corporate social responsibility and voluntary sustainability standards. *Business: Understanding a Rapidly Emerging Economy*, 27.

Arshad, I. S., Muhammad, T., Yahia, A., & Al Astal, M. (2015). Empirical study on corporate social responsibility in United Arab Emirates. *International Journal of Scientific and Research Publications, 5*(7), 262–265.

Duthler, G., & Dhanesh, G. (2018). The role of corporate social responsibility (CSR) and internal CSR communication in predicting employee engagement: Perspectives from the United Arab Emirates (UAE). *Public Relations Review, 44*(4), 453–462.

Ekergil, V., & Özgür Göde, M. (2017). According to Global Reporting Initiative (GRI) Standards Analysis and Evaluation of Sustainability Reports of Selected Hotels. *Business and Economics Research Journal, 8*(4), 859–871.

Farouk, S., & Jabeen, F. (2018). Ethical climate, corporate social responsibility and organizational performance: Evidence from the UAE public sector. *Social Responsibility Journal, 14*(4), 737–752.

Frederick, W. C. (1960). The growing concern over business responsibility. *California Management Review, 2*(4), 54–61.

Freeman, R. E., & Reed, D. L. (1983). Stockholders and stakeholders: A new perspective on corporate governance. *California Management Review, 25*(3), 88–106.

Gallego-Álvarez, I., Lozano, M. B., & Rodríguez-Rosa, M. (2018). An analysis of the environmental information in international companies according to the new GRI standards. *Journal of Cleaner Production, 182*, 57–66.

Johnson, H. L. (1971). *Business in contemporary society: Framework and issues.* Wadsworth.

Kolsi, M. C., & Attayah, O. F. (2018). Environmental policy disclosure and sustainable development: Determinants, measure and impact on firm value: Evidence from ADX listed companies. *Corporate Social Responsibility and Environmental Management, 25*(5), 807–818.

Kumar, D. A., & Balakrishnan, V. (2011). Corporate social responsibility: Existing practices Vs CSR framework. *Global Journal of Management and Business, 11*(9).

Masdar.ae. (2020). Retrieved 2 April 2020, from https://www.masdar.ae

Mezher, T., Tabbara, S., & Al-Hosany, N. (2010). An overview of CSR in the renewable energy sector: Examples from the Masdar Initiative in Abu Dhabi. *Management of Environmental Quality: An International Journal, 21*(6), 744–760.

Miralles-Quiros, M., Miralles-Quiros, J., & Arraino, I. (2017). Sustainable development, sustainability leadership and firm valuation: Differences across Europe. *Business Strategy and the Environment, 26*(7), 1014–1028.

Nobanee, H., & Ellili. N. (2016). Corporate sustainability disclosure in annual reports: Evidence from UAE banks: Islamic versus conventional. *Renewable and Sustainable Energy Reviews*, 1336–1341.

Sarraj, D. (2018). *Examining materiality in sustainability reporting: Evidence from GCC countries* (Dissertation). Auckland University of Technology.

Suchman, M. (1995). Managing legitimacy: Strategic and institutional approaches. *Academy of Management Review, 20*, 571–611.

Trueman, B., & Titman, S. (1986). Information quality and the valuation of new issues. *Journal of Accounting and Economics, 8*(2), 159–172.

Wójcik-Jurkiewicz, M., & Sadowska, B. (2018). Non-financial reporting standards and evaluation of their use illustrated with example of Polish listed companies. *Journal of Service Management, 27*(2), 539–545.

Managing the Risks of Investment Deposit Account in Islamic Banks: An Examination of Mudharaba Contract Between MENA and International Markets

Asma Hkimi and Neila Boulila Taktak

1 Introduction

In recent years, the Islamic banking sector has grown significantly to become a major financial system. It has also drawn attention and interest of many specialists such as accountants, economists, regulators, auditors, etc. The financial crisis doesn't have a significant effect on the performance of Islamic banks and even their development around the world. Today, there are more than 300 Islamic financial institutions in 50 economies around the world, in both Muslim and non-Muslim countries, with assets close to 1.9 billion of dollars (Izzaouihda & Chami, 2018). Like classical banks, the goal of Islamic banks is to affect and to mobilize resources in an optimum way, but these banks offer instruments

A. Hkimi (✉) · N. Boulila Taktak
IHEC, University of Carthage, Carthage, Tunisia
e-mail: asmahkimi@hotmail.fr

N. Boulila Taktak
e-mail: neila_boulila@yahoo.fr

© The Author(s), under exclusive license to Springer Nature Singapore Pte Ltd. 2022
A. Echchabi et al. (eds.), *Contemporary Research in Accounting and Finance*, https://doi.org/10.1007/978-981-16-8267-4_8

in accordance with Islamic law and encourage productive investment, to offer a competitive remuneration compared to their conventional counterparts. The exception of Islamic financial system is the principle of profit and loss sharing (PLS) between Islamic banks as a mudharib or agent, shareholders, depositors, and entrepreneur (Hamza & Saadaoui, 2013).

By practicing this principle, Magalhães and Al-Saad (2013) and Toumi et al. (2011a, 2011b) confirm that the relationship between all partners has been modified and replaced by a new partnership based on the equitable sharing of profits and losses. Therefore, the rule of Islamic law considers this principle as the central axis of contractual relations in Islamic finance (Aysan et al., 2015; Faishal Ibrahim et al., 2012; Hamza, 2015; Hamza & Saadaoui, 2013; Olson & Zoubi, 2008; Toumi & Viviani, 2013). Consequently, The Shariah law prohibits Islamic banks to pay or receive any interest in their lending and investing operations. By the application of PLS mechanism, the main resources of Islamic banks come especially from the profit sharing investment accounts (PSIA), which is considered as a form of short term funds investment (Archer et al., 1998). The PSIA holders are called Musharaka and Mudharaba.

The remainder of the paper is organized as follows: The second section presents the literature review on the mudharaba contract and hypotheses development. Data and methodology, based on dynamic panel model, are presented in the third section. The fourth section discusses the empirical results. The final section concludes our paper.

2   LITERATURE REVIEW AND HYPOTHESIS DEVELOPMENT

2.1   *Literature Review*

The mudharaba contract represents the principal source of funds for the Islamic banks. This instrument is based on profit loss sharing principle. It can be defined as a partnership agreement between one or more investors providing funds (Rabl al mal) and an entrepreneur (Mudharib or agent) who ensures the work and the project management.

Under the mudharaba contract, IBs as asset manager (mudharib) and IAHs as fund-provider agree to divide profit is shared for both partners in accordance with a prearranged profit-sharing ratio. However, loss is borne only by owners of funds except in the case of misconduct, negligence, fraud, or violation contractual clauses by IBs (Elasrag, 2014; El Melki,

2011; Farooq & Vivek, 2012; Ghayad, 2008; Ismal, 2010; Zarai & Zarai, 2013).

Moreover, the form of mudharaba contract used by IBs create a double agency problem. In other words, IB can be acted as a mudharib (agent), where it enters into a profit sharing with depositors and principal, where it enters into a profit sharing with an entrepreneur who only participates with his/her experience and management skills (Chong & Liu, 2009; El Melki, 2011; Farooq & Vivek, 2012; Ghayad, 2008; Ismal, 2010; Li et al., 2012; Ruimy, 2008; Sarker, 2000). Hence, this bilateral relationship exposes IBs a second asymmetric information problem with businessman who exploit investors' funds to finance their projects.

According to Hamza (2015) and Li et al. (2012) asymmetric information and conflict of interests between the bank as a fund-provider and the entrepreneur as a manager (agent) can affect negatively the relationship between IBs and IAHs in terms of relevant and transparent information about the risks. This mode of financing does not guarantee either capital or return. So, it encourages IBs to take excessive risk which affects negatively IBs performance solvency and thus the rate of return paid to depositors (Hamza, 2015; Hamdi & Zarai, 2013; Li et al., 2012). And, this, in turn, produces additional agency conflicts.

In Islamic banks the shareholders and deposit investment account are the main provider of funds. However, compared to the shareholders, the depositors do not have the right to manage or to control and monitor project financed by their funds, and they entrust their deposits to the management of IBs which is nominated by shareholders (Li et al., 2012). Besides, IAHs may not have access to information about IB risk exposition, and they cannot obtain all information about the performance of assets financed by their funds or on the method by which their profit rate is calculated (Hamza, 2015; Kammer et al., 2015). Additionally, they cannot vote for or against the use of prudential reserves (PER and IRR), and they have no representative on the board of directors.

According to Hamdi and Zarai (2013) «*They also agree to give up any right they have to these reserves when they stop their relationship with the IBs. Plus, the calculation and the use of IRR are decided by IBIs administration based on their own discretion and there are no specific supervisory disclosure requirements about this. Indeed, the publicly available information about these reserves is relatively limited*».

Grassa and Matoussi (2014) and Magalhães and Al-Saad (2013) note that the investment deposit account complicates the governance system and increases asymmetric information problem between IBs and IAHs. Investment deposit accounts are full of different types of risks. Among the risks faced by the unrestricted investment account holders, we present the displaced commercial risk (DCR) and profit rate risk which are the specific and unique risks (Esam & Ezzat, 2014; Hamza, 2015; Hamdi & Zarai, 2013; Htay et al., 2013; Ramly et al., 2018; Toumi et al., 2018).

Displaced commercial risk (DCR) refers to the massive withdrawal funds risk. In other words, if depositors are not satisfied they withdraw their funds to another Islamic or conventional bank offering a higher return. Thus, to protect themselves from this risk, IBs managed the rate of return paid to depositors at the expense of the return paid to shareholders (AAOIFI, 1999; Archer & Karim, 2006; Hamza, 2015; Hamdi & Zarai, 2014; Htay et al., 2013; IFSB, 2010; Ramly et al., 2018; Toumi et al., 2011c). However, the excessive risk taken by the bank does not allow them to provide a rate of return based on the pre-established ratio and, this in turn, exposes them to the rate of return risk. Consequently, the IAHs will be receiving a lower rate of return rather than suggested by conventional or Islamic banks.

Such as, IBs use a prudential reserves namely profit equalization reserve (PER) and investment risk reserve (IRR) as smoothing practice to protect themselves from the massive withdrawal funds. Furthermore, they resort to another practice which can be used to smooth the rate of return namely adjusting mudharib share (MS) and the transfer from shareholders' funds (Aysan et al., 2015; Hamza, 2015; Hamza & Saadaoui, 2013; Hamdi & Zarai, 2013; Htay et al., 2013; Li et al., 2012; Sundararajan, 2008).

According to AAOIFI, IFSB (2005) and BNM: «*PER is an amount appropriated by the Islamic bank out of the mudaraba (profit and loss sharing contract) income, before allocating the mudarib (entrepreneur) share and its purpose is to ensure that the market rate of return able to pay to IAHs and increase owner's equity. It is mainly intend for protection of a financial firm against the risk of ruin due to existence of systematic risk that is prevalent in the industry and issue of adequate capital and cost of raising it to mitigate the risk. Similarly, IRR is an amount appropriated by the Islamic bank after allocating the mudarib share, in order to cater against future losses for the IAHs*» (Htay et al., 2013).

For the second type of reserves, IBs can adjust their commission as a mudharib or reduce of the shareholders' income to IAHs, in order to remunerate the latter a rate of return close to the market benchmark. The use of these reserves as a practice of smoothing allows IBs to cover their periodic losses (Hamza & Saadaoui, 2013; Farooq & Vivek, 2012; Toumi et al., 2011c).

Theoretically, IBs are not obliged to smooth the rate of return paid to depositors. But, in reality either the supervisory authority pressure or the massive competition required them to smooth the returns. In some countries like Qatar, Malaysia, Bahrain, etc., the supervision authority indicates that Islamic banks should not allow depositors to support a loss of their capital or a significant decrease in their return. As a result, the voluntary practice of smoothing becomes compulsory and deposit investment account holders are considered as guaranteed deposits treated as conventional deposits accounts (Archer & Karim, 2006; Fiennes, 2007; Toumi et al., 2011c).

2.2   Hypothesis Development

In order to diminish the volatility of the profit rate, IBs can use a PER to maintain a stable or increasing remuneration paid to depositors (Archer & Karim, 2006; Hamza, 2015; Sundararajan, 2008). Under the mudharaba contract, depositors agree in advance on the return portion that may be attributable to reserve account, which is fixed and calculated by the bank at their own discretion. According to Hassan and Mervyn (2007) in Hamdi and Zarai (2013), the percentage of return is usually invested by IBs to produce further returns to IAHs. In fact, in periods of small return caused by moral hazard behavior the IBs can decide to diminish the amount of reserve in order to distribute a competitive remuneration in that period. In contrast, in the case of excessive profits the IBs can transfer part of income and profits from investment deposit account to the reserve accounts in that period.

The PER is used to stabilize the payment of periodic profits and not to cover periodic losses because IBs as a «Mudharib» cannot cover the losses that normally supported by the depositors' funds (Rab almal). It should be noted that the PER is qualified as a reserve and not a provision (Archer et al., 2010). We note that PER which belongs to shareholders and IAHs serve to smooth a low and positive rate of return (Toumi & Viviani, 2013). We propose to test the following hypothesis:

H1. The PER has a positive impact on the volatility of the rate of return paid to IAHs.

The second recourse which IBs use to smooth the rate of return paid to IAHs is investment risk reserve (IRR). It is created from profits paid to IAHs after deduction of the banks' share as a mudharib in order to maintain or cover losses attributable to IAHs. Like PER, the provisioning for this reserve is mentioned in the contract and determined by the IBs management at their own discretion (Archer et al., 2010; Hamza & Saadaoui, 2013; Hamdi & Zarai, 2013; Ramly et al., 2018; Sundararajan, 2008).

According to Hamdi and Zarai (2013), the use of IRR has some resemblances with reserves used by conventional banks to smooth the dividends distributed to shareholders whereas in IBs investment deposit accounts are treated as quasi-shareholders, and they are exposed to major governance issues. As a result, IAHs do not have governance right to suggest or to control investment decisions. In addition, they do not have the right to manage or to monitor the project financed by their funds. Additionally, they do not have the right to vote on the use of IRR (Archer & Karim, 2006; Farooq and Vivek, 2012; Hamza & Saadaoui, 2013; Kammer et al., 2015).

Moreover, in context of asymmetric information, IBs acting as mudharib contributes to the increase of agency problem and encourages managers' moral hazard. Moreover, asymmetric information between banks as a provider of funds and an entrepreneur as a mudharib can affect negatively the relationship between banks and IAHs. Therefore, the increase of agency conflicts increases the agency costs. And this, in turn, leads to the loss of depositors' confidence and exposes IBs to withdrawal funds risk (Hamza, 2015; Hafsa Orhan Astrom, 2013). Under this contract, the dual roles played by the IBs can affect negatively the relationship between bank's manager not only in their dealing with IAHs and in those with shareholders, but also between investors (shareholders and investment deposit account).

Additionally, information on the calculation and the use of IRR is characterized by the lack of transparency. Besides, the IRR account encourages IBs to take greater risk by the allocation of depositors' funds in PLS assets supposed to be less risky than debt assets. Consequently, the existence of IRR account encourages management discretion through moral hazard behavior (Hamza, 2015). Under certain circumstances, the concept of profit loss sharing is far from being a real practice for IBs (Sundararajan, 2008). The sign of this variable is expected to be negative.

H2. The IRR has a negative impact on the volatility of the rate of return paid to IAHs.

In theory, IBs as a «Mudharib» do not guarantee either capital or a fixed rate of return to IAHs. However, market pressure requires IBs to treat investment account holders as guaranteed accounts and must provide a competitive rate of return to satisfy their investors and to protect themselves from withdrawal funds risk. In addition, certain IBs are required to apply the regulatory framework which noted that deposit investment account holders should be treated as guaranteed accounts. Indeed, in many countries IBs are subject to the same regulatory framework as conventional banks (AlShattarat & Atmeh, 2016; Maali & Atmeh, 2015).

Under contractual terms, the maximum part in predetermined profit is allocated to the bank as a mudharib whereas the actual share distributed varies from year to year according to the profit rate provided by assets (Archer & Karim, 2006). So, when PER and IRR are insufficient, IBs diminish or renounce their mudharib share below to the contracted terms to offer a remuneration equivalent to a competitive remuneration and absorb a part of loss which is normally are borne by IAHs, in order to stop withdrawal funds (Farooq & Vivek, 2012; Sundararajan, 2008).

According to Diaw and Mbow (2011), IAHs are not able to exert power over bank management, and they cannot negotiate the profit-sharing ratio which can significantly affect their returns because the diminish or the wave of mudharib share allocated to IAHs is fixed by the administration of IBs at their own discretion. Consequently, this situation increasing agency problem between banks as a mudharib and IAHs who do not have right to propose or to control investment decisions.

It should be noted that there are no empirical validations we allow to measure the effect of the mudharib share (MS) on the rate of return paid to IAHs. So, to enrich the debate, in our research, our third hypothesis is as follows:

H3. The mudharib share has a positive impact on the volatility of the rate of return paid to IAHs.

3   METHODOLOGY

3.1   Sample

Our sample is composed of 41 Islamic banks observed over the period stretching from 2005 to 2016. Data are collected manually from the international site of Islamic banks «IBIS» and the site of each Islamic bank. The deposit interest rate and the rate of inflation are mainly from the site of World Bank. Table 1 shows the selected sample. The sub-sections below describe all variables and their measurement used in the estimation (Table 2).

3.2   Variables Measurement

3.2.1   Measurement of Dependent Variable

We define the fluctuation rate of return paid to depositors by:

$$\text{VRIAH} = \frac{\text{Return}_{(t)} - \text{Return}_{(t-1)}}{\text{Return}_{(t-1)}}$$

where, VRIAH = Volatility of the rate of return paid to depositors.

Table 1 Sample

Countries	Number of Islamic banks
Malaysia	10
Sudan	10
Bahrein	7
United Arab Emirates	4
Qatar	3
Jordan	2
Indonesia	2
Bangladesh	2
United Kingdom	1
Total countries: 9	Total IBs: 41

Source Authors' calculation based on data collected from IBIS and annual reports

Table 2 Dependent and independent variables

Variables	Definition	Measure
Dependent variable		
VRIAH	Volatility return paid to depositors	Return (t) − Return $(t − 1)$ / Return $(t − 1)$
Independent variables		
PER	Profit equalization reserve	PER/Total assets
IRR	Investment risk reserve	IRR/Total assets
MS	Mudharib share	Mudharib share/Total assets
Control variables		
Size	Bank size	Log of total assets
BA	Bank age	logarithm of the number of years since the bank was established
IDI	Islamic deposit insurance	binary variable that is equal to 1 if there is Islamic deposit insurance and 0 otherwise
Crisis	Subprime crisis	binary variable that is equal to 1 for the crisis period (2007–2008) and 0 otherwise
AAOIFI	Islamic accounting standards	binary variable which is equal to 1 if the country of the bank requires the application of the AAOIFI's standards and 0 otherwise
INF	Inflation rate	Consumer price index
DIR	Deposit interest rate	

Source Developed by the authors

3.2.2 Measurement of Independent Variables

In order to estimate the effect of the specific mechanism on return paid to investment account holders, we use three proxies. First, profit equalization reserve measured by the ratio PER to total assets. Second, investment risk reserve measured by the ratio IRR to total assets. Third, mudharib share (MS) measured by the ratio mudharib share to total assets.

We introduce seven control variables. Bank size (size) is the logarithm of the bank's total assets; Bank age (BA) is the logarithm of the number of years since the bank was established; Islamic deposit insurance (IDI) is a binary variable which is equal to 1 if there is Islamic deposit insurance and 0 otherwise; Crisis is a binary variable which is equal to 1 for the crisis period (2007–2008) and 0 otherwise; AAOIFI is a binary variable which is equal to 1 if the country of the bank requires the application of the AAOIFI's standards and 0 otherwise; INF is the inflation rate; DIR is the deposit interest rate paid to deposit account holders.

We suggest the model below to study the impact of the new and specific mechanism used by IBs to smooth the return paid to investment accounts holders (IAH).

$$VRIAH_{it} = \beta_0 + \beta_1 VRIAH_{i,t-1} + \beta_2 PER_{i,t} + \beta_3 IRR_{i,t} + \beta_4 MS_{i,t}$$
$$+ \beta_5 LNTA_{i,t} + \beta_6 LNAB_{i,t} + \beta_7 ASSD_{i,t} + \beta_8 CF_{i,t}$$
$$+ \beta_9 AAOIFI_{i,t} + \beta_{10} INF_{i,t} + \beta_{11} TINTD_{i,t} + \varepsilon_{i,t}$$

where i indicates the bank ($i = 1,...,..., 41$), and t indicates the annual time period ($t = 2005,..., 2016$).

$VRIAH_{it}$ is the volatility of investment deposit return of the bank i in year t. β_0 is the constant. β_1 is the parameters to be estimated for the lagged dependent variable. $\beta_2,... \beta_{11}$ are the parameters to be estimated. ε_{it} is the error term.

The estimation method using for this dynamic panel is the system Generalized Method of Moments (GMM). It was developed by Arellano & Bover (1995) and Blundell and Bond (1998). Compared to other econometrics methods, GMM system is considered the more efficient estimator to control endogeneity of variables (Hamza, 2015; Hamza & Saadaoui, 2013; Trabelsi & Trad, 2017).

4   RESULTS AND DISCUSSION

4.1   Descriptive Statistics

Descriptive Statistics in Table 3 indicates that the average of the dependent variable VRIAH is 4.32 with a standard deviation equals to 49.818 showing that observations are widely dispersed around the mean. Islamic banks hold an average of 0.032 of profit equalization reserve (PER). The mean of investment risk reserve (IRR) is 0.215. The mudharib share (MS) average is equal to 3.056.

For other variables, the average bank size (Size) is 17.946 with minimum value of 10.255 and maximum of 27.678. The age average of IBs is equal to 2.704. Inflation (INF) variable is ranged from −4.9 to 37.4 with an average of 7.266. The mean of deposit interest rate (DIR) variable is estimated at 3.547 while its minimum and maximum values are 0.981 and 11.721, respectively. Table 4 shows that only 30.54% of IBs

Table 3 Descriptive statistics of the dependent variable and control variables

Variables	Mean	SD	Skewness	Kurtosis	Median	Min	Max
VRIAH	4.321	49.818	15.496	256.549	2481.853	−1	880.255
PER	0.032	0.156	7.543	71.167	0.024	0	1.861
IRR	0.215	0.961	4.887	27.229	0.923	0	7.181
MS	3.056	13.490	5.580	34.850	181.998	0	101.745
Size	17.946	3.642	0.315	3.002	13.270	10.255	27.678
BA	2.704	0.896	−0.762	3.218	0.804	0	4.143
INF	7.266	8.838	2.056	6.867	78.125	−4.9	37.4
DIR	3.547	2.259	1.461	4.923	5.106	0.981	11.721

Source Authors' calculation based on data collected from IBIS and annual reports

enters into insurance contracts. A total of 16.92% of IBs are influenced by the crisis. A total of 50.76% of the banks belongs to countries which apply the AAOIFI standards.

4.2 Cross-Correlation Matrix and Test Variance Inflation Factor

The analysis of the cross-correlation matrix in Table 5 indicates that the independent variables are not highly correlated and are less than the limit (0.8) proposed by Kennedy (1998) whereas the variable deposit interest rate (DIR) is significantly correlated with the variable Size (0.724). According to Hamilton (2004), the correlation matrix cannot find all the problems tied with multicollinearity.

As a result, we use the Variance Inflation Factor test (VIF), which is more dependable in detecting multicollinearity. This latter confirms the presence of multicollinearity problem. To resolve this problem, we apply the principal component analysis method, and this tool transforms highly correlated variables into a new variables de-correlated from each other.

Table 4 Frequency of binary control variables

Variables	IDI		Crisis		AAOIFI	
Modality	1	0	1	0	1	0
Frequency%	0.3054	0.6945	0.1692	0.8307	0.5076	0.4923

Source Authors' calculation based on data collected from IBIS and annual reports

Table 5   Cross-correlation matrix

	VRIAH	PER	IRR	MS	LNTA	LNAB	INF	TINTD	VIF
VRIAH	1.0000								
PER	−0.0024	1.0000							
IRR	0.2154	0.0063	1.0000						
MS	0.0817	−0.0445	0.2748	1.0000					
LNTA	−0.0545	0.1560	−0.2730	0.3352	1.0000				
LNAB	0.0626	−0.1096	0.2087	0.0315	0.0907	1.0000			
INF	−0.0897	0.2068	0.0136	0.1395	0.3649	0.0115	1.0000		
TINTD	−0.0089	0.2317	0.0277	0.3342	0.7246	0.0243	0.5489	1.0000	

Source Authors' calculation based on data collected from IBIS and annual reports

4.3   Discussion and Policy Implications

In order to reach the results of our study, we have successively introduced the variables so as to take into account all the variables in the fourth model.

In Table 6, we report the results of the estimation. The lagged value of VRIAH coefficient is statistically significant at 1% with a negative sign. Regarding the effect of profit equalization reserve, the coefficient estimate indicates that the impact of (PER) is statistically significant at 1% with a positive sign. This finding contradicts the result of Hamza (2015) for a sample of 60 Islamic banks during the period extending from 2004 to 2012, which indicates that the use of PER to smooth the rate of return paid to IAHs is not significant. However, this result has been confirmed by Aysan et al. (2015) which reveals that the share of the shareholders' reserves in the (PER) influences positively the rate of return provided to the IAHs.

The significant effect of (PER) first, is justified by the success of the PLS principle which is considered as the central axis of contractual relations in Islamic finance (Aysan et al., 2015; Hamza, 2015). Second, this result can be explained by the reinvestment mechanism of reserve adopted by most Islamic banks to generate other returns to IHAs (Archer & Karim, 2006). Third, the shareholders' decision to accept or renounce all or part of their profits means that they support the displaced commercial risk arising from the portfolio of assets financed in part or in full by IAHs funds (Hamdi & Zarai, 2013). It should be noted that the acceptance of DCR is justified by the phenomenon of commercial pressure or

Table 6 Results of GMM estimation

Variables	Model 1			Model 2			Model 3			Model 4		
	Coef	T	P>|t|	Coef	T	P>|t|	Coef	T	P>|t|	Coef	T	P>|t|
VRIAH												
VRIAH$_{(t-1)}$	0.1127911	2.65	0.014**	0.1975752	5.18	0.000***	0.2141644	4.39	0.000***	0.2647374	5.89	0.000***
PERt	14.00022	5.05	0.000***	21.93313	6.63	0.000***	23.03063	7.13	0.000***	20.46395	5.68	0.000***
IRRt	0.8908671	1.36	0.186	-0.2186968	-0.23	0.820	-0.4268471	-0.41	0.683	-0.9423488	-0.98	0.337
MSt	0.4165542	3.02	0.006***	0.1269904	0.67	0.506	0.0899874	-0.46	0.653	0.0458405	0.23	0.821
BA	3.337859	2.77	0.011**	3.392263	2.55	0.018*	3.936211	2.47	0.021*	3.89233	2.90	0.008***
IDI				17.59916	3.31	0.003***	19.47472	3.49	0.002***	20.28588	3.22	0.004***
Crisis							6.7211	4.40	0.00***	6.727603	4.04	0.000***
AAOIFI										1.074962	0.34	0.736
INF	-1.294609	-6.53	0.000***	-1.263174	-7.62	0.000***	-1.79503	-7.26	0.000***	-1.604773	-6.56	0.000***
Factor*	-1.105213	-1.45	0.161	-2.036077	-1.52	0.142	-1.870599	-1.48	0.151	-1.041487	-0.55	0.590
Cons	-4.315113	-2.07	0.050	-5.79743	-2.09	0.048	-6.844754	-2.07	0.049	-7.222734	-2.12	0.044
Observations	217			217			215			215		
Hansen test (p-value)	(0.280)			(0.758)			(0.563)			(0.667)		
Arellano-Bond test (AR2)	(0.564)			(0.307)			(0.300)			(0.594)		

*Significant at 10% level, **Significant at 5% level, ***Significant at 1% level
Source Authors' calculation based on data collected from IBIS and annual reports

supervisory authority pressure which encourage the majority of IBs to smooth the remuneration of IAHs at the expense of remuneration served to shareholders (Hamdi & Zarai, 2013; Toumi & Viviani, 2013).

On the other hand, due to competition with other Islamic financial institutions both Islamic or conventional, to protect themselves of the withdraw funds, IBs must offer a competitive rate of return and encourage their specific investors (IAHs) to reinvest their funds and use their different products (Archer & Karim, 2006 in Hafsa Orhan Astrom, 2013; Khan & Ahmed, 2001).

Due to competition, commercial pressure and pressure made by the supervisory authorities, IBs made the smoothing practice mandatory and considered the unrestricted investment accounts holders as guaranteed accounts treated as conventional deposits AlShattarat and Atmeh (2016), Maali and Atmeh (2015) and Toumi and Viviani (2013). H1, is thus supported.

The finding of Table 6 also shows that the investment risk reserve (IRR) has a negative and no significant impact on rate of return paid to IAHs suggesting that the creation of IRR encourages moral hazard and increase the level of the risk taken by managers. In addition, under the hypothesis of asymmetric information between the bank as a provider of funds (Rab almal) and entrepreneurs as a manager (agent) encourages IBs to expose depositors' funds to a higher level of risk which could affect negatively their performance and solvency and therefore the relationship between banks and IAHs (Hamza, 2015). It seems that IBs invest their depositor's funds in riskier projects since their commission as a mudharib will not be affected by any types of risk and since the amount of IRR is determined after deduction of their mudharib share (Hamdi & Zarai, 2013). Moreover, the losses on investment of IAHs funds could be covered, fully or partially by IRR which is created only by the depositor's funds and not by shareholder's funds.

According to PLS principle where the profit, the loss and the risk are shared between banks and IAHs, the agency problems are more complicated. According to Hamza and Saadaoui (2013), the lack or inadequacy of transparent information about performance solvency, risk, etc., pushes investors to investigate the real information they need. Consequently, this initiative increases the agency problem and produces additional agency costs.

IAHs do not negotiate the rate of return and the percentage of their income that will be transferred to the investment risk reserve account.

According to Sundararajan (2005), they also renounce their part on IRR when they stop relationship with IBs. Indeed, the access to information about the use and the calculation of IRR seems to be limited.

Furthermore, this negative impact can be explained by the insufficient amount of IRR. Toumi and Viviani (2013) supposed that the amount of IRR depends not only on the decision of IB administration but also on the history of the profitability of the investments financed by IAH's funds. So, in this case if the return history is low, the amount of IRR will be insufficient to cover losses. On the other hand, a surplus of IRR also raises another problem which is additional cost supported both by the bank and IAHs. Thus IBs should have sophisticated statistical techniques to manage their reserve accounts more carefully.

According to Hamza and Saadaoui (2013), another explanation which might justify this result is that the IAHs face the risk of misconduct of their funds which expose the IBs to a higher level of risk and under-capitalization problem (IFSB, 2010, §44).

Moreover, this negative effect is due to the governance structure of IBs which does not give IAHs the right to monitor and control effectively investment decision taken by the bank. Besides, IBs do not disclose the full disclosures on performance of the portfolio financed by their funds or on calculation of PER and IRR or on the method by which the remuneration is determined. This leads us to conclude that the actual practices of corporate governance in IBs are not effective enough to protect the rights of IAHs (Hamza, 2015; Kammer et al., 2015; Magalhães & Al-Saad, 2013).

We conclude that asymmetric information, moral hazard behavior, excessive risk taking, and the limited right to control the depositor's funds lead to the loss of depositor's confidence, which in turn creates a liquidity imbalance and insufficient reserves (Hafsa Orhan Astrom, 2013) and expose IBs to withdrawal funds risk. H2 is supported.

The effect of mudharib share (MS) is positive and no significant. It means that Islamic financial institutions may face competition costs which require the share of part or full of their mudharib share to depositors to offer a profit rate similar to market-based deposit interest rates (Sundararajan, 2005). As a result, investment account holders are treated as guaranteed accounts and must provide a competitive rate of return discouraging partners from withdrawing their funds (AlShattarat & Atmeh, 2016; Maali & Atmeh, 2015).

Farooq and Vivek (2012) reveal that when the PER and IRR are insufficient, and Islamic banks should reduce their commissions as a mudharib below the contractually agreed percentage. Hence, this mechanism can be used only in the absence of losses because the contractual condition of the mudharaba contract indicates that the losses are supported by the IAHs themselves. H3, is thus supported.

Regarding the effect of the other variables, the coefficient associated with Size variable is negative and no significant. This findings confirm the result of Hamza (2015). The negative relation implying that the large banks cannot reduce asymmetric information and agency costs compared to small banks. This can also be explained by the appropriate strategy adopted by small banks to diversify risk and reduce withdrawal funds risk. So, large banks aiming to increase portfolio generate excessive risk and offer a low return to their depositors (Essam & Ezzat, 2014; Hassan & Bashir, 2005). Consequently, small banks are more stable, and they are able to offer a competitive return to IAHs (Hamza, 2015; Nawaz, 2017). BA variable is positive and significant, which indicates that the stabilization of return paid to depositors depends on the experience acquired by the IBs in monitoring, controlling, and management of their funds (Aysan et al., 2015). This result suggests that the older IBs can produce a higher returns compared to younger IBs and face withdrawal funds risk (Hamza, 2015; Mkadmi & Halioui, 2013; Ben Slama Zouari & Boulila Taktak, 2014). However, the variable IDI reveals a positive coefficient and is statistically significant suggesting that the countries where existing a system of Islamic deposit insurance compliant with Shariah, allow IBs to protect themselves from withdrawal funds and offer a competitive rate of return (El-Gamal & Inanoglu, 2003; Maali & Atmeh, 2015). This finding contradicts the result of Hamza (2015). The coefficient of crisis is statistically significant at 1% with a positive sign on the rate of return. It means that the success of IBs over the period of crisis depends on the requirements of Sharia law (Ahmad & Abdul Majid, 2017; Khediri et al., 2015). The positive impact can be also explained by the success of (PLS) principle that has reduced financial risk and return variation. According to Almanaseer (2014), the increase of owner's equity has reduced the effect of the crisis on the bank's performance. During the crisis period, Islamic banks are more stable than their conventional counterparts (Fakhfekh et al., 2016). AAOIFI variable is positive and no significant indicates that the harmonization of Islamic bank's accounting standards and practices around the world leads IBs to prepare and publish information to meet the needs of different users, thus limiting the problems related to the transparency of published information (Quttainah, 2012). This positive effect can also be explained by users' confidence in Islamic accounting standards (El hamma, 2015). Finally, the results show that INF has a negative and a significant impact on rate of return. IDR variable is negative where the coefficient is not significant.

5   Conclusion

The objective of this paper is to examine the effect of prudential reserves on the rate of return paid to IAHs. In other words, verifying if PER and IRR allow IBs to stabilize the rate of return and thus allow them to offer a low volatility rate of return. However, when the reserves are insufficient, there are other practices used by IBs to smooth the rate of return. The first alternative is to reduce part or all of their commission as a mudharib below the contracted share. Secondly, IBs can donate some portion of the shareholders' income to IAH in order to present a stable and competitive remuneration.

To verify our hypothesis, we conducted our study on a sample of 41 Islamic banks during the period stretching from 2005 to 2016. We applied the generalized method of moments (GMM system). The results show that the use of PER and mudharib share affects positively the rate of return paid to depositors. So, the use of PER indicates the success of IBs to generate more profit by the invest of PER, and the positive sign of mudharib share (MS) reveals the absence of losses which means that IBs are able to reduce their risk by the diversification of investment portfolio. However, IRR is characterized by a moral hazard, asymmetric information, hence excessive risk taking which could impact negatively the relationship between banks not just in their dealings with IAHs and in those with the shareholders, but also as between the interests of both categories of investors (shareholder and investment account holder). It is also revealed that small Islamic banks offer a better remuneration to their depositors. Bank age, Islamic deposit insurance, AAOIFI, and crisis affect positively the rate of return paid to IAHs. However, deposit interest rate and inflation have a negative coefficient.

To the best of our knowledge, our paper is the first to diagnose the impact of reserves (PER, IRR, MS) on the rate of return attributable to investment account holders. Besides, we incorporate a new measure to evaluate empirically the impact of prudential reserves (PER—IRR) and mudharib share (MS) on the rate of return paid to depositors. This study attempts to fill the gaps in the literature by providing new empirical evidence. In other words, results emphasize the role played by the reserves to protect banks of withdrawal funds risk and allow us to enrich our knowledge regarding the relation between the smoothing mechanism and the volatility of the profit rate paid to depositors (UIAHs).

Finally, our results provide crucial evidence which could meet the needs of different users such as academics, investors, banking, regulators, etc., and make a humble contribution to the literature on the study of the specific practice of smoothing used by Islamic banks to face withdrawal funds risk.

Despite these contributions, the absence of information on transfers from shareholders' funds as a practice of smoothing prevented us from testing its impact on the rate of return of IAHs.

References

AAOIFI. (1999, March). *Statement of the purpose and calculation of tha capital adequacy ratio for Islamic banks*. AAoifi.

Ahmad, Z., & Abdul Majid, N. H. (2017). Islamic bank financing, financial crisis and, monetary policy in Malaysia: An interaction in the long run. *Equilibrium, 2*(1), 15–23.

Almanaseer, M. (2014). The impact of the financial crisis on the Islamic banks profitability—Evidence from GCC. *International Journal of Financial Research, 5*(3), 176–187.

AlShattarat, W. K., & Atmeh, M. A. (2016). Profit-sharing investment accounts in islamic banks or mutualization, accounting perspective. *Journal of Financial Reporting and Accounting, 14*(1), 30–48.

Archer, S., Ahmed, R., & Al-Deehani, T. (1998). Financial contracting, governance structures, and the accounting regulation of Islamic banks: An analysis in terms of agency theory and transaction cost economics. *Journal of Management and Governance, 2*, 149–170.

Archer, S., & Karim, R. A. A. (2006). On capital structure, risk sharing and capital adequacy in Islamic banks. *International Journal of Theoretical and Applied Finance, 9*(3), 269–280.

Archer, S., Karim, R. A. A., & Sundararajan, V. (2010). Supervisory, regulatory, and capital adequacy implications of profit-sharing investment accounts in Islamic finance. *Journal of Islamic Accounting and Business Research, 1*(1), 10–31.

Arellano, M., & Bover, O. (1995). Another look at the instrumental variable estimation of error component models. *Journal of Econometrics, 68*(1), 29–51.

Aysan, A. F., Disli, M., Ozturk, H., & Turhan, I. M. (2015). Are Islamic banks subject to depositor discipline? *The Singapore Economic Review, 60*(1), 155.

Ben Slama Zouari, S., & Boulila Taktak, N. (2014). Ownership structure and financial performance in Islamic banks. *International Journal of Islamic and Middle Eastern Finance and Management, 7*(2), 146–160.

Blundell, R., & Bond, S. (1998). Initial conditions and moment restrictions in dynamic panel data models. *Journal of Econometrics, 87*(1), 115–143.

Chong, B. S., & Liu, M.-H. (2009). Islamic banking: Interest-free or interest-based? *Pacific-Basin Finance Journal, 17*(1), 125–144.

Diaw, A., & Mbow, A. (2011). A comparative study of the returns on Mudharabah deposit and on equity In Islamic banks. *Humanomics, 27*(4), 229–242.

Elasrag, H. (2014). Corporate governance in Islamic finance: Basic concepts and issues. *SSRN Electronic Journal.*

El-Gamal, M. A., & Inanoglu, H. (2003). Efficiencies and unobserved heterogeneity in Turkish banking: 1990–2000. *SSRN Electronic Journal.*

El hamma, A. (2015). La Comptabilité Des Produits Financiers Islamiques: Normes AAOIFI vs. IFRS. *Revue de Management et de Stratégie, 1*(2), 10–22.

El Melki, A. (2011). Le principe de partage des profits ou des pertes dans le cadre des banques islamiques: illustration modélisée des contrats de financement participatifs moudaraba et moucharaka. *Global Journal of Management and Business Research, 11*(11).

Essam, M., & Ezzat, A. (2014). Do principal-agent conflicts impact performance and risk-taking behavior of Islamic banks?

Faishal Ibrahim, M., Eng Ong, S., & Akinsomi, K. (2012). Shariah compliant real estate development financing and investment in the Gulf Cooperation Council. *Journal of Property Investment & Finance, 30*(2), 175–197.

Fakhfekh, M., Hachicha, N., Jawadi, F., Nadhem, S., & Idi Cheffou, A. (2016). Measuring volatility persistence for conventional and Islamic banks: An FIEGARCH approach. *Emerging Markets Review, 27*, 84–99.

Farooq, M. O., & Vivek, S. (2012). Displaced Commercial Risk (DCR) and Value of Alpha (α%) for Islamic Banks in Bahrain. *Islamic Finance: Risk, Stability and Growth, 2*, 237–262.

Fiennes, T. (2007). Supervisory implications of Islamic banking: A supervisor's perspective. In D. S. Archer & R. A. A. Rifaat, *Islamic finance: The regulatory challenge* (pp. 11–39, 247–256). Wiley.

Ghayad, R. (2008). Corporate governance and the global performance of Islamic banks. *Humanomics, 24*(3), 207–216.

Grassa, R., & Matoussi, H. (2014). Corporate governance of Islamic banks: A comparative study between GCC and Southeast Asia countries. *International Journal of Islamic and Middle Eastern Finance and Management, 7*(3), 346–362.

Hafsa Orhan Astrom, Z. (2013). Credit risk management pertaining to profit and loss sharing instruments in Islamic banking. *Journal of Financial Reporting and Accounting, 11*(1), 80–91.

Hamdi, F. M., & Zarai, M. A. (2013). Earnings management and investment accounts holders interests in Islamic banking institutions. *Research Journal of Business and Management Invention, 2*(9), 22–35.

Hamdi, F. M., & Zarai, M. A. (2014). Corporate governance practices and earnings management in Islamic banking institutions. *Research Journal of Finance and Accounting, 5*(9), 81–96.

Hamilton, J. D. (2004). *Time series analysis*. Princeton University Press.

Hamza, H. (2015). Does investment deposit return in Islamic banks reflect PLS principle? *Borsa Istanbul Review, 16*(1), 32–42.

Hamza, H., & Saadaoui, Z. (2013). Investment deposits, risk-taking and capital decisions in Islamic banks. *Studies in Economics and Finance, 30*(3), 244–265.

Hassan, M. K. & Bashir, A.-H. M. (2005). Determinants of islamic banking profitability. *Islamic Perspectives on Wealth Creation*, 118–140.

Hassan, M. K., & Mervyn, K. L. (2007). *Islamic banking: An introduction and overview*. Handbook of Islamic Banking.

Htay, S. N. N., Salman, S. A., & Shaugee, I. (2013). Invisible hands behind the corporate governance practices in Malaysia. *World Journal of Social Sciences, 3*(1), 119–135.

IFSB. (2005). *Guiding principles of risk management for institutions (other than insurance institutions) offering only Islamic financial services*. Islamic Financial Services Board.

IFSB. (2010). *Guidance note on the practice of smoothing the profits payout to investment account holders*. Islamic Financial Services Board.

Ismal, R. (2010). Strengthening and improving the liquidity management in Islamic banking. *Humanomics, 26*(1), 18–35.

Izzaouihda, K., & Chami, M. (2018). Lissage des Rendements des Comptes d'Investissement Participatif en Banques Islamiques Quelle pertinence? *International Journal of Economics and Strategic Management of Business Process, 10*, 7–17.

Kammer, A., Norat, M., Pinon, M., Parasad, A., Towce, C., & Zeidane, Z. (2015). *Islamic finance: Opportunities, challenges, and policy options*. SDN/15/05. IMF.

Kennedy, P. (1998). *A guide to econometrics*. Blackwell.

Khan, T., & Ahmed, H. (2001). *Risk management: An analysis of issues in Islamic financial industry*. Islamic Development Bank.

Khediri, K. B., Charfeddine, L., & Youssef, S. B. (2015). Islamic versus conventional banks in the GCC countries: A comparative study using classification techniques. *Research in International Business and Finance, 33*, 75–98.

Li, Y., Hassan, A., Abdirashid, E., Zeller, B., & Du, M. (2012). The impact of investor protection on financial performance of Islamic banks: An empirical analysis. *Corporate Ownership & Control, 9*(4).

Maali, B. M., & Atmeh, M. A. (2015). Using social welfare concepts to guarantee Islamic banks' deposits. *International Journal of Islamic and Middle Eastern Finance and Management, 8*(2), 134–149.

Magalhães, R., & Al-Saad, S. (2013). Corporate governance in Islamic financial institutions: The issues surrounding unrestricted investment account holders. *Corporate Governance: The International Journal of Business in Society, 13*(1), 39–57.

Mkadmi, J. E., & Halioui, K. (2013). Analyse de l'impact du conseil d'administration sur la performance des banques conventionnelles Malaisiennes. *La Revue Gestion et Organisation, 5*(1), 16–26.

Nawaz, T. (2017). Momentum investment strategies, corporate governance and firm performance: An analysis of Islamic banks. *Corporate Governance: The International Journal of Business in Society, 17*(2), 192–211.

Olson, D., & Zoubi, T. A. (2008). Using accounting ratios to distinguish between Islamic and conventional banks in the GCC region. *The International Journal of Accounting, 43*(1), 45–65.

Quttainah, M. A. (2012). *Four essays on the impact of Shari'ah (Islamic Law) as an institutional governance mechanism on organizational performance and managerial behavior* (Thèse de doctorat en Sciences de gestion). Institut Polytechnique Rensselaer/USA.

Ramly, Z., Datuk, N. & Nordin, M. H. (2018). Shariah supervision board, board independence, risk committee and risk-taking of Islamic banks in Malaysia. *International Journal of Economics and Financial Issues, 8*(4), 290–300.

Ruimy, M. (2008). *La Finance Islamique, Collection 'Finance d'aujourd'hui.* Edition SEISBN 9782896031412.

Sarker, M. A. (2000). Islamic business contracts, agency problem and the theory of the Islamic firm. *International Journal of Islamic Financial Services, 1*(2).

Sundararajan, V. (2005, November 22–24). *Risk measurement, and disclosure in Islamic finance and the implications of profit sharing investment accounts.* Paper prepared for the Sixth International Conference on Islamic Economics, Banking, and Finance, Jakarta, Indonesia.

Sundararajan, V. (2008). Issues in managing profit equalization reserves and investment risk reserves in Islamic Banks. In S. Archer, A. Rifaat, & V. Sundararajan, *Islamic finance: The regulatory challenge* (pp. 40–68). Wiley.

Toumi, K., & Viviani, J. L. (2013). Le risque lié aux comptes d'investissement participatifs: un risque propre aux banques islamiques. *Revue des Sciences de Gestion,* 131–142.

Toumi, K., Viviani, J.-L., & Belkacem, L. (2011a). Actual risk sharing measurement in Islamic banks. In W. Sun, C. Louche, & R. Pérez (Eds.), *Finance* and sustainability: Towards a new paradigm? A post-crisis agenda (Critical studies on corporate responsibility, governance and sustainability) (Vol. 2, pp. 325–347). Emerald Group Publishing Limited.

Toumi, K., Viviani, J.-L., & Belkacem, L. (2011b). Islamic banks exposure to displaced commercial risk: Identification and measurement (CR2M - CC028 - Université Montpellier 2).

Toumi, K., Viviani, J.-L., & Belkacem, L. (2011c). A comparison of leverage and profitability of islamic and conventional banks. SSRN Electronic Journal.

Toumi, K., Viviani, J. L., & Chayeh, Z. (2018). Measurement of the displaced commercial risk in Islamic banks. The Quarterly Review of Economics and Finance.

Trabelsi, M. A., & Trad, N. (2017). Profitability and risk in interest-free banking industries: A dynamic panel data analysis. International Journal of Islamic and Middle Eastern Finance and Management, 10(4), 454–469.

Zarai, M. F., & Zarai, M. A. (2013). Earnings management and investment accounts holders interests in islamic banking institutions. International Journal of Business and Management Invention, 22–35.

WEBSITES

www.ibisonline.com
www.worldbank.org
www.ifsb.org

Customers' Preference and Selection of Takaful Insurance Products: The UAE Case

*Mohamed Adel Saleh, Abdolkarim Abootaleb Abbasi,
Ali Ahmad Al Falasi, Mohammad Bader Almheiri,
and Abdelghani Echchabi*

1 Introduction

The United Arab Emirates has one of the largest economies in the GCC region. The economy's growth has expanded mainly as a result of the oil boom. The growth in the economy has improved the financial industry. However, there has been a slowed growth in the insurance industry and its

M. A. Saleh · A. A. Abbasi · A. A. Al Falasi · M. B. Almheiri · A. Echchabi (✉)
Department of Business, Higher Colleges of Technology,
Dubai, United Arab Emirates
e-mail: aechchabi@hct.ac.ae

M. A. Saleh
e-mail: H00327134@hct.ac.ae

A. A. Abbasi
e-mail: H00366924@hct.ac.ae

A. A. Al Falasi
e-mail: H00276697@hct.ac.ae

A. Echchabi et al. (eds.), *Contemporary Research in Accounting
and Finance*, https://doi.org/10.1007/978-981-16-8267-4_9

217

contribution to the economic growth of the country. Nevertheless, historically, insurance has been considered an important part of the finance industry. Religious laws, that are influential in the making of the UAE laws, have been a key reason for the slowed growth of the insurance industry (Jaffer & Irshad, 2020). However, the Takaful approach has played a critical role in promoting the scalability of the insurance industry from both Islamic and conventional perspectives. Takaful products are being preferred to other competing services as a result of their stringent adherence to Shariah laws.

By 2018, the assets of Islamic countries were valued at $4.2 trillion, where Takaful currently has a share of 1.25% of these assets (Dinç, 2019). Despite the share being minimal, it is substantial compared to other industries in the country. The overall growth rate is still low, with a 2020 report by the Gross Written Premium revealing a growth rate of 3.9%, compared to over 19% of what was recorded by other conventional insurance companies. As such, there is still a low uptake of Takaful products.

Takaful has been under-researched compared to the conventional insurance industry, primarily due to the fact that it is largely focused on Islamic religious principles, and their services may be unfamiliar to non-Muslims (Dahnoun & Alqudwa, 2018). Historically, insurance companies that are not affiliated with any religion were more popular, primarily because of the fact that they appeal to all religions. Religious-affiliated companies will often have a limited audience since their audience is limited. The above reason elucidates why the research on Takaful has been relatively scarce. Accordingly, the Takaful market has been largely based in Islamic countries, with little existence in minority-Muslim countries (Sherif & Hussnain, 2017).

There are certain areas that should be improved to increase the Islamic insurance outcome, which will consequently foster the customers' satisfaction. First, there should be changes in how customers access products while at the same time maintaining their affordability. Second, it is imperative to ensure that the products are affordable. Third, there should be an increased focus on how to foster trust since it is one of the factors that

M. B. Almheiri
e-mail: H00324340@hct.ac.ae

is inhibiting the uptake of this product compared to other conventional insurance products.

Accordingly, the study aims at unraveling some of the factors that influence the customers' selection of Takaful services and the obstacles that push the customers away from these services. The study will then provide recommendations to Takaful firms and relevant government agencies on how they can foster the Islamic insurance industry. Particularly, the study attempts to achieve the following objectives:

1. To identify the factors that influence the selection and preference of Takaful products and services.
2. To identify factors that can promote the growth and contribution of the Takaful industry to the country's financial development.

2   LITERATURE REVIEW OF TAKAFUL INSURANCE PRODUCTS

2.1   Takaful History

According to Hassan (2019), Takaful can be traced to the second century AD when there was an influx of Muslims in the Far East, Asia, and India. It was based on the principle of people guaranteeing one another when one member of a group is experiencing misfortunes.

With the progression of trade around the world, Muslims from the Ottoman empire developed help practices to foster trade. The plan involved the development of a Waqf fund that aimed to provide insurance to the members. However, the development of the program was inhibited by the proliferation of western practices in the region. A factor that was influenced by the proximity of the region to Europe. Hassan (2019) further reported in a subsequent study that the Ottoman and Egyptian empires have also approved the use of western financial principles such as those on insurance, which prevented the growth of Islamic insurance (Öz & Işık, 2019). The growth of the Islamic financial services such as insurance policies was slowed by Islamic laws that did not support business continuity through the Waqf system, which was also against some aspects of a business being a legal entity. The religious aspects made it difficult for Muslims to venture into various businesses. In the seventeenth century, several modern insurance policies were developed, and subsequently spread to different regions worldwide, including different Islamic nations.

There was an increase in the number of businesses in these regions, that used the principle of insurance adopted in different nations across the world to protect themselves from unprecedented uncertainties. However, the practice was earlier perceived as immoral by many Muslims and was not accepted according to the Shariah jurisdictions. The lack of alternatives to the actions made it difficult for the Muslims to reject the insurance traditions.

Some perceived the continued use of conventional insurance policies as destigmatizing to the Muslim community due to their Islamic principles leading to the development of Takaful insurance (Khan et al., 2016). However, after the introduction of the insurance program, there was a slow adoption among Muslim governments. Only after the intervention by religious and economic experts was the program integrated into Shariah laws. The debates on this subject first emerged in 1976 in Saudi Arabia by the Islamic Economics committee. Despite the lengthy debates on the subject, most of the major terms were not fully agreed upon.

The first agreement was made in 1986 when the first model of Takaful was made. The model was established during the second session by the Islamic *Fiqh* Council (Hassan, 2019). Sudan was reported as the first country that adopted the model. The other countries that were among the first to adopt this model included Saudi Arabia, Malaysia, Bahrain, and the United Arab Emirates. Takaful later spread its wings to Africa and some parts of Europe. Takaful has now spread across the world. It is currently regarded as an important insurance alternative among Muslims. Saudi Arabia currently accounts for over 80% of all Takaful operations in GCC countries (Guendouz & Ouassaf, 2018). The other countries include Bahrain, UAE, Malaysia, and Oman.

2.2   *The Differences Between Takaful and Conventional Insurance*

Conventional or traditional insurance is a concept that is used to refer to insurance policies emanating from the western world. The earliest known conventional insurance model was initiated in Barcelona in the fifteenth century and aimed to capture maritime activities as captured in the Hammurabi Laws (Dahnoun & Alqudwa, 2018). The current insurance environment is determined by legal risks, macroeconomics, geopolitical, and natural disasters.

It is noteworthy that the earning of interest is prohibited in the three primary religions, i.e., Judaism, Islam, and Christianity. However, the aspect of interest rates has been relaxed in Judaism and Christianity, which emanated from the sea trade. Islam considers interest rates as haram (prohibited), even though it is the basis of international trade. Contrary to conventional insurance companies, Takaful operates strictly under Shariah laws, which conforms to Islamic tenets.

Takaful has evolved from cooperation on voluntary contribution, which in Islamic terms is referred to as *ta'awun* and *tabarru'* (Dahnoun & Alqudwa, 2018). It involves different people who contribute money and pool them in a way that is easily accessible by the Takaful vendor. It involves a concept of sharing risks among the members, which differs from conventional insurance, where the obligation to pay for the risk is transferred from the members to the insurance operators. The funds paid incur profits when they are held at the fund, and when some members suffer the loss, they are repaid using money that has been developed from the pool. Muslims have also ascertained that Takaful products eliminate the aspect of uncertainty, gambling, and high interest rates. It is based on aspects of mutual responsibility, harmony, and benefit to all the members. Three primary bodies govern Takaful, namely, the local insurance governing body in every country, the international insurance supervision association, and the international board of financial services.

Takaful became a formal insurance method in 1986 (Dahnoun & Alqudwa, 2018). Despite facing criticism at the beginning from Islamic scholars, it was finally accepted and adopted. The majority of the Islamic nations have embraced this insurance policy. Nonetheless, this approach has slowed growth, which augments the need to solve some of the gaps.

2.3   *Factors Influencing Customers Selection of Takaful Products*

Several factors influence the customers' intention to adopt Takaful services. Based on different studies, the usage of Takaful is mainly affected by a variety of social and economic factors. Elements such as positive behavioral beliefs, religiosity, social influence, income, and cost of premiums are considered the main determinants of whether a customer will subscribe to Takaful services or otherwise (El-Tahir, 2021).

Particularly, Takaful is based on the Islamic religious principles centered on the avoidance of interest, gambling, and uncertainty (Al Mahi et al., 2017). These dimensions make customers more confident in the

Takaful products' religious conformity. This perception among adherent Muslims makes Takaful a more desirable product, compared to conventional insurance. Furthermore, the sense of community support presented by mutual contribution makes Takaful products more attractive to some consumers. Therefore, the consumer's attitude is a major contributor to the likelihood of a person buying a product. Takaful products have also presented customers with the opportunity to provide mutual help to advance various virtues, such as helping those that need help (Shabiq & Hassan, 2016). The above fact proves that religious aspects are the most significant factor that influences customer preferences, and it is affirmed by the large presence of Takaful in Islamic countries.

On the other hand, support from family and social friends, and peers can also contribute to a person subscribing to Takaful services. This encouragement from people around a potential customer leads to the development of positive subjective norms. It has been asserted that the conviction that a specific important member of a social circle would approve of the behavior contributed to a person purchasing the product. The approval acts as a motivator forcing a person to opt for Takaful services (El-Tahir, 2021). The social influences are heavily based on the interactions in Mosques, and Islamic media, where most of the Takaful products are advertised. Takaful mainly advertises on Islamic television and religious stations and platforms, which may have fueled the purchase of Takaful products within Islamic countries.

Another factor that influences the usage of Takaful is the price of its products and services. Low prices tend to affect customers' selection of either Takaful or conventional insurance services. Their range of products includes medical insurance, professional indemnity insurance, WIBA insurance, livestock insurance, products in the heavy engineering industry, and an array of other insurance products such as fire, burglary, and risk. Having a wide variety of these services, with easy access to customers is an additional reason for customers to opt for their preferred type of insurance.

Other factors that influence the customers' selection of their insurance services include relative advantage, compatibility, social influence, awareness, and religiosity (Husin et al., 2015). In this regard, the religiosity dimension is present in all the aforementioned factors, as Takaful insurance is implementing the Shariah compliance in every aspect of its operations (Shabiq & Hassan, 2016). On the other hand, relative advantage can be regarded as the additional advantages that this firm provides compared to the other companies. Particularly, Takaful provides the customers with the added benefits of Islamic affiliation, which has been highlighted as an integral factor that influences the purchase of the product. The customers have the added assurance that the company will protect their religious beliefs and principles.

Compatibility also refers to the idea that the products that Takaful provides are compatible with the needs of most customers, which makes it easy for the customers to purchase the products (Husin et al., 2015). The company has focused on integral areas that capture the needs and interests of many customers, especially in risk mitigation, medical, professional indemnity, work-related, and livestock insurance. Therefore, Takaful provides an added advantage in the fact that the products are in conformity with the cultural needs of most customers (Johnson et al., 2019).

Awareness is another factor that influences the purchase of Takaful products, as affirmed herein in this literature. The amalgamation of the above-mentioned factors has increased the awareness of Takaful products in Islamic communities and consequently influenced their purchase (El-Tahir, 2021). The awareness has further been heightened through mainstream Islamic television and radio stations and through different social media sites. The use of these sites has made it possible for a large number of people to understand Takaful products and consequently purchase products based on this awareness. Awareness and lack of awareness refer to the Takaful principles, operations, advantages brought about with Takaful products, and the values created by the Takaful industry.

There is a direct correlation between awareness toward a certain product and the choice of the customers toward how they utilize the product. Awareness is an integral function that determines the functions and usability of a product. It further makes it easy to unravel the remedies and benefits that can be derived from a certain product or service. There is an apparent lack of awareness of Islamic financing and Takaful among non-Islamic countries and certain Islamic countries, which inhibits access to Takaful products (Riazi, 2017). However, there is an apparent customer awareness in the majority of the Islamic countries on Takaful products, which has been an integral factor in promoting the adoption of these products and the relevant customer choices that have been made (Bhatti & Husiri, 2019). Hassan (2019) and Bryman (2016) also obtained similar findings, where factors like awareness, social influence, compatibility, and relative advantage had a significant impact on customers' intention to opt for Takaful services.

Moreover, family consumption in the form of income per capita is another aspect that influenced the adoption of Takaful insurance policies (Sekaran & Bougie, 2016). The ability to afford Takaful insurance plans among households was an integral factor influencing the demand and uptake of Takaful plans. Higher-income earners had a high uptake of Takaful products, unlike the low-income earners, since most of them cannot afford the premiums. Similarly, high inflation often leads to an increase in the price of basic products and services including Takaful, consequently, lowering income.

It is noteworthy that Medical Takaful plans were the most preferred and popular services offered by Takaful firms, followed closely by motor vehicle policies. Work-based Takaful policies were the third most preferred product. The fourth most preferred insurance product was livestock Takaful, influenced by the fact that a significant number of customers in many parts of the world are livestock owners (Ishak, 2017).

3   Research Model and Factors Definition

3.1   Social Impact

Social impact is potentially a determining factor influencing the selection of Takaful services. It measures the social pressure or pressure from friends, family, and peers to perform a certain action. Subjective norm is mainly derived from customer behavior and the psychological factors that influence the purchase decisions. It is the basis through which customers make purchases on any product (Shabiq & Hasan, 2016). Depending on the social pressure, there are some positive or negative aspects that can result from the subjective norms. Subjective pressures can influence decisions and consequently affect the type of purchase behaviors of individuals. Several studies indicated that subjective norms and intentions to purchase are correlated, which implies that a positive relationship between them in the case of Takaful is also likely.

The subjective norms from Islamic communities have been an integral factor in influencing the purchase of products and services with a religious aspect. Subjective norms have also been created through advertisement platforms such as television, radio, and in Islamic meetings where different Muslim groups share knowledge on different Takaful products, and consequently impacting the purchase decisions (Shabiq & Hasan, 2016).

3.2   Uncertainty

Uncertainty is also a significant factor that eventually influences Takaful's purchase decisions. Uncertainty is the unfavorable behavior of customers toward the outcome of certain products or services. Uncertainty reflects risk dimensions that an individual has developed toward a certain product or service, and the customer is aware of the negativity that may result from their decisions. Uncertainty might also emerge when people purchase a product or order a service they have not used before (Shabiq & Hasan, 2016).

The relationship between intention and uncertainty is often negative, and it is one of the most important aspects influencing the purchase of Takaful products. Uncertainty possibly influences the purchasing decisions because people have often perceived the risks of Takaful products as high compared to the other conventional insurance products. Nevertheless, the stringent compliance to Shariah laws is one aspect that relatively diluted the perceived risk and its influence on the purchase of Takaful products.

3.3   Perceived Compatibility

Perceived compatibility is another factor that has influenced the uptake of Takaful products. Innovation is a critical component that influences perceived compatibility in the use of Takaful products. The innovation that has been witnessed in the company has consistently been in sync with values, past experiences, and needs that have been adopted throughout the company (Husin et al., 2015). Additionally, the perceived compatibility implies that innovation awareness has not been changed over the years in relation to reality. These factors have influenced the decision of the customers toward Takaful products since customers have often preferred Takaful products since they are useful to them (Nugraheni & Muhammad, 2019).

3.4   Relative Advantage

The other factor that eventually influences purchase behavior in Takaful is a relative advantage. Relative advantage refers to the advantage of providing additional benefits to the customers through certain products or services. Takaful products allow customers to obtain certain additional benefits that they would not have obtained with other conventional insurance products. These benefits include lower overall cost, which is almost unrivaled by the conventional counterparts, the social prestige provided by Takaful especially in an Islamic context, easiness, and efficiency in terms of claims, etc. (Shabiq & Hasan, 2016). It can also include perks aspects, such as dividends (McCluskey et al., 2010). Customers will often select products that provide additional benefits to them. Particularly, Takaful has some additional benefits compared to the insurance counterparts. As such, it is likely to attract more customers relative to the conventional insurance schemes.

3.5   Customers Awareness of Takaful Services

The majority of customers in Muslim countries are still not aware of the Takaful services. The awareness has been limited by the perceived ambiguity of the Takaful operations. Likewise, there are still major misunderstandings regarding the legality of the insurance policies that Takaful is providing (Husin et al., 2015). Consequently, it has resulted in disagreements between different Muslim scholars. In addition, there is limited knowledge among the general public on how insurance policies work. Prevalent misinterpretations and propaganda on Islamic laws have also affected the uptake of Takaful services (Atlas, 2017). Since it was introduced as a legitimate scheme dealing in insurance policies in 1979, customer awareness has been low due to the limitations that have existed in this industry over the years. Takaful currently has a presence in 75 countries, which are mainly in Muslim countries. It has established operations in Southeast Asia and the Middle East. Compared to conventional insurance companies in these countries, customer awareness, growth rate, and understanding of Takaful insurance are relatively low. However, in the GCC countries, the growth rate of Takaful still supersedes that of conventional insurance (Alshammari et al., 2019).

4 Methodology

4.1 Research Design

It was important to use research methods that incorporate both quantitative and qualitative approaches, to gain deeper insights of the current topic (Headley & Plano Clark, 2020). The approach focused on examining the real-life contexts to obtain comprehension and multilevel perspectives, and social influences and connections. The use of Takaful insurance services is mainly associated with the religious aspect of Islam, which makes the approach ideal. Mixed methods research design involves the incorporation of an array of influences of various variables that have an intensive exploration on the meaning of the subject through a qualitative approach (Creswell & Clark, 2017).

The study seeks to understand customers' perception of Takaful insurance services using a mixed method with qualitative and quantitative items. The combination of both qualitative and quantitative methods will enable the researchers to draw from the strengths of both approaches to promote a holistic interpretation of the subject under discussion. The mixed research method incorporates different approaches that will enable the researcher to understand the concepts and applications better. This approach is important for the study since it aims to unravel the perceptions of potential and existing customers in this field (Bazeley, 2017). Quantitative methodologies have been significantly used to investigate factors that influence the preference of Takaful services in several countries. As such, additionally using qualitative methods will add a significant value to the study (Alramz, 2017). Specifically, the triangulation aspect of the mixed methods was conducted by comparing and consolidating the findings from both the quantitative and qualitative approaches.

4.2 Data Collection and Analysis

The study targets the entire UAE population, that are eligible to purchase insurance premiums. In this regard, a significant number of individuals is covered in this category due to the improved economic status in the country. However, because of the current challenges in accessing the entire population, only a sample of 300 respondents was considered including current and potential Takaful customers. In addition, ten industry experts were involved in the qualitative interviews.

Since the study applied both quantitative and qualitative methods of data collection, researchers incorporated the use of a survey to collect data from the existing customers. The study also incorporated the use of interviews to gather information from professionals. As such, the study incorporated both qualitative interviews and quantitative questionnaires (Schoonenboom & Johnson, 2017). Survey questionnaires were distributed randomly to individuals from various UAE states. Health precautions were strictly observed to foster the health and safety of the participants and those of the researchers since the study was conducted in the midst of the COVID-19 pandemic. The questionnaire was developed into two sections. The first section captured the factors that could affect the preferences and selection of the customers of the Takaful products in the United Arab Emirates. These factors were measured on a 5 points Likert scale to give the respondents more flexibility in terms of rating those factors and their importance. The quantitative data analysis was performed using descriptive statistics, regression, and t-test analyses. It is noteworthy that the analysis was conducted using SPSS software.

On the other hand, online interviews were conducted through Zoom video conferencing application. In this regard, the researchers approached different organizations that are involved in offering Takaful services and requested their assistance in being part of the interview process. The target interviewees were mainly at the management rank. Out of the approached firms, 10 interviewees finally agreed to be part of the interviews. The interviews were recorded and were transcribed subsequently. Subsequently, the interviews' output was analyzed thematic approach.

5   FINDINGS

5.1   *Quantitative Results*

5.1.1   *Respondents Profile*
The respondents' profile in Table 1 indicates that 66% of the respondents were male, while 34% were female respondents. Further, the table shows that 76% of the respondents are single while the remaining 24% represent married respondents.

In terms of age distribution, the results indicate that 67% are between 20 and 30 years old, 15% are less than 20 years old, 12% are between 31 and 40 years old, and 6% of the respondents are between 41 and 50 years old.

Table 1 Respondents' profile

Factor	Categories	Percentage
Gender	Male	66
	Female	34
Age	Less than 20	15
	20–30	67
	31–40	12
	41–50	6
Educational Level	Diploma	23
	Bachelor	67
	Master	2
	Ph.D	6
	Professional certificate	3
Marital Status	Single	76
	Married	24
Occupation	Student	52
	Public sector	23
	Private sector	18
	Self-employed	7
Takaful customers	Yes	56
	No	44

Source Authors' calculation based on the collected data

Regarding the education level, the results reveal that 67% of the respondents hold a Bachelor's degree, 23% hold a Diploma, 8% hold postgraduate degrees, and 3% of the respondents hold a professional certificate.

Finally, in terms of type of occupation, roughly, 52% of the respondents are students, 23% work in the public sector, 18% work in the private sector, and 7% of the respondents are self-employed. It is noteworthy that 56% of the respondents are currently using Takaful services, while 44% are not.

5.1.2 Regression Analysis

The regression analysis summary is presented in Table 2. The findings reveal that compatibility, social impact, and awareness have a significant positive impact on the customers' intention to adopt Takaful services, with awareness having the highest impact on behavioral intention. On the other hand, uncertainty was found to have significant negative effect on customers' intention to adopt Takaful services. Nevertheless, relative

Table 2 Regression analysis summary

	Coefficients	Standard Error	t Stat	P-value
Intercept	0.028748732	0.212689	0.135168	0.892659
Uncertainty	−0.09188273	0.043066	−2.13351	0.034499
Relative Advantages	0.079791646	0.077704	1.026869	0.306124
Compatibility	0.293130325	0.063426	4.621625	0.00000
Social impact	0.194320666	0.048782	3.983432	0.000105
Awareness	0.545074464	0.051194	10.6473	0.00000

Source Authors' calculation based on the collected data

advantage had no significant effect on the intention to adopt Takaful services.

The results are in line with those conducted by Hassan and Abbas (2019), which revealed that compatibility, awareness, and social influence were some of the contributing factors to the behavioral intention. However, it contradicts the findings of Hassan and Abbas (2019) regarding relative advantage. It is likely that the respondents do not clearly and prominently the comparative advantages that Takaful products offer in contrast to the conventional insurance services. As such, they might perceive them as similar in terms of advantages and benefits. Accordingly, relative advantage was not found to be a determining factor in the selection of Takaful versus conventional insurance.

It is noteworthy that the model's R square value is 0.81, indicating that the models' significant factors explain 81% of the variation in the intention to adopt Takaful services. In other words, these factors can predict the customers' selection of Takaful services by 81%.

5.1.3   T-test Analysis

The t-test results summary for the behavioral intention items is presented in Table 3. The objective in this regard is to compare the individual items' mean value with the test value of 3 (neutral value), to test the willingness of customers to use/continue using Takaful services.

In this regards, the results indicate all the p-values for the t-test are less than 0.05, which implies that the individual items' mean values are significantly different from the test value. In addition, the t values are positive, which implies that the mean difference is positive for all the intention items. As such, this is an indication that the customers are intending to

Table 3 t-test summary

	T	Df	P
INT1	6.028	153	0.000
INT2	4.681	152	0.000
INT3	5.158	153	0.000
INT4	5.706	153	0.000
INT5	6.053	153	0.000
INT6	5.646	151	0.000

Source Authors' calculation based on the collected data

use/continue using Takaful services in future. The findings are in line with the findings of Hassan (2019) and Husin et al. (2015), where the authors assessed the factors that influence customers' selection of Takaful products and identified a high willingness of customers to use Takaful services.

5.2   Qualitative Findings

5.2.1   Performance Between Takaful and Conventional Insurance Firms

Regarding the perceptions about differences between Takaful and conventional insurance products, all the interviewees stated that the awareness and use of conventional insurance surpassed that of Takaful products because of the age differences between the two. Nonetheless, there was a consensus that Takaful presented the better growth opportunity when compared to conventional insurance services. Particularly, the interviews revealed that the conventional insurance had a larger market share compared to Takaful since it had been in the market for a longer time, consequently becoming more efficient and performing better.

On the other hand, the interviews showed that the performance of Takaful could surpass that of conventional firms provided they reduce risks through assets-based contracts. In other words, there is a room for improvement in Takaful even though it is still relatively new. Nevertheless, Takaful companies also embarked on an unexplored target market that would spur the growth and profitability, compared to conventional insurance companies.

5.2.2   Competitiveness of Takaful Companies Versus the Insurance Companies

Regarding the competitiveness of Takaful services compared to the conventional insurance services, most of the interviewees were of the opinion that the conventional insurance industry still has a significantly bigger market share compared to the Takaful industry. The respondents further stated that the efficiency and performance of conventional insurance companies superseded that of Takaful since they had been in the market for a long time. However, the Takaful companies were also catching up rapidly.

Some of the factors that were perceived to contribute to increasing the competitiveness and performance of Takaful companies include the Takaful products and services pricing as well as the Shariah compliance aspect of these services. These two dimensions are interconnected since the customers usually compare prices of products and services, taking into account also the compliance of the Takaful services to the Islamic religious principles. The latter was a major factor in distinguishing Takaful services from the conventional insurance services, since customers generally accept to pay a small premium for Takaful services to obtain a service that is in line with their religious beliefs.

The interviewees mentioned some of the actions that can improve the competitiveness and performance of Takaful companies in the UAE. This includes providing the right financial and logistic infrastructure that would reflect the religious principles upon which Takaful is built. Moreover, to foster financial development, the interviewees called for heightened compliance to Shariah laws. In addition, the interviewees recommended that awareness about Takaful operations should be enhanced. This can be achieved through awareness advertisements and campaigns, public lectures, extensive usage of social media network, etc. Additionally, the interviewees indicated that some other factors such as financial technology development and careful pricing could also enhance the competitiveness and popularity of Takaful services.

On the other hand, the government's support in increasing the significant of Takaful in the UAE can include developing appropriate regulations that promote growth and development of Takaful through mergers and acquisitions for instance. Some additional aspects that could also foster the Takaful development include the allocation of appropriate premiums to projects with different risk levels.

5.2.3 Issues Faced by Takaful Companies that Are Preventing Them from Optimal Performance

Shariah compliance was consistently mentioned as one of the major issues that inhibit the performance and competitiveness of Takaful insurance products. This was echoed by all the interviewees. Moreover, the interviewees stated that some additional factors that negatively affect the performance of Takaful include competition from the other insurance companies, complex laws, limitation of Shariah courts, and limited specialized marketing resources and human capital. In addition, the interviewees revealed that operation inefficiencies were also one of the challenges that negatively affected the performance of Takaful. The inefficiencies have triggered the increase of costs and reduction of revenues. Finally, Takaful is also experiencing a challenge of limited liquidity and capital.

6 CONCLUSION AND RECOMMENDATIONS

The main objective of the study was to examine the customers' willingness to use/continue using Takaful services in the UAE, as well as the factors that influence their decisions. In addition, the study attempted to explore the perception of Takaful and insurance professionals regarding the competitiveness and performance of both industries. The study used a mixed methodology approach, by relying on both quantitative and qualitative aspects of data collection and analysis.

The findings revealed that customers in the UAE are keen to use/continue using Takaful services. Further, the findings showed that uncertainty has a negative influence on the intention to adopt Takaful services. While compatibility, social impact, and awareness were found to have a significant positive influence on the intention to adopt Takaful services in the UAE. Moreover, it was consistently highlighted in the interviews that though the Takaful industry is still relatively new compared to conventional insurance, it has better growth prospects and can highly benefit from the "catch up" effect, since this area was not as explored as the long-existed conventional insurance industry. Furthermore, issues like Shariah compliance, pricing, lack of financial technology usage, and liquidity limitations should be addressed, in order to improve the performance and competitiveness of Takaful industry.

These findings are highly significant and provide significant contribution to the Takaful industry, as well as the policy makers in the UAE and similar settings. Particularly, the awareness of Takaful should be raised through advertising and awareness campaigns, public lectures, and optimal usage of social media networks. The compatibility of Takaful should be highlighted in these campaigns. This includes compatibility with religious belief, existing insurance/Takaful needs, and other financial needs. This is because compatibility and awareness were found to have a significant effect on the intention to adopt Takaful services. These campaigns should also rely on social influence of major influence groups, such as peers, family members, and media influence.

In relation to the above, the Takaful practitioners and policy makers should also ensure that the perceived uncertainty and ambiguity of Takaful services are reduced. This will encourage customers to adopt Takaful services instead of the conventional insurance services. This aspect can also be emphasized in the awareness campaigns.

A primary limitation of the study is that it was conducted in the midst of the COVID-19 outbreak, which made it complicated to obtain to obtain more questionnaire responses and also to conduct the interviews in more appropriate conditions. In addition, the study focused only on retail customers and did not consider corporate customers. As such, the findings may not be applicable to corporate customers as well. Accordingly, future studies are recommended to cover a comprehensive and larger sample of both retail and corporate customers to obtain more meaningful results that can be generalized to the UAE context.

References

Al Mahi, A. S., Sim, S., & Hassan, A. F. (2017). Religiosity and demand for Takaful (Islamic insurance): A preliminary investigation. *International Journal of Applied Business and Economic Research, 15*(24), 485–499.

Alramz. (2017). *The UAE insurance sector: High time for a change. Equity research.* https://webcache.googleusercontent.com/search?q=cache:gpw6oU-fzv0J:https://alramz.ae/Researcharchives/download/Ramz_UAE_Insurance_Sector_27-SEP-2017.pdf+&cd=1&hl=en&ct=clnk&gl=ke

Alshammari, A. A., Alhabshi, S. M., & Saiti, B. (2019). The impact of oil prices and the financial market on cost efficiency in the insurance and Takaful sectors: Evidence from a stochastic frontier analysis. *Economic Systems, 43*(3/4), 410–427.

Atlas, M. (2017, April 14). Emergence and evolution of Takaful insurance. *Atlas Magazine.* https://www.atlas-mag.net/en/article/emergence-and-evolution-of-takaful-insurance

Bazeley, P. (2017). *Integrating analyses in mixed methods research.* Sage.

Bhatti, T., & Husin, M. M. (2019). An investigation of the effect of customer beliefs on the intention to participate in family Takaful schemes. *Journal of Islamic Marketing, 1*(3), 709–727.

Sekaran, U., & Bougie, R. (2016). *Research methods for business: A skill building approach.* Wiley.

Bryman, A. (2016). *Social research methods.* Oxford University Press.

Creswell, J. W., & Clark, V. L. P. (2017). *Designing and conducting mixed methods research.* Sage.

Dahnoun, M., & Alqudwa, B. (2018). Islamic insurance: An alternative to conventional insurance. *American Journal of Humanities & Islamic Studies, 1*(1), 4–7.

Dinç, Y. (2019). *Improving the Takaful sector in Islamic countries.* COMCEC. http://www.comcec.org/en/wp-content/uploads/2019/11/2-Presentat ion-Slides_Improving-the-Takaful-Sector-in-Islamic-Countries_17....pdf

El-Tahir, H. (2021). *The global Takaful insurance market: Charting the road to mass markets.* Deloitte. https://www2.deloitte.com/content/dam/Del oitte/lu/Documents/financial-advisory/1947_global-takaful-insurance-mar ket_AAM.pdf. Accessed 26 April 2021.

Guendouz, A. A., & Ouassaf, S. (2018). Determinants of Saudi Takaful insurance companies profitability. *Academy of Accounting and Financial Studies Journal, 22*(5), 1–24.

Hassan, H. A. (2019). Takaful models: Origin, progression, and future. *Journal of Islamic Marketing, 11*(6), 1801–1819.

Hassan, H. A., & Abbas, S. K. (2019). Factors influencing the investors' intention to adopt Takaful (Islamic insurance) products. *Journal of Islamic Marketing, 11*(1), 5–13.

Headley, M. G., & Plano Clark, V. L. (2020). Multilevel mixed methods research designs: Advancing a refined definition. *Journal of Mixed Methods Research, 14*(2), 145–163.

Husin, M. M., Ismail, N., & Rustam, N. (2015). *The effects of compatibility, social influence, and awareness in the adoption of Takaful.* Worldresearch-library.org. https://www.worldresearchlibrary.org/up_proc/pdf/22-142815 1841104-107.pdf. Accessed 26 April 2021.

Ishak, N. H. (2017). Concept paper: Customer satisfaction in Malaysian Takaful industry. *International Journal of Academic Research in Business and Social Sciences, 7*(3), 380–391.

Jaffer, S., & Irshad, A. (2020). *UAE insurance industry report 2019.* Milliman. https://milliman-cdn.azureedge.net/-/media/milliman/pdfs/art icles/uae_insurance_industry_report_2019.ashx

Johnson, R. B., Russo, F., & Schoonenboom, J. (2019). Causation in mixed methods research: The meeting of philosophy, science, and practice. *Journal of Mixed Methods Research, 13*(2), 143–162.

Khan, I. R., Rahman, N. N. B. A., Yusoff, M. Y. Z. B. M., & Nor, M. R. B. M. (2016). History, problems, and prospects of Islamic insurance (Takaful) in Bangladesh. *Springerplus, 5*(1), 1–7.

McCluskey, T., Broderick, A., Boyle, A., Burton, B., & Power, D. (2010). Evidence on Irish financial analysts' and fund managers' views about dividends. *Qualitative Research in Financial Markets, 2*(2), 80–99.

Nugraheni, P., & Muhammad, R. (2019). Innovation in the Takaful industry: A strategy to expand the Takaful market in Indonesia. *Journal of Islamic Marketing, 11*(6), 1313–1326.

Öz, S., & Işık, M. A. (2019). Islamic insurance system: Takaful insurance. *International Journal of Commerce and Finance, 5*(2), 211–218.

Riazi, A. M. (2017). *Mixed methods research in language teaching and learning.* Equinox Publishing.

Schoonenboom, J., & Johnson, R. B. (2017). How to construct a mixed methods research design. *KZfSS Kölner Zeitschrift Für Soziologie Und Sozialpsychologie, 69*(2), 107–131.

Shabiq, A., & Hassan, Z. (2016). Factors affecting adoption of Takaful (Islamic Insurance) in the Maldives. *International Journal of Accounting and Business Management, 4*(1), 86–97.

Sherif, M., & Hussnain, S. (2017). Family Takaful in developing countries: The case of the Middle East and North Africa (MENA). *International Journal of Islamic and Middle Eastern Finance and Management, 10*(3), 371–399.

Customers' Acceptance of E-banking During the COVID-19 Pandemic: The Case of Oman

Salim Al-Hajri, Abdelghani Echchabi, Syed Ghayas, and Mohammed Ali Akour

1 INTRODUCTION

In the era of technology advancement and development, businesses globally found themselves obliged to upgrade their operations to some degree of technology usage, which subsequently improved the services and operations of businesses (Ksenofontov et al., 2019). Such is the case of financial institutions and particularly banks. The latter have customers that intensively conduct daily banking operations involving considerable amounts of money. It has been demonstrated in the previous studies (e.g. Echchabi & Olaniyi, 2012; Naz & Farooq, 2016) that one of the main

S. Al-Hajri · S. Ghayas · M. A. Akour
Department of Management Information Systems, A'Sharqiyah University,
Ibra, Oman
e-mail: drsalim_amor@asu.edu.om

A. Echchabi (✉)
Department of Business, Higher Colleges of Technology,
Dubai, United Arab Emirates
e-mail: aechchabi@hct.ac.ae

criteria for customers to select their respective banks is the quality and effi-ciency of services, implying that banks that have an efficient, handy and secure E-banking system are more likely to attract and retain customers (Echchabi, 2018).

On the other hand, the businesses sudden migration to technology usage was recently dictated by the spread of COVID-19 which forced businesses worldwide across sectors to shift their operations and services' offering to the online mode, wherever possible. Exceptions were made for vital sectors, and businesses were unable to operate online. This partially includes the banking services that were forced to temporarily close a significant proportion of their branches. However, the main branches remained operating physically with reduced number of working hours. During this period, the E-banking systems implemented by these banks played a significant role in facilitating the conduct of banking transactions efficiently on a remote basis.

As such, the aim of this paper is to examine the extent of adop-tion of E-banking services in Oman, and the factors that contribute to their adoption. The Omani context is selected for several reasons. Mainly, because Oman is ranked one of the highest in terms of overall stability among the Middle East and North African (MENA) countries. This allows the country to continue attracting workers and employees from around the world. The latter perform significant remittances towards their home countries, which bring high income for the Oman-based banks in terms of fees, beside the common daily transactions performed by the customers. Secondly, the country has recently witnessed the establish-ment of many banks, conventional and Islamic, local and foreign. This renders the competition between the banks more ferocious. Hence, banks with better services are likely to attract more customers and enhance their overall performance.

In order to investigate the E-banking services acceptance and usage in Oman in a comprehensive way, four prominent behavioural theories and innovations adoption models are incorporated in the current study. These models are Innovations diffusion theory (IDT), theory of reasoned action (TRA), theory of planned behaviour (TPB), and technology accep-tance model (TAM). These theories are briefly presented in the following sections, and the aspects relevant to the current study are incorporated.

The rest of the paper is structured as follows: In Sect. 2, the previous studies in the area of E-banking, as well as the related theoretical models are discussed. Section 3 outlines the methodology used and the respondents' profile. Section 4 presents the main analysis outcomes. Finally, Sect. 5 links the study results with significant practical and theoretical implications, as well as valuable recommendations for future studies.

2   LITERATURE REVIEW

2.1   Theoretical Model

2.1.1   The Theory of Reasoned Action

TRA states that an individual's behavioural intention depends on two major dimensions, one is personal in nature, and one is social. The personal dimension is defined by behavioural beliefs and the individual's evaluation of the behavioural outcomes. On the other hand, the social dimension is defined by normative beliefs and the individual's motivation to comply with these beliefs. Accordingly, Ajzen and Fishbein (1980) conceive that a person's attitude and his/her subjective normative belief within the social environment can determine the individual's behavioural intention, which then determines the actual behaviour. Subjective normative belief was introduced in TRA to reflect the perceptions and expectations of third parties about a specific behaviour, and the person's willingness to comply with these expectations (Otieno et al., 2016).

TRA has been used in various fields to predict and explain human behaviour. This includes strategic Information Systems (IS) adoption (Zabedi, 2016), information technology (IT) adoption (Otieno et al., 2016), Internet adoption (Buabeng-Andoh, 2018), and in the specific case of E-banking usage and adoption (Nor et al., 2008; Turan, 2012).

Early scholars such as Sheppard et al. (1988) supported the robustness of the TRA model from a comprehensive study of 87 empirical studies employing TRA in different contexts and fields. Nevertheless, several other authors like Warshaw and Davis (1985) and Davis et al. (1989) questioned TRA performance and its predictive ability. In particular, Bonfield (1974) and Harrell and Bennett (1974) found a low and negligible correlation between behavioural intention and physicians' actual prescribing behaviour. Hence, many scholars suggested a further enhancement of TRA, which came in the form of TPB.

2.1.2   The Theory of Planned Behaviour

TPB is the immediate extension that addresses shortcomings of TRA regarding the insufficiency of the explanatory factors of behavioural intention. In this regard, Ajzen (1991) argues that behavioural intention is dependent upon three factors, namely, attitude, subjective normative belief and perceived behavioural control. Subsequently, behavioural intention influences the actual behaviour directly. The introduction of perceived behaviour control at this level incorporates the perception of the difficulty to perform the behaviour to fill the gap witnessed in the TRA framework (Kiriakidis, 2017).

Several studies applied and supported TPB, including the adoption of IT tools by businesses (Alwahaishi & Snasel, 2013), and the adoption of online learning tools to use Internet (Al-Hajri et al., 2018; Hadadgar, et al., 2016). TPB was also used in the area of E-banking services in different settings (AL-Ajam & Nor, 2013; Echchabi, 2018).

Nevertheless, some studies such as Liao et al. (1999) who comprehensively studied TPB did not find any empirical and scientific support for its foundation. In addition, studies such as Randall and Gibson (1991) demonstrated weak evidence for the whole TPB framework. As such, the above studies revealed varied findings and arguments regarding the theory which suggests further improvements and adjustments by including other dimensions, or by decomposing the existing constructs into more concise and coherent dimensions.

2.1.3   The Technology Acceptance Model

TAM was developed by Davis (1989) to analyze and assess factors that influence users' acceptance behaviour of new systems and innovations. He identified two major determinants/dimensions of behavioural intention, namely, perceived usefulness and ease of use. According to Davis (1989), perceives usefulness measures the extent to which the usage of a given innovation or system would enhance the task performance of a person. On the other hand, perceived ease of use describes the extent to which using a given innovation or system would be easy for the person in terms of overall deployed efforts.

Several studies applied and supported TAM in different fields and settings, including the E-banking area (Alkailani, 2016; Fawzy & Esawai, 2017; Maduku, 2014; Santouritis & Kyritsi, 2013; Xiao et al., 2017). These studies found strong relationships between the model's explanatory and dependent variables. Nevertheless, some other studies showed weak relationships or no relationships between the model's dimensions (e.g. Anandarajan et al., 2000; Karahanna & Limayem, 2000). Thus, these mixed and inconclusive results suggest that further improvements and extensions of the model are needed. Notably by including dimensions from the remaining behavioural theories and models.

2.1.4 The Innovations Diffusion Theory

Rogers (2003) developed IDT to analyze and assess the comprehensive process through which innovative systems are communicated and channelled to the ultimate users. The author identified five major determinants of systems' usage and acceptance, namely, relative advantage, compatibility, trialability, observability, and complexity. He postulates that the usage of innovative systems and technologies is negatively influenced by complexity, and positively influenced by the other four factors.

Brown et al. (2004) studied the Rogers's characteristics of innovation and later found support for Roger's IDT. Subsequently, many studies used IDT for the investigation of various technological tools adoption including E-banking (Abu-Assi et al., 2014; Grabner-Krauter & Breitenecker, 2011; Kalaiarasi & Srividya, 2013). These studies provided meaningful empirical support to IDT in different fields.

However, other studies showed mixed and inconclusive results. From a meta-analysis of 75 studies, Tornatzky and Klein (1982) reported that only three dimensions, namely, relative advantage, complexity, and compatibility are significant in determining the technology adoption. Another study by Moore and Benbasat (1991) reported that only relative advantage is a significant determinant of technology adoption.

2.2 Empirical Studies

The area of E-banking services adoption received significant attention in empirical literature, in parallel to the above-mentioned important theoretical developments. In this regard, Alwan and Al-Zu'bi (2016) investigated the factors that increase the acceptance and adoption of online banking services in Jordan, for a sample of 476 bank customers. Using linear regression, the study found that factors like perceived privacy, perceived security, perceived ease of use, service quality, and customers' trust, have a significant effect on customers' acceptance and adoption of online banking services.

In the same context, Anouze and Alamro (2020) analyzed the factors that influence E-banking usage in Jordan and the reasons of its slow usage in the country. The study was focused in Amman area and used multiple regression and neural networks for data analysis. The findings identified perceived ease of use, perceived usefulness, security, and reasonable price, as the main determinants of online banking adoption.

Xiao et al. (2017) attempted to unravel the main factors that influence customers' acceptance of E-banking services in China. The authors used a survey of 52 bank customers combined with four in-depth interviews of selected customers. The findings showed that perceived credibility and usefulness have a significant positive influence on consumers' acceptance of E-banking. In addition, the obstacles that stand against the usage of E-Banking services included the difficulty to operate them, the unnecessity to use them in many cases, and the questionability regarding their security.

Likewise, Echchabi (2018) examined the factors that influence customers' acceptance of E-banking services by Islamic banks' customers in Thailand. The study covered a sample of 500 Islamic banks' customers from different districts in Thailand, and used t-test and regression analysis for data collection. The results showed high willingness of Islamic banks' customers to adopt E-banking services. Particularly, the findings revealed that perceived ease of use positively and significantly influences perceived usefulness. Similarly, perceived usefulness and perceived ease of use positively and significantly influence customers' acceptance of E-banking services.

Magboul and Abbad (2018) investigated the factors that influence E-banking services adoption in Sudan, covering a sample of 211 employees of private banks in Khartoum city. Using structural equation modelling, the results showed that perceived usefulness, top management support, perceived ease of use and user acceptance have a significant impact on customers' acceptance of E-banking.

Echchabi et al. (2019) analyzed the acceptance of E-banking services by Islamic banks' customers in Oman. In this regard, a survey covering 300 Islamic banks' customers was administered across several Omani cities. Using linear regression, the findings indicated that relative advantage, self-efficacy, ease of use, and facilitating conditions have a significant effect on the acceptance of E-banking services in Oman.

Lin et al. (2020) analyzed E-banking services acceptance in Taiwan and the related relevant factors. The study used a survey of 398 banks' customers from different regions on Taiwan and applied structural equation modelling technique. The findings indicated that trust has the highest level of significance and impact on E-banking acceptance.

Teka (2020) also examined the acceptance and usage behaviour of E-banking in Ethiopia. For this purpose, the author analyzed a sample of 420 Banks' customers using structural equation modelling. The results showed that perceived usefulness, perceived ease of use, personal attitude, perceived behavioural control, subjective norms, awareness, and availability of internet services have a significant positive impact on E-banking usage. In addition, perceived risk has a significant negative effect on E-banking.

In summary, the above-mentioned studies showed diverse and inconclusive findings, as they covered a wide range of technologies' adoption and usage, and used different behavioural models. In addition, very little attention and efforts were deployed to extend the existing model to enhance the understanding of behavioural intention towards theory. As such, the current study extends the existing behavioural models by focusing on five dimensions that are most applicable in the case of E-banking adoption in the case of Oman, namely, perceived ease of use, perceived uncertainty, perceived relative advantage, perceived facilitating conditions, and perceived self-efficacy.

3   METHOD

The study focuses on the total population of banks' customers in Oman. The sample size was statistically estimated in 200 respondents which is in line with similar comparable studies (e.g. Bartlett et al., 2001; Echchabi, 2018; Echchabi & Aziz, 2013; Nulty, 2008). From the total 200 distributed questionnaires, only 131 were properly filled and returned back for analysis. This reflects a generally accepted response rate of 65.5%.

In line with the above objective, a customized questionnaire was specifically developed to collect and analyze customers' perception of E-banking services, and their assessment of various aspects of these services in the case of Oman. The measurement of E-banking adoption and its aspects was measured through 29 items derived from the previous similar studies highlighted above (e.g. Echchabi, 2018; Echchabi et al., 2019). In addition, the questionnaire also gathered information related to respondents' profile, namely, respondents' gender, age, education level, etc. It is noteworthy that the survey questionnaire was originally developed in

English, but it was distributed to respondents on both Arabic and English depending on their language preference.

The data analysis was performed using linear regression and one-sample t-test techniques, guided by Hair et al. (2010). It is noteworthy that the statistical analysis was conducted using SPSS software version 23.

As shown in Eq. 1, behavioural intention is the dependent variable, while the independent variables are perceived ease of use, uncertainty, relative advantage, facilitating conditions, and self-efficacy, respectively.

$$\beta I = \beta_0 + \beta_1 PEU + \beta_2 U + \beta_3 RA + \beta_4 FC + \beta_5 SE + \varepsilon \qquad (1)$$

The demographic profile in Table 1 shows that 90% of the study sample are female, while 10% of them are male respondents. Regarding age classification, 87% of the sample are between 20 and 30 years old, 9.9% are between 31 and 40 years old, and 3.1% of are aged between 41 and 50 years old.

Regarding education level, 40.5% of the study sample are Bachelor degree holders, 34.4% are Diploma holders, 20.6% are Higher Diploma holders, while 2.3% of the sample are High School Certificate holders and another 2.3% are Postgraduate degrees holders. It is noteworthy that the 34.8% of the respondents are customers with Islamic banks, 33.9% are customers with conventional banks, while 31.4% have accounts in both the banks.

4   FINDINGS

The results in Table 2 indicate that perceived ease of use has a significant positive impact on the acceptance and usage of E-banking services. This is in line with the previous studies' findings including Davis (1989), Echchabi et al. (2019), and Echchabi (2018). This implies that aspects such as the easiness to conduct the daily transactions using E-banking tools, the clarity and simplicity of the E-banking procedures, as well as the easiness at which E-banking can be used for the daily follow-up of banking and financial transactions, play an important role in E-banking adoption and usage. Hence, these aspects should be emphasized and optimized to improve E-banking services and platforms in order to increase their usage. This is particularly valid during period of crises and medical crises like COVID-19 where customers and financial institutions attempt to minimize direct contact to protect all the parties. As such, simplifying

Table 1 Profile analysis

Demographics	Categories	Percentage
Gender	Male	10
	Female	90
Age	Less than 20 years	–
	20–30 years	87
	31–40 years	9.9
	41–50 years	3.1
	More than 50 years	–
Education level	High school certificate	2.3
	Diploma	34.4
	Higher Diploma	20.6
	Bachelor's degree	40.5
	Postgraduate degrees	2.3
Type of bank	Islamic bank	34.8
	Conventional bank	33.9
	Both	31.4

Source Authors' calculation based on the collected data

the E-banking systems and making it easier to use by customers would certainly minimize their resort to the banking institutions to perform their transactions.

Furthermore, the uncertainty has a significant and negative effect on the adoption and usage of E-banking. This finding confirms the suggestions of Rogers (2003) regarding this dimension. This implies that the Omani bank customers still perceive the E-banking services as relatively risky/not trustworthy, and ultimately cannot be completely relied upon for executing large volume banking transactions. This finding is alarming considering the pace and scope of E-banking adoption around the world, whereby it is currently one of the common tools of conducting banking transactions. This negative perception about E-banking implies that is not likely to be adopted and used by customers in Oman in the short term, but it also means that it would be relatively more complicated to survive through crises like COVID-19, since customers lack trust in these services, and hence are less likely to use them.

Likewise, facilitating conditions significantly and positively affect the acceptance and usage of E-banking. This finding affirms the relationships outlined by Ajzen and Fishbein (1980). In the current study, this dimension comprises of the government authorities' encouragement and backing of E-banking services, network support for the selection of E-banking services from a social perspective, the country's safety, as well as the political and economic stability. Thus, these aspects need to be enforced by the country's authorities, especially in periods like COVID-19 where the customers need to be ensured safety is observed, by implementing various operating measures that allow customers to conduct their daily transactions in a safe and secure environment.

In addition, self-efficacy has a substantial positive effect on E-banking adoption and usage by customers in Oman. This finding confirms the findings of Ajzen and Fishbein (1980). This result indicates that the bank customers perceive that they have the required skills and knowledge that permit them to use E-banking services. Nevertheless, the customers need to be aware of any safety measures taken by the banks to protect customers during periods like COVID-19. This can be done through short messages and emails that explain these measures, but it can also be through notifications in the first interface of the banks' phone applications, that the customers can view before using the application.

In contrast, relative advantage has no significant effect on the acceptance and usage of E-banking services by bank customers in the Oman. This contradicts the suggestions put forward by Tan and Teo (2000) and Rogers (2003). This suggests that the customers do not primarily consider the relative advantage in terms of costs, for using E-banking services. Rather, they focus on the aspects discussed earlier.

Finally, the *t*-test outcome in Table 3 reveals that the mean values for all the behavioural intention items are significantly greater than the test value of 3. This shows that there is a high tendency of the Omani

Table 2   Linear regression result

Model	Unstandardized Coefficients		Standardized Coefficients	*t*	*Sig*
	B	Std. Error	Beta		
(Constant)	0.443	0.334		1.326	0.187
Perceived Ease of Use	0.214	0.083	0.199	2.573	0.011
Uncertainty	−0.203	0.060	−0.229	−3.391	0.001
Relative Advantage	0.137	0.088	0.142	1.569	0.119
Facilitating Conditions	0.467	0.121	0.366	3.854	0.000
Self-Efficacy	0.223	0.079	0.222	2.812	0.006

Source Authors' calculation based on the collected data

Table 3   one sample t-test result

| | Test Value = 3 | | | | | |
| | t | Df | Sig. (2-tailed) | Mean Difference | 95% Confidence Interval of the Difference | |
					Lower	Upper
Behavioural Intention	12.612	130	0.000	0.77354	0.6522	0.8949
BI1	9.480	130	0.000	0.794	0.63	0.96
BI2	13.149	130	0.000	1.046	0.89	1.20
BI3	12.817	130	0.000	0.885	0.75	1.02
BI4	15.631	130	0.000	1.023	0.89	1.15
BI5	9.861	130	0.000	0.725	0.58	0.87
BI6	10.216	130	0.000	0.802	0.65	0.96

Source Authors' calculation based on the collected data

customers to adopt E-banking services and/or continue using them, depending on their satisfaction of the above dimensions. Previous studies' findings such as Echchabi (2018) and Echchabi et al. (2019) support these findings.

5   Discussion and Conclusion

The primary aim of the study was to analyze the acceptance and usage of E-banking services in Oman in the light of COVID-19 pandemic, with the help of linear regression and one-sample t-test techniques. Overall, the results revealed high acceptance tendency for E-banking services by customers in Oman. The findings also indicated that perceived ease of use, facilitating conditions as well as the self-efficacy has a significant positive effect on E-banking services acceptance and usage. In contrast, uncertainty has a significant negative effect on E-banking services acceptance.

The current study and its findings provide a valuable extension of the behavioural theories and model, especially TAM. This extension is at two different levels. Firstly, the study extends the model by incorporating and introducing new relevant dimensions. Secondly, the study uses the established model in a new and relatively different area. Accordingly, the study provides support to the model in terms of robustness and suitability to this area of study. Moreover, the findings provide new and significant information to policymakers, regulators, and banking practitioners in Oman concerning the aspects to strengthen, in order to widen the market and increase the usage of E-banking in the country.

Specifically, the practitioners should focus on the uncertainty issue, which is still highly perceived by the customers as well as potential customers. In this regard, the banks and authorities are required to improve the safety and security of E-banking services, as well as the visibility of these dimensions. It is noteworthy that many customers have had bad experiences concerning the safety and security of the system which renders them hesitating to use it intensively. Furthermore, the authorities are required to put in place all the necessary logistics and laws that allow for the proper and safe running of the system.

Finally, it is noteworthy that the current study typically considered the banks' customers in an aggregated form, combining commercial banks as well as Islamic banks customers, local and foreign banks customers. A major contribution of future studies would be to segregate the sample and analyze it separately for commercial and Islamic banks, as well as local and foreign banks. The future studies are highly recommended as well to study the cross groups' differences e.g. gender difference, age difference, education levels difference, etc.

REFERENCES

Abu-Assi, H. A., Al-Dmour, H. H., & Al-Zu'bi, Z. M. F. (2014). Determinants of internet banking adoption in Jordan. *International Journal of Business and Management, 9*(12), 169–196.

Ajzen, I. (1991). The theory of planned behaviour. *Organizational Behavior and Human Decision Processes, 50*(2), 179–211.

Ajzen, I., & Fishbein, M. (1980). *Understanding attitudes and predicting social behaviour*. Prentice-Hall.

Al-Ajam, A. S., & Nor, K. M. (2013). Customers' adoption of internet banking service: An empirical examination of the theory of planned behaviour in Yemen. *International Journal of Business and Commerce, 2*(5), 44–58.

Al-Hajri, S., Ghayas, S., & Echchabi, A. (2018). Investigating the e-learning acceptance in Oman: Application of structural equation modelling approach. *Journal of Computer Science, 14*(3), 368–375.

Alkailani, M. (2016). Factors affecting the adoption of internet banking in Jordan: An extended TAM model. *Journal of Marketing Development and Competitiveness, 10*(1), 39–52.

Alwahaishi, S., & Snasel, V. (2013). Modelling the determinants influencing the diffusion of mobile internet. *Journal of Physics: Conference Series, 423*(1), 1–8.

Alwan, H. A., & Al-Zu'bi, A. I. (2016). Determinants of internet banking adoption among customers of commercial banks: An empirical study in the Jordanian banking sector. *International Journal of Business and Management, 11*(3), 95–104.

Anandarajan, M., Igbaria, M., & Anakwe, U. (2000). Technology acceptance in the banking industry. *Information Technology and People, 13*(4), 289–312.

Anouze, A. L. M., & Alamro, A. S. (2020). Factors affecting intention to use e-banking in Jordan. *International Journal of Bank Marketing, 38*(1), 86–112.

Bartlett, J. E., Kotrlik, J. W., & Higgins, C. C. (2001). Organisational research: Determining appropriate sample size. *Information Technology Learning and Performance Journal, 19*(1), 43–50.

Bonfield, E. (1974). Attitude, social influence, personal norm, and intentions as related to brand purchase behaviour. *Journal of Marketing Research, 11*(4), 379–389.

Brown, I., Hope, R., Mugera, P., Newman, P., & Stander, A. (2004). The impact of national environment on the adoption of internet banking: Comparing Singapore and South Africa. *Journal of Global Information Management, 12*(2), 1–26.

Buabeng-Andoh, C. (2018). Predicting students' intention to adopt mobile learning: A combination of theory of reasoned action and technology acceptance model. *Journal of Research in Innovative Teaching & Learning, 11*(2), 178–191.

Davis, F. D. (1989). Perceived usefulness, perceived ease of use and user acceptance of information technology. *MIS Quarterly, 13*(3), 319–340.

Davis, F., Bagozzi, R., & Warshaw, P. (1989). User acceptance of computer technology: A comparison of two theoretical models. *Management Science, 35*(8), 982–1003.

Echchabi, A. (2018). E-banking acceptance in Thailand: An emphasis on Islamic banks' customers. *European Journal of Islamic Finance, 9*, 1–4.

Echchabi, A., Al-Hajri, S., & Tanas, I. (2019). Analysis of E-banking acceptance in Oman: The case of Islamic banks' customers. *International Review of Business Research Papers, 4*(5), 120–128.

Echchabi, A., & Aziz, H. A. (2013). An empirical survey on the prospects of Mobile money in Morocco. *Studies in Business and Economics, 8*(1), 46–54.

Echchabi, A., & Olaniyi, O. N. (2012). Malaysian consumers' preferences for Islamic banking attributes. *International Journal of Social Economics, 39*(11), 859–874.

Fawzy, S. F., & Esawai, N. (2017). Internet banking adoption in Egypt: Extending technology acceptance model. *Journal of Business and Retail Management Research, 12*(1), 109–118.

Grabner-Krauter, S., & Breitenecker, R. J. (2011). Factors influencing online banking adoption: Evidence from the Austrian market. *International Journal Internet Marketing and Advertising, 6*(4), 333–351.

Hadadgar, A., Changiz, T., Masiello, I., Dehghani, Z., Mirshahzadeh, N., & Zary, N. (2016). Applicability of the theory of planned behaviour in explaining the general practitioners eLearning use in continuing medical education. *BMC Medical Education, 16*(1), 1–8.

Hair, J. F., Black, W. C., Babin, B. J., & Anderson, R. E. (2010). *Multivariate data analysis* (7th ed.). Prentice Hall.

Harrell, G., & Bennett, P. (1974). An evaluation of the expectancy/value model of attitude measurement for physician prescribing behaviour. *Journal of Marketing Research, 11*(3), 269–278.

Kalaiarasi, H., & Srividya, V. (2013). An investigation on online banking adoption. *International Journal of Business Innovation and Research, 7*(1), 99–112.

Karahanna, E., & Limayem, M. (2000). E-mail and V-mail usage: Generalizing across technologies. *Journal of Organizational Computing and Electronic Commerce, 10*(1), 49–66.

Kiriakidis, S. (2017). Perceived behavioural control in the theory of planned behaviour: Variability of conceptualization and operationalization and implications for measurement. In A. Kavoura, D. Sakas, & P. Tomaras (Eds.), *Strategic innovative marketing* (pp. 197–202). Springer Proceedings in Business and Economics.

Ksenofontov, A. A., Ksenofontov, A. S., Kirpicheva, M. A., & Trifonov, P. V. (2019). The use of management technology to improve business efficiency. *IOP Conference Series: Materials Science and Engineering, 483*(1), 1–4.

Liao, S., Shao, Y., Wang, H., & Chen, A. (1999). The adoption of virtual banking: An empirical study. *International Journal of Information Management, 19*(1), 63–74.

Lin, W., Wang, Y., & Hung, Y. (2020). Analyzing the factors influencing adoption intention of internet banking: Applying DEMATEL-ANP-SEM approach. *Plos One, 15*(2). https://doi.org/10.1371/journal.pone.0227852.

Maduku, D. K. (2014). Customers' adoption and use of e-banking services: The South African perspective. *Banks and Bank Systems, 9*(2), 78–88.

Magboul, I., & Abbad, M. (2018). Antecedents and adoption of e-banking in bank performance: The perspective of private bank employees. *Interdisciplinary Journal of Information, Knowledge, and Management, 13*, 361–381.

Moore, G., & Benbasat, I. (1991). Development of an instrument to measure the perception of adopting an information technology innovation. *Information Systems Research, 2*(3), 192–222.

Naz, A., & Farooq, A. (2016). Customers' patronage in selection criteria of Islamic banks in Pakistan. *International Journal of Business and Management,* 4(100), 361–366.

Nor, K. M., Abu Shanab, E. A., & Pearson, J. M. (2008). Internet banking acceptance in Malaysia based on the theory of reasoned action. *Journal of Information Systems and Technology Management,* 5(1), 3–14.

Nulty, D. D. (2008). The adequacy of response rates to online and paper survey: What can be done? *Assessment and Evaluation in Higher Education,* 33(3), 301–314.

Otieno, O. C., Liyala, S., Odongo, B. C., & Abeka, S. (2016). Theory of reasoned action as an underpinning to technological innovation adoption studies. *World Journal of Computer Application and Technology,* 4(1), 1–7.

Randall, D., & Gibson, A. (1991). Ethical decision making in the medical profession: An application of the theory of planned behaviour. *Journal of Business Ethics,* 10(2), 111–122.

Rogers, E. M. (2003). *Diffusion of innovations* (5th ed.). Free Press.

Santouritis, I., & Kyritsi, M. (2013). Investigating the determinants of internet banking adoption in Greece. *Procedia Economics and Finance,* 9(1), 510.

Sheppard, B., Hartwick, J., & Warshaw, P. R. (1988). The theory of reasoned action: A meta-analysis of past research with recommendations for modifications and future research. *Journal of Consumer Research,* 15(3), 325–343.

Tan, M., & Teo, T. S. H. (2000). Factors influencing the adoption of internet banking. *Journal of the Association for Information Systems,* 1(1), 1–42.

Teka. B. M. (2020). Factors affecting bank customers usage of electronic banking in Ethiopia: Application of structural equation modeling (SEM). *Cogent Economics & Finance,* 8(1). https://doi.org/10.1080/23322039.2020.176 2285

Tornatzky, L., & Klein, K. (1982). Innovation characteristics and innovation adoption implementation: A meta-analysis of findings. *IEEE Transactions on Engineering Management,* 29(1), 28–45.

Turan, A. H. (2012). Internet shopping behavior of Turkish customers: Comparison of two competing models. *Journal of Theoretical and Applied Electronic Commerce Research,* 7(1), 77–93.

Warshaw, P., & Davis, F. (1985). Disentangling behavior intention and behavioral expectation. *Journal of Experimental Social Psychology,* 21(3), 213–228.

Xiao, Y., Sukumar, A. P. C., Tipi, L., & Edgar, D. (2017). Factors influencing people's intention to adopt e-banking: An empirical study of consumers in Shandong Province, China. *Asian Journal of Computer and Information Systems,* 5(3), 26–43.

Zabedi, A. M. (2016). Adoption of information systems (IS): The factors influencing IS usage and its effect on employee in Jordan telecom sector (JTS): A conceptual integrated model. *International Journal of Business and Management,* 11(3), 25–36.

Blockchain in Dubai: Toward a Sustainable Digital Future

Sarra Baroudi and Sonia Benghida

1 INTRODUCTION

Blockchain is one of the new technologies that have laid the groundwork for a revolution not only in the financial sector but also in the energy, tourism, medical, industrial, and supply chain sectors among others (Di Vaio & Varriale, 2020).

In 2016, the Gulf States started to show interest in blockchain technologies. It began in the UAE, Bahrain, and Saudi Arabia, particularly in the financial and public services sectors. When Bahrain concentrated on researching the regulatory implications of blockchain, the United Arab Emirates and Saudi Arabia focused their efforts on studying and reviewing existing and potential blockchain technologies for government, industrial, and commercial services (Alsubaei, 2019).

This book chapter is an exploratory qualitative study that investigates the effectiveness, obstacles, and advantages of blockchain technology,

S. Baroudi (✉)
Department of Accounting, Heriot-Watt University, Edinburgh, Scotland, UK
e-mail: s.baroudi@hw.ac.uk

S. Benghida
Sociology Department, McGill University, Montreal, QC, Canada

A. Echchabi et al. (eds.), *Contemporary Research in Accounting and Finance*, https://doi.org/10.1007/978-981-16-8267-4_11

with a particular emphasis on five blockchain-powered case studies in Dubai. The application of blockchain technology in Dubai is recent, with very few peer-reviewed published papers in the field. This research is an exploratory investigation of blockchain for sustainability, with a focus on the state-of-the-art of this technology in the Emirates. Its main target audiences are policymakers, strategists, and researchers with an interest in sustainability.

Several studies on Blockchain technology have appeared worldwide in the last decade; nevertheless, there is a lack of research focus on the Mena area. The latter covers a huge geographical region with 20 countries (UNICEF, 2021) having different economic, social, and political conditions. Due to its proven impact on the economy, blockchain's contribution to the concept of financial inclusion has been globally propagandized and endorsed in recent years.

The chapter addresses three main questions: what is the current state of blockchain in the Arab world? What differences can blockchain technology make for the development of Arab countries? Especially after the global disruptions, the COVID-19 crisis has caused. What sustainability potentials exist for using this technology in the Emirates? This chapter begins by presenting blockchain technology, contrasting its various types, providing an overview of blockchain in Dubai, and then discussing how blockchain promotes sustainability via the use of examples from Dubai initiatives. Finally, the importance of Blockchain technology is emphasized.

2   BLOCKCHAIN TECHNOLOGY

An asymmetry of information between the financial industry and investors marked the global financial crisis of 2008, voicing concern about how the financial sector operates. FinTech proposed a solution to the lack of transparency in this context. FinTech has undeniably opened doors for the financial sector, due to its digitalized processes. FinTech combines "Finance" and "Technology", it's a catch-all term for any technology that involves blockchain, data capture, data analysis, and artificial intelligence used to digitize traditional financial services.

There is no consensus around the origin of FinTech, some authors suggest that it was associated with Internet finance in China (Lee & Low, 2018), while others claim it was linked to Silicon Valley in 2000 (Ma & Urpelainen, 2018; Treiblmaier & Beck, 2019).

Satoshi Nakamoto is said to be the first to introduce bitcoin to the world via a white paper peer-to-peer electronic cash system (Nakamoto, 2008). Blockchain, the underlying technology that developed Bitcoin and its innovations in the Global Payments industry, has had a far-reaching effect far beyond the core finance domain. Blockchain is now regarded as a unique form of a distributed ledger. It safely and securely records peer-to-peer transactions that are carried out through smart contracts using advanced cryptography protocols. This provides secure and transparent transactions. It allows for the transfer of cryptocurrency ownership without the use of an intermediary, such as the bank, to validate the transactions (Lee & Low, 2018). This is made possible because the records, stored as blocks, are distributed across all the network's computer nodes. i.e., all the computers will have the same information given at the same time frame to all network users. This is similar to the cloud-based software process where individuals can work collaboratively and update the records without the authorization of the administrator.

When it comes to Bitcoin, blockchain is used in a decentralized manner, meaning that no single individual or group of individuals has/have authority- rather, all users have control collectively. Furthermore, decentralized blockchains are permanent, meaning that it is difficult to alter entered data on the system without alerting the entire network. As a result, blockchain technology eliminates the risk of fraud, making it highly secure. As Magnuson (2020) puts it: «It [blockchain] is purpose-built to avoid the perils of Big Tech».

Blockchain technology was designed initially as a platform for bitcoin trading, however, its applications expanded beyond the financial industry. Disintermediation of social media websites and e-commerce marketplaces is posing a significant threat to multinational companies like Google, Amazon, Apple, or Facebook. Thanks to Blockchain, these companies could solve misaligned incentives with blockchain-based initiatives.

The threat of counterfeit products in global pharmaceuticals, auto parts, and high-end, high-quality exported goods is driving the market for tamperproof, on-demand authentication. Enterprise blockchain applications make it possible to trace and monitor products from "source to consumption," from "farm to store," and from "farm to fork."

Similarly, new applications in marine goods, farms, and other food products can be monitored across supply chains through multiple industries using blockchain networks that abstract many components using sophisticated smart contracts and ingeniously implemented consensus protocols.

It is no surprise that food giants such as Walmart have introduced Food Trust to ensure the authenticity of items sold in their stores. Before the emergence of blockchain apps, the skepticism engendered by academic credentials, land records, permits, and inaccurate health records for insurance claims was not conclusively addressed.

Citizens' and customers' identification records, as well as birth, academic, credentials, medical records, property ownership, marriage certificates, and death certificates, are now considered to be immutably and indefinitely registered on the blockchain, removing the need to hold paper-based records. Government services such as marriage registration, patent management, and income tax services will benefit from blockchain technology (Akins et al., 2014). Estonia, Switzerland, Singapore, and the UAE are the first to adopt the blockchain paradigm wholeheartedly and are expected to go paperless soon. The blockchain industry is maturing, and by 2021, it could be more widely adopted.

3   Comparing the Different Types of Blockchains

When it was first used to operate bitcoin, blockchain was considered a public permissionless technology, but since then other forms of blockchains have emerged and there is currently mainly public or open blockchain, private or closed blockchain, consortium blockchain, and Linux based Hyperledger. Each category or type of blockchain is best suited to a particular number of case studies. When deciding on a type, one must consider the trade-offs.

The transactions in the blockchain are irreversible. i.e., a new information block is added to the ledger every time there is a new record. To be approved, the cryptographic problem associated with the transaction (the "hash algorithm") must be solved. This hash algorithm will be sent to all computer nodes and will generate a unique identifier that will be incorporated in the new information block. Since, the hash of this recent transaction embeds the hash of the earlier transaction, modifying one block implies changing the hash of all previous transactions' blocks, including the blocks related to their cryptographic validation.

Since the transactions are transparent, anybody, including users, miners, developers, and community members may participate in the public blockchain because it is an accessible network with no privilege to a specific person. This means that all participants have access to all of the records' details and their history, but they cannot see the identity of the initiators because it is kept anonymous. One drawback of the public blockchain is the significant amount of computing power needed to keep a distributed ledger running at a large scale (Andoni et al., 2019). A private blockchain is a closed network where only pre-approved individuals have access to the network and can view data. Unlike a public blockchain, participants have information about the identities of all participants in the network before transacting.

The consortium model is a version of the private blockchain where the blockchain works under the leadership of a team. This type of blockchain allows sharing the copy of transactions to only authorized users. Authorization of new entrants can be guaranteed by existing users or regulatory authorities. Linux-based Hyperledger is a closed blockchain network that helps to facilitate the creation and applications of blockchains in banking, insurance, supply chain, manufacturing, and infrastructure.

Overall, a private Blockchain, as opposed to a public blockchain, offers greater privacy in transactions which is essential for sensitive information such as medical and financial information. Additional benefits include improved protection, reduced costs, increased reliability, and an increased degree of confidence since only pre-verified individuals could start an additional node in the blockchain.

Despite their differences, open and closed blockchains share certain similarities, most notably that they are both decentralized peer-to-peer systems in which each participant maintains a copy of the distributed ledger.

4   BLOCKCHAIN STRATEGY IN DUBAI

The United Arab Emirates is the world's sixth-largest oil producer and one of the wealthiest nations, with a gross domestic product (GDP) per capita exceeding $ 43,000 in 2019, according to the World Bank. In line with its "Vision 2021," this oil and the natural gas-dependent economy are committed to sustainable development to become the most diverse economy of the Gulf Cooperation Council (GCC). This includes the digitization of the economy, which has become a high priority during the COVID-19 pandemic.

The UAE government has long invested in the economy to diversify its income sources and reduce its reliance on oil. Twelve years ago, the majority of Dubai's GDP was based on oil exports, but times have changed as oil now has only contributed less than 1% of Dubai's GDP. The Emirates offers competitive services in varied fields like tourism, real estate, banking and finance, and healthcare. It has evolved into a multinational city and has gained notoriety as an international business and investment hub over the last 40 years.

This explains why, in order to avoid the demise of fossil fuels, Dubai has become a more varied and diversified market. According to estimates published on Statista (2021), the gross domestic product (GDP) fell 10.8 percent in 2020. However, considering the global economic impact of the COVID-19 pandemic, this fallout falls beyond the predicted spectrum of economic recession.

The Institute for Management Development (IMD) presented a 2020 Smart City Index where both Abu Dhabi and Dubai are tagged as the region's smartest cities. Understandably, the concept of a «Smart City» is one of the most increasingly evolving issues of modern sustainability trends. Dubai has transitioned to a Smart City platform taking up all the challenges including technological, political, socioeconomic, local talent capital, regulation, cyber, and infrastructural dimensions (Samad & Azar, 2019). The financial and trade center of the country has been essential in promoting government efficiency, ingenuity, technology, and scientific research.

According to the second edition of the Smart Centre Index (SCI), Dubai is the best smart center in the Arab world for developing talent, innovation, and delivering innovative technologies. Dubai is ranked first in the Arab world for innovative strength, creativity, and distribution of new technology. Dubai is emerging as one of the early pioneers in the development of an integrated, intelligent city that integrates digital technology into all aspects of its operations. The city has indeed made great strides in the field of smart transformation, taking advantage of all advanced technologies to synchronize these technologies to meet residents' needs. Dubai has confidently launched bold and pragmatic initiatives and programs that leverage technology to make people's lives easier and happier.

Since 1995, Dubai has been a leader in governance and digital city development. Dubai Internet City (DIC), established in October 1999 by TECOM Group, was the UAE's first communication technology plan. After only one year of its launch, the new business succeeded in attracting a hundred companies; and since then, there has been considerable development. These measures paved the way for the establishment of Dubai's E-Government service in 2001, as well as the opening of a new government office a decade later. By 2015, Dubai Internet City, Dubai E-government, and then both Dubai Smart Government and the Smart Dubai Office were all established.

The Ruler of Dubai, Sheikh Mohammad bin Rashid Al Maktoum, is the one who emphasizes "human well-being" as the heart of Smart Dubai. His priority has long been the progress and happiness of Dubai and the UAE's residents. For over twenty years, he has driven the rapid technology growth and deployment in all levels of the public and private sectors in Dubai.

In October 2016, Dubai announced a city-wide blockchain plan. Because of Dubai's exponential growth in different economic sectors, Traditional practices had to be regularly revised to ensure good performance. Hence, the efficiency of government has become increasingly important. The expansion of the industry, construction, and tourism industries, in particular, revealed that the government required tighter controls on activities such as permits, transaction monitoring, and tracking.

Blockchain is one of the most advanced technologies that humankind has reached in recent years, yet the world is still hesitant at times and at other times refusing to explore and use this technology to its full potential. This, of course, does not apply to Dubai, whose government launched the blockchain Dubai Strategy, becoming the first government in the world to completely abandon paperwork and conduct all its business through blockchain technology from 2020.

While policymakers worldwide are slowly exploring various blockchain developments, Dubai has already recognized the full potential of this technology on a citywide scale. The Dubai government aims to build an atmosphere conducive to the success of Blockchain technologies.

Three pillars endorse the Blockchain strategy (Bishr, 2019):

1. Improve government effectiveness by implementing blockchain technology in all related government buildings.
2. Enterprise Development: Promote the growth of the blockchain industry by developing a welcoming atmosphere for start-ups.

3. Local and International Thought Leadership: Take the lead in global thought around blockchain technologies and establish it as a center for blockchain human capital and competencies development.

The implementation of Blockchain is ideally aligned with the vision of embracing technological advancement across the region, allowing Dubai to have the most effective, streamlined, secure, and impactful experiences.

5   BLOCKCHAIN IMPLEMENTATION

Dubai has developed a detailed roadmap focused on the three pillars of the Blockchain strategy as shown in Fig. 1. The next steps for the city's blockchain objectives are outlined in this framework. Each of the strategy's pillars has actionable initiatives in Dubai's plan.

- **Government trust and Efficiency**
  In 2018, the Smart Dubai Office (SDO) introduced the "Payment Reconciliation and Settlement" System. It was the first blockchain application. Instead of the six-week manual process, this new process

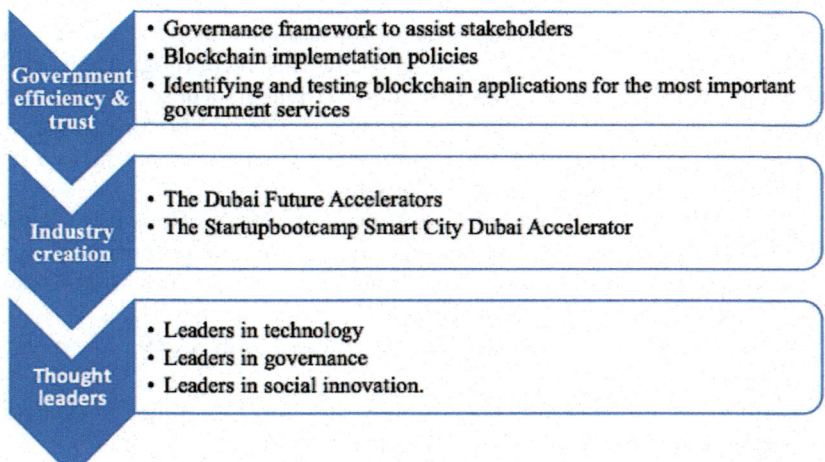

Fig. 1   Dubai blockchain strategy (*Source* Developed by the authors)

reconciles transactions between government departments and banks in seconds.

Dubai recognized the importance of implementing a governance system mainly to ensure that all stakeholders are receiving the necessary assistance notably in terms of clarifying blockchain policies in several areas. The Smart Dubai Office conducted workshops with stakeholders individually to determine their best potential pilots and to provide them with any technical tools they might need.

- **Industry creation**
  Dubai made it possible to attract significant interest from multinational banking and FinTech companies. Dubai has taken part in two accelerators: Dubai Future Accelerators and Start-up Bootcamp Smart City Dubai Accelerator (Bishr, 2019).

  In 2018, more than 200 submissions were received for the second Global Blockchain Challenge from 85 cities eager to demonstrate their brightest blockchain solutions. 17 out of the 200 proposals were selected to be presented in Dubai, and three out of them won prizes and were invited to collaborate with local government agencies to test Blockchain deployment.

- **Thought Leaders**
  Thought leaders prominent leaders in their respective disciplines who can bring a unique and useful outlook on blockchain in Dubai (Bishr, 2019).

- Leaders in technology: who present a guide in blockchain, cryptocurrencies, and distributed ledgers, then move on to case studies of blockchains and "smart contracts" in action.
- Leaders in governance are more expert in explaining the cooperation between innovators, policymakers, and tax authorities.
- Leaders of social innovation introduction of the usage of Blockchain in sustainability news.

6   BLOCKCHAIN AS A VITAL TOOL TO BOOST SUSTAINABILITY: CASE STUDIES FROM THE EMIRATES

Sustainability advocates achieving economic development while preserving the environment and the society is possible (Purvis et al., 2019). Sustainability has three core pillars: economic, environmental, and social.

Being aware of the promise of blockchain, the United Nations suggests the need of understanding how a blockchain-based framework would solve sustainability challenges while ensuring a safe, reliable, and cost-effective system. In this light, the United Nations Environment Programme (UNEP) has established a set of long-term targets to accomplish by 2030 for all state members. This initiative acknowledges the relevance of blockchain technology to these targets. In this section, we discuss how blockchain technology can benefit sustainability by looking at its application in different sectors in Dubai.

6.1   Can Blockchain Prevent Corruption? Case of UAE Trade Connect (UTC)

Financial institutions in the UAE have become more focused on the small and medium-sized enterprise (SME) market. The lack of digitalization involved in data verification has resulted in a substantial risk of fraud. More SMEs are interested in invoice discounting, which means more controls are required to prevent the occurrence of duplicated invoices to lenders which will be problematic given that several banks will have to deal with fake invoices and finance the same invoice due to a lack of coordination among these banks.

Blockchain is a distributed ledger initially designed to record cryptocurrencies. Therefore, its application is heavily tested by the accounting and finance sectors especially its potential to offer a digital alternative to hard copy and an automated solution to manual recordings. It has been suggested that blockchain technology improves the process of authentication of transactions and audit and offers a more efficient transaction reporting system (Schmitz & Leoni, 2019). Furthermore, Iansiti and Lakhani (2017) suggest that smart contracts help automate transfers by connecting them with GPS features and updating the transactions at various locations. This will prevent fraudulent transactions and contribute to social responsibility.

This is the reason why UAE Trade Connect (UTC) as a blockchain-based solution will prevent fraud, by detecting duplication of invoices. Using blockchain technology eliminates the risk of submitting the same invoices several times. There will be automatic "red flags" to alert the Trade Office to potentially corrupt activity.

This platform went live recently on 19 April 2021 after a rigorous phase of testing. At present, the main scope of this project is fraud detection in the trade finance sector, particularly it prevents:

- Invoice duplication scenarios: This system detects if a particular invoice is submitted to the same bank several times to obtain different invoice finance.
- Invoice Financing: The project detects if the same invoice is submitted to different banks.
- Sanctions Risks and financial crime: This system highlights instances of over-invoicing and under-invoicing, money laundering, and transfers involving classified accounts. The developers aim to expand the application of this technology to detecting money laundering, sanctions evasion, and e-invoicing.

The success of the UTC platform depends on the number of entities participating in this project and their commitment level. At present, there are eight UAE banks taking part in this project. Since all records can be viewed by all users of the network, and since it is difficult to alter the records, fraud perpetrators will be prevented from committing frauds.

Despite their corporate governance structures differences, the network participants are working to achieve a common objective of combating the risk of double invoicing thanks to the leadership of an external party, i.e., the Etisalat group who played as a neutral facilitator. In this regard, Blakstad and Allen (2018) suggest that the main advantage of blockchain technology relates to its transparency, irrevocability, and decentralization.

As Fig. 2 shows, corruption and fraud are linked to confidentiality, privacy, and the possibility of alteration of the records, while blockchain provides transparency and irreversibility. Additionally, corruption and fraud are linked to the centralization of power.

Although the UTC platform foundation of this project is blockchain, it makes use of other technologies where relevant. For instance, it requires artificial intelligence and machine learning to detect more advanced fraud techniques such as document fabrication and to identify over and under-invoicing and over-invoicing. Blockchain-based procurement allows UTC to disinfect its system by using varied technologically induced solutions.

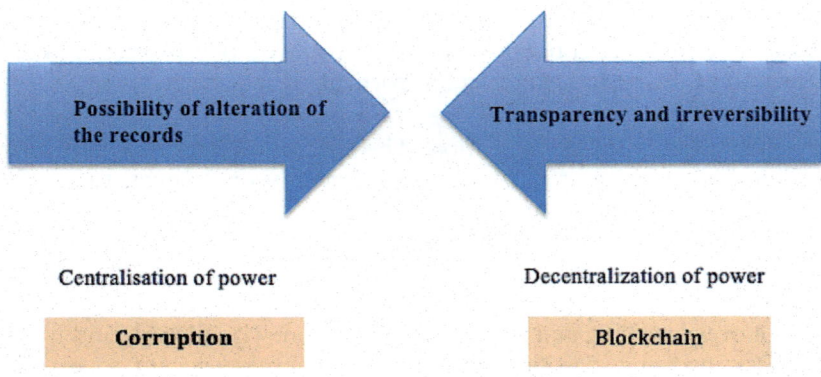

Fig. 2   Blockchain to stunt corruption (*Source* Developed by the authors)

6.2   *How Blockchain Is Applied to Crowdfunding Platforms? Case of Ideology and Smart Crowd in Dubai*

According to crowdfunding experts, four key benefits of blockchain explain why crowdfunding has become extremely useful. First, the decentralization offered by blockchain means that start-ups will no longer rely on platforms to raise funds. Second Tokenization means that start-ups can provide investors with equity and adopt employee-owned enterprise models. Third, high availability and immediate provision, means that it is easier for projects to get funded, finally Smart Contracts features used to enforce funding terms provide greater accountability in crowdfunding. In this light blockchain enables equitable access to capital for entrepreneurs (Dierksmeier & Seele, 2020; Greenberg & Mollick, 2017) and helps socially responsible investments to see the light (Schulte, 2013). Furthermore, it offers higher traceability of investments and ownership, thus minimizing the probability of fraud, dishonest use of funds, and data alterations.

Being aware of the potential that blockchain can offer to crowdfund, different platforms implemented this technology in Dubai such as Ideology and Smartcrowd Ideology is a crowdfunding platform that connects entrepreneurs, developers, and investors. It offers community members a full ecosystem that encompasses the steps required to set up a project from initial idea to raising funds. Applications should go through a rigorous review process by the Ideology team. Once the project is approved, it proceeds to the voting stage where members vote on the project. however, if the reviewer team has concerns over the project, it will be referred to the upcoming projects section. Applicants will be given feedback on how to improve their proposal and they will be given another chance of submitting a new application once they addressed the reviewer team feedback. A fixed fee charge is applied to entrepreneurs when they submit their proposals, and a commission is applied when they collect the funds raised.

Furthermore, Blockchain technology has been applied to real estate crowdfunding by the Smart crowd project which is the first financially regulated digital investment platform where members caninvest together in a specific real estate and gain additional income by crowdfunding. Smart crowd manages individual contributions on behalf of the crowd funders, ensuring the timely payment of the rent income and overseeing the sales process. This project solves two main challenges of the real estate market: the high lump sum cash required and the market illiquidity: In fact, Smart crowd enables small/novice or large/expert investors to crowdfund their projects without the need of a high deposit, this will encourage investors to enter the real estate markets.

6.3   Supply Chain Management: Case of DP World

Supply chain management is one of the most successful implementations of digital blockchain technologies. Blockchain can assist supply chain partners by providing an effective, open, and tamperproof history of information flows, product flows, and financial flows in transactions. Indeed, blockchain enhances supply chain management thanks to its transparency, traceability, and security (Venkatesh Kang, et al., 2020). Blockchain also helps monitor long and complex supply chains by recording the relevant data over the life journey of the product starting from the raw material to the final product offered to the consumer (Xu et al., 2019). This helps in identifying and getting rid of any inefficient processes. Furthermore, blockchain records give evidence about the extent of using environmentally friendly raw materials, the extent of respecting basic human rights and avoiding child labor of all supply chain participants (Dierksmeier & Seele, 2020).

As an example of supply chain management, there is the DP World project. It is implemented by an Emirati company that provides supply chain solutions while highlighting the importance of sustainable development goals (SDGs) to their strategy. In 2019 they joined the UN global compact, and they are committed to platforms at the world economic forum. This project is currently still in a trial phase to ensure the efficiency of its system before full implementation.

This project aims to reduce the cost and confusion of consumers. Blockchain technology can reduce the cost by incorporating automated procedures and confusion by providing consumers with clear information about how the products have been made without the need to look at various documents. This helps ethical buyers to make informed decisions in a reasonable time.

Implementing Blockchain tracking technology requires a complex infrastructure, which is expected to be expensive, potentially increasing the cost of green products. Furthermore, consumers' trust in blockchain depends on the trustworthiness of the information that is entered into it; therefore, this ambitious project should have a system that guarantees this to avoid the confusion of consumers and achieve its main objective.

Many businesses use sustainability as a marketing tool; however, customers may find it difficult to recognize the greenwash practices of businesses that use this technology because it necessitates a thorough understanding of blockchain technology. Since DP world is committed to sustainability goals, it is expected to search its network for greenwash practices of the businesses.

One big challenge of this project is that not all companies want to participate in such a transparent system because their practices would be scrutinized by the public, particularly if they are not socially and environmentally sustainable.

6.4   Health Care Management

By digitizing and decentralizing information in a distributed archive, blockchain is efficient in enhancing health management systems. As a result, patient information would be accurate, complete, and accessible only by the relevant users.

Smart contract functionality improves delivery systems by automated processes such as updating and prescribing medications (Engelhardt, 2017), preventing health care fraud (McGhin et al., 2019), and assisting in the withdrawal of toxic or defective medicines (Wu & Lin, 2019).

The mission of the UAE Ministry of Health and Prevention (MOHAP) is to improve the health of its residents by delivering robust, creative, and equitable healthcare services in compliance with international norms. In addition to serving as a regulator and supervisor of the health-care industry, the MOHAP is evolving with advanced technologies by implementing blockchain technology to help the healthcare system.

NMC hospital group collaborated with DU in 2018 to upgrade its electronic health reports and integrate blockchain technologies. This tech-nology enables various healthcare providers to remotely view patients' data in real-time. Patients can be treated at many hospitals or clinics without having to physically transfer their records. In this context, Yue et al. (2016) argue that blockchain's simultaneous data access enables patients to access, share, and upload their health records. As a result, the patient information infrastructure will be enhanced. General princi-ples of ethics and social responsibility advocate for patient data protection, which can be achieved because blockchain parties can only see the details that they have been allowed to see (Engelhardt, 2017). Further-more, Private Encrypted Blockchain enables access to interconnected databases, resulting in data reliability in terms of completeness and speed (Engelhardt, 2017; McGhin et al., 2019; Yue et al., 2016).

According to Carlos Domingo, chief new business and innovation officer at Du: "By digitizing all health records, and putting them in blockchain technology, data can be shared and distributed across all hospi-tals. We are looking at fully digitizing the health system with blockchain technology to assure data integrity with zero error and guarantee end-to-end accountability of the patients' records." The goal of this project is to guarantee data accuracy and to protect data confidentiality.

The application of Blockchain technology is not limited to patient records management in Dubai, it also covers healthcare professionals licensing. Relevant governmental organizations will connect smart licensing systems e.g., Masaar e-services portal and Sheryan regardless of the location of the candidate. Blockchain technologies can assist health partitioners in identifying the requirements of various licenses and the processes involved.

Furthermore, Blockchain technology is being used to improve and secure organ donation. The UAE Ministry of Health and Prevention (MOHAP) implemented "Hayat," a register that is used to document donors' legal will. This system would make it easier to access organ donation offers, as well as optimize and accelerate the transplantation process.

6.5   Blockchain-Powered Autonomous Taxis: For a Sustainable Transportation Planning

With the continuous blockchain development and the increasing demand for self-driving cars, Dubai has opted for the blockchain digital ecosystem to store and manage vehicles' digital records: "vehicle identification, possession, warranties, wear and tear, mileage, leases, loans, parts, and service information for automobiles" (Grewal, 2020). This information will be saved in a decentralized, shared ledger. Authorized parties will have partial access to this ledger data based on their access rights. As a result, blockchain different stakeholders will be able to use credentials instantaneously.

By 2030, Dubai City expects driverless modes of transportation to account for 25% of all trips. Meeting this goal would be a significant step forward especially that it is projected to produce 22 billion AED of annual economic revenues (UAE, 2021). The Dubai Autonomous Transportation Strategy is aiming at:

- Lowering transportation costs up to 44 %, resulting in annual savings of more than AED 900 million.
- Preventing accidents, reducing losses by 12%
- Rising individual efficiency by 13%
- Reducing time wasted in traditional transportation, resulting in saving 396 million hours on transportation trips yearly.
- Decreasing environmental carbon emissions and pollution by 12%, resulting in savings of up to AED 1.5 billion per year.
- Reducing the allocated parking spaces.

7   CONCLUSION

A decade ago, bitcoin was supposed to be both the biggest cryptocurrency and the greatest revolution in the financial ecosystem when it was first introduced to the world, but this revolution is still a long way off. Bitcoin was afflicted with scaling problems, controversies, missteps, and price swings and has received a fusillade of criticism after the slump in its price to 51,541 in April 2021. Despite a turbulent decade with bitcoin, investors did not hesitate to predict a profound economic, social, and political change, where trust would prevail over mistrust, horizontality over verticality, decentralization over-centralization.

Blockchains are changing the way we trade money, buy assets, manage food safety, track patient data in healthcare, control supply chains, and vote in elections, among other things. Decentralization, openness, immutability, and automation are all advantages of blockchain technology. The world is increasingly prone to benefit from blockchain networks and their positive effects on all economic spheres, growth, and quality of life change.

Since the Emirates already has a well-developed ICT market, their government departments, financial institutions, and educational institutions acknowledged the promise of Blockchain as a key to a better future. Consequently, many companies are currently piloting programs to understand how to apply blockchain to improve operating processes and structures while developing alternative approaches for delivering services in collaboration with specialist international firms.

The unprecedented turmoil caused by the COVID-19 pandemic has devastated societies and ecosystems in the Mena area and all around the world. The pandemic has compelled many companies to incorporate more technological solutions, and more businesses understand the importance of adopting emerging technologies, such as blockchain. Hence it is crucial for the Arab countries to learn from Dubai, and to restart their trading network by turning the harsh lessons into action. As said Mariam Obaid AlMuhairi, a project manager at the Centre for the Fourth Industrial Revolution UAE: *"If there were any lingering doubts over the value of blockchain platforms to improve the transparency of businesses that depend on the seamless integration of disparate networks, COVID-19 has all but wiped them away"* (Smart cities, 2020).

REFERENCES

Akins, B. W., Chapman, J. L., & Gordon, J. M. (2014). A whole new world: Income tax considerations of the Bitcoin economy. *Pittsburgh Tax Review, 12,* 25.

Alsubaei, D. (2019). Blockchain adoption in the Gulf states. In Association with the Bahrain Center for Strategic International and Energy Studies (DERASAT) *Policy Paper 2019–2022.*

Andoni, M., Robu, V., Flynn, D., Abram, S., Geach, D., Jenkins, D., McCallum, P., & Peacock, A. (2019). Blockchain technology in the energy sector: A systematic review of challenges and opportunities. *Renewable and Sustainable Energy Reviews, 100,* 143–174.

Bishr, A. B. (2019). Dubai: A city powered by blockchain. *Innovations: Technology, Governance, Globalization, 12*(3–4), 4–8.

Blakstad, S., & Allen, R. (2018). *FinTech revolution* (pp. 121–132). Springer.

Di Vaio, A., & Varriale, L. (2020). Blockchain technology in supply chain management for sustainable performance: Evidence from the airport industry. *International Journal of Information Management, 52*, 102014.

Dierksmeier, C., & Seele, P. (2020). Blockchain and business ethics. *Business Ethics: A European Review, 29*(2), 348–359.

Engelhardt, M. A. (2017). Hitching healthcare to the chain: An introduction to blockchain technology in the healthcare sector. *Technology Innovation Management Review, 7*(10), 22–34.

Greenberg, J., & Mollick, E. (2017). Activist choice homophily and the crowdfunding of female founders. *Administrative Science Quarterly, 62*(2), 341–374.

Grewal, J. (2020). *Blockchain-powered autonomous automobiles can be the answer, in IBM*. https://www.ibm.com/blogs/blockchain/2020/04/blockchain-powered-autonomous-automobiles-can-be-the-answer/. Accessed on 20 April 2021.

Iansiti, M., & Lakhani, K. R. (2017). *Do not copy or post*.

Lee, D. K. C., & Low, L. (2018). *Inclusive fintech: Blockchain, cryptocurrency, and ICO*. World Scientific.

Ma, S., & Urpelainen, J. (2018). Distributed power generation in national rural electrification plans: An international and comparative evaluation. *Energy Research & Social Science, 44*, 1–5.

Magnuson, W. (2020). *Blockchain democracy: Technology, law and the rule of the crowd*. Cambridge University Press.

McGhin, T., Choo, K. K. R., Liu, C. Z., & He, D. (2019). Blockchain in healthcare applications: Research challenges and opportunities. *Journal of Network and Computer Applications, 135*, 62–75.

Nakamoto, S. (2008). *Bitcoin: A peer-to-peer electronic cash system*. https://bitcoin.org/bitcoin.pdf. Accessed 24 February 2020.

Purvis, B., Mao, Y., & Robinson, D. (2019). Three pillars of sustainability: In search of conceptual origins. *Sustainability Science, 14*(3), 681–695.

Samad, W. A., & Azar, E. (2019). *Smart cities in the Gulf*. Springer.

Schmitz, J., & Leoni, G. (2019). Accounting and auditing at the time of blockchain technology: A research agenda. *Australian Accounting Review, 29*(2), 331–342.

Schulte, U. G. (2013). New business models for a radical change in resource efficiency. *Environmental Innovation and Societal Transitions, 9*, 43–47.

Smart cities. (2020). *Why Covid-19 makes a compelling case for the wider integration of blockchain*. https://www.smartnations.com/why-covid-19-makes-a-compelling-case-for-the-wider-integration-of-blockchain/. Accessed on 28 February 2021.

Treiblmaier, H., & Beck, R. (2019). *Business transformation through blockchain.* Palgrave Macmilan.

UAE. (2021) *Dubai autonomous transportation strategy.* In the United Arab Emirates Government portal. https://u.ae/en/about-the-uae/strategies-initiatives-and-awards/local-governments-strategies-and-plans/dubai-autono mous-transportation-strategy. Accessed on 25 April 2021.

UNICEF. (2021). *MENA.* https://www.unicef.org/mena/topics/mena. Accessed on 20 April 2021.

Venkatesh, V., Kang, K., Wang, B., Zhong, R. Y., & Zhang, A. (2020). System architecture for blockchain-based transparency of supply chain social sustainability. *Robotics and Computer-Integrated Manufacturing, 63,* 101896.

Wu, X., & Lin, Y. (2019). Blockchain recall management in pharmaceutical industry. *Procedia CIRP, 83,* 590–595.

Xu, X., Lu, Q., Liu, Y., Zhu, L., Yao, H., & Vasilakos, A. V. (2019). Designing blockchain-based applications a case study for imported product traceability. *Future Generation Computer Systems, 92,* 399–406.

Yue, X., Wang, H., Jin, D., & Jiang, W. (2016). Healthcare data gateways: Found healthcare intelligence on blockchain with novel privacy risk control. *Journal of Medical Systems, 40*(10), 1–8.

Feasibility and Exploratory Study of Implementing the Blockchain Technology in the UAE Financial Markets

Sonia Abdennadher, Maher Salem,
Saeed Ahmed Saeed Alkaabi, and Ali Salem Alshebli

1 INTRODUCTION

Also known as Distributed Ledger Technology (DLT), Blockchain technology has become one of the newest advancements in the financial markets (Miraz & Donald, 2018). Blockchain is a distributed database shared over a larger computing network. There is a copy of the shared ledger in each one of the computers on the network. The Blockchain is a group of blocks. Every block has unique hash to differentiate from other hashes. The Blockchain helps the transaction to become more secured through DLT. It works with spreading the information of transaction

S. Abdennadher (✉) · M. Salem · S. A. S. Alkaabi · A. S. Alshebli
Department of Business, Higher Colleges of Technology,
Al Ain, United Arab Emirates
e-mail: sabdennadher@hct.ac.ae

S. A. S. Alkaabi
e-mail: H00303019@hct.ac.ae

A. S. Alshebli
e-mail: H00292223@hct.ac.ae

© The Author(s), under exclusive license to Springer Nature
Singapore Pte Ltd. 2022
A. Echchabi et al. (eds.), *Contemporary Research in Accounting and Finance*, https://doi.org/10.1007/978-981-16-8267-4_12

among users to make sure they cannot be hacked. It needs verified transaction from all users. Every block on the chain is a piece of data, which has been mathematically encrypted. Therefore, there are numerous protocols required before each block is validated. This needs consensus from several others before it is added to the existing chain. Because of the complex and highly encrypted design, the Blockchain has no single point of failure. Hackers cannot simply attack one computer node to use fraudulently data. They would need to attack every node on the chain, simultaneously.

As claimed, Blockchain technology will make simpler and safer the way personal information is stored and how transactions for goods and services are made. Blockchain technology creates a permanent and immutable record of every transaction. This impenetrable digital ledger makes fraud, hacking, data theft, and information loss almost impossible. Several companies are working to become early adopters of Blockchain. Banks and other financial institutions (FIs) are already using Blockchain to optimize their services, reduce fees for customers and fraud as well.

This technology is being adopted by developed and developing countries to solve complex issues of transactions to augment transparency and accessibility of financial records. Blockchain technology allows digital records to be decentralized but in a manner that they cannot be altered. As technology advances, hackers are also evolving due to increased cyber fraud cases. Corruption is also a huge problem motivated by the largely unregulated environment in which cryptocurrencies are used. The reason behind the Blockchain technology initiative is rising to the global level of innovation by increasing transparency and incorruptibility in financial markets. The purpose of introducing Blockchain technology in the financial markets in the UAE is to curb the inefficiencies of traditional methods of transactions and benefit from new technology through an integrated process that suits all business models. The technology stored the transaction history records irreversibly and once the transaction has happened, it becomes a part of a permanent Blockchain database. The data are secured and linked to other people or companies using secure cryptography, meaning they become safe from hacking or tampering in any way. The un-erasable or impenetrable data can then be distributed without duplication or modification. The emergence of cryptocurrency, especially bitcoins, has encouraged the use of Blockchain technology because of the limited control online trading platforms and the unscrupulous nature of the dark web (Beyondskills, 2020).

There are several Blockchain financial services use cases gaining momentum such as cross-border transactions and international trade to transferring money, trade banking platforms, and credit reporting and scoring. For instance, the impact of Blockchain in international trade consists to have fast money movement and reduction of the transaction time. The transfer itself posts immediately and it takes only about few minutes for payments to be validated in the Blockchain. Also, the taxes and fees will be lower than before because cryptocurrency is peer-to-peer monetary system, and there is no third party. Furthermore, there is no exchange rate because everyone is using the same cryptocurrency with the same value. The Blockchain created from cryptocurrency transactions is clear and secure records that is trackable and verifiable. In the last few years, there is a global interest on Blockchain technologies. Hence, UAE is also willing to use Blockchain for digital transactions, giving each customer a unique identification number that shows his/her information on the secure chain.

The financial markets in the UAE have, for so long, dependent on the traditional banking system until recently, when the Global Blockchain council was formed to facilitate the adoption of Blockchain technology in UAE. In fact, the government launched the Emirates Blockchain Strategy 2021 where 50 percent of the government transactions should be generated by the technology. By adopting Blockchain technology, the UAE government expects to save money in transactions and documents processed routinely, millions of printed documents and working hours annually. In terms of banking sector, several banks started their end-to-end Blockchain transactions of cross-border trade finance, Know Your Customer (KYC) platform to verify KYC data sharing between licensing authorities and FIs, and issued checks to strengthen their authenticity and minimize potential frauds.

In 2017, Abu Dhabi Securities Exchange (ADX) used Blockchain technology for a new e-voting system for shareholders accessing and participating in listed annual general meetings. In 2018, ADX signed a partnership with Equichain, a London-based FinTech firm, to bring efficiencies to capital markets. The objective is to look for a way to make the Blockchain easier and safer for investors to use it. When thinking about the need to change from one system to another, there are reasons for this change. In this study, our aim is to answer to the following questions: What are the challenges of using Blockchain technology in the stock exchange markets? What are the possible impacts of using Blockchain technology in the trading, clearing, and settlement?

Therefore, this research article will intensively examine the possibility of adopting Blockchain on UAE market from stakeholders' perspectives. It has conducted several interviews and surveys to extract several performance metrics and criterions regarding the feasibility of adopting Blockchain in UAE.

2   Literature Review

2.1   Opportunities in the Financial Markets

Blockchain technology has numerous opportunities as far as financial transactions are concerned. In addition to fostering transparency, minimizing internet banking fraud, and eliminating the corruptibility of files and financial data, this technology is also known to decrease transaction costs, eliminate intermediation, and increase operational efficiencies (Miraz & Donald, 2018; Workie & Jain, 2017). Researches have been conducted to describe the Blockchain and the effects of new technology on financial markets especially in the stock markets (Alexis, 2016). FIs in the UAE can greatly benefit from adopting this technology because of the related advantages. The rest of the world is slowly embracing Blockchain technology and is aware about its future in the financial markets.

Blockchain technology has proven to be quite useful to be used when transferring and keeping track of financial instruments or assets. The investors are more willing to invest their money in the financial markets where they trust on them. The trust is required for the development of the financial markets and maintaining its resilience (Mayer, 2008; Tomasic & Akinbami, 2011). While the way the financial markets function today is good, there are still some flaws that exist today, and this is why the Blockchain has come to improve upon. Investors can participate in financial markets trusting that the storage unit where they keep their financial assets record is safe from getting hacked and manipulated. This helps them to be more willing to enter those financial markets and be more active. Basically, every user in the network would have a computer which has a copy of the data making this device a node. For a hacker, to be able to get access, he would have to hack and alter the data in every node which is quite impossible. An attack on the central node can effectively bring down the entirety of that network which means that it would be much easier for hacker to target a centralized ledger than a decentralized one (Chiu & Koeppl, 2019).

2.2   Applications in the Stock Markets: Use Cases

The Blockchain has been invented in 2008. Until now, the financial markets especially the stock markets resist to adopt the new revolution because the current systems and technologies used by the stock markets are working relatively well and no need to replace them by Blockchain. It's hard to convince the investors by telling them we will change the current system. It is not easy to replacing the existing systems with a new technology haven't yet proven concretely its effectiveness. Meanwhile, the Australian Securities Exchange (ASX), with a total market capitalization of around AUD $2 trillion, will change its current software CHESS by Blockchain in 2022 because of the COVID-19 crisis (Ledgerinsights.com). ASX has announced to its clients in 2017 that they will adopt the Blockchain as a new system. The new revolution will reduce the cost for investors giving advantage to ASX through reducing the time of clearing and settlement and keep all information secured. Also, it will stop the intervening of humans to decrease their errors and additionally switch all system to be online. It will lead to increase the number of investors because ASX will become more attractive aiming to be the first stock market adopting the Blockchain in their clearing and settlement process. The investors will see the difference between the old system and the new, and they will see how to get benefit from using the new one. The clearing and settlement take (T + 3 or T + 5) but with Blockchain the mechanism would change and will be (T + 0). Globally, the financial world is waiting for ASX to see how the Blockchain can benefit the financial market.

Moreover, Hong Kong Exchanges and Clearing Limited (HKEX) started a partnership with Digital Asset in 2018 to introduce the first Blockchain platform for financial services in Hong Kong. Digital Asset is also involved in the Australian Securities Exchange's CHESS settlement system. The technology of Digital Asset uses a smart contract modeling language. The Digital Asset protocol was also subject to recent third-party tests of basic functionality by Depository Trust & Clearing Corporation (DTCC) the major equity clearing and settlement services provider showing the ability of this technology to ensure 6,300 trades per second sustained for five hours. Accenture found that DLT is capable to support volumes of more than 100 million trades per day. By comparison, Hyperledger Fabric can handle 2,250 transactions per second. Further tests need to determine whether DLT is able to ensure resiliency, security, anonymity, and regulatory requirements to meet the needs of the markets at different sizes and maturities. Several consultants and IT providers were started to do these tests and trials on their own platforms such as Digital Asset, R3, IBM, and Accenture.

3   POTENTIAL IMPACTS ON INVESTMENT AND SECURITIES INDUSTRY

3.1   *Impacts Related to the Main Characteristics of Blockchain*

The main four features of the Blockchain are decentralization, trustless, safety, and Transparency (Kremenova & Gajdos, 2019). (1) The term called decentralization is the important element in Blockchain technology. The decentralization gives each block the responsibility to maintain and protect the data. Although the data are safe and the protection has guaranteed, once these data are attacked by hackers, the entire data will get lost or changed by them, no one can stop the damage if it's happened. In a decentralization system, the data are secured and impossible to be hacked because the hacker should control over 50% of users if he wants to get control (Kshetri, 2017); (2) Trustless: The situation in Blockchain is different since the trusted third party does not exist in the process, which means the buyer and seller do not need to have a guaranteed party in-between to press the bottoms to agree on the transaction. With Blockchain, the third party is the system itself. It works as the "bridge" between the buyer and seller with a totally trusted transaction that happened immediately without taking a long time or having a high commission; (3) Safety and transparency are important for the system to face unexpected issues and creating environment based on the information where customer enters onto the system and no one can change it because the information is secured by a unique hash. In addition, every user can review the transaction to ensure if it is correct or not, so this means that anyone can use the technology without fearing anyone who could attack and stole information or details (Kshetri, 2017).

3.2   Trading, Clearing, and Settlement Trade Procedure Through DLT

DLT has the power to effect different ways of the financial markets, including market efficiency , transparency, post-trade processes, and operational risk. But, we cannot predict the exact change that will happen (Workie & Jain, 2017). The accurate recording capabilities of Blockchain may take one day and make current clearing and settlement procedures redundant, resulting in faster transactions and reduced costs for FIs. Blockchain is enabling a digital identity authentication where banks and other FIs are able to identify individuals using Blockchain-enabled IDs. When customer identifying secured information with using Blockchain, the FI can increase public trust while protecting against fraud and speeding up the verification process significantly. Blockchain technology applied in the financial markets will lead to less clearance time, meaning automating the post-trade process, smart contracts of trades, and legal ownership transfers of the securities.

The relationship between the investors and the selling parties is controlled by an intermediary who depends on holding a system of payment to exchange the equity for the money, also these holding parties "custodians" may be international. For instance, the European Central Securities Depositories (CSDs) drive their settlement services to T2S (target 2 securities) platform operated by the European system. The target here is to integrate the securities settlement infrastructure through a centralization of settlement in Europe. Before DLT settlement operational seems imperfect, and the integration is weak (Pinna & Ruttenberg, 2016). The process of settlement usually goes through many steps, and it takes in most of the exchange markets two working days. DLT have a potential to reduce the settlement time for securities transactions by making easy the exchange of digitally traded assets. Even though that the settlement time will be reduced, it is still unclear because of some market participants having indicated that the ability to net transaction occurring over a period is blurred. There may be some affect in case of short sales or trade cancelations. Adopting the DLT may not be necessarily leading to implement real-time settlement, but it has the power to time-stamp the settlement position of the parties (Workie & Jain, 2017).

3.3   *Transparency and Market Efficiency*

DLT technology entails maintaining a database that have all the information about the history of securities transactions and any related information that happens on the network. It can provide all or some information in one time for all the participants on the network. For example, any network participant can find some similar information without the need to make new report infrastructure. The DLT technology could help by facilitating transparency but it will not resolve all the questions about transparency from a policy perspective. Some of the users would like to keep some information secretly from some competitors. If the confidential information was policed that might make an informational disadvantage for non-network users (Workie & Jain, 2017). Hence, Blockchain considered as a revolutionary tool that automates transactions, simplify the post-trade settlement, reduces intermediaries, establishes market for security tokens, enhances transparency, and enables fund raising and new crypto exchange traded funds.

Now, while we exposed the Blockchain and its uses, its advantages and its improvements, it is judicious that we explore its risks and limitations to notice that Blockchain is still has its flaws like any other technology.

4   Weaknesses and Limitations

The first disadvantage is the fact that Blockchain technology uses a lot of energy. Having multiple computers running at all times to keep a network fully updated and functional means that you will have to consume a lot of power to keep them up. Moreover, while this technology can be used to help keep trading information transparent, it can also help those who want to participate in an illegal activity anonymously. Buying illegal products while keeping the identity secret is very much possible with the Blockchain technology. Another limitation of Blockchain technology is its lack of flexibility. When a transaction is recorded onto the Blockchain system, it cannot be easily canceled, changed, or reversed. This is because all of the blocks are related and correlated. Posting another transaction on the Blockchain requires to be duplicated and validated by other users. A Blockchain based on a Proof of Work (PoW) protocol deals with changing transaction history backwards. The Blockchain has to be dynamically consistent in the sense that current transaction has to be linked to transaction in previous block. Consequently, if a person attempts to revoke a transaction in the past, he has to propose an alternative Blockchain and provide a new PoW for each newly proposed block. Thus, it is costly to rewrite the history of transaction backwards if the part of the chain that needs to be replaced is long. Consequently, the "older" transactions have more users that can trust them (Chiu & Koeppl, 2017).

To implement the Blockchain system in the UAE financial market, we need first to make sure that the Blockchain is going to work well in the UAE. To know whether the system is going to benefit the financial market, we need to evaluate its benefits and risks, and whether it will meet the rules and regulations set in the country and whether this system will be welcomed by the users, investors, and managers.

5   RESEARCH METHODOLOGY

5.1   Model

Blockchain technology and its decentralization are of great importance monitored by government agencies and authorities in developed countries that seek to develop their systems. This research collects point of views from experts and workers in FIs and companies in the UAE. A survey has been addressed to investors, representatives of ADX, DFM, SCA, brokers, and managers of listed companies. Height variables have been considered in which there are several items as shown in the following Table 1.

All variables are dependent and based on the managers and users we interview. We can represent them as shown in the following Fig. 1.

We propose the conceptual model in the previous flowchart to represent the managers and users point of views about the introduction of the Blockchain technology in the financial markets. This model takes in account the attitude of investors toward this technology and those expressed by the managers. In information system field, attitude represents the set of values, beliefs, and expectations attributed to the system (Triandis, 1971; Zmud, 1979). According to Zmud (1979), organizational actors have attitudinal predispositions toward IS roles in the organization. The author shows that the specificities of the actors, designated by individual differences, have cognitive and attitudinal impacts on the success of an IS. Fischben and Ajzen (1975) define attitudes as the predispositions acquired by the individual to react consciously in a decision-making situation. The research aims to study if the investors/shareholders (final users) are reluctant or not toward the Blockchain technology. This psychological state linked to the insecurity of the new technology is a barrier to use the new system. However, managers and executives strongly believe in unblocking and easing this reluctance in near future. Unfavorable users and adopters' engagement could be explained by three motivational factors (Ives & Olson, 1984): (1) resistance to change due to reluctance to technological change; (2) lack of ownership of the system due to lack of usage habit; (3) lack of availability of user participation in the implementation and development of IS (Abdennadher & Cheffi, 2020; Brav et al., 2019; He & King, 2008; Spears & Barki, 2010). We study the attitudes of the users (individual shareholders) and adopters

Table 1 Questionnaire items

Variable	Items
V1. Organizational barriers to adopt Blockchain technology	1.1. Implementation (replacing or adapting existing legacy systems) 1.2. Regulatory uncertainty 1.3. Potential security threats 1.4. Lack of in-house capabilities (skills and understanding) 1.5. Uncertain ROI (Return On Investment) 1.6. This technology is unproven 1.7. Not currently identified as a business priority 1.8. Expensive implementation due to migration costs 1.9. We don't see any barrier 1.10. Not Sure/Other
V2. Technical challenges/risks/issues of Blockchain	2.1. Interoperability issues among Blockchain infrastructures (where interfaces are not completely understood to work with other existing or future systems in either implementation or access and with possible restrictions) 2.2. Compatibility issues of Blockchain with existing enterprise information systems 2.3. Scalability issues (where the Blockchain system is not able to continue to function well when it changes to a larger size or volume) 2.4. Vulnerabili ty issues (when credentials can be compromised or stolen and when there are programming errors) 2.5. Smart contract issues (related to the automatically execution of pre-defined conditional statements of "if–then") 2.6. Other

(continued)

Table 1 (continued)

Variable	Items
V3. Potential impacts of Blockchain on the trading, clearing and settlement in the financial markets	3.1. The Blockchain gives the possibility to undertake stock lending and borrowing 3.2. The Blockchain gives the possibility to undertake short selling 3.3. Blockchain gives the possibility to better control the short selling and lending practices 3.4. Blockchain reduces the level of liquidity caused by the latency problem (which is the "time for a transaction to confirm") 3.5. The latency of DLT can cause unfair competition between traders 3.6. Because of the trades that could be made anonymously due to the technology of encryption, this can create market misconducts 3.7. Blockchain has not yet managed to address the prevention of money laundering 3.8. Blockchain has not yet managed to provide an effective implementation of international trading standards 3.9. Reduction of the time necessary for trading, clearing and settlement 3.10. Reduction of trading costs 3.11. With providing an "automated third party verification", Blockchain will reduce reliance on brokerage for executing trading transactions 3.12. Profound redefinition of investment profession 3.13. Allowing real-time delivery versus payment 3.14. Blockchain will disrupt the Investment industry 3.15. The role of brokers is less to execute the customer orders but ensuring the validity and legality of the smart contracts 3.16. The profile of brokers will change as it will be more IT driven 3.17. The new Blockchain system provides technical possibilities for cheapest opportunities to invest savings and funds in securities 3.18. Other (to be specified by the respondent)
V4. Attitude (for the final user—the investor)	4.1. Using Blockchain will be enjoyable 4.2. Using Blockchain will be not enjoyable 4.3. Overall, using Blockchain for trading will be a pleasant experience 4.4. Overall, using Blockchain for trading will be an unpleasant experience

(continued)

Table 1   (continued)

Variable	Items
V5. Intention (for the final user—the investor)	5.1. I plan to use Blockchain trading platform when it will be implemented 5.2. I intent to use Blockchain trading system as a routine part of my trading 5.3. I intent to use Blockchain trading system at every future opportunity 5.4. I want to participate in the implementation process of the new Blockchain trading system in the UAE financial markets. I would like to be contacted for this purpose 5.5. Not sure/Other
V6. Adoption (for organizations and investors)	6.1. I am following the development of Blockchain in UAE or aboard (by different means such as press, web, participation in working groups, formal and informal meetings with various actors) 6.2. I am favorable for the introduction of Blockchain as a replacing existing trading system 6.3. Many organizations in UAE are planning to replace their current systems (e.g., financial ledgers or sub-ledgers, customer relationship management systems, enterprise resource planning [ERP]) with Blockchain solutions 6.4. Many listed companies in UAE are planning to replace their current systems (e.g., financial ledgers or sub-ledgers, customer relationship management systems, enterprise resource planning [ERP]) with Blockchain solutions 6.5. Organizations will lose a competitive advantage if they don't adopt Blockchain technology
V7. Usefulness (for organizations and investors)	7.1. Using a new Blockchain trading system will improve my ability to make good investment decisions 7.2. Using a new Blockchain trading system will allow me to do my trading transactions more quickly 7.3. Using Blockchain system will enhance the effectiveness on trading 7.4. Using Blockchain system will enhance the trust of investors on the financial markets 7.5. The new Blockchain system ensures soundness and accuracy of transactions 7.6. The new Blockchain system protect investors through establishing fair and proper dealing principles between various actors 7.7. The new Blockchain system imposes strict controls over securities transactions to ensure sound and transparent procedures 7.8. The new Blockchain system enhances the liquidity and stability of prices of the listed securities 7.9. There are several limits and dysfunctions within the existing trading system likely to encourage the use of Blockchain If you do agree, please specify such existing limits: ... 7.10. Other ...

Source Developed by the authors

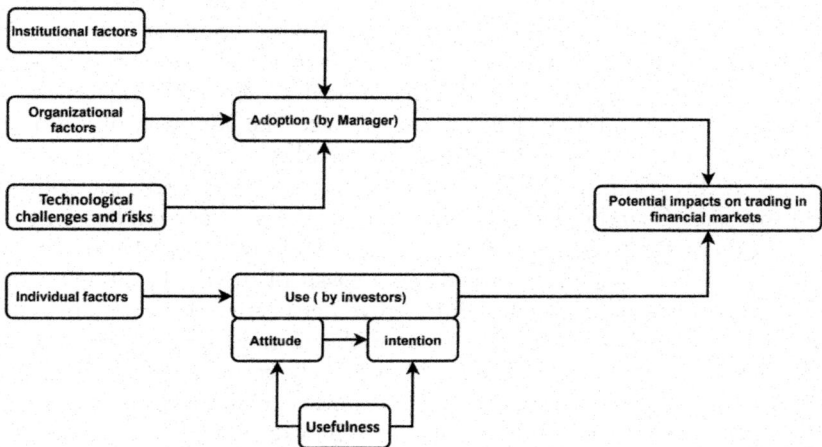

Fig. 1 Analysis model of the adoption and use of the Blockchain technology in the financial markets (*Source* Developed by the authors)

(brokers, managers of the stock market, managers of listed and non-listed companies, and financial market authority representative) through the analysis of their answers to the survey. This is also through the socio-demographic and individual factors influencing their attitudes and motivational behaviors.

This exploratory quantitative study shows that the emergence of the Blockchain technology in the financial markets leads to an overhaul of the managers-investors relationship. We develop a conceptual model representing the implementation process of the Blockchain system in the financial markets as a whole: (1) context and factors of adoption and use, (2) adoption and use behaviors, and (3) consequences or impacts of adoption and use. This global processual approach encompasses the roles assigned to the Blockchain system by the managers and the investors in general, as well as the individual and organizational impacts in terms of trading more specifically. Our pursued conceptual approach follows Orlikowski (1993) through the three aspects of the process. In fact, to design the model, we were particularly interested in integrating contextual factors, particularly organizational, individual, and technological factors to describe and explain the impacts of Blockcahin and the process generating them. We describe the blockchain implementation process taking into consideration the organizational and technological contexts that explain the emergence of the new system and the adoption behaviors of managers and the investors use. This conceptual model presents the implementation process of the Blockchain system in hole. The adoption of a global approach contributes to provide different market participants (managers of the stock exchange institutions, regulator, brokers, listed companies, and investors/shareholders) additional insights for understanding of the slow start of Blockchain adoption and its implications in the securities trading. This study aims to provide an analysis of the implications of the Blockchain technology from an integrative perspective that combines the viewpoint of the investors with that of the managers. This perspective prevents a partial portrait because of the likely convergences and divergences between the two protagonists in terms of the risks and benefits resulting from the adoption of the new Blockchain technology in the financial markets in the UAE.

5.2   Research Design

The major idea of this research is to elicit valuable and effective information based on the items in Table 1 from experts and securities related institutions and agencies regarding the adoption of Blockchain technology in UAE. Therefore, it was very important to select the best research method with the best questions to gather such valuable data.

5.3   Sampling Method

The planned sample in this research was 100 people, but 53 responses have been obtained so far. The sample size has been selected based on the several factors such as data size and members as well as other statistical factors (Delice, 2010). The questionnaire was addressed to economists working in FIs such as the Abu Dhabi Stock Exchange, ADNOC Investments, speculators, financial agents, and others. We tracked young economists on social media platforms and made sure to participate in the survey that was published on these platforms.

The questionnaire, as mentioned, carries several sections: they vary in terms of technology adoption, the extent to which the responsible authorities are ready to implement it, and the extent of technology's effects on the financial system in the UAE. We have taken great care to ensure that these questions are comprehensive and serve the purpose of investigation.

The responses from the questionnaire has been collected and revised to make the reactions easier to read. The questionnaire is based on 9 sections and most of the answering system was linear scale whereas, 1 strongly agrees with the proposal and 5 is severely weak or strongly disagree.

6   DATA ANALYSIS

Table 2 reports the summary frequency responses of our variables of interest representing the significant findings of the survey analysis.

Our data analysis is structured around the following four significant axes: (1) Barriers and challenges of implementing, (2) Potential impacts on trading and clearance, (3) Technical challenges, and (4) Blockchain limitations and risks.

6.1   *Barriers and Challenges of Implementing*

The survey analysis shows that most of the asked experts confirm that the Blockchain will be the next innovative solution for stock markets and more than 40% agreed on this. We have conducted this survey to elicit the feasibility of implementing Blockchain in the UAE institutions in different sectors. But, financial sector is one of the most important sectors in which UAE is looking to adopt Blockchain technology on it. But, does Blockchain affect any time reduction in the stock market, or does it reduce the cost or it needs expensive costs for migration process? All of these Likert scale and open questions have been also answered by the experts and agencies.

Regarding the distribution of people on weather implementing Blockchain technology, replacing or adapting the existing legacy systems is considered the most important barrier with 46% of the responses strongly agree and agree, 27% are neutral and only 26% disagree or strongly disagree. The costs of migration is not representing a significant barrier. It is rather the organizational and technical change for the replacement and the integration of the new system which represents this reluctance. The migration cost barrier will disappear and many investors will be able to participate, eventually increasing their investment.

Compared to the regulation uncertainty where the legislators are not "prepared", the results are not so pronounced. Indeed, 40% of responses are neutral with only 32.5% agree; 42.5% of the respondents do not see any barrier to the development of the new system. This result requires

Table 2 Summary of survey responses

	Strongly agree	Agree	Neutral	Disagree	Strongly disagree
Implementation (replacing or adapting existing legacy system)	23%	20%	27%	3%	23%
Expensive due to migration costs	11	19	34	26	8
Reducing time necessary for trading	23%	32	11	9	25
Reducing the trading costs	28%	21%	13	11	26
Regulation uncertainty	–	32%	40%	28%	–
Any seen barrier	–	31%	27%	42%	–
Enhancing the liquidity and stability of prices	22%	28%	23%	21%	6%
Not currently identified as a business priority	13%	30%	28%	17%	12%
Compatibility issues with existing systems	19	38	17	17	8
Scalability issues	23	19	28	26	4
Vulnerability issues	30%	21%	25%	17%	6%
Possibility to undertake stock lending and borrowing	21%	32%	11%	11%	23%
Possibility to undertake short selling	28%	21%	13%	11%	27%
Possibility to better control the short selling and lending practices	11%	19%	34%	26%	8%

Source Authors' own calculation based on the collected data

further exploration. The findings show that the cost does not constitute an obstacle to replacing and implementing the new Blockchain system for stock trading. For reducing the trading costs, the acceptance rate exceeded 49%, but there are some of the respondents believe that barriers and obstacles exist to prevent the new implementation and they constitute approximately 30%. Furthermore, for the readiness of legislation and legislators, the responses were somewhat equals for each of the agreeing, neutral, and disagreeing. We infer from these responses that replacing the old system with a new system using Blockchain technology will save time and replacing it will not afford so much cost, but of course it requires development and exploration over time. While legislation will be in line with the development of the Blockchain technology to serve the financial sector in the UAE.

6.2   Potential Impacts on Trading and Clearance

Concerning the potential impacts on trading, clearing, and settlement, some results are interesting. In fact, the responses on the reaction on whether Blockchain technology can improve the liquidity of securities and the stability of their prices show obviously that most of respondents are agreed (28%) or even strongly agreed (22%), and few are disagree and strongly disagreeing with it (21% and 6%, respectively). One of the interesting results of this preliminary study is that 55% of the respondents agreed that the new system will reduce the trading time. The respondents agreed also that Blockchain could give the possibility to undertake stock lending and borrowing (53%), short selling (49%), and control those practices (30%). One of the interviewed experts (a senior manager in the stock exchange) highlights the possibility to create a Securities Lending and Borrowing (SLB) Blokchain based platform. "Currently not all types of investors have the capability to be a lender and could offer his/her shares for SLB purpose". This platform will allow not only the trading transactions but also the SLB transactions in a digital, smooth way with less human intervention, and with using smart contracts. The data are distributed among experts who see time and cost reduction and some who believe no reduction at all (25%). While reducing the trading time from T + 2 to T + 0 is feasible, the cost is still not clear since the migration process really needs to be thoroughly investigated.

6.3   Technical Challenges

This research has also considered the compatibility and scalability of Blockchain with other enterprise infrastructure as valuable items of the study. Blockchain is not still standardized and declared as a system-compatible or scalable. Indeed, most of experts (57%) claim that Blockchain is not easy to install or configure on the current platforms.

There will be several issues to be fixed before and even after deploying it. Although Blockchain promised to reinforce the security and to protect the data, it has also some vulnerabilities that could be exploited by an experienced hacker. We believe Blockchain has still some vulnerabilities issues such as in coding and architecture (Alkhalifah et al., 2019). Most of the asked experts (51%) agree on the existence of vulnerabilities issues on Blockchain.

Other item such as if the Blockchain is considered a priority has been also examined to find out if the technology is one of the future innovations. The responses here are varying and reflecting individual experiences and expectations. The majority with more than 40% are considering Blockchain currently as not a priority. However, there are also experts agreeing with considering it as a business priority (29% of the respondents).

6.4   Blockchain Limitations and Risks

Most Blockchain are designed as a decentralized databases that function as a distributed digital ledger. These Blockchain ledgers record and store data in blocks, which are organized in a chronological sequence and are linked through cryptographic proofs. The creation of Blockchain technology brought up many advantages in a variety of industries, providing increased security in trustless environments. However, its decentralized nature also brings some disadvantages. For instance, when compared to traditional centralized databases, Blockchain presents limited data modification and requires increased storage capacity.

As per the results and the literature about advantages and challenges of the Blockcain, we propose some recommendations to better deploy this technology in the stock market. These are:

1. New Trading Approach: Immediate trading matching and equating the order creating a payment system like PayPal that will exchange the money for the certificate of the shares plus the validation of the participants. Once the payment is received, the buyer will receive the shares by conducting a smart contract that will be prepared automatically by the system. This is depending on the type of security and regulation. Blockchain technology will allocate all the information about the Clearing house, brokerage companies, investors, and authorities. An approach of automating reports and payment systems

requires to set up a simulation for the entire transaction process. Therefore, the approval of the Stock Exchange about the acceptance of a transaction process would appear automatically if the matching went with no flags.

2. Good financial management and enough capital: Any company that decided to implement Blockchain must first have enough capital because its implementation is costly and not many organizations can afford it in long-term.

3. Security and privacy: Ensuring a high level of security and privacy is especially important. It is possible to encryption algorithms, personal identifier, passwords, and other privacy. The Blockchain can be a safer environment for trading.

4. Team Well-Trained: To Make Blockchain Implementation and Service Performing Well. Specified Teams with Different Expertise and Training Course Are Required.

5. Intelligent algorithms with mathematical complexity: Blockchain needs the help of complex mathematics running behind high-end computing power in intelligent algorithms with mathematical complexity. This also includes smart algorithms to run efficiently every second behind the trading transactions.

6. New Generation of an Interactive Platform that React Live: It Must Be Implemented to Show the Real Settlement Trading with a Time of Transaction of 0 day.

7. Analytics and user interfaces: Analytics capacities can permit their clients to execute basic Blockchain trading. The operations are simple to do. Comers could be served within few minutes. In this way, investors and users feel that it is open and helpful system. Three main characteristics should be ensured (Kuzlu et al., 2019): (a) throughput (successful transactions per minute), (b) latency (response time per transaction), (c) scalability (number of participants and investors serviceable).

8. We recommend creating a financial system for adequate payment between money authorities, investors, listed companies, and financial intermediates where the central bank or one of the banks will be appointed to play the direct role in money transfer operations.

9. Creating a new Blockchain trading platform in which it relies on smart contracts that are implicitly built for each company listed in the stock market. These contracts interact with each other and communicate about stock prices and number of shares that have been purchased.

7   Conclusion

We aspire to reach those researching this technology within the United Arab Emirates or outside of this country with simplifying the idea of switching from the old financial systems to the new financial system that adopts Blockchain technology.

The purpose of this research is to study the susceptibility and the readiness of the UAE financial markets to implement Blockchain technology and what are the challenges and impacts of this adoption. Throughout a survey analysis, the findings shown that the infrastructure of the UAE financial markets is ready and prepared for development and includes an elite of technical economists as well. However, this step of transition requires the inclusion of a new technical team expert in Blockchain, and mainly it requires the involvement and assistance of the financial intermediaries and all parties concerned in the trading transactions. The decision to replace the existing system requires the cooperation of all counterparties.

Then, the questionnaire and interviews were launched with a group of respected economists who are also known on social trading platforms, and we had an interview with an investor from ADNOC Investment and collected responses on which we built analyzes that led to our recent inference that the transformation in financial systems needs everyone's initiative and a courageous decision.

References

Alkhalifah, A., Ng, A., Kayes, A. S. M., Chowdhury, M., Alazab, M., & Watters, P. (2019). *A taxonomy of blockchain threats and vulnerabilities*. https://doi.org/10.20944/preprints201909.0117.v1.

Abdennadher, S., & Cheffi, W. (2020). An exploratory study of the e-corporate governance effectiveness: The case of Internet voting at shareholders' annual meetings in France. *Corporate Governance Journal, 20*(4), 673–702. https://www.emerald.com/insight/content/doi/10.1108/CG-04-2019-0116/full/html

Beyondskills. (2020). *A 2020 perspective on blockchain technology: Key trends to follow* [Ebook] (pp. 1–11). Beyondskills inc.

Brav, A., Cain, M. D., & Zytnick, J. (2019 May, 15). Retail shareholder participation in the proxy process: Monitoring, engagement, and voting. *Engagement and Voting*. https://papers.ssrn.com/sol3/papers.cfm?abstract_id=3387659

Chiu, J., & Koeppl, T. V. (2017). The economics of cryptocurrencies–bitcoin and beyond. https://papers.ssrn.com/sol3/papers.cfm?abstract_id=3048124

Chiu, J., & Koeppl, T. V. (2019). Blockchain-based settlement for asset trading. *The Review of Financial Studies, 32*(5), 1716–1753. https://academic.oup.com/rfs/article-abstract/32/5/1716/5427772

Delice, A. (2010). The sampling issues in quantitative research. *Educational Sciences: Theory and Practice, 10*(4), 2001–2018.

Fishbein, M., & Ajzen, I. (1975). *Belief, attitude, intention, and behavior: An introduction to theory and research Reading.* Addison-Wesley.

He, J., & King, W. R. (2008). The role of user participation in information systems development: Implications from a meta-analysis. *Journal of Management Information Systems, 25*(1), 301–331.

https://u.ae/en/about-the-uae/strategies-initiatives-and-awards/federal-governments-strategies-and-plans/emirates-Blockchain-strategy-2021

Ives, B., & Olson, M. H. (1984). User involvement and MIS success : A review of research. *Management Science, 30*(5), 586–603.

Knirsch, F., Unterweger, A., & Engel, D. (2019). Implementing a Blockchain from scratch: why, how, and what we learned. *EURASIP Journal On Information Security*(1). https://doi.org/10.1186/s13635-019-0085-3

Kremenova, I., & Gajdos, M. (2019). Decentralized networks: The future internet. *Mobile Networks and Applications, 24*(6), 2016–2023.

Kshetri, N. (2017). Blockchain's roles in strengthening cybersecurity and protecting privacy. *Telecommunications Policy, 41*(10), 1027–1038. https://www.sciencedirect.com/science/article/abs/pii/S0308596117302483

Kuzlu, M., Pipattanasomporn, M., Gurses, L., & Rahman, S. (2019, July). Performance analysis of a hyperledger fabric blockchain framework: Throughput, latency and scalability. In *2019 IEEE international conference on blockchain (Blockchain)* (pp. 536–540). IEEE.

Ledger Insights. (2019). *UAE bank ADCB adopts Blockchain for trade finance.* https://www.ledgerinsights.com/Blockchain-trade-finance-uae-adcb-dltledgers/

Lubin, J., Anderson, M., & Thomason, B. (2017). https://www.mitpressjournals.org/doi/pdf/, https://doi.org/10.1162/inov_a_00263

Maslin, M., Watt, M., & Yong, C. (2019). Research methodologies to support the development of blockchain standards. *Journal Of ICT Standardization, 7*(3), 249–268. https://doi.org/10.13052/jicts2245-800x.734

Mayer, C. (2008). Trust in financial markets. *European Financial Management, 14*(4), 617–632. https://onlinelibrary.wiley.com/doi/abs/10.1111/j.1468-036X.2008.00454.x

Miraz, M., & Donald, D. (2018). *Application of blockchain in booking and registration systems of securities exchanges.* 2018 International Conference on

Computing, Electronics & Communications Engineering (Iccece), 35–40. https://doi.org/10.1109/iccecome.2018.8658726

Mire, S. (2018, October 26). *Blockchain for stock markets: 11 possible use cases*. Disruptor Daily. https://www.disruptordaily.com/Blockchain-use-cases-stock-trading/

Mohammad Bin Rashid launches the Emirates Blockchain Strategy 2021. (2018, April 11). *Gulf News*. https://gulfnews.com/technology/mohammad-bin-rashid-launches-the-emirates-Blockchain-strategy-2021-1.2204107

Orlikowski, W. J. (1993, September). CASE Tools as organizational change: investigating incremental and radical changes in systems development. *MIS Quarterly, 17*, 309–340.

Pinna, A., & Ruttenberg, W. (2016). *Distributed ledger technologies in securities post-trading: Revolution or evolution?* ECB occasional paper series. https://www.ecb.europa.eu/pub/pdf/scpops/ecbop172.en.pdf Accessed 27 October 2020.

Spears, J. L., & Barki, H. (2010). User participation in information systems security risk management. *MIS Quarterly, 34*, 503–522.

Staff Report. (2018). https://gulfnews.com/business/markets/adx-signs-partnership-with-equichain-for-Blockchain-tech-1.2227927

Tomasic, R., & Akinbami, F. (2011). The role of trust in maintaining the resilience of financial markets. *Journal of Corporate Law Studies, 11*(2), 369–394. https://www.tandfonline.com/doi/abs/10.5235/147359711798110628?casa_token=11iLlMe9FX0AAAAA:6Nsr6QkQEkYO_AVd7Gvi58_lF93qnjk3z7HZL3uqU75ue4acVM_TWR5wos_El0UcuNIBQW6DodmOw

Triandis, H. C. (1971). *Attitude and attitude change*. Wiley.

Workie, H., & Jain, K. (2017). *Distributed ledger technology: Implications of Blockchain for the securities industry*. HSTalks. https://hstalks.com/article/201/distributed-ledger-technology-implications-of-bloc/.

Wu, B., & Duan, T. (2019). The application of blockchain technology in financial markets. *Journal of Physics: Conference Series, 1176*,. https://doi.org/10.1088/1742-6596/1176/4/042094

Zmud, R. W. (1979). Individual differences and MIS success : A review of the empirical literature. *Management Science, 25*(10), 966–979.

Would Blockchain Disrupt the Accounting and Auditing Professions? An Exploratory Study in the UAE

Hareb Abdulla, Abdulla Alfalasi, and Rihab Grassa

1 INTRODUCTION

Technology and the increased digitization of the business landscape continue to influence and change not only how business functions but, also, how this information is communicated to external stakeholder groups (Price, 2016). Blockchain emerged as a real-world technology option in 2016 and 2017. It is poised to change IT in the same way that open-source software did twenty-five years ago (Mearian, 2019). Blockchain is a disturbed ledger technology that allows data to be stored globally on thousands of servers while, also, allowing anyone on the network to see everyone else's entries in near real-time. This makes it

H. Abdulla · A. Alfalasi · R. Grassa (✉)
College of Business, Higher Colleges of Technology, Dubai, United Arab Emirates
e-mail: rgrassa@hct.ac.ae

H. Abdulla
e-mail: H0033032@hct.ac.ae

A. Alfalasi
e-mail: H00350155@hct.ac.ae

difficult for one user to gain control of the network (Mearian, 2019). In other words, Blockchain is a public ledger of information that is collected through a network that sits on top of the Internet. This means of recording information gives Blockchain its groundbreaking potential (lisk, n.d.).

With the rapid development of technology and digital currency, accounting and audit firms have expressed interest in Blockchain. Indeed, Blockchain is a revolutionary and promising technology that can help to reduce risk; stamp out fraud; and promote transparency of the financial statements (builtin, n.d.). It enables automated, reliable, and verifiable preparation of financial statements for routine business transactions. The Big Four audit firms have been the pioneers in adopting important initiatives to keep up with the new technologies (Bajpai, 2017). In 2014, Deloitte launched a Blockchain initiative (Deloitte 2016). In 2017, Ernst & Young (EY) developed several applications and services to implement the Blockchain technology across the firm (EY, 2017). PWC used Blockchain to launch its digital asset services. In addition, they aim by 2020 to implements Blockchain in live production systems (PWC, 2017). KPMG aims to use Blockchain technology on business propositions and processes (KPMG, 2017).

This chapter explores the perceptions of the impacts of Blockchain technology on the UAE's accounting and auditing profession. Indeed, as an innovative approach, Blockchain may change their accounting and auditing practices. Therefore, it is worthwhile to explore the perceptions of practitioners on the potential and challenges of this new technology on the UAE's accounting and auditing profession and to explore the extent to which this discipline may be transformed. Therefore, in this paper, we try to provide an initial discussion on how Blockchain can enable a real-time, verifiable, and transparent accounting ecosystem. Moreover, Blockchain has the potential to transform current auditing practices and create a more precise and timely automatic assurance system.

The aim of this paper is twofold. First, since there have been few research studies on Blockchain and accounting profession, we provide insights and discuss the few previous works in this field. Second, in this paper, by conducting interviews with the accounting and audit managers of several important companies operating in the UAE, we try to explore their perceptions on the effect of Blockchain technology on the country's accounting and auditing profession.

The reminder of this paper is organized as follows. Section 2 offers insights into the literature review. Section 3 presents the methodology used in this paper. Section 4 is dedicated to discussion and conclusions and identifies, also, future areas for research.

2   Literature Review

A very small number of studies have discussed the effect of Blockchain technology on the accounting and audit profession. Dai and Vasarhelyi (2017) argue that, in order to avoid any unauthorized data or record changes, Blockchain plays the role of the accounting information system by distributing the power of transaction verification, storage, and management to a group of nodes. This mechanism facilitates the close to real-time reporting of reliable accounting information to stakeholders at several aggregation levels based on their roles and demands. Consequently, Blockchain can authenticate any audit-related information. Indeed, auditors can rely on the truthfulness of the data because Blockchain safeguards the data posted on it. In turn, this help the auditors to perform numerous substantive tests. Faccia and Mosteanu (2019) argue that Blockchain technology can help to move from a double entry to a triple entry accounting system; reduce the risk of error; and detect fraudulent transactions.

Liu et al. (2019) introduce two forms of Blockchain: namely, permissionless and permissioned; and they discuss their opportunities and challenges to auditors. Auditors must prepare for the changes imposed by the development of the Blockchain technology and they need to promote themselves in the roles of strategic partners (Karajovic et al., 2019). As matters stand currently, auditors should gain competency in Blockchain technology and governance of Blockchain; contribute actively to Blockchain development with an emphasis on risk control; and move to continuous auditing (Liu et al., 2019).

Brender and Gauthier (2018) see that the auditing profession has to become more IT-oriented because the key objective of financial audit is changing. Indeed, it becomes to ensure that the blockchain technology is set up and deployed properly. Moreover, since controls can be encoded into blockchain technology and automated, the blockchain technology itself can guarantee the existence, accuracy, and completeness of transactions. Furthermore, the authors assume that the auditors are able to perform an in-depth blockchain source code and parameter review. Therefore, auditors are primarily "IT engineer auditors" whose main roles are to certify the blockchain technology. On the other hand, auditors have to certify their clients' financial statements as these stand currently (Brender & Gauthier, 2018). Overall, with the rapid development of technologies everywhere and, more particularly, blockchain technology, it is imprtant that the auditing firms think about what future auditing will look. Moreover, the utilization of blockchain technology includes the auditing profession making an example shift of at two points. Firstly, the scope of the audit shifts from giving an opinion on the fiarness of the financial statements to test the accounting information systems and, also, confirming if the blockchain is properly implemented or not. Secondly, deprending of the regulators, the attestation profession will swtich from a backward-looking activity to a forward-looking activity which involves strategic analysis and advice based on big data. Lastly, the attestation service must clarify if their employed audit teams have the necessary skills in order to dealwith possible changes in the auditing profession. Moreover, up to the present time, the Big4 accounting firms have invested in technologies, for instance data analysis and software, and all of them have endangered blockchain-related projects (Brender & Gauthier, 2018).

Most previous studies have discussed the theoretical effect of blockchain on the accounting and auditing profession, and very few studies have explored this relationship emperically. Brender et al. (2019) have exploered how, in Switzerland, auditors anticipate the impacts of blockchain technology on their activities. They arrived at the following three assumptions. First, the accounting and auditing profession does not anticipate fully blockchain's potential effect on it. Second, the profession needs to become more IT orientated and forward looking. Third, the profile, the mission and the auditors' role will change.

3   METHODOLOGY

We believe that the interview methodology can be the most appropriate means for this type of research. Therefore, during the spring of 2019, we interviewed 8 audit and accounting directors from the UAE's largest companies, and 2 audit managers from two BIG4 company and 3 auditors/accountants from local accounting firms. We conducted online interviews from which we felt that we covered all the raised issues. Initially, we contacted our interviewees by emailing them a summary of the research agenda and assuring them of the confidentiality of their answers. Due to the COVID-19 issue, we performed all the interviews through Zoom. On average, each interview took about one and a half hours.

As shown by the results in Table 1, all interviewees are concerned by the Blockchain issues and challenges for their companies' accounting and auditing departments. Therefore, we believe that, when compared to other company members, the interviewees were able to provide more worthwhile and informed responses to our questions.

We conducted semi-structured interviews and encouraged our interviewees to discuss the issues and challenges that Blockchain technology presented to the UAE's accounting and auditing profession. We asked broad questions about the Blockchain technology's effect on accounting and auditing discipline. These general questions led us to a deeper debate of the interviewees' perceptions on the topic.

All interviewees were asked the same basic questions. However, following each new interview, we revised and improved our questions and, if necessary, considered new suggestions. This method meant that we adjusted the research questions as the study developed. Therefore, theory and practice progressed together from the collected data without an initial agenda being imposed upon the research study. We micro-analyzed the collected information to reveal the themes that arose from the interviews. These allowed us to recapitulate the interviewees' perceptions.

Table 1 summarizes the interviewees' perceptions on Blockchain's effect of on the UAE's accounting and auditing profession, the industrial sector, and the size of each company. This allowed us to ascertain any possible connection between the interviewees' perceptions on Blockchain and their companies' trend toward the new technology. Moreover, it helped us to understand if the companies' characteristics (mainly sector and size) correlated with the interviewees' perceptions.

4   Discussion of the Findings

We identified five main themes from our analysis of the interviews. These are: (i) the purpose of Blockchain; (ii) Blockchain's effect on auditing method/accounting; (iii) advantages of using Blockchain for auditing; (iv) software to audit Blockchain; (v) how Blockchain affects accounting/auditing firms' daily operations. We noted a significant uniformity in our interviewees' views concerning the uncertainty surrounding Blockchain (Table 1).

Table 1 Perceptions of blockchain technology

Code	Interview role	General view	Sector	Size
C1	Chief Internal Auditor	It is easier to keep track of transactions on a Blockchain software as all data are stored in a single database, and this allows efforts to be refocused on strategic goals and delivers actionable results	Public healthcare	Large
C2	Audit manager	It has the potential to increase the accounting profession by cutting down the cost of ledger maintenance in reconciling ledgers. Also, by assuring transparency, it provides ownership of assets	BIG 4 audit firm	Large
C3	Internal audit manager	By streaming their processes and audits, it will assist accountant/auditors in ensuring the transactions recorded are accurate	Energy	Large
C4	Accounting manager	Blockchain is already impacting on those organizations' CPA auditors since the use of Blockchain to record transactions and the rate of adoption is expected to continue to increase	Healthcare	Large
C5	Audit manager	Ability to audit the whole population with a click Ability to do instant auditing Provide live recommendations	Government	Large
C6	Accounting manager	Secure recording of transactions between untrusted parties	Industry	Large

Code	Interview role	General view	Sector	Size
C7	Head accounting	Both audits have different objectives so, in my perception, it is difficult to compare. Auditing Blockchain. It can be part of auditing financial statements if a company uses Blockchain for its transactions. Therefore, I see both audits are complementary and not substituting each other	Pharmaceutical	Large (multinational)
C8	Audit manager	It is extremely difficult (if not impossible) to manipulate a Blockchain transaction. This is due to the decentralized approach of recording the transactions in different ledgers	Big 4 audit company	Large
C9	Partner	Auditors must be involved in the early processes of implementing Blockchain	Local accounting firm	Medium
C10	Accounting manager	It will save time, effort, and cost	Industry	Large
C11	Audit manager	It will bring new challenges to the audit profession	Local accounting firm	Medium
C12	Audit manager	It will enhance the accounting profession and simplify the recording process	Financial	Large
C13	Internal audit manager	It offers a new secured environment for conducting business transactions	Financial	Large

Source Authors preparations based on distributed survey

Table 2 Interviewees perceptions on blockchain technology

	In favor	Not in favor	undecided
Accounting profession	8	5	0
Audit profession	6	5	2

Source Authors owns calculations based on distributed survey

Table 2 summarizes the interviewees' perceptions on Blockchain technology. As shown, 8 accounting profession managers favored Blockchain technology, and 5 were not in favor of it. 6 audit profession managers favored Blockchain technology, 5 were not in favor of it, and 2 were undecided.

4.1   The Purpose of Blockchain Technology

Based on our findings, all our interviewees argue that Blockchain technology reinforces the development of digital currency such as Bitcoin, Litecoin, and Ethereum. Indeed, Blockchain allows digital information to be distributed rather than to be copied. Therefore, each piece of data can only have one owner. In other words, Blockchain represents a system of computers in which information is stored and shared among all the network's participants and a public journal of information collected through a network that sits on top of the Internet. Moreover, our interviewees explained, also, that how the information is recorded is what gives Blockchain its revolutionary potential. A data structure holds transactional records and ensures security from untrusted parties, authentic business transaction, transparency, and decentralization.

4.2   Blockchain Effect on Accounting and Auditing Methods

Our findings show that all the interviewees argue that Blockchain has important effects on the accounting process and auditing methods. Blockchain can affect the future of accounting/auditing/ procedures by keeping separate records based on transaction receipts. Also, companies can write their transactions directly into a joint register and, thereby, create an interlocking system of enduring accounting records. Moreover, by streamlining their accounting process and audits, Blockchain assists them, also, in ensuring that the recorded transactions recorded are accurate. Furthermore, Blockchain has made an impact already on those firms' auditors. It is anticipated that there will be a considerable increase in the use of Blockchain technology to record business transactions. In addition, Blockchain technology helps to verify transactions easily without reconciliation and offers a new secure environment for conducting business transactions.

4.3   Advantages of Blockchain Auditing When Compared to the Auditing of Companies' Financial Statements

All our findings show that all our interviewees agree that, as compared to the auditing of companies' financial statements, the advantages of Blockchain auditing include:

- Blockchain may eliminate the need for a join financial statement audit.
- Blockchain has the potential to reduce ledger maintenance costs of by reconciling ledgers. In addition, by assuring transparency, Blockchain provides, also, ownership of assets.
- Blockchain verifies recorded data recorded without having to return to the third party and most of the stored data are time sampled (Chronological order). Therefore, the transactions, recorded in the ledger, can be tracked to either the date or point of origin.
- Despite these complexities, Blockchain offers an opportunity to streamline financial reporting and the audit process. In today's world, account reconciliation, trial balances, journal entries, subledger extracts and supported spreadsheet files are provided to a CPA auditor in a variety of electronic and manual formats.
- Blockchain can audit a whole population with a single click.
- Blockchain can audit instantly.
- Blockchain provides live recommendations.
- Blockchain technology is innately resistant to recorded transactions being changed/modified.
- Blockchain technology can assist as an open distributed record that, in permanent way, can record and verify transactions efficiently between two parties.
- Blockchain permits the verification of reported transactions.

- Blockchain helps to build an efficient governance , risk management and puts in place controls in from the start than having to retrofit them after an issue arises.

4.4   Software to Audit Blockchain

Based on our findings, none of our interviewees have been given currently the opportunity to use any Blockchain software for audit purposes. In other words, none of the companies, to which we distributed our questionnaire, have implemented Blockchain technology. However, they have provided training and seminars on Blockchain so that their employees are knowledgeable about Blockchain technology.

4.4.1   Software for Auditing Blockchain
Most of our interviewees cannot recommend a software with which they are unfamiliar. However, those, who are familiar with the software, recommend Audit Program—ISACA and PwC's Blockchain validation solution because it combines the patent-pending risk framework with the auditing software. Currently, within the area of Blockchain technology, it is the only existing solution for risks and controls relating to private businesses' Blockchain processes. Moreover, there is, also, Ethereum or Hyperledger which is the leading Blockchain software that encompasses so many features. Furthermore, Python is recommended, also, for backend web development, data analysis, artificial intelligence, and ad scientific computing.

4.4.2   Track of Transactions on Blockchain
The most used accounting software is QuickBooks. Many of our interviewees cannot give a clear answer since they are unfamiliar with Blockchain software. However, based on the interviewees, who answered yes to this question, Blockchain software makes it easier to keep track of transactions because all data are stored in a single database, and this allows efforts to be refocused on strategic goals and the delivery of actionable results. In addition, since all businesses track information and face the challenge of reconciling data with counterparties, Blockchain technology has the potential to be relevant to everyone.

Intuit Inc. developed the first version of the software in 1998 to address the need for simplified accounting platforms. Therefore, the first major adoption, may transform business processes and old legacy systems that are cumbersome to maintain. Furthermore, every node has a copy of Blockchain. Once a block reaches a certain number of approved transactions, a new block is formed. The software automatically updates itself every 10 min. Blockchain technology has the potential to reduce maintenance costs and reconcile ledgers to enhance and provide absolute certainty over the ownership and history of assets. Blockchain technology can help accountants, also, to gain clarity over their organizations' available resources and obligations in addition to freeing up resources to concentrate on planning and valuation rather than recordkeeping.

4.4.3   Blockchain's Effect on Accounting/Auditing Daily Operations

Our interviewees argue that Blockchain affects the operation of both accounting and audit. Some experts in the field argue that Blockchain technology may eliminate the need for a joint financial statement audit. Moreover, just as computers and the Internet have changed workplaces across all industries, Blockchain offers the industry solutions to varied issues. Indeed, business models are reevaluated currently to implement Blockchain solutions. In addition, they need to ensure accuracy of the code rather than validity of the transaction and demonstrate changes in how they verify transactions and balances.

Based on our findings, all the interviewees argue that it is not be difficult to use Blockchain software to track transactions. The software has been designed to help the team's manager view their activities transparently and effectively in a shared and secured environment. Moreover, every node has a copy of Blockchain and, once a block reaches a certain number of approved transactions, a new block is formed. The Blockchain technology updates automatically every 10 min. In addition, each transaction is labeled with the required approvals. Furthermore, by creating a Blockchain, a solution has been created to solve a specific problem. Then, specific transactions or interactions should be determined along with who can have access to each part of the transaction.

4.4.4   Evidences and Blockchain Software

Based on our findings, the audit evidence should include all data. The auditors' duties and skills may change as new Blockchain based techniques and procedures arise. For example, approaches for the purpose of obtaining sufficient appropriate audit evidence need to consider both traditional stand-alone general ledgers and Blockchain ledgers. Moreover, other data types, auditors can gather various types of evidence such as nonfinancial data extracted from modern ERP's or online database, RFID and networked sensors, social media, and even stores' closed-circuit television (CCTV) videos. As in the normal process, this provides a full series of the document but it is stored electronically in a format using more formulas. Also, it allows to establish: (i) whether or not segregation of duties policies are being respected by checking whether or not the appropriate employee is authorized to do so; (ii) verify whether stated commissions are in accordance with determined set; and (iii) verify whether or not differences exist between sales (or purchase) orders, invoices, and payments.

4.4.5   Authenticity of Transaction Recorded

Our interviewees argue that all the transactions, recorded using Blockchain, are authentic and not fraudulent. They think all such transactions are secured and that all transactions are linked by hashing algorithms. Moreover, Blockchain's functionality is complicated. Digital records combine to from blocks. These blocks make a chain cryptographically and chronologically connecting the network with each other through sophisticated mathematical algorithms. Each block has a unique set of records with a connection to the preceding one. Any new block is added only to the end of the Blockchain.

Industries, product suppliers, and distributors are switching to Blockchain technology as a means of reducing the risk of fraud. A decentralized, unchallengeable record of each product's journey promotes authenticity. However, Blockchain suffers from some disadvantages. These are such as: (i) *Slow Performance*—compared to a centralized database, a decentralized database is much slower. (ii) *Signature Verification*—unlike a centralized database, a public private cryptograph digital signature verification is requested for every Blockchain transaction (generally by using Elliptic Curve Digital Signature Algorithm (ECDSA)). This procedure ensures that the transaction takes place between the accurate nodes. In order to prove each node's authenticity of, it is required to validate itself with a digital signature; this complicates the whole process. (iii) *Consensus Approach*—all nodes must approve the record of a valid transaction in the ledger; this denotes an extensive effort. Well, before the earlier described process, all the nodes need to go through the various back and forth communications; this is again a lengthy process. (iv) *Redundant Data*—unlike a centralized database, the Blockchain system requires

is a larger volume of necessary computations. Every node consecutively on this common network needs to experience the same process independently. (v) *Energy Consumption*—to validate each transaction, all the nodes, existing in the Blockchain network, attempt 450 thousand trillion solutions in each passing second; this represents an important consumed volume of computer power.

4.4.6   Mistakes During Recording

Our interviewees explain that is neither easy nor permissible to fix the mistake. However, we can add another block and use an extra data field to indicate that old data is wrong and that the new one is being used instead. Moreover, when a transaction is recorded onto the Blockchain, it cannot be altered and it cannot be reversed. Even many advanced cryptocurrency users can recall an incident when they have failed to double-check their transaction details and, accidently, they have sent funds to the wrong recipient or sent the wrong amount. As unfortunate as it is, cryptocurrency transactions on Bitcoin, Ethereal, and Bitcoin Cash Networks are designed to be irreversible, and we have no control over them. Furthermore, since coding and transaction mistakes happen, mis-booked information may be confined or required by law to be removed.

4.4.7   Manage Information

Based on our findings, information overload is a phenomenon connected mainly to the information age. It is not like that information overload has been born with the information age. It has "been around" actually for quite some time. Moreover, Blockchain can be used in various shipping applications and can bring about an evolution after the information is stored in the block. The information cannot be changed or deleted unless the efficiency ship is chartered in the era of the information overload. Furthermore, a combined use is highly practical when it comes to mastering data management as businesses scale up in this digital age. Typically, master data consists of information such as names of products, staff, vendors, equipment, tools, and places. It is a glossary of information that helps to make sense of transactional data which is a static data.

5   Conclusion

Blockchain technology has been introduced recently into the UAE. In this research paper, we tried to explore the potential impact of Blockchain on the UAE's accounting and auditing profession. Based on the findings from several interviews, almost all accountants and auditors, who had experience of Blockchain technology, believed that it had a lot of positive benefits on accounting practices and very few negative impacts. Blockchain technology provides a secure platform where all the items of information on transactions are protected against illegal access or tampering. Furthermore, Blockchain technology offers several features that help to track transactions. Irrespective of the amount of the transaction, Blockchain technology can still track it and help in managing it efficiently. One of the most useful features of Blockchain technology is the automatic update whereby every 10 minBlockchain automatically updates all transactions in the system and waits for approval to ensure that the labeling of the transaction is correct. Overall, while Blockchain technology improves efficiency , it has some shortfalls. Currently, within the UAE, the biggest disadvantage is the lack of experience of Blockchain technology due to it only recently being introduced within the UAE. According to our data, once the necessary experience is gained, accountants will face fewer difficulties in using Blockchain technology, and this will lead to an increase in efficiency . However, Blockchain technology lacks a feature, which most accountants think is crucial. The missing feature is that Blockchain is unable to adjust to a transaction added to the system and to go back to the transaction and fix the problem, a new block must be created.

We think this paper's findings can be on interest to the UAE's accounting and auditing profession and to companies responsible for the training of accountants and auditors. Moreover, our research paper offers two recommendations to business and practitioners. First businesses should consider their goals and identify the problems that they are trying to solve. In this regard, they need to consider how Blockchain or distributed ledger technology helps to solve such problems and what aspects of the Blockchain technology provide the necessary competitive edge or benefit specific products or services. Three is a need to identify the appropriate market and the affected customers, relevant competitors and key legal risks. Blockchain technology can help to tackle legal challenges head on and there are certain uses of the distributed ledger technology that, undoubtedly, will raise legal uncertainties. Therefore, we recommend that companies engage with regulators to help to educate the employees about the solutions and benefits provided by Blockchain technology (Smith, 2018).

Second, we recommend that the UAE's accounting and auditing profession engage with other industries and, more especially, with the country's financial sector to maximize the potential advantages of certain applications of Blockchain technology. However, consensus may need to be achieved on an industry wide basis to maximize the value that can be added by individual players. Furthermore, because many manifestations of Blockchain technology may not yield significant immediate benefits, businesses can assess costs versus the benefits of small to medium efficiency gains in both the short term and the long term. For a business to achieve greater long term efficiency improvements, they must accept substantial costs in both the short to medium terms (Smith, 2018).

This chapter contributes also, to both the existing Blockchain and accounting/auditing literature by providing the accountants' and auditors' perceptions of Blockchain technology's impact on this profession.

Finally, we stress the limited nature of our paper's findings. Its purpose was to serve as an initial exploration on the impact of Blockchain technology on the UAE's accounting and auditing profession. We recommend that our research findings need to be validated by future research studies. More particularly, we recommend that further studies be conducted in different countries to explore the empirical impact of Blockchain technology on the accounting and auditing profession and in putting into context the results of this UAE-based study.

References

Bajpai, P. (2017). *Big 40 accounting firms are experimenting with blockchain and Bitcoin.* Available at: https://www.nasdaq.com/article/big-4-accoun ting-firms-are-experimenting-with-blockchain-and-bitcoin-cm812018. Last accessed May 21, 2021.

Brender, N., & Gauthier, M. (2018). *Impacts de la blockchain sur le métier d'auditeur.*

Brender, N., Gauthier, M., Morin, J.-H., & Salihi, A. (2019). The potential impact of blockchain technology on audit practice. *Journal of Strategic Innovation and Sustainability, 14*(2). https://doi.org/10.33423/jsis.v14i2. 1370

Builtin. (n.d.). *What is blockchain technology? How does blockchain work?: Built in.* Retrieved February 1, 2020, from https://builtin.com/blockchain. Last accessed May 21, 2020.

Dai, J., & Vasarhelyi, M. (2017). Toward blockchain-based accounting and assurance. *Journal of Information Systems, 31*(3), 5–21.

Deloitte. (2016). *Tech trends 2016—Innovating in the digital era.* Deloitte University Press. Last accessed May 21, 2020.

Ernst & Young (EY). (2017). *EY infuses blockchain into enterprises and across industries with launch of EY Ops Chain.* Available at: https://eylaw.ey.com/2017/05/03/ey-infuses-blockchain-into-enterprises-and-across-indust rieswith-launch-of-ey-ops-chain/. Last accessed May 29, 2020.

Faccia, A., & Moşteanu, N. R. (2019). *Accounting and blockchain technology from double-entry to triple-entry.* Published in Proceedings of 8th International Conference on Business and Economic Development (ICBED), New York.

Karajovic, M., Kim, H. M., & Laskowski, M. (2019). Thinking outside the block: Projected phases of blockchain integration in the accounting industry. *Australian Accounting Review, 29*(2), 319–330.

KPMG. (2017). *KPMG and microsoft blockchain services.* Available at: https://home.kpmg/xx/en/home/insights/2016/09/kpmg-and-microsoft-blockc hain-services.html. Last accessed July 2020.

KPMG. (2020). *KPMG and Microsoft announce new "Blockchain Nodes".* Available at: https://home.kpmg.com/us/en/home/media/press-releases/2017/02/kpmg-and-microsoft-announce-new-blockchain-nodes.html. Last accessed 20 May 2020.

Lisk. (n.d.). *What is blockchain?* Retrieved February 1, 2020, from https://lisk.io/what-is-blockchain. Last accessed 20 May 2020.

Liu, M., Wu, K., & Xu, J. J. (2019). How will blockchain technology impact auditing and accounting permissionless versus permissioned blockchain. *Current Issues in Auditing, 13*(2), 19–29.

Mearian, L. (2019). What is blockchain? The complete guide. Retrieved February 1, 2020, from https://www.computerworld.com/article/3191077/what-is-blockchain-the-complete-guide.html. Last accessed May 21, 2020.

Price, E. (2016). Fed: Blockchain is transformative. *International Financial Law Review, 1.*

PWC. (2017). *Redrawing the lines: FinTech's growing influence on financial services.* Available at: https://www.pwc.com/gx/en/industries/financial-services/assets/pwc-fintech-exec-summary-2017.pdf. Last accessed May 19, 2020.

Smith, S. S. (2018). Blockchain augmented audit—benefits and challenges for accounting professionals. *The Journal of Theoretical Accounting Research, 14*(1), 117–137.

Opportunities and Challenges Facing SMEs' Access to Financing in the UAE: An Analytical Study

Teheni El Ghak and Hajer Zarrouk

1 INTRODUCTION

In the United Arab Emirates (UAE), Small and Medium Enterprises (SMEs) are regarded as a cushion for unstable economic conditions and play a crucial role in strengthening global economic development. Zimmermann and Thomä (2016) mentioned that SMEs are the sustainer of job creation and economic growth and a crucial source of competitiveness in the globalized markets. Schilirò (2015) stated that SMEs enable creating a skilled workforce and share expertise to enhance innovation and strengthen the pillars of the knowledge economy. In the same order of ideas, Miniaoui and Schilirò (2017) argued that innovative SMEs are key

T. E. Ghak (✉)
Laboratory of International Economic Integration, Faculty of Economic Sciences and Management of Tunis, University Tunis El Manar, Tunis, Tunisia
e-mail: elghateheni@yahoo.fr

H. Zarrouk
PS2D, Faculty of Economics Sciences and Management, University Tunis El Manar, Tunis, Tunisia
e-mail: hzarrouk@hct.ac.ae

A. Echchabi et al. (eds.), *Contemporary Research in Accounting and Finance*, https://doi.org/10.1007/978-981-16-8267-4_14

311

drivers of economic diversification, employment creation, and sustainable growth in the Gulf Cooperation Council (GCC). Baby and Joseph (2016) and Jones and Mosteanu (2019) also stated that SMEs play a pivotal economic role. In fact, SMEs represent 99.2% of the Emirate number of establishments in 2019 (In absolute numbers, there are currently 400,000 SMEs) (Dubai SME, 2019). SMEs employ up to 52% of the total workforce in the Emirate. The contribution of the SME sector to the GDP of the country is 60%. The UAE Government's Vision 2021 projects SME contribution in the non-oil economy to reach 70% by 2021. In terms of the Segment-wise split, 73% of SMEs are operating in the wholesale and retail sector, 16% in the services sector, and 11% in the industry sector. SMEs provide jobs for more than 86% of the private sector's workforce (The Official Portal of the UAE' Government, 2019a). The growth and diversification of Dubai's economy are due to the overwhelming number of SMEs in the UAE. These SME businesses make up nearly 99.2% of all companies and have recorded a 9% compounded annual growth rate (CAGR) since 2008. Services account for a majority of SMEs (48%), followed by Trading (47%) and Manufacturing (5%). SMEs contributed nearly 50% of Dubai's GDP. Regarding employment and job creation, SMEs account for 51% of the workforce (The Official Portal of the UAE' Government, 2019b).

Given the importance of SMEs, the Government has a high spotlight on improving the SME sector's performance, productivity, and contribution to the economy. Furthermore, the Government keeps implementing policies to empower the SME sector to become the driving force of Dubai's sustainable economic growth. SMEs are at the core of the UAE Vision 2021. The UAE' Government and a national bank, by blueprints to provide expertise, technical support, and training, plan to improve the SME area's capacities to accomplish more superior outcomes, especially in innovation. The SME Expo will give the small and medium-sized national entrepreneurs a platform to meet leading industry experts and collaborate. SMEs and miniature ventures are welcome to take an interest in aggregate activity to accomplish the objectives.

SMEs face various challenges throughout the lifecycle, including raising funds, maintaining cash flow, improving sales, and enhancing customer services. Nevertheless, financing SMEs with appropriate sources is an essential tool for growth and wealth creation. Access to finance is crucial for SMEs' improvement, development, and success (Abdulsaleh & Worthington, 2013; Ou & Haynes, 2006).

SMEs, namely, employ three financing methods: initial internal sources (owner–manager's personal savings and retained earnings); informal outside sources (family and friends' funds, trade credit, venture capital, and angel financiers); and traditional external sources (banks, financial institutions, and securities markets) (Abdulsaleh & Worthington, 2013). Although the UAE' Government is taking a significant role in establishing initiatives and programs to help with funding sources, SMEs are confronted with many issues and challenges, such as access to financing. In this context, a recent study conducted by Zarrouk, Sherif, et al. (2020) revealed that financial barriers, difficulties accessing bank financing, and legal issues inhibit 'SMEs' growth. The results are relevant to research from Bakhouche et al. (2020). The authors mentioned that SMEs face many challenges, including the absence of governance structure, lack of appropriate industry training requirements, innovation capabilities, business experience, and limited access to finance.

Against this backdrop, this chapter investigates the challenges inhibiting SMEs from accessing credit in the UAE and proposes possible solutions. The remainder of the chapter is structured as follows. Section 2 discusses the potential sources of SME financing and highlights funding' challenges. Section 3 offers some policy implications. Section 4 concludes the chapter.

2   FINANCING OPTIONS FOR SMEs IN THE UAE: REALITY AND CHALLENGES

2.1   *Government Policies to Support SMEs*

To support SMEs that are 100% owned by UAE nationals and registered with the new federal SME Programme, the Federal Government introduced Federal Law No. (2) of 2014 on SMEs ("SME Law") that sets the foundations for a future definition of SMEs by the UAE cabinet (generally upon the following criteria: employment levels, turnover, or capital investment). The SME law also foresees the establishment of an SME Council and the creation of a national SME program. Under the new SME Law, the Emirates Development Bank should allocate at least 10% of its annual financing to develop SME financing (OECD, 2016). This effort can be reinforced by providing feedback to SMEs, which have had their funding application declined. There is a strong need to improve the finance dialogue between SMEs and banks in all business stages, mainly when finance cannot be provided. There are acceptable practices in many countries that ensure an effective and efficient relationship between financial providers and businesses in this context. The European Commission (2017), for example, has encouraged the banking institutions to give appropriate feedback to declined SME credit applications. The clear communication of credit institutions with their SME customers about their expectations that form the basis for a successful application is critical to comprehend the reasons behind the denial of the credit request. It is essential for SMEs to understand what needs to be done and help them to be better prepared before approaching lenders.

Besides, new regulatory measures, including bankruptcy law, were introduced. Under the UAE Federal Law No. (6) of 2010, the Al Etihad Credit Bureau, a Public Joint Stock Company, has launched a credit scoring system by aggregating and analyzing credit information from financial and non-financial institutions. Borrowers and financial institutions could make better-informed decisions through access to data. However, there is no specific credit scoring on SMEs (the scoring method is the same for all companies).

The UAE issued a new Federal Law No. (4) of 2020 on "Securing Interest with Movable Property". It expands the scope of previous legislation by enabling companies operating in various business sectors, especially SMEs, to secure their bank and commercial loans by using their "tangible and intangible" movable properties (such as equipment and tools, receivables, cash flows, crops, and others).

The UAE Green Agenda Programs (2015–2030), launched in January 2012, focus on improving bank guarantees for green SME manufacturing with access to low-interest rates. The agenda also considers helping them climb up the global value chain ladder (The Federal Competitiveness & Statistics Authority, 2017 p. 92).

2.2   Major UAE Policy Responses to COVID-19 Pandemic Effects on SMEs

The effect of the COVID-19 pandemic on SMEs is severe. Many SMEs expect businesses to closure because of higher vulnerability levels and lower resilience related to their size. "*In sampled countries in the Middle East and North Africa and North America, the proportion of firms that reported a drop in sales compared to the same 30-day period in 2019 fell by 11 percentage points, with substantial drops observed in the UAE (down 22 percentage points) and the USA (down 15 percentage points)"* (Facebook/OECD/World Bank, 2020). The Wave II update of the *Global State of Small Business Report* (2020) has found that one of the most significant issues facing SMEs is access to capital. In the UAE, the proportion of small and medium-sized businesses (SMBs) that mentioned cash flow as an ongoing challenge in June was 47%, down just 1% from figures in May, and 42% of SMBs on Facebook revealed a lack of support compared to the 29% in May. As part of its effort to help small businesses in their economic recovery following COVID-19, Facebook announced a grant of $544,609 for eligible SMEs in Dubai (Mansoor, 2020).

Besides, the UAE' Government activates emergency stimulus measures promptly to mitigate the consequences of the COVID-19 outbreak on SMEs. It focused on banks' low lending levels to SMEs to soften the coronavirus pandemic's impact on smaller businesses. Banks need to be more supportive to ensure easy access to capital at affordable prices. In April 2020, Abu Dhabi's finance department announced a credit guarantee scheme for SMEs registered, operating, and headquartered in the Emirate, providing First Abu Dhabi Bank PJSC and Abu Dhabi Commercial Bank PJSC more incentives to lend smaller businesses. The Government will guarantee up to 80% of the scheme's value extended to SMEs (Abu Dhabi's Department of Finance, 2020). A similar scheme was already in place in Dubai by Dubai SME and Beehive but is limited to SMEs at least 51% owned and operated by UAE nationals (Beehive, 2020). With this unprecedented move, UAE's top lenders with Government need to maintain and revise such Credit Guarantee Scheme extended to small and medium-sized businesses. For instance, Credit guarantee schemes remain the most broadly used tool in OECD countries, and their design is regularly revised to keep up with emerging needs that promote SME growth.

2.3   SME's Public-Sector Lending

In addition to venture capitalists, several financing programs outside the banking system are established to fund SMEs. These include essentially:

- Dubai SME: the primary goal is to promote innovation and leadership across all segments of SMEs;
- Mohammed bin Rashid Fund for SMEs established in 2012;

- Khalifa Fund launched in 2007;
- Tejar Dubai;
- Hup71;
- Abu Dhabi Investment Office (ADIO) launched in 2018.

Direct investments by Governments through funds or co-investment funds (e.g., ADIO—Ghadan Ventures Fund) had been considered an effective means of addressing supply-side gaps in the capital availability for startups since they can expand the scale of SME markets. However, options are not aplenty. Since 2018, the UAE's Securities and Commodities Authority (SCA) has been working to create a platform to finance SMEs. It will be implemented once the regulatory and legislative framework for funding SMEs is developed (Bakhouche et al., 2020).

2.4   SME's Banks Funding

The total number of banks operating in the state reached 59 by the end of October 2019, including 21 national banks and 38 foreign banks (The Official Portal of the UAE' Government, 2019a). Banks in the UAE have an essential responsibility to fund the SME sector. Banks tend to provide a large number of different products with credit facilities ranging from loans for working capital and investment to receivables, asset-backed and real estate loans, and overdraft facilities, and vary according to the business purpose, collateral, term, amount, and other characteristics (IMF, 2015). Statistics issued by the Central Bank of the UAE (CBUAE) stated that, during the first quarter of 2020, UAE banks gave 4.3% more loans to SMEs compared to the fourth quarter of 2019 (AED93.4 billion and AED89.5 billion, respectively). The loans given represent 8.1% of the total cumulative balance of credit facilities provided to all private-sector commercial and economic businesses in the first quarter of 2020, reported to AED1.149 trillion (FAB, 2020).

Nevertheless, the UAE has a relatively poor track record of bank funding for these firms than regional and global norms (IMF, 2015; Baby & Joseph, 2016; Jones & Mosteanu, 2019). In 2012, an SME Bank Friendliness Index was launched to provide feedback to banks about what SMEs think of their products and services. Based on surveys of 30,000 SMEs and more than 20 banks, the research findings provided valuable insights: only 14% of SMEs used bank finance to fund their growth plans. Only 50 of every 100 companies that approach banks for finance get it.

Three-quarters of SMEs surveyed also use the services of more than two banks. Unfortunately, this problem persists until today. *"Typical lending requirements applied by commercial banks are quite strict and include collateral assets worth at least AED 500 000 and preferably audited financial statements. Interest rates on business loans are also high. The range of financing products offered by banks to clients is also relatively simple and comprises letters of credit, overdrafts, secured loans, and unsecured loans"* (OECD, 2016 p. 24). Approximately 50–70% of SMEs' applications for funding are rejected by conventional banks (The Official Portal of the UAE' Government, 2020). Bank lending to SMEs is negligible; about 4% of system-wide bank loans in the UAE are allocated toward SMEs. This percentage is below levels in the Middle East and North Africa, and OECD (9.3 and 22%, respectively), despite a massive stimulus package in April 2020, approaching $69.7 billion of funding support at zero cost—around 17% of GDP—from the Federal Government of the UAE (NBK, 2020).

Recent studies underlined several challenges faced by SMEs in getting funds from banks. The cost of finance, lack of long-term financial products, high reliance on real estate collateral, and limited availability of other types of collateral are cited among the hurdles faced by SMEs. Besides, leasing, factoring, and other credit products are underdeveloped (IMF, 2015 p. 24). According to the UAE' Government, *"Conventional lenders are sometimes unwilling or unable to support SMEs given their limited assets or lack of a proven record of company operations. This makes it difficult for SMEs to make business and finance provisions can be expensive or inflexible"* (The Official Portal of the UAE Government, 2020). Zarrouk, Sherif, et al. (2020) revealed that SMEs have insufficient information on different funding sources. The banks are seen as the first port of call for SMEs in search of funding.

SMEs complain about the difficulties involved in dealing with banks. An earlier study made by Baby and Joseph (2016) mentioned that banks tend to have limited involvement in financing SMEs, providing many skip cases. SME departments are shouted down in some banks. SME financing meets troubles because of poor financial discipline, dishonest people in business, accommodation to help friends, launching other companies without proper planning or feasibility study, etc.

2.5   SME's Non-bank Funding

Other means of raising funds have been gaining traction in recent years. Kiva, Accion, and Liwwa are micro-lenders that provide small amounts of financing (up to $5,000) to startups and entrepreneurs. Other options are crowdfunding sites, namely Eureeca, I own token, and Humming Crowd Reality (RAKBANK, 2019). Crowdfunding is a method of raising small amounts of capital (fund) through a joint effort of a large number of individual investors (crowd) who are part of the network and pool their resources to support projects or ventures initiated by other people or organizations (De Buysere et al., 2012 p. 9). It is done mainly through dedicated online platforms. There are four types: reward-based, equity-based, debt-based (peer-to-peer lending), and donation-based. In 2016, the Dubai Financial Services Authority (DFSA) launched a regulatory framework for loan and investment-based crowdfunding platforms, considered the GCC's first framework. Global loan-based crowdfunding is predicted to reach more than USD 300 billion, and global equity-based crowdfunding is estimated to exceed USD 93 billion by 2020 (The Dubai Financial Services Authority, 2017). Loan-based crowdfunding in the UAE is set to be exposed to stricter controls to introduce a new regime for the licensing and regulation of crowdfunding platforms. The CBUAE has launched on October 28, 2020 a new Regulation of new activity on "Loan Based Crowdfunding" in mainland UAE that spells out the rules for issuing Crowdfunding Licenses under the CBUAE. Equity and donation-based crowdfunding investment platforms are exempt from this regulation.

Crowdfunding, an alternative source of funding for SMEs, is gaining traction because it offers several benefits such as cost reduction, retaining management control over the company, removing geographic barriers to investment, etc. (Golić, 2014).

Launched in November 2014, Beehive is the first peer-to-peer lending platform offering a new funding service to assist SMEs in the region seeking finance from AED 100,000 for up to 3 years. Beehive has launched its SME Invoice Financing and Trading products. The new Invoice Finance solution helps established SME businesses to solve their cash-flow problems. Businesses will list invoices that are payable within 60–120 days and receive financing within 24–48 hours at rates starting from 0.75% per month. Invoice Trading is the process in which SMEs sell their outstanding invoices, individually or in bundles, online in an auction to obtain the cash within 48 hours. It helps support cash flow and increase revenue. Besides, funding is scalable to business growth. Funds can be released in days rather than weeks.

In 2016, Dubai established an angel investor service to facilitate SME financing. Angel investors (generally high net worth individuals) provide investment in exchange for an equity share in the company. Besides, Private equity (PE) and venture capital (VC) are slowly picking up in the UAE as funding sources. Still, they are generally located offshore where there is sureness encompassing requirement of their privileges. The UAE is characterized by a burdensome licensing process, legal and regulatory restrictions, vulnerabilities of the legal system, and challenges in structuring investments.

However, there is a limited demand for alternative financial instruments. According to the OECD (2017b p. 8), *"Many entrepreneurs lack financial knowledge, strategic vision, resources and in some cases, the willingness to attract sources of finance other than straight debt."*

In 2020, steps were taken by Nasdaq Dubai to support the expansion of SMEs. The initiative aims to help SMEs achieve the next phase of their growth by raising capital via an initial public offering (IPO).

Financial technology (FinTech) is becoming an additional source of financing for SMEs with acquiring business capital. Through FinTech platforms to process requests, their services are more accessible and faster to SMEs. For instance, Salary, a digital business loan and credit line platform, provides flexible and affordable financing for small businesses. Tabby, however, a Dubai-based FinTech is an additional financing source for SMEs; it allows boosting strong sales with buy now pay later. Customers can pay when they want, but the firm will be paid right away. InstaVal is vital in supporting small businesses through new, innovative routes through its digital investment banking platform to promote equity investments in startups, scaleups, and SMEs. MyMoneySouq and Moneyball provide a comparison of all UAE SME bank loans. Invoice Bazaar offers many financing services accessible to small businesses, including but not limited to invoice financing, payment gateway financing, and inventory financing.

3   POLICY IMPLICATIONS AND RECOMMENDATIONS

Based on the overview of the existing financing options available to SMEs, this section focuses on the practice aiming at improving SMEs' access to finance. This section looks at the various practices adopted in many countries worldwide and can be implemented in the UAE.

3.1   Enhancing SMEs Access to Existing Financing Instruments

3.1.1   Referral Scheme

It is a fact that SMEs are mostly dependent on traditional banks to raise money. To improve the effective use of finance platforms, implementing a bank referral scheme can provide an efficient process to find the best match between those moneylenders and SMEs. This initiative had been adopted by the United Kingdom (UK) to connect small firms that were rejected for a traditional bank loan to alternative moneylenders. Schammo (2019) highlighted the added value of a bank referral. It helps SMEs on their journey to find external finance by searching for alternative options of funding after the rejection of finance applications by their banks. Simultaneously, it allows alternative lenders to have more visibility in the SME funding market and facilitates access to businesses with external funding needs.

3.1.2   Education and Awareness to Successfully Attract Finance

Both supply and demand-side barriers constitute obstacles to access to alternative sources of finance. On the demand side, many SMEs owners lack financial knowledge of the alternative financing method that affects their willingness or awareness to successfully attract finance other than straight debt (Zarrouk, Sherif, et al., 2020). The lack of appetite by business owners for alternative financial products can be attributed to the scarcity of financing options and regulatory barriers. Therefore, financial instruments for SMEs often operate in narrow, illiquid markets, with a limited number of participants, which, in turn, drives down demand from entrepreneurs and discourages potential providers of finance (Nassr & Wehinger, 2016; OECD, 2017a).

In this context, an Advisory Hub similar to a European Investment Advisory Hub (EIAH) can be considered to strengthen access to finance. It will act as a single point of contact to customized advisory and technical assistance services for SME owners in the UAE. There is another example adopted in France that can be implemented. The Banque de France has established a network of regional correspondents, about 100 advisors, which advice emerging financial issues to a tiny local firm.

Targeted financial education programs can help entrepreneurs improve their skills, develop a long-term strategic plan for business funding, increase understanding of the economic and financial environment relevant to their business, pick up and reach investors and financial providers, and understand and handle financial risk related to different instruments. For example, Portugal has a national strategy to foster financial literacy, focusing on SMEs. Small and medium businesses' financial education needs are addressed comprehensively under the "National Plan for Financial Education."

Furthermore, the UAE' Government can collaborate with the ELITE business support program—launched in the UK by the London Stock Exchange Group in 2014. The program provides the most dynamic small companies with advice, guidance, training, direct connection to the financial community, and mentoring to help them through their next growth stage. For instance, a successful partnership with the Italian' Government started in 2017.

3.1.3   SMEs Credit Rating

Difficulties faced by SMEs in accessing finance are generally attributed to a lack of credit information. Information asymmetries prevent investors from reliably evaluating the risks and potential benefits of investing in SMEs. Setting up a credit risk assessment infrastructure may play an essential role in overcoming deficiencies and ameliorating transparency in the SME finance sector (Word Bank Group, 2018).

Developing information infrastructures specific for SMEs, such as credit bureau, registries, or data warehouses, will accurately provide the risk level associated with SME financing and encourage investors and finance providers. In Thailand, The National Credit Bureau started in 2016, offering FICO SME scores to lenders to better evaluate SMEs' creditworthiness. The FICO SME Score provides banks and financial institutions with a useful tool for credit risk SMEs assessment, allowing them to make faster and more accurate lending decisions.

For instance, in 2020, the Khalifa Fund for Enterprise Development has come up with a digital 'SME Rating' to help businesses identify their strengths and weaknesses, allowing them to grow and improve. However, Khalifa Fund's counselors will use this digital classification system when assessing applicant businesses for the fund. Furthermore, UAE Etihad Credit Bureau, launched in 2010, provides risk assessment for companies, but there is no specific SME rating.

In the UAE, to encourage financing SMEs through traditional and non-traditional financial providers, a setup of information infrastructures for SME credit risk assessment can reduce higher borrowing costs typically associated with small and medium businesses: evidence from Japan, where Credit Risk Database (CRD) has been established in 2001. The CRD delivers credit risk scoring, data sampling, statistical data, and associated services that facilitate SMEs' direct access to the financial institutions and facilitates access to the lending market by allowing the securitization of claims.

3.1.4   Implementation of a Normalized SMEs' Accounting System

The irregularity of the SMEs' accounting system generates asymmetric information between financial providers and enterprises. Normalization of the accounting system will help to reduce information asymmetry and costs. This financial data generated disclose the operation of firms and therefore determines whether financial institutions can provide financing for businesses. A formal and accurate financial statement reflecting SMEs' business information helps minimize information deficiencies between financial institutions and enterprises. Therefore, normalizing the financial system will reduce information costs and smooth access to financial institutions' loans. Many quantitative studies conducted on SMEs operating in the UAE used many data sources, non-standardized, to conduct their research (Sherif et al., 2019).

3.1.5   Insolvency Regulation

The ease of SME financing through insolvency practices plays a pivotal role in the small businesses lending process due to the insolvency laws that include the default recovery rules that influence creditors. However, the regulatory framework in the UAE is not conducive to risk. Insolvency regulations in the UAE are not well-established, and, as a result, non-performing business liabilities can still be treated as a criminal offense (Zarrouk, Galloway, et al., 2020). There is some evidence suggesting that targeted SME-friendly insolvency practices facilitate SME funding (World Bank Group, 2018).

3.2   Alternative Financing Instruments for SMEs

An increasing range of alternative financing instruments has become available to SMEs; however, only accessible to a small share of these firms. These instruments for SMEs include asset-based financing, alternative forms of debt, hybrid tools, and equity-based financial instruments suitable for UAE small enterprises.

3.2.1   Asset-Based Finance Instruments

In several OECD and emerging countries, asset-based finance is the most common instrument of external finance used by many SMEs to overcome their working capital needs, support domestic and international commerce, and, in some scenarios, for investment reasons (OECD, 2015). According to the OECD (2018 p. 12), "*asset-based finance has grown steadily over the last decade, despite repercussions of the global financial crisis on the supply side.*" This type of financing takes numerous forms: asset-based lending, factoring, purchase order finance, warehouse receipts, and leasing.

In the UAE, there is a lack of financial companies providing asset-based financing to SMEs (IMF, 2015). Asset-based lending is a specialized method of providing working capital and term loans secured by property, accounts receivable, inventory, or equipment.

Factoring is a financing method in which a business sells its creditworthy accounts receivable (i.e., invoices) at a discount (generally equal to interest plus service fees) and receives immediate cash from a third party (factor) (Klapper, 2006). In many countries, especially in emerging economies, the factoring volumes are expanding significantly over the last decade. The instrument has become more largely used and accepted as an alternative option to cash-strapped SMEs (OECD, 2018). A successful example of factoring practices was implemented by Nacional Financiera (NAFIN) in Mexico. NAFIN provides reverse factoring services to SMEs through its productive chains program. The program aims to link small, risky suppliers with large, creditworthy firms that buy from them. SMEs can then use the receivables from their larger customers to secure loans, and consequently, cash is immediately generated, as opposed to waiting for buyers to settle their payment.

Asset-based finance instruments can flourish easily as they embed low risks to investors, even in the absence of transparent and normalized credit data. Access to asset-based finance relies on the backed asset's liquidation value instead of the firm's creditworthiness (OECD, 2015).

3.2.2   SMEs Fund Raising Through Capital Market

The UAE' Government could reform the financial market by implementing a registration of micro, small and medium enterprises system. The implementation of this system might improve SMEs' fundraising significantly. However, with a convenient system in place, publishing enough information is the most crucial thing. An adequate framework of appropriate laws and regulations should be formulated to establish a sound legal system to make the financial market attractive for SEMs to raise capital. Development of incentive measures and a supervision environment are needed to support firms to step into the capital market.

For instance, most SMEs can raise capital from the National Association of Securities Deal Automated Quotations market (NASDAQ). Direct financing is a convenient additional way for SMEs to raise money from the capital market. The equity segment of Nasdaq First North (Sweden, Finland, and Denmark), considered SME Growth Markets, aims to facilitate SMEs' access to capital (NASDAQ, 2019). Over several consecutive years, it has been categorized as one of the leading European marketplaces for SMEs (NASDAQ, 2019). In this regard, awareness in different Emirates, specifically in Abu Dhabi, is needed to let more SMEs benefit from the potential capital injection and the public listing.

3.2.3   Microfinance Institutions to Bridge the Credit Gap

Microfinance companies can help to bridge the lending gap by providing small loans to small firms. These microcredit loans use collateral such as group guarantees and can grow over time based on sound reimbursement patterns. In East Africa (Uganda, Kenya, and Tanzania), the Women's Microfinance Initiative loan program's goal is to assist rural women in starting businesses that can generate income to ameliorate household living standards (Word Bank Group, 2018). Similar examples can be implemented in the UAE in collaboration with Businesswomen Councils based in different Emirates to further strengthen the UAE women's involvement in the business market through small- and medium-sized and micro-enterprises. Microcredit might help overcome difficulties, especially financing, faced by households vs. female entrepreneurs and, therefore, help develop and sustain their businesses.

4   Conclusion

The SMEs sector plays a vital role in the UAE' Economy. Banks and the UAE' Government traditionally gave the bulk of the credit to SMEs. Beyond traditional lending, crowdfunding and peer-to-peer lending are recent alternatives. Nevertheless, SMEs face significant financing obstacles; this might endanger economic growth and employment in the UAE. This chapter highlights difficulties faced by SMEs in accessing credit, which is extremely important for every SME during all development stages of operation. It also explores possible solutions to help mitigate these challenges. Further supporting public policies are needed, and innovative ideas could help SMEs obtain better access to finance. Credit reporting, secured lending, and insolvency regulation could be adequate solutions for these problems. Besides, capital market and microfinance institutions have great potential to play an essential role in creating a funding ecosystem.

This paper is a revised and expanded version of a paper entitled "Access to Finance, Entrepreneurial Orientation and SMEs Businesses in UAE: A GABEK Analysis" presented at The 41 Annual Conference of the Institute for Small Business and Entrepreneurship.

Acknowledgment The authors acknowledge the financial support from Abu Dhabi Education and Knowledge (ADEK).

References

Abdulsaleh, A. M., & Worthington, A. C. (2013). Small and medium-sized enterprises financing: A review of literature. *International Journal of Business and Management, 8*(36), 36–54. https://doi.org/10.5539/ijbm.v8n14p36

Abu Dhabi's Department of Finance. (2020). *Abu Dhabi Government SMEs credit guarantee program.* https://www.adib.ae/en/Pages/Business_SME-Credit-Guarantee-program.aspx. Accessed 10 December 2020.

Baby, A., & Joseph, C. A. C. (2016). Bank finance challenges faced by UAE SME sector. *Kuwait Chapter of Arabian Journal of Business and Management Review, 6*(1). https://doi.org/10.4172/2223-5833.S1-005.

Bakhouche, A., Elchaar, R., & Emam, M. (2020). Survey of financing options and key challenges faced by SMEs in the UAE: Economic environment, finance, and regulatory landscape. In *Entrepreneurial Innovation and Economic Development in Dubai and Comparisons to Its Sister Cities* (pp. 115–145). https://doi.org/10.4018/978-1-5225-9377-5.ch006

Beehive. (2020). *Dubai SME and Beehive's capital guarantee scheme for Emiratis*. https://www.beehive.ae/dubai-sme-capital-guarantee/. Accessed 10 December 2020.

De Buysere, K., Gajda, O., Kleverlaan, R., & Marom, D. (2012). *A framework for European crowdfunding*. http://eurocrowd.org/wp-content/blogs.dir/sites/85/2013/06/FRAMEWORK_EU_CROWDFUNDING.pdf. Accessed 12 December 2020.

Dubai SME. (2019). *The state of Small & Medium Enterprises (SMEs) in Dubai 2019*. http://economicforum.ae/wp/wp-content/uploads/2019/12/SME-REPORT-2019-v9-2019.12.10-copy.pdf. Accessed 12 December 2020.

European Commission. (2017). *Survey on the access to finance of enterprises in the euro area, October 2016 to March 2017*. https://www.ecb.europa.eu/pub/pdf/other/ecb.accesstofinancesmallmediumsizedenterprises201705.en.pdf?17da4ff2a730b7ababea4037e4ce8cae

FAB. (2020). *Market insights & strategy*. https://www.bankfab.com/-/media/fabgroup/home/cib/market-insights/daily-morning-news/daily-morning-news-pdfs/2020/may/20-05-2020.pdf?view=1. Accessed 10 December 2020.

Facebook/OECD/World Bank. (2020). *The future of business survey*. https://dataforgood.fb.com/global-state-of-smb. Accessed 10 December 2020.

Golić, Z. (2014). Advantages of crowdfunding as an alternative source of financing of small and medium-sized enterprises. *Proceedings of the Faculty of Economics in East Sarajevo, 8*, 39–48.

IMF. (2015). *United Arab Emirates: Selected issues* (IMF Country Report No. 15/220). https://doi.org/10.5089/9781513524634.002

Jones, A., & Mosteanu, N. R. (2019, April 8–9). *Entrepreneurship in the UAE dynamic market—Financing, challenges, and obstacles*. 8th International Conference on Business and Economic Development (ICBED). New York, USA. https://www.abrmr.com/myfile/home/home_firstpdf/con_fst_36901.pdf. Accessed 12 December 2020.

Klapper, L. (2006). The role of factoring for financing small and medium enterprises. *Journal of Banking and Finance, 30*(11), 3111–3130.

Mansoor, Z. (2020). *Cash flow key challenge in the recovery of UAE-based small and medium businesses—A survey*. https://dataforgood.fb.com/global-state-of-smb. Accessed 10 December 2020.

Miniaoui, H., & Schilirò, D. (2017). Innovation and entrepreneurship for the diversification and growth of the gulf cooperation council economies. *Business and Management Studies, 3*(3), 69–81.

NASDAQ. (2019). *Nasdaq First North is now an SME growth market*. https://www.nasdaq.com/SME-growth-market. Accessed 10 December 2020.

Nassr, K. I., & Wehinger, G. (2016). Opportunities and limitations of public equity markets for SMEs. *OECD Journal: Financial Market Trends, 2015*(1), 49–84. https://doi.org/10.1787/fmt-2015-5jrs051fvnjk

NBK. (2020). *Economics in focus.* https://www.nbk.com/dam/jcr:ad3dcb1a-cff4-4b5f-be87-f8bceaf96947/NBKEconomicsinFocusUAEtourism202092E.pdf. Accessed 14 December 2020.

OECD. (2015). New approaches to SME and entrepreneurship financing: Broadening the range of instruments. *OECD Publishing.* https://doi.org/10.1787/9789264240957-en

OECD. (2016). *Entrepreneurship, SMEs, and local development in ABU DHABI: Boosting the entrepreneurial Ecosystem.* https://www.oecd.org/employment/leed/AbuDhabi-Ecosystem-Final-Web.pdf. Accessed 12 December 2020.

OECD. (2017a). *Fostering markets for SME finance: Matching business and investor needs.* OECD Working Party on SMEs and Entrepreneurship.

OECD. (2017b). *Financing SMEs and entrepreneurs.* https://www.oecd.org/cfe/smes/Financing%20SMEs%20and%20Entrepreneurs%202017b_Highlights.pdf

OECD. (2018, February 22–23). *Enhancing SME access to diversified financing instruments* (Discussion Paper). SME Ministerial Conference. Mexico City. https://www.oecd.org/cfe/smes/ministerial/documents/2018-SME-Ministerial-Conference-Plenary-Session-2.pdf. Accessed 10 December 2020.

Ou, C., & Haynes, G. W. (2006). Acquisition of additional equity capital by small firms–findings from the national survey of small business finances. *Small Business Economics, 27*(2), 157–168.

RAKBANK. (2019). *How to get startup funding for innovative businesses?* https://rakbank.ae/blog/posts/get-funding-for-innovative-businesses. Accessed 12 December 2020.

Schammo, P. (2019). Undisruption' in the SME funding market: Information sharing, finance platforms, and the UK bank referral scheme. *European Business Organization Law Review, 20*(1), 29–53.

Schilirò, D. (2015). Innovation in small and medium enterprises in the United Arab Emirates. *International Journal of Social Science Studies, 3*, 148–160.

Sherif, M., Galloway, L., & Zarrouk, H. (2019). Performance and entrepreneurial orientation in SMEs: The case of Abu Dhabi. *International Journal of Accounting, Auditing, and Performance Evaluation, 15*(3), 241–261. https://www.inderscience.com/info/inarticle.php?artid=102247

The Dubai Financial Services Authority. (2017). *Dubai's DFSA launches a crowdfunding framework on 01 August 2017.* https://www.finextra.com/pressarticle/70244/dubais-dfsa-launches-crowdfunding-framework. Accessed 12 August 2019.

The Federal Competitiveness and Statistics Authority. (2017). *UAE and the 2030 agenda for sustainable development excellence in implementation 2017*. https://sustainabledevelopment.un.org/content/documents/201 61UAE_SDGs_Report_Full_English.pdf. Accessed 12 December 2020.

The Official Portal of the UAE' Government. (2019a). *Annual economic report 2019* (27th ed.).

The Official Portal of the UAE' Government. (2019b). *The impact of SMEs on the UAE's economy*. https://u.ae/en/information-and-services/business/crowdfunding/the-impact-of-smes-on-the-uae-economy. Accessed 12 August 2019.

The Official Portal of the UAE' Government. (2020). *Crowdfunding*. https://u.ae/en/information-and-services/business/crowdfunding. Accessed 12 December 2020.

Word Bank Group. (2018). *Improving access to finance for SMEs: Opportunities through credit reporting, secured lending, and insolvency practices*. https://www.doingbusiness.org/en/reports/thematic-reports/improving-access-to-finance-for-smes. Accessed 12 December 2020.

Zarrouk, H., Sherif, M., Galloway, L., & El Ghak, T. (2020). Entrepreneurial orientation, access to financial resources, and SMEs' business performance: The case of the United Arab Emirates. *Journal of Asian Finance, Economics, and Business, 7*(12), 465–474.

Zarrouk, H., Galloway, L., Sherif, M., Elkaroui, E., & Al Mulla, A. (2020b). Entrepreneurial orientation in small firms: A qualitative exploration in the context of an emerging economy. In S. Parsha, J. Gibb, M. Akoorie, & J. M. Scott (Eds.), *Research handbook on entrepreneurship in emerging economies: A contextualized approach*. Edward Elgar Publishing. https://www.e-elgar.com/shop/research-handbook-on-entrepreneurship-in-emerging-economies. Accessed 12 December 2020.

Zimmermann, V., & Thomä, J. (2016). *SMEs face a wide range of barriers to innovation-support policy needs to be broad-based*. KfW Research Focus on Economics, 130, Frankfurt/M.

INDEX

Printed by Printforce, United Kingdom